Race and State

Race and State

Edited by

Alana Lentin and Ronit Lentin

Cambridge Scholars Publishing

Race and State, Edited by Alana Lentin and Ronit Lentin

This book first published 2006. The present binding first published 2008.

Cambridge Scholars Publishing

12 Back Chapman Street, Newcastle upon Tyne, NE6 2XX, UK

British Library Cataloguing in Publication Data
A catalogue record for this book is available from the British Library

Copyright © 2008 by Alana Lentin and Ronit Lentin and contributors

All rights for this book reserved. No part of this book may be reproduced, stored in a retrieval system, or transmitted, in any form or by any means, electronic, mechanical, photocopying, recording or otherwise, without the prior permission of the copyright owner.

ISBN (10): 1-84718-774-9, ISBN (13): 9781847187741

TABLE OF CONTENTS

Introduction
Alana Lentin and Ronit Lentin
Speaking of Racism 1
    Why "race" and state? 3
    The double face of the racist state 7
    Ireland as a textbook case 10
    Reading "Race and State" 12
    References 14

Part I
Theorising Race and State

Chapter One
Deva-stating disasters: Race in the shadow(s) of New Orleans
David Theo Goldberg 15
    References 29

Chapter Two
The problem of the immigration line: state racism and bare life
Les Back 32
    New borderlands and pariahs 35
    The named and the nameless 38
    References 51

Chapter Three
De-authenticating Fanon: Self-organised anti-racism and the politics of experience
Alana Lentin 53
    Introduction 53
    Mis-recognising Fanon: Taylor and the questionable roots of identity politics 56
    Problematising the authenticity of experience 61
    Experience and representation in contemporary anti-racism 63
    Conclusion 66
    Notes 68
    References 69

Chapter Four
The leviathan black hole and the hydra it beholds: State, racism and the modern/colonial habitus
Festus Ikeotuonye 71
    Introduction 71
    Colouring the world with imperial reason 74
    Black hole and hydra dialectic 78
    Coloniality as the motions of modern self constitution 83
    The modern state as empire in brief 85
    The problem of order and "other" in state formation 91
    Notes 97
    References 98

Chapter Five
Asylum seekers and the nation-state: Putting the "order" back into "borders" in Australia and the Republic of Ireland
Steve Garner and Anthony Moran 103
    Introduction 103
    The nation-state and asylum seekers 104
    Republic of Ireland 105
    a) The Supreme Court ruling on the residence rights of "Irish-born children", 2003 107
    b) Referendum on Citizenship, 2004 108
    Australia 110
    Conclusion 116
    Notes 117
    References 118

Chapter Six
Contingent regulations: Nazi sexual politics of race in the occupied territories of the soviet union, 1941–1945
Regina Mühlhäuser 121
    Different concepts of "Racial Purity" and "Racial Mixing" 123
    Dominant images of soldierly masculinity and sexual conquest ... 125
    Changing demands in the everyday situation of war and occupation 127
    Conclusion 130
    Notes 131
    References 133

Part II
Racial States After the 11ᵗʰ of Septmber, 2001 137

Chapter Six
Wars on our doorstep: Islamicising "race" and militarising everyday life
Gargi Bhattacharyya 138
  Thinking about what we mean by racist state - again.............. 138
  Occupation policing: Is this business as usual?................... 139
  Policing and the racist state 140
  a) Force and over-reaction.. 141
  b) Tampering with evidence and fit-ups............................ 141
  c) Stop and search 142
  d) Immigration 143
  Does state racism always have a shadow of militarisation?......... 144
  Racial supremacy and global alliances............................. 146
  The Islamicisation of "race": how anti-muslim state racism infects racisms against other communities................................. 148
  How to respond?... 149
  References.. 150

Chapter Seven
The production of the imaginary terrorist as an object of fear: Orientalism in the Twenty First century
Chris Sparks.. 152
  Fear.. 153
  Orientalism as a feature of the war on terror 154
  The war of terror: A dialectic of instigation and eradication..... 156
  Media, democracy and rumour mill 157
  The political context: the current politics of fear 160
  Politics and enmity 161
  Post 9/11 Orientalism 162
  How terrorism works... 164
  The function of mediated images in the inter-subjective construction of a common sense of fearful situations............................ 165
  Using mass media to produce incapacitating fear 166
  References.. 167

Chapter Eight
Elusive genealogies: Conceptualizing race in the wake of 11 September, 2001
Malreddy Pavan Kumar 169
Introduction 169
Colonialism and cultural mapping 171
Anthropometric Geography and racial mapping 176
Imperialism and territorial mapping: 178
Conclusion 183
Notes 184
References 184

Part III
The Racial State(s) of Ireland

Chapter Nine
From racial state to racist state? Racism and immigration in twenty first century Ireland
Ronit Lentin 187
Introduction: Racism in Ireland, the contradictions 187
Ireland as a racial state 190
Biopolitics: From racial state to racist state 192
The law in the service of the racial state 193
The Citizenship Referendum 198
Market-driven migration in the service of the racial state 199
Conclusion: Multiculturalism, "integration", and the promise of "racelessness" 202
Notes 205
References 206

Chapter Ten
Rethinking immigration and the state in Ireland
Steven Loyal and Kieran Allen 209
Introduction 209
The cultural turn in Sociology 210
State and citizenship 214
The Irish State and racism 217
The migrant as asylum seeker 220
The migrant as bonded labourer 222
The migrant as owner of valuable skills 224

Conclusion 225
References 227

Chapter Eleven
"Special powers": Northern Ireland and racism in a permanent state of exception
Robbie McVeigh 229
    Northern Ireland and the State of Exception 233
    Managing racism in a racial statelet 235
    "Good relations" and State racism 239
    "Good relations" and racism in a permanent state of exception 244
    Conclusion 248
    Notes 249
    References 252

Chapter Twelve
"A slice of Africa". Whose side were we on? Ireland and the anti-colonial struggle
Piaras Mac Éinrí 255
    Ireland: a special relationship with the Majority World? 255
    Ireland as coloniser and colonised 258
    Official discourses 259
    Locating the historical perspectives 260
    Pre-independence 262
    The Second Boer War 1899-1902 263
    Irishness as whiteness? 265
    Irish-Indian contacts 267
    Conclusion 269
    Notes 270
    References 270

Chapter thirteen
Re-racialising the Irish state through the census, citizenship, and language
Rebecca Chiyoko King-O'Riain 274
    Race, Racialisation and the Racial State 275
    Irish Racial State 278
    Census 280
    Citizenship 282
    Language 284
    Conclusion 289

References 289

Chapter Fourteen
Routinised practices and technologies of the state: Dialectical constitution of Irishness and Otherness
Elaine Moriarty 292
    Introduction 292
    Racialised regime of representation 296
    The routinisation of racialisation in the Irish State 298
    The ethical engagement 303
    Conclusion 306
    Acknowledgements 307
    Notes 307
    References 308

Contributors 312

ACKNOWLEDGEMENTS

This collection is based on a conference titled Race and State, held at Trinity College Dublin in March 2005. The conference was organised by the MPhil in Ethnic and Racial Studies, Department of Sociology, Trinity College, in association with the British Sociological Association's Race and Ethnicity Study Group, and the Sociological Association of Ireland (SAI).

The editors wish to thank all the contributors and the conference committee, Dr Max Farrar, School of Social Studies, Leeds Metropolitan University; Elaine Moriarty, Department of Sociology, TCD; and Dr Karim Murji, Open University, UK. Thanks are also extended to Emily Rauscher, David Landy, Chu Chun Yu and Ama Peters, all graduates of the MPhil in Ethnic and Racial Studies, and to Partho Sen Gupta, for their assistance on the day. Thanks to Robbie McVeigh for his help in preparing the final text for publication.

Ronit would like to lovingly thank Alana for sowing the inspirational radical seed of the apple tree. Alana would like to thank Ronit for tending the ground so that the tree could flourish.

Alana and Ronit dedicate this book to Lia, in memoriam.

INTRODUCTION

ALANA LENTIN AND RONIT LENTIN

SPEAKING OF RACISM

It has never been easy, but speaking about racism in the western political climate of the first decade of the twenty-first century is more difficult than ever before. There is a feeling in post-colonial and post-immigration societies that the blatant, overt racism of the past is no longer as pressing. We hear more and more talk of euphemisms such as discrimination, intolerance or the challenges of living with diversity than of the bluntness of racism. Racism evokes times past: the extermination of the "racially impure", the trade in captured slaves, the lynchings, the injustices of Apartheid… It is unimportant that the legacies of these histories continue to define societies in many areas of the world. What is important is that "we" can relegate these horrors to times and peoples past. Anything that reminds us of them—the chanting neo-nazi "thugs", their excrement through letter boxes, the jokes in bad taste—are written off as ignorance at the margins, psychologically challenged individuals to be either helped and educated or written off.

There is a deep discomfort about admitting racism, in Europe in particular, because common wisdom, fed by national and supranational policy, tells us that racism opposes everything that we believe in as citizens of democratic, "civilised" modern states; at least the virulent racism we associate with ghettos and genocide. When it comes to the everyday issues of discrimination in employment, education and access to services, unjust policing and the racialisation of minority religion and culture we question whether this can really be called racism. Isn't it in fact rather arbitrary? Isn't just a question of a few "bad apples" to be weeded out?

In reality, racism goes well beyond the everyday discrimination that continues to affect the children and grandchildren of immigrants and indigenous minorities. Today's racism descends directly from the pernicious history of twentieth century Europe. This is the racism of the immigration regime: the rounding up of "illegal" immigrants, their incarceration in detention centres, their expulsion—bound and gagged—on chartered planes. There is the scapegoating of Muslims for the threat posed to western culture and civilization, the attack on the civil liberties of those racially profiled brown-skinned others, blamed for bringing the Middle East onto our streets, and the equation of every political action taken by a black or brown person with fanaticism, barbarism and primitivity. Finally, there is the antisemitism that political leaders insist on blaming on abstractly defined Muslims, purposefully avoiding the implications of pitting minority groups against each other and leaving officials free to rail against Jew hatred while drafting even stricter policy to curtail asylum and immigration.

In other words, racism both past and present is inextricably linked both to the policy instituted by states and to the political climate engendered by governmental leaders playing the proverbial "race card". The fact that it is impossible to disentangle it from the role of the state in its perpetuation is what makes it so difficult to talk about racism, in either politics, academia or just among our friends and acquaintances. Few brought up in the culture of national education systems that preach the supremacy of western democracy are capable of admitting the interdependency between racism and the functioning of the state. Furthermore, the anti-racism that the majority white population is exposed to is not based upon the lived-experience of those who face racism, but on vague principles of tolerance, solidarity and respect for human dignity that tend to leave out a lot of the detail. It is hardly surprising, therefore, that people facing racism are often accused of exaggeration and self-victimisation.

Under these conditions, it is all the more important that the interconnections between "race" and state are brought out. The papers collected in this book all seek to draw attention to these relationships from either historical, theoretical or contemporary sociological perspectives and, in some cases, in specific relationship to the Irish case. These papers are bound together by their being unapologetically political. In opposition to the contemporary tendency to dissociate sociological phenomena from contemporary political processes and events—not least the ongoing "War on Terror"—the contributors to *Race and State* seek to engage theory, history and sociology with the world which inspires them. This collection aims to contribute to the revitalisation of a politicised approach to doing social science through the specific prism of "race". As both Eric Voegelin (1933) and Michel Foucault (2003), two key figures in the theoretical background to the discussion of "race" and state, have pointed out, the discussion of "race" and racism is interesting because of what it can tell us about the nature of the state and politics. While the contributors to this volume are more committed to the study of racism for its own sake, the point is well taken and serves to validate the importance of insisting on treating racism politically and not, as is too often the case, as pathology.

Why "race" and state?

In George Mosse's seminal examination of the rise of Nazism, he reminds us that we do not have to possess any special powers to understand the origins of racism, we have merely to "integrate the study of racism within our study of the modern history of Europe" (1978: 236). As this is true historically for understanding the rise of racism, colonialism and genocide, so it is true for interpreting racism today. The way in which the modern nation-state in the West has evolved, from the Enlightenment to neo-colonialism, determines the patterns of inclusion and exclusion that dominate relationships between the state and individuals and groups in society, and between the West and "the rest".

By highlighting the way in which "race" and state, and racism and state practices are interwoven, this collection of papers hopes to contribute to a significant, if minoritarian, body of literature on the politics of "race" and racism. The official histories of the West at best portrayed racism as a bloody blot on the memory of the twentieth century rather than, as Zygmunt Bauman (1989) has shown, as politically inseparable from the modern project. The work of authors such as Voegelin and Foucault, along with others including Frantz Fanon, Aimé Césaire, Hannah Arendt, C.L.R. James, George Mosse and, more recently, Etienne Balibar, David Theo Goldberg, Howard Winant, Enzo Traverso, Ivan Hannaford and Barnor Hesse, stands in stark contrast to the received tradition in thinking on the history and sociology of modern racism.

The title of this collection and that of the conference from which it emerges is borrowed from Eric Voegelin. In 1933, Voegelin, a German philosopher forced to seek exile from his native country due to the rise of Nazism, published two volumes on "race": *Rasse und Staat* and *Die rassenidee in der Geistesgeschichte von Ray bis Carus*. The first volume in particular outlines Voegelin's theoretical approach to "race" which he views as crucial to a theory of state and, therefore, as inherently political. He completely rejects the potential usefulness of scientific racism, separating between what he calls the "race concept" and the "race idea". While the pseudoscientific "race concept" is accepted by Voegelin as the basis for the "race idea", he focuses on the political implications of "race" and sees them as entirely more pernicious than the false science that he takes the concept to be. Voegelin's work on "race" is part of a much wider project to establish a theory of state. He saw such a theory as based upon a set of body ideas, or "any symbol which integrates a group into a substantial whole through the assertion that its members are of common origin" (Voegelin 1940: 286). In other words, what Voegelin was trying to theorise was the basis for the idea that human beings should live in defined territories known as nation-states with which they are supposed to identify. He sought to uncover the theoretical glue holding together the initially nebulous idea of the unity of nation-states and the reasons for which, despite this, they have come to be the only accepted and legitimated means of organising societies.

In constructing his theory, Voegelin saw "race" as the most important of all the body ideas. This is because the state takes action, according to Voegelin, on the basis of a vision of the type of people belonging to its political community and an assumption about the type of collective moral experiences they have had. At the time of Voegelin's writing *Rasse und Staat*, the belief that racial categorisation was the sole means of making sense of human difference and the consequent organisation of society had reached its peak. The amalgam of science and politics used to bring the "race idea" to full fruition meant that it was particularly prone to the type of myth-making that perpetuated its appeal. It could therefore dominate over other equally important body ideas by drawing on pre-modern myths, such as medieval Jew hatred or the danger posed by the Barbarians, for example, and combining them with the modern, rational argument for strong "race nations", binding together individuals born into a common destiny.

Voegelin, by drawing on the writings of several "race" theorists, demonstrates how the birth of the nation-state turns history into the servant of politics. This nationalisation of history, its orientation towards benefiting the creation of nations in the place of states, contributes also to the rise of "race". Because the nation needs to constitute itself as unique, it benefits from the stamp of scientific approval that "race" provides. It is when embodied by the state and integrated into its institutions that the unique "race nation" can constitute itself as more than a mere ideal.

The theorists of "race" and racism that have inspired our thinking on "race" and state focus on the intrinsically modern nature of racism. They link it, in methodological terms, to the emergence of Enlightenment thought, and in political terms, to the birth of the nation-state. Hannaford (1996) proposes that the possibility of thinking about humanity in racial terms comes about with the shift from monogenesis to polygenesis: the rejection of the singular belief in Creation. Once it is considered that all humankind may not originate from the work of one god, it becomes possible to think about groups of human beings as being inherently physically and mentally different from each other. The Enlightenment made this shift in thinking concrete by providing the tools for 'a more logical description and classification that ordered humankind in terms of physiological criteria based on observable "facts" and tested evidence' (Hannaford 1996: 46).

Focusing on the rise of modern antisemitism, Hannah Arendt, Zygmunt Bauman and Enzo Traverso have all related its emergence and the process leading to the Holocaust to the nature of modernity as embodied by the state. Bauman (1989) shows how the assimilation of the Jews, enabled by the advent of the modern secular nation-state, made their existence strange where once it was natural; closed off in ghettoes and therefore identifiably distinct. Assimilated Jews become, for Foucault (2003), the "race" present among all "races", the dreaded threat within. When the perception of this threat is coupled with the rationalisation upon which modern state societies are built, racism taken to its extremes is made possible. Bauman's by now infamous metaphor of the gardener associates modern societies with the order and rationality of gardening as opposed to the laissez-faire attitude of the pre-modern gamekeeper. To maintain the order of the garden, the gardener must weed out 'every self-invited plant which interferes with his plan and vision of order and harmony' (Bauman 1989: 57). So too, the success of a racialised vision of the nation, made up of individuals with a common heritage and shared destiny, made it necessary to order populations, sorting between insiders and outsiders, between us and them. The scientific legitimation that came with racial science by the mid-nineteenth century led to a perfect marriage between science and politics, uniting theory and practice in the body of the modern, rational, territorially-bound and unified nation-state.

The work of Etienne Balibar is also central to the analysis of the relationship between "race" and state. He focuses (1991a) more precisely on racism and nationalism, yet does not treat them as abstract ideologies but as tools of the state. It is only as a function of state power that racism, as it intersects with nationalist ideology, becomes significant. Balibar describes the relationship between racism and nationalism as one of "reciprocal determination". They are not reducible to each other, but each determines the other's political potential within the context of the growth of both the nation-state itself and its project of imperialist domination.

By the end of the nineteenth century, racism could be said to have two main political functions. The first was to establish the terms of conflict between "race nations", the European states themselves, each considered to unify a "race" of people within them. The second, more durable and ultimately pernicious task was to distinguish between different groups of people both within and between societies based on a system of hierarchies which placed the European at the top. Racism was originally employed as a discourse against the presumed "weakness" of the working class, thought to dilute the strength of the "race nation" (Balibar, 1991b; MacMaster, 2000). However, when the outbreak of the First World War and mass conscription necessitated the rallying of the working class, racism sought different targets. It took on both an internal and external dimension which were nonetheless mutually complementary. Externally, racism was used to explain the differences between Europeans and the "natives" in the colonies, legitimating both their direct domination and the civilising mission woven into the colonial enterprise. Internally, racism theorised the enemy within; be it the often invisible and thus particularly dangerous Jew, or the sharp reminder of the long-time diversity of European societies represented by Gypsies, blacks and immigrants.

The need to classify human beings that the nation-state gave rise to and which racism fulfilled is related by Balibar to universalism. Balibar sees racism and universalism as opposites which determine each other. This is why, he explains, 'each of them has the other inside itself—or is bound to affect the other *from the inside*' (Balibar 1994: 198). Racism and universalism are so intimately connected because the power of racism is in its ability to define the frontiers of humanity. The reason why racism has endured past the end of slavery, the Holocaust and into the postcolonial era is that it was able to institute ideas about the purportedly inherent differences between West and East, "civilised" and "primitive", or in other words, between the "raceless" and the "raced". Racism and universalism reflect each other because it is impossible to dissociate racism from the project of defining a "general idea of man" at the core of universalism. In order to define universally rational man, in the sense of the Enlightenment philosophers, it was also necessary to define who such a being was not. It is here that the hierarchical categorisation of "races" from the superior to the inferior, upon which racism is based, is fundamental. Because the idea of universal humanity was constructed in the image of the white European, against the non-European, the blacks in the colonies and the internal others, the application of the essence of humanity, as it was defined by European thinkers, to all men and women was impossible from the outset. It is simply not possible for those who do not comply with a definition of humanity—rationality, individuality, white aesthetics—to be considered (fully) human. It is for this reason that Hesse (1999) has insisted on referring to *European* universals in an attempt to point out the specificity of the ideal of humanity proposed by Europeans. It is only because of the rise in Europe's power and its domination over the rest of the world that this perspective could be presumed to be universal. This question remains central to today's debate over a "clash of civilisations", theorised in the West against a supposedly politically immature, irrational and dangerous East.

The connection between racism and the quest to define an ideal vision of what it is to be human, is illustrated by looking specifically at how racism evolved in the colonies. David Goldberg (2002) theorises a separation between "naturalist" and "historicist" racism. The former lasted from the seventeenth to approximately the mid-nineteenth century and was defined by the idea that racial inferiority was inherent and scientifically provable. Historicist racism comes later but continues to overlap with naturalism. It is based on the idea that racial progress is possible. In other words, through exposure to Europeans in the colonies, education and assimilation, "inferior" racial groups could eventually evolve and attain a higher level of humanity. This progressivist approach is at the heart of contemporary debates on the integration of immigrants and their descendents, as though imposing "our way of life" upon them were sufficient to make differences disappear and end racism. Historicist racism is the relationship between racism and universalism in practice. It endures when virulent, overt naturalist racism is weakened because it functions under the guise of offering others the possibility to become like us, although we never ask whether this is in fact desired.

Goldberg demonstrates how historicist racism, the attempt to assimilate colonised and immigrant peoples into a European standard that was considered a higher way of life, continues to determine racism today. The assimilation of difference is the prerequisite for "racelessness" or the belief that we live in a post-racial age when the divisions "race" creates have lost significance. For Goldberg, this position emerges from dominant white thought, in which only whiteness is racially neutral. It is by failing to engage with the experience of racism that it is possible to claim that "race" has faded away and is no longer significant for individual lives and societies. While biological racial differences are inexistent, the effects of the racism that nevertheless persist make it impossible to relegate the experience of "race" to the shadowy past. Racism in contemporary western societies is experienced, above all else, as the discrepancy between the promise encapsulated by the *idea* of the West (integration, democracy, human rights…) and the reality; that it is always nearly there, but ultimately just out of reach.

The double face of the racist state

Today the postcolonial, post-immigration societies of the western world present us with a political paradox that has a strong influence over how we interpret and struggle against racism. Put simply, the discourse and practice of western states are both racist and anti-racist. What does this mean? The end of the Second World War and the realisation of the horrors of the Holocaust brought with it a commitment to eradicate racism. Governments and international institutions introduced programmes of education, public information and legislation to this end. Their approach was founded upon the idea that racism is an external force that invades the body politic but that the state itself, contrary to the argument this collection seeks to make, is unconnected from this process. Racism is seen as an aberration of the politics of democratic nation-states, the work of posthumously named fanatics as epitomised by Adolf Hitler. Following the Holocaust, the bringing to an end of colonialism and the beginning of large-scale non-European immigration to the West, it was important to officially prove the falsity of racism as a scientific idea. The emphasis of organisations such as UNESCO in the 1950s, which strongly influenced government policy, on providing alternative explanations for human difference by focusing on culture and ethnocentrism rather than "race" and racism, had an important effect on policy-making (Lentin 2004). Successive governments over the last fifty years have officially promoted the importance of confronting and punishing racism, while at the same time both instituting policies that could only be described as racist and failing to challenge a culture of discrimination that ensures the persistence of racism.

The contemporary political situation throws this paradox into relief. There is an increasing concern in the West with identity or what it means to belong to a particular national entity, to Europe, or to what is considered western civilisation. This identity is being pitted against a non-western essence, that has entered the metropolis and which for many runs the risk of overrunning the West itself. Difference from western cultural norms, which has always been strange and vaguely threatening, has come now to symbolise an attack on values that have taken on proportions of "we-ness" that greatly exaggerate the realities of the majority of those living in today's diverse societies.

Since the eleventh of September, 2001 this threat has been mainly associated with Islam. The religion itself and Muslims have been associated with barbaric actions and inhumane attitudes. This notion has not confined itself to rhetoric, but has been practically transformed into the "War on Terror", a war on all fronts that has the potential to attack our neighbours in Paris, Amsterdam and London as much as those in Iraq and Afghanistan. The "collateral damage" caused by this war is the erosion of everybody's civil liberties, a fact that the politics of fear have managed to convince the majority of us is for our own good. It is impossible to dissociate the fear and hatred of Islam and Muslims from the actions of states in their quest to eliminate the scourge of terrorism. Although we can make coherent arguments that demonstrate the rise in Islamophobia since "9/11", it is rare that the racial profiling of the brown-skinned in general is perceived as racism. The dominance of "human security" above all political concerns has made this a question of commonsense. It is important to recall that, in Europe, the historical precedent for this is the widespread social antisemitism that indirectly enabled the gas chambers.

In the approach of western states and supranational institutions today there is no sense of the contradiction between the discrimination bred by the human security regime and what racism is officially understood to be. Racism, as an aberration from the "natural" course of modern state politics has always been seen as marginal. It has been treated psychologically, as a problem of individuals, the result of ignorance or socioeconomic disadvantage. Rarely has it been treated as a problem of elites and, even less so, as the business of states. Even the landmark admission of the institutionalised racism of the British police force in 1997 (The Stephen Lawrence Inquiry 1997) focused on the perceived importance of introducing greater numbers of minority ethnic police officers into the force, as though police racism was uniquely a result of individuals' lack of sensitivity.

This dominant attitude makes it possible for the paradox at the heart of official approaches to dealing with racism and discrimination to function. On the one hand, governments admit that great numbers of the population face discrimination in employment, education, health care, and in social and political life. This discrimination is put down to a variety of factors and is rarely cognisant of the role played by states, and the political culture in which they are moulded, in bringing it about. On the contrary, the state is seen as a source of protection against discrimination through its declared commitment to principles of democracy, equal rights and the rule of law. Moreover, the state actively intervenes against discrimination in various ways, including the funding of campaigns, training programmes, employment schemes, educational programmes etc.

On the other hand, states across the West actively participate in the practice of racism in many ways. Most significantly, they do so by distinguishing between citizens and non-citizens on the basis of racialised criteria. Immigration policies are differentially oriented according to country of origin. To curtail the flow of unwanted western-bound immigration, all western states have embarked upon a politics of detention and deportation that violates the treaties that they themselves have signed to protect human rights. There is an increased link drawn between immigration and asylum and terrorism, creating the impression that those wishing to come to the West are a potential threat to "our" security. Finally, children and grandchildren of immigrants do not escape this general association of the "foreigner" with danger or threat. It is more and more common to hear about the radicalisation of young people of immigrant origin, almost always associated with Islamic fundamentalism whether or not these claims have any bearing in reality. Despite the living together of generations of young people of different origins in western metropolises for decades, an image has been created that gangs of ethnically segregated young people endanger our neighbourhoods and that, in the worst cases, they have links to terror organisations that bring the threat to our very existence into the heart of society.

The uprisings of young people in the *banlieues* of France for three weeks in November 2003 highlighted the nature of contemporary western racism. The response of the French government was to admit to the social disadvantage faced by residents of these poor and under-serviced areas and to promote the importance of greater *"mixité sociale"* as a solution to the discrimination faced by young people of minority ethnic origin. This response nevertheless came after the French interior minister, Nicolas Sarkozy, called the rioters "scum". It was also tempered by the overriding belief that solutions to the problems of the "difficult neighbourhoods", as they are euphemistically referred to in French, could be overcome by a reinstatement of "French values" (Lentin 2006). Encouraging diversity, or *"mixité sociale"*, as a solution to the police brutality that actually triggered the riots or the daily racism faced by brown and black people in a myriad of spheres, reveals the extent to which racism is divorced from acts and practices carried out in the name of the state and analytically confined to the domain of intercultural communication. The insistence in France, but also in other examples from the US, that these young people are in fact French sends out mixed messages when they are also culturally reified as different from their peers of "French stock".

The racism of western states cannot be separated from their publicly declared commitment to anti-racism. This is because the definition of racism upon which official anti-racism is built is often very far removed from what the lived-experience of racism tells us that it is. This dissociation of racism from the state and its resultant depoliticisation is what ultimately leads to the bubbling over of rage that became the French riots of late 2005. Until there is a widespread realisation of the need to analyse racism from a perspective that sees the state as central to its origins, its persistence and perhaps its resolution, it will remain impossible to redress the injustices that racism has left as legacies imprinted upon societies and individuals.

Ireland as a textbook case

It is not only because the conference from which this collection derives was held in Ireland that there is a whole section in this collection which deals with the "racial states" of Ireland. Ireland is indeed uniquely positioned among European nation-states. Though a former colony, the Irish nation-state has imagined itself as based on a racialised notion of identity and on a desire to demonstrate that the claim to statehood was in part based on the assertion that the Irish nation was not different from other European nations and did therefore differ from subaltern non-European peoples. However, in recent years common wisdom has it that Ireland has only just changed from being a "sending country" to being an "immigration destination". While the case of the Republic of Ireland can be used as a laboratory case in illustrating the nexus of "race" and state, the "racial statelet" of Northern Ireland, the capital of which has recently been declared as "the race hate capital of Europe" (see McVeigh in this volume), serves as an even more peculiar illustration of the intersection of the colonial and the racial.

Since the growth of the economy of the Republic of Ireland in the 1990s and the arrival of a small yet significant number of immigrants—asylum seekers, labour migrants, and undocumented migrants—the Irish state has both denied racism and consistently minimised the effect of state policies on the lives of racialised populations. On the one hand, emphasis has been placed on the need for more migrants to sustain the economic growth of the "Celtic Tiger". On the other hand, the state has made explicit its commitment to restricting immigration and increasing deportations of those not deemed "useful" to global Ireland. What seemed like a contradiction between the state's avowed commitment to anti-racism and its restrictive immigration politics is actually, as is the case elsewhere, entirely consistent. If the Republic of Ireland was facing substantial in-migration for the first time in its history, it goes without saying that racism was perceived to have been imported by migrants rather than being the product of state policies enacted by white, Christian, settled Ireland. The state had to do something, and the result was racial categorisation and state racism, a racism the state uses to defend "its own" population, a racism that society exercises against itself (Foucault 2003).

If from the start, the arrival of immigrants in Ireland was conceived as a "problem", there were specific developments in the Republic of Ireland which make it a textbook example of a contemporary "racial state". Of particular significance is the referendum held in June 2004 which asked the electorate to constitutionally change the *jus solis* citizenship entitlement to all people born on the island of Ireland, an entitlement which prevailed since the establishment of the state in 1922, into an entitlement based on *jus sanguinis* according to which only the children of citizens can become citizens at birth. The proposed change needs to be understood not only in the context of the formation of the state in Ireland, or the move from institutional to constitutional racism, with Irish historicism increasingly regarding non-Irish others as inadequate candidates for citizenship, employing patently racist legislation to criminalise, regulate and control both in-migrants and indigenous populations, but also in the context of globalisation. The racial state gives citizenship to some—including its own co-opted "ethnic minorities"—inside what can be termed a "gated community". Those, including labour migrants, indigenous and other racialised people, although not deemed eligible, are, as Michel Foucault (2003) would have it, "made live and let die". At the same time, the rest of the globalised world—through a series of imperialist and neo-imperialist moves—is "made die", and if they are lucky, "let live". Thus the globalised world shifts from sovereign power to biopower, in historical and structural terms, separating those within the gated community of the racial state from those without. Contemporary Ireland, declared by the Centre for the Study of Globalisation and Regionalisation as topping the globalisation index, is a prime example of the deliberate separation—using commonsense, legal, constitutional means—between those who can and those who cannot access citizenship.

The government's campaign for the Citizenship Referendum, sprung on the electorate without sufficient time to debate and explore the meanings of such a change, portrayed migrants as taking advantage of Ireland's supposedly "generous" immigration laws. Migrant mothers, in particular, were singled out for deliberately subverting "the integrity of Irish citizenship" by having Irish citizen babies (see Lentin and McVeigh, 2006). Privileging a progressivist vision about the integration of immigrants, particularly those labour migrants needed by the "Celtic Tiger" economy, the state was quite clear which categories of people it regarded as waste material, including, in particular, asylum seekers.

Admittedly this is not different from other European states, all of which boast a reduction in the numbers of people seeking asylum while omitting to admit that large numbers are not given permission to lodge their asylum applications in the first place. What is different about Ireland is that the Citizenship Referendum, posited by the government as essential to the "integrity of Irish citizenship", was passed with a majority of four to one. With this result, the state now argued, neither the government nor the majority of Irish people could be considered racist. On the contrary, both the electorate and the government are deemed to be anti-racist, even though the government has replaced its anti-racist policy with a focus on diversity that emphasises Irish racelessness while at the same time leaving "race" and racism out of official discourse.

Reading "Race and State"

The chapters in this book are organised into three parts, reflecting the structure of the conference from which this collection emerged. Not all the papers presented at the conference are included here. There are also three papers that were not presented at that occasion but which we felt could add to the argument the authors in this book collectively seek to make. These are the articles by David Theo Goldberg and Alana Lentin in Part I and of Ronit Lentin in Part III.

Part I of the book looks at theoretical issues in conceptualising the relationship between "race" and state. The authors centre their focus on how to build on historical and contemporary observation in order to construct a theory of "race" and state. Crucially, "race" and racism are always understood to emerge out of an historicised context, of modernity and the nation-state, of Nazism (Muelhauser), of colonialism (Lentin, Ikeotuonye) and of the contemporary politics of states such as the US and Ireland (Goldberg, Garner and Moran). Moroever, racism is always set in its political context so that there is no doubt that it must be viewed, in the opinion of these authors, from a politicised perspective that leaves no room for the reduction of racism to pathology. Of importance also is the authors' location of the origins of racism in the West. While there has been a growing tendency to generalise the phenomenon of racism both to non-western contexts and to pre-modern times, it is important to identify the advance of racism as we know it today within the modern setting, its roots firmly implanted in Europe.

Racism has often been theorised as capable of taking on many guises and of adapting itself politically to time and context. Part II examines racism in its most pernicious contemporary manifestation, namely in the racialisation of "terror". While Kumar focuses on the historical and theoretical precedents, particularly in anthropology and geography, for the current racism of the "war on Terror", Sparks's and Bhattacharyya's pieces relate directly to contemporary politics. The significance of this section of the book is its ability to make concrete the link between racism and today's politics of fear by showing how, through the media (Sparks) and by the militarisation of everyday life (Bhattacharyya), the object of society's fears is a racialised being. The fears of western people for their personal security, justified as they may be to some extent, are channelled through a presentation of the threat in the figure of a brown-skinned man. Through the state's direct targeting of these internal outsiders as potential terrorists society is unable to formulate a contradictory impression that would reveal the tenuous link made between terrorism and the Muslims living among us.

The chapters in Part III, on the racial state(s) of Ireland, must be read against the background of post-Referendum Ireland, where new census categorisations will divide the population in "racial" terms (King-O'Riain), and where the debates on migrant labour privilege the interest of global capital (Allen and Loyal). The fact that Ireland has been convincing itself of its "monoculturalism" and non-colonial past is refuted by Mac Éinrí's discussion of Irish alliances with colonial whiteness. That Ireland has moved from being constructed in racial terms to being an explicitly—though not admittedly so—racist state (Lentin) is illustrated by the routinisation of racist discourse (Moriarty). These chapters, taken together, are an important addition to such a collection which, for the first time, focuses on Ireland as a "test case" for demonstrating and interpreting the relationship between "race" and state.

"Race and state" aims to contribute to breaking the taboo that clearly exists in the West regarding the racism of the state. We can no longer pretend that racism was only a passing phase through which some states passed, momentarily overtaken by anti-democratic fanaticism. Racism is not reducible to Nazism and fascism. It is very much a part of the lives of millions of individuals. Were it merely the "natural" feelings that lurk in us all, as many would have it, it could quite simply not cause the, often fatal and irreversible, damage it incurs on our bodies and minds. It would not impinge upon how we live together in diverse societies, nor would it bring about such injustices and inequalities. For racism to function, it needs a political apparatus. That apparatus is the state, its bureaucracy and its institutions which in turn influence the hearts and minds of the people who live within it. It is how it functions that this book seeks to interrogate in the hope, always, of pointing towards a better future.

References

Arendt, Hannah. 1966. *The Origins of Totalitarianism*. New York & London: Harcourt Brace Jovanovich.
Balibar, Etienne. 1991a. Racism and Nationalism, in Etienne Balibar and Immanuel Wallerstein, *Race, Nation, Class: Ambiguous Identities*. London: Verso: 37-67.
Balibar, Etienne. 1991b. Class Racism, in Etienne Balibar and Immanuel Wallerstein, *Race, Nation, Class: Ambiguous Identities*, London: Verso, 1991, pp. 204-216.
Balibar, Etienne. 1994. *Masses, Classes, Ideas: Studies on politics and philosophy before and after* Marx. New York: Routledge.
Bauman, Zygmunt. 1989. *Modernity and the Holocaust*. Cambridge: Polity Press.
Fanon, Frantz. 1967. *Black Skins, White Masks*. London: Pluto Press.
Foucault, Michel. 2003. *Society Must be Defended*.
Goldberg, David Theo. 2002. *The Racial State*. Malden, Mass. and Oxford: Blackwell.
Hannaford, Ivan. 1996. *Race: The history of an idea in the West*. Baltimore: Johns Hopkins University Press.
Hesse, Barnor. 1999. "It's Your World": Discrepant M/multiculturalisms, in Phil Cohen (Ed.), *New Ethnicities, Old Racisms*. London : Zed Books.
Lentin, Ronit and Robbie McVeigh. 2006. *After Optimism? Ireland, Racism and Globalisation*. Dublin: Metro Eireann Publications.
Lentin, Alana. 2004. R*acism and Anti-Racism in Europe*. London: Pluto Press.
Lentin, Alana. 2006. Racism, Anti-Racism and the Western State, in G. Delanty, R. Wodak and P. Jones (eds.) forthcoming 2006, *Migrant Voices:Discourses of Belonging and Exclusion*. Liverpool: Liverpool University Press.
MacMaster, Neil. 2001. *Racism in Europe 1870-2000*. Houndmills: Palgrave.
Mosse, George. 1978. *Towards the Final Solution: A history of European racism*. London: J.M. Dent & Sons Ltd.
The Stephen Lawrence Inquiry. 1999. Report of an Inquiry by Sir William MacPherson of Cluny. Presented to Parliament by the Secretary of State for the Home Department by Command of Her Majesty. London: The Stationary Office.
Voegelin, Eric. 1933a. [2000]. *Race and State*. Baton Rouge and London: Louisiana State University Press. (trans. Ruth Heim).
Voegelin, Eric 1933b. *Die Rassenidee in der Geistesgeschichte von Ray bis Carus*. Berlin: Junker & Duennhaupt.
Voegelin, Eric. 1940. The Growth of the Race Idea, *The Review of Politics* July: 283-317.

Part I

Theorising Race and State

CHAPTER ONE

DEVA-STATING DISASTERS: RACE IN THE
SHADOW(S) OF NEW ORLEANS

DAVID THEO GOLDBERG

For at least the past half-century, America has advanced itself as committed to racial justice, pointing to the Civil Rights Movement and the wave of non-discrimination, anti-segregationist, and equal rights legislation that followed the series of Supreme Court rulings from the late 1940s onwards. These were important developments, and in many ways shifted the racial ground on which America historically has stood. Less noticed in the political sphere—certainly less celebrated—however, are the counter-trends in ideological representation, prevailing political commitment, and dominant social arrangement that these gains prompted as a backlash from the 1980s onwards (Gold 2004).

Old segregationist racism, from post-Reconstruction to *Brown v. Board of Education* (1954), was what can properly be characterised as an *activist* segregation. It involved for the most part an active intervention in politics, economics, law, and culture self-consciously designed to produce segregated city, town, and neighborhood spaces. To combat this activism, to undo its pernicious and debilitating effects and implications, the Civil Rights Movement likewise was compelled to act responsively on every social, political, legal, and cultural register. Coalitional anti-racist resistance and struggle, perhaps by definition, are activist pursuits. Laws needed changing, the web of racial covenants and redlining promoting residential segregation needed unraveling, the closed doors of segregated schools and universities had to be unlocked, inaccessible workplaces had to be entered and transformed from the inside out, voting practices reproducing all-White city halls and legislatures had to be dramatically restyled and voting districts reapportioned (People 2005). None of this would have changed on its own, economic determinists of one stripe or another notwithstanding.

Prompted by the tensions between political pressures at home and abroad, the period from roughly post-World War II to the 1970s was one of tension and contradiction between the ancient regime of racist structures and anti-racist possibilities. It was a period of promise and projection, expectation and elevation, denial and in some debilitating ways ultimately dashed hope. It was a period, in short, of desegregating commitment and the seeds of a re-segregating mobilisation. The logic of the old segregation supposedly was swept aside— only to be replaced by the whisper of the new, the subtle and silent, the informal and insidious, what elsewhere I have characterised as "the born-again" (Goldberg 2004). This newly expressed segregation, the newly privatising segregation at the heart of the model I designate *racial americanisation*, is no longer activist but conservative, a segregation in the literal sense conservationist.

To say that racism in the United States got to be born-again is not to say it ever disappeared. It shifted its modalities and expression, its articulations and dispositions, its ways of being. The public legalities aimed at undoing explicit racist practice in the name of the state redirected principal racist expression and reproduction to the private sphere, institutionally and personally. And in doing so it emphatically sought to protect privatised racist expression from state intervention. But this principal form of contemporary racial americanisation, of what I am calling born-again racism, proceeds not simply by reducing the social to the preferential, the state to the privatisations of (in)civil society. Preferences are not expressed, enacted, and experienced in a political and institutional vacuum. Rather, public spheres—and the state especially—structure the conditions of possibility on the basis of which choices are to be made, preferences pushed and indeed whether, when, and what punished or rewarded. State structures channel, shape, and mould both the boundaries and the terrain of choice-making and their implication; and preferences expressed and enacted reinforce existing state formation even as they inflect and color them.

Conservationist segregation thus fashions the model of racial americanisation. This model proceeds by *undoing* the laws, rules, and norms of expectation the Civil Rights movement managed to put in place. It attacks those laws and the social order predicated on them as unconstitutional, as the only sort of racial discrimination with which we should be concerned today. Embracing *race neutrality*, racial americanisation nevertheless licenses "limited" racial profiling for purposes of security maintenance, targeted policing and medical research as legitimate for combating the moral panics of terror and the disasters producing it, socially or naturally prompted. The Racial Privacy Act initiative, first introduced in California and now traveling to other states identified by racial conservationists as racial battlegrounds, embodies even in its title the logic at work. Racial expression was not to be excised from the body politic. Rather, it was to be privatised, and protected in its privatisation (Post 2001).

In the absence of the Civil Rights spirit, and now in its active undoing, accordingly, the present period *conserves* (and deepens) the hold of racial preference schemes historically produced *as if they were the nature of things*. So racial americanisation is produced by a mix of doing nothing special, nothing beyond being guided by the presumptive laws of the market, the determinations of the majority's personal preferences, and the silencing of all racial reference with the exception especially of racial profiling for purported purposes of crime and terror control. This silencing fails to distinguish between exclusionary *racist* designs and practices, on the one hand, and redressive or ameliorative *racial* interventions, on the other, reducing the latter to the former for the most part as the only contemporary racist expressions worth worrying about.

William Bennett, self-ascribed arbiter of America's moral virtues, exemplifies the logic in play here. He recently responded to a call-in question on his radio show that, while morally reprehensible and ridiculous, aborting all Black babies would result in a sharp reduction in the US crime rate (Bennett 2005). His "hypothetical" if not hypocritical call, effectively genocidal, is protected as the sort of free speech the wall of privatisation around civil society is designed to render critically unreachable. Bennett's "observation" trades on a cache of widespread if no longer explicitly expressed presumptions: that the crime rate in the US is overwhelmingly fueled by Black criminality, that such criminality is a more or less natural and so inescapable condition of especially the Black poor, but also that it is not unacceptable to issue eugenicist judgments about the implications of hypothetical genocide in the case of African Americans in ways it would mostly not be for any other group today (Muslims included). This latter presumption trades on the Africanity of African Americans, the normalcy if not naturalness of early death in the case of the descendants of the despised continent. Hidden from view here is the less extreme logic on which the claim trades, for it is as surely the case that any aborting of babies of any ethnoracial background would likely reduce the crime rate, given that some percentage of that rate, large or small, is made up by members of every ethnoracial group. Bennett's racial eugenicism advances itself only at the price of the expendability of Black lives.

Only slightly less extreme, because not quite as explicit, the libertarian pluralist motto of "live and let live" licenses a surplus of possibility and opportunity for the affording few at the expense of the impoverished many. It might more accurately be replaced with the motto, "live free or die," most explicitly identified with the state of New Hampshire, implying that those who cannot afford the freedom will be left to perish. There is, as commentators on euthanasia have long pointed out, a thin line between (social) killing and letting die. Between making live and letting die, as Foucault has put it in *Society Must be Defended* (Foucault 2003), are histories whitewashed and refashioned, activist interventions restricted, the racial status quo resurrected, revived, (re)fixed in place.

The privatisation of racially exclusionary and debilitating preference expression that expresses racial americanisation today makes it more or less unreachable by state intervention. But to secure the shift, to make it truly unreachable by state amelioration, to restrict the competition for social resources in the face of the increasing heterogenising of the society, racial conservationists are keen to supplement their gains by a radical curtailment of state possibility. In this mode, the current commitment by fundamentalist fiscal radicals to defund social programs in education, health care, emergency management and response, popular culture and the arts through extreme forms of tax reduction while increasing military, security, and prison expenditures and investments brings public funding to the point of bankruptcy. Grover Norquist, contemporary Republicans' philosopher-king, has giddily proclaimed that his aim is so to starve government of revenues that he "can drown it in a bathtub" (Dreyfuss 2001). The overwhelming social commitment to spiraling support for state institutions of violence, their enactment and (re)enforcement—military, policing, homeland security—in the face of an at best static if not diminishing treasury burdened most notably by dramatic tax reductions for the wealthiest 1 per cent of the population entails that the increases in such expenditures can only be supported by squeezing social welfare and support revenues.

In the past couple of budget cycles, hyper-conservatives have targeted programs for the poor both because these programs offer easy fiscal targets and convenient ideological rationalisation. At the same time, defense budgets, whether narrowly or broadly interpreted, have spiraled. Thus, the defense budget for FY2006 amounts to $435 billion, up 5 per cent from the previous year and almost 25 per cent from its 2002 total of $344 billion. The projected $40 billion worth of cuts in the 2006 budget projections focus overwhelmingly on social programs such as student loans, health care and welfare for the poor etc (Washington Post 2005). If one factored into the figure for the defense budget the entire range of institutional apparatuses sustaining military presence at home and around the world, including $35 billion for Homeland Security, funds to fight in Iraq and Afghanistan, and the considerable sums for their respective reconstructions, the total would reach a staggering $900 billion, up roughly 30 percent since 2002 (Higgs 2004).

At the same time, funding for education, health, housing, and transportation as well as emergency relief has been cut repeatedly. Since 2003, when it was incorporated into the Department of Homeland Security, the Federal Emergency Management Agency (FEMA) has been reduced by 10 per cent (if President

Bush had had his way the cuts would have come closer to 25 per cent). These cuts have had a debilitating effect on disaster preparedness and reconstruction, undercutting the agency's ability to sustain support for those most in need, as we have witnessed in the wake of Katrina, and ceding to uncoordinated private charities the responsibilities of evacuation, clean-up, reconstruction, and care. The results, as we now know, have been disastrous.

As with personal or corporate bankruptcy, this emaciation of the social support sector of government revenues forces a radical restructuring of public programming and state governmentality. The immediate implication of such state restriction and ultimately devastation is to redistribute wealth upwards. The point, explicitly articulated by neo-conservative pundits and neoliberal politicians, is to put more wealth into the hands of the already wealthy. Expenditures of the wealthy, we are repeatedly told beguilingly, are supposed to trickle down into jobs for the less well off. But the mission, as much as any, is also to elevate the decision making, social engineering, and effective powers of the well off. The social effect of state emaciation, accordingly, is not that social spending should end completely. Rather, in being redirected into private hands, it is fashioned by the social and political interests of those with capital to spare.

So private (toll) roads, the recent emergence of private electrical grids in the face of blackouts, dramatically expanded privatisation of funding for radio stations, policing functions (at least supplementally), certainly schools and in some instances such as Philadelphia entire school districts, hospitals, and universities (even public ones) are thrown increasingly into the hands—and so at the discretion of—those who can afford and choose to support them. Even the authoring of key legislation is handed over to corporately sponsored lobbyists— the K Street Project in Washington DC—who craft laws for lawmakers too stretched, resourceless, or corrupt to do it themselves. The effect is not that all funding support for public programming ends but that funding for almost anything other than explicit behavioral control programs becomes pointedly privatised. The state is reduced to little more than keeping law and order, staving off the violent and increasingly the merely critical, at home and abroad. State interests, on this view, are thus directed, if not reductively determined, by the wealthy with disposable income or investment capital to plunge into political exploits.

Now the elevated factions of social class in a racial state like the US have traditionally been White, or more precisely representing the interests of those occupying the structural class position of whiteness (and masculinity). The US Census Bureau reports that in 2000 the top 5 per cent of White wage earners received wages almost double those of the top 5 per cent of Black wage earners. Unsurprisingly, the largest contributors by far to political campaigns in the US are White men. Under this mandate of radical privatisation, funded institutions, programs, and activities accordingly become dramatically less diverse both in their programming, scope and commitments and notably in their employment patterns even than they were until recently, and certainly than they could or ought to be. Hence the fundamentalist conservative outrage expressed by the likes of Abigail Thernstrom, Ward Connoly, Linda Chavez, and the Center for Individual Rights at the temporary set-back in their well-heeled plans regarding the Supreme Court's recent upholding in *Grutter v. Bollinger* (2003) of law schools' limited affirmative action programs for the sake of maintaining a diverse student body. Neo-conservative critics committed to a "race-free" America (note, not *racist* free) have blasted the diversity commitments of the Court's majority as "murdering the Fourteenth Amendment" (Ward Connerly 2003)), as "diversity drivel" (Michael Greve), and discriminatory (Linda Chavez), indeed, even "racist" (Abigail Thernstrom) (Chronicle 2003). If it is no longer possible explicitly and discriminatorily to restrict demographic diversity, the culture wars can be won by defunding progressive cultural commitments, by shrinking the cultural horizons of heterogeneity.

There are supplementary sociological factors in play underpinning and sustaining the current cauldron of anxieties, paranoias, redirections, and renewed restrictions for some and social possibilities for others around racial matters. Black Americans are no longer the largest minority in the US. Latinos are growing as a percentage of the overall population (12-13 per cent and rising more quickly than any other major demographic group), as too are Asian Americans though in far smaller numbers and a lower growth rate. African Americans (11 per cent of the population) thus are shrinking proportionately, or at least not growing. Social leverages, relatively speaking, are accordingly shifting. Latinos see themselves connected with some pride to Latin America, or nations in Latin America (most notably at World Cup time, or when the US soccer team plays Mexico or Brazil, or baseball teams occasionally play Cuba). To some degree, and with varying effect, they also have leaders of Latin American countries speaking (up) on their behalf, whether trying to negotiate better conditions for recent (im)migrants to the US or in the case of both Castro and Chavez offering more visible assistance to America's racial poor in the wake of natural disasters than seems to emanate from Washington. Asian Americans see themselves connected as a result of family ties, heritage, and nostalgia (if not now also investment) to countries in Asia—notably China, Taiwan, Hong Kong, Vietnam, Japan and Korea. Those connections are affirming, a sense of pride, regions that represent at least some success and that, at least in the public imaginary, are less ostensibly or forcefully racially inscribed.

African American connection to Africa, by contrast, is at best imagined, ideological, in any case deeply ambivalent, fueled on one side by pride in

Africa's rich cultural and civilisational legacy, its expansive beauty, even its fortitude in the face of colonial degradation but on the other side by its current poverty stricken, famine common, and war torn conditions. The tale of anti-apartheid jubilation and the relative success of the new South Africa have paled before Africa's broadening debilitation. And, of late, the concern with overcoming African poverty has become the new White liberal cause celebre. Witness Bono, Angelina Jolie, and their social influence, as important and heart felt as they may be. Here, Black Americans, who have long rallied in support of Africa, are now edged if not elbowed to the social sidelines.

Related to these demographic shifts and their attendant conditions of possibility and implication, debates about race in the US have shifted quietly if dramatically over the past five years. Today the two seminal considerations regarding the americanising of matters racial have to do with the twin towers of immigration and terrorism. Their ideological connectivity is evidenced in the remarks of the Republican Texas congressman John Culberson. In recently sponsoring legislation to arm civilian militias—"boots on the ground," as he puts it ominously—to patrol the Texas border with Mexico, Culberson explicitly characterizes illegal border crossers from Mexico as "terrorists' (or when speaking more carefully as "harboring terrorists") (Culberson 2005). This identification evidences the increasing shift of racial inventedness in the wake of 9/11 to the slippery figure of the terrorist as Muslim, a slippage often prompting the (il)logical reversal in the public mind notwithstanding politically rationalising denials.

Here too relational logics affect ambiguous outcomes. So as the "war on terror" is mobilised globally and critical attention is pressed upon especially radicalised and radicalising Muslims, African Americans fade into the fabric of America, becoming less African, so to speak, and more American. Iconic Black figures such as Colin Powell and Condoleeza Rice suggest the constrictive possibility of climbing effectively to positions of power, of climbing out of *African* Americanness as the devil's choice might have it. On the other hand, this slow dissolution of African America in the remaking of contemporary America (a dissolution thick with traces, of course) is consistent with longer trends of social invisibilities and disappearances. Roughly a third of African American men have suffered through the criminal justice system in one way or another, leaving them at the margins of civil society and largely without voice. African American youth under eighteen tried as adults are ten times more likely than White youth convicted of similar crimes to receive life sentences without possibility of parole (in California it is twenty-two times more likely). Racial profiling continues to shine a debilitating spotlight on Black men in the dark of night. And racially inflected impoverishment (like unemployment rates) continues to grope at Black Americans more than at others in its spiral upwards

(12 per cent of Americans but 25 per cent of African Americans live in poverty now, mostly without state support or health insurance). Two further factors fuel this deepening social invisibility, leaving African Americans with a social dilemma more acute than members of other demographic groups. First, America continues to walk away from the commitment to affirmative action. The California experiment is indicative of future trends. In the wake of Proposition 209 in 1998, banning the use of state funds for affirmative action programs in hiring, promotion, and college admission or support, registration of Black students at the better ranked University of California campuses as well as the hiring and retention of Black faculty (not to mention women in the sciences, as it turns out) have dropped precipitously. In the Fall 2005 freshman Engineering class at UC Berkeley, for instance, of the 800 new students not a single one was African American. The numbers of African American students attending Boalt Hall, the University of California's flagship law school, were close to comparable. It is not over-dramatising the condition to say that Blacks in California are becoming dramatically less visible in higher education, and by extension in the professional workplace that carries status and influence, as a consequence (Brown et al 2003).

The second factor is even more fraught. Since at least *Brown v. Board of Education*, the Supreme Court desegregation ruling in 1954, the principal stress has been on formal equality before the law. That equals should be treated equally before the law has entailed the veiling of the substantially disequating effects as a result. Those without the means are treated far differently than those with. Conservatives see this as an unavoidable, even necessary, constitutive feature, if regrettable, of the American order and social fabric. Once again, we find principal evidence for this in the attempt to make California the laboratory by pushing to privatize racial discrimination in the name of protecting it for the most part from public scrutiny. But it is evidenced also in the attacks on civil rights protections specific to named racial groups as "special treatment". Underlying this rejection of supposedly special treatment is a drive less to dim the spotlight than to shift it from the public to the private realm, effectively pushing Black and Brown Americans, especially the racial poor, more deeply into the shadow of social disappearance, eroding self-confidence in the face of expanding invisibilities. The already vulnerable are made to feel even more so.

The fate of New Orleans in the wake of Hurricane Katrina in late summer 2005 illustrates these trends with furious force. A city of almost half a million, its population as the hurricane hit was 67 per cent African American. One in eight Americans now live in poverty and double that number of Black Americans; in New Orleans the poverty rate for Black residents was closer to 50 per cent as a result of the multiplying logic of high racial concentration Nancy

Denton has identified more generally (Denton 1994). Privatising the conditions of wellbeing has meant the wealthy White have the best medical care while the multitude have little or none. The well off live in gated communities high on the hill while the poor in the city as elsewhere have lived in polluted neighborhoods vulnerably below sea level with close to no garbage collection and few options. (Nationwide, White Americans are 79 per cent less likely than African Americans to live in locations threatened by the significant health hazards prompted by industrial pollution (Pace 2005).) The powerful drive larger and larger gas-guzzling SUVs while the impoverished have had no public transportation to speak of. The newly rich drink imported bottled water while the struggling have had only polluted tap water. The wealthy can dine daily in restaurants while the poor barely have had anything to eat at all, and could afford nothing by the end of each month as they await paychecks or welfare subsistence, or both. The wealthy get tax breaks and stock options while the poor can't even depend on the most rudimentary of educations. The lives of the rich are guarded from those of the poor whose fate is more likely prison than work.

In the case of Katrina all this has meant that the federal resources to make the city less vulnerable to the wrath of nature were rendered less and less available while urban decadence could ultimately be drowned in its own vulnerabilities. The well-to-do could scramble for safety in their air conditioned army-like vehicles while the poor were reduced to a decaying and in some cases deadly domed stadium. The tens of thousands unable to flee the evacuation order in New Orleans as the hurricane bore down were overwhelmingly Black, as revealed at the Superdome and Convention Center. Family and other networks could support the mobile while the immobile were left to flounder in a flooded and rotting city, many losing contact even with the family members sharing their fate. The less lucky lost their lives. The wealthier got to watch from afar while the stricken got to share the streets with floating bodies (sometimes of their own relatives), excrement, oil pollution. The privileged seemed to need no medical care while the poor restricted to the city got close to none, even where doctors from further afield were valiantly and vaingloriously volunteering their help. The rich were free to roam the country, the poor rounded up and subjected to prison-like conditions even when bussed off to safer turf, their crime nothing else than abject poverty and the color of their skin.

Amartya Sen has famously argued that famines, far from simply natural disasters, are politically produced, the product of strife, war, political conflict and turmoil (Sen 1981). It is these latter factors that more or less inevitably prevent the delivery of food and medical aid to avoid or alleviate starvation and death. The same could be said in this case.

In the name of securing the city, post-Katrina New Orleans was quickly turned into an armed military camp. Combat ready forces went door-to-door urban warfare style, kicking down locked entrances searching for survivors to evacuate at the end often enough of fully loaded AK47s. While critics were rightly bemoaning the dehumanising conduct of war abroad, few seemed to notice that for domestic purposes America was mimicking tactics of militarisation honed in the desert war. America, in short, has taken to turning itself into armed and gated camps at home. Our regime of social truth today is shaped principally by a military mind-set circulated and recirculated by all those retired generals appearing on the nightly news programs advising the public on how to read the day's events. President Bush even went so far as to make a case for turning over disaster response from civil to military agencies, the latter supplemented by if not subsidising private enterprise. And privately employed soldiers of fortune, recently repatriated by the likes of Blackhawk Security company from tours of duty protecting politicians and corporate entities in Iraq, invaded the city, requisitioning forcibly abandoned apartments in the French Quarter as headquarters, and firing randomly upon perceived looters and loiterers with the tacit blessing of the more constrained National Guard.

Post-Katrina New Orleans, in a nutshell, is simply Iraq come home.

The rebuilding of New Orleans will be instructive too. A city with few residents for the foreseeable future, it will be turned into a Disneyland for the oil industry where the racial poor will not be welcomed back (after all, they have been disbursed and dispersed to larger more heterogeneous cities where their presence ultimately will become less noticed) (Guardian Unlimited 2005). New Orleans will alchemize overnight from a Black majority to White majority city, a nightmare explicitly stated by the head of the US Department of Housing and Urban Development (HUD), Alphonso Jackson, himself ironically (and perhaps tragically) African American (DeBose 2005). A safe Democratic haven deep in the red-state South is being metamorphosed into another southern Republican stronghold. The working class will service the oil rich and worry free. The pollution will be rendered invisible in landfills and waterways once again to afflict the most vulnerable. A new sports stadium supporting privately owned sports teams valued at hundreds of millions of dollars each will be sponsored by public revenues. Mardi Gras will be turned from the conviviality of an organic urban celebration to the plasticity of tourist fanfare. New Orleans spirit reduced to the cloned parades of Mickeys and Minnies. Welcome back, well, to Houston.

For those residents of the Gulf who managed to survive the devastation, life after Katrina has meant putting themselves back together with diminishing government support to rely on, all the public relations rhetoric and promiscuous political promises notwithstanding. It is revealing that a large effort of private giving to hurricane relief has been heralded in contrast to the forlorn public revenues enabled (all the wondrous Presidential promises of more or less unlimited support notwithstanding), amidst handwringing about having to slow down extending existing tax cuts, most notably on capital gains and dividend payouts, and rendering permanent the ending of the estate tax.

Thus, those among the hundreds of thousands of Gulf Coast homeowners whose homes were decimated by the hurricane and flooding and who sought federal support to rebuild and revive their properties were directed to apply for low interest disaster loans from the Small Business Administration (SBA). A staggering 82 per cent of the 276,000 loan applications received to date have been rejected, overwhelmingly because incomes are too meager or credit ratings too low to qualify. The loans that have been approved have gone exclusively to wealthier and Whiter neighborhoods in New Orleans, those thus more readily able to rebuild. Rejected applicants are eligible for home repair grants from the FEMA but the grant amount in each case is capped at about one-seventh the loan amounts available from the SBA. The likes of the Ninth and Lower Ninth Wards largely remain empty, mildewed, cordoned off disaster areas with little relief in sight (Kestin, O'Matz, and Maines, 2005). Federal policy reinstates the privatised racial divide between the haves and the "would rather not have around."

The respective experiences of universities in the city serve to bear this out. Tulane University, private, overwhelmingly White, and wealthy, is well on the way to being cleaned up and set to welcome back its student body and (albeit diminished) faculty in January 2006; Black city schools such as Dillard, Xavier, and Southern, their physical plant more or less completely ruined by Katrina's flooding, will be fortunate if they reopen any time at all. The federal government has lived up to President Bush's promises to do whatever it takes to rebuild New Orleans at best partially—in both sense of the term (Crenson 2005).

So post-Katrina New Orleans has simply made bare for all of us what neocon America amounts to. Privatising the support system means just that, sustaining and securing the structures of support for private, corporately channeled interests and less for everyone else.

When Kanye Wesst declared on the national telethon to raise money for the victims of Katrina that George Bush "doesn't care about Black people", he personalised and individualised what for the past twenty years has been turned effectively into a deeply institutional rationality (Associated Press 2005). Since the Reagan administration, and exacerbated dramatically under George W. Bush, the state is being structured in such a way that poor people generally, which means especially Black citizens, are not to be taken into consideration, cared for, or exhibited compassion by the institutional apparatuses representing the state.

The effect of the Civil Rights successes for conservatives in the US was to read the state as being in the service of Black Americans. It had become, for African Americans, the largest post-segregation employer, the instrument of affirmative action, the educator of choice if not necessity, the guarantor of welfare rights when all else failed (or in this dismissive scheme of things more likely as the first resort), the underwriter of housing for those who might otherwise have none. In short, the state was seen by racial conservationists to have been metamorphosed by the Civil Rights revolution into a Black institution, or at least one whose mission was now foremostly to serve the interests of African Americans. The most effective counter on the conservationist view, both instrumentally and to avoid being seen as racist, would be to go after the institution of the state itself. Kill Goliath and the philistines with a single fling: Restrict Black advancement, thus cutting out the possibility of additional competition; and delimit state power, long a central conservative tenet. And so that it cannot respond to perceived crisis after crisis of racially driven impoverishment—gangs, crack cocaine, HIV/AIDS, educational failure, intensified poverty, urban blight—other than through criminalising the most vulnerable, the state is being steadily denuded of the resources of response.

Underlying these effects, prompting them both directly and indirectly, is a set of ideological presumptions and at least implicit discursive articulations that define racial americanisation. Most basically, homogenised apartness is taken as the norm of a deracialised—a declaratively raceless—polity. It is taken as the assumed, the natural, the given. Integration, or at least desegregation, accordingly comes over as unnnatural, literally absurd and irrational in the prevailing order of things, requiring intervention by the state at the cost of liberty (the freedom to choose where one lives or is educated, who one hires or works with, where one hangs out, worships or may be laid to rest). Racial americanists often ask what is so wrong with wanting to live only among one's own, among those culturally (and so presumptively racially) like one. Besides the fact that such presumed homogeneity necessarily takes for granted the coherence, purity, boundedness, and racial identity of cultural likeness, such homogeneity can only be purchased with the coin of severe repression, of purging difference and denying its influence if not its miscegenating seed. Homogeneity produces an ethnoracial class the insistent extension of which necessitates segregation. If the suburb of Gretna, a bridge away across the Mississippi, was to maintain its self-promoting fantasy as safe haven, the African American inhabitants of New Orleans had to be kept at arms length by forcefully closing the bridge, even at the cost of drowning those seeking refuge as Katrina flooding lapped at their waists (Cadenhead 2005).

The second assumption is that standards of civility, sociality, morality, self-determination, and wellbeing are represented overwhelmingly as White, that is, as those associated with the structure of whiteness. These are assumed as the norm, as the criteria of judgment, as representing what everyone else should aspire to. It was the blackness of the Superdome inhabitants and street looters that the media stressed ("they are *so* Black," declared Wolf Blitzer of CNN, in an ambiguous mix of paternalistic pathos and disgusting disdain), their slothfulness and gangsterism, their lack of civility and ability to fend for themselves.

Third, Whites are projected as the real victims of the excess of antiracist pathos (of leftist antiracist racism, of political correctness, of liberal soft-headedness, of the ideology of egalitarianism). New Orleans Mayor Ray Nagin was repeatedly portrayed as incompetent, as too slow to the response, as having no effective emergency plan in place. By contrast, until his incompetence proved irrepressible and he had to go, the fall guy for an incompetent and morally bankrupt administration, the narcissistically out of place head of FEMA, Michael Brown, was lauded publicly by the President for the "heckuva job he was doing". We find in a nutshell in this contrast all the ironies surrounding affirmative action and its criticisms: a Black, democratically elected official chastised for failing to deliver emergency resources he is repeatedly denied despite his plaintive pleas through the media when his offical requests fell on deaf ears and empty offices; by contrast, a White, politically connected FEMA director lacking any of the competencies or qualities for the position to which he is appointed by the President solely because of his fundraising support for the President's re-election campaign. The deeper tragedy is that in the New Orleans of tomorrow a Black mayor will be less likely electable because of the racial facelift the city is undergoing in its redesign. Urban regeneration and gentrification, we have long known, produce racial reapportionment and political "rectification". The difference this time round, in contrast say to the DeLay-ing tactics recently in Texas, will concern only the means of delivery.

Residential segregation tends to be reflected in and reinforced by what we might call "political segregation." African American voters tend overwhelmingly to vote for Democratic Party candidates. Of the 225 Republican members of the US House of Representatives none is Black and the three Hispanics are all Cuban-American. Of the more than 3500 Republican members of state legislatures, just sixteen are Black and thirteen Hispanic. Democrats other than White, by contrast, number sixty-seven US Representatives, and 20 per cent of Democratic members of state legislators. In recent presidential elections Republicans accordingly have taken to strategies of discouraging Blacks from voting, going so far as to intimidate elderly Black people from showing up at polling booths or requiring forms of voter identification that unduly burden poor (and so disproportionately Black or Hispanic) voters (Haines 2005). Thus uniformed state troopers in swing states such as Florida have asserted themselves visibly in the doorways of polling stations to remind African Americans of the historical horrors of casting a vote, and older Black people, registered Democrats all, have been visited at home by investigators on trumped up charges of voter fraud. Even where Republicans have gestured at diversifying their voter base, much as they might their investment portfolio, their overriding strategy in the face of rapidly heterogenising multiculture has been twofold. First, because White voters tend largely to vote Republican, to ensure that they vote in elections. And second, to reproduce White legislative majorities—by running almost exclusively White candidates—at more or less all levels of elected government. New Orleans is simply a more costly version of the recent Texas reapportionment strategy. By any means necessary?

So, in terms of the institutionalisation and reproduction of racial americanisation, these new forms of segregation have managed to *informalise* what used to be formally produced, both to *realise* and *virtualise* segregative exclusions. Race continues to define, globally as domestically, where one can go, what one can do, how one is seen and treated, one's social, economic, political, legal and cultural, in short, one's daily experience and prospects. Global circulation, like local city space, is increasingly contradictory: As there is greater heterogeneity and multiplicity so segregation is refined; as visible openness and accessibility are enlarged exclusionary totalisation is extended; as interaction is increased access is monitored, traversal policed, intercourse surveilled. As boundaries and borders become more permeable, they are re-fixed in the social imaginary, shifting from the visible to the virtual, from the formalised to the experiential, from the legal to the cultural and economic.

National (including now "homeland") security has become the abiding insomnia of American paranoia. Where segregation has been privatised along with much else in American life, its logic has come to dominate US foreign policy. Segregation was never about the complete dislocation of one racially conceived group from another, a final solution of another sort, so much as it was conceived as a logic of ongoing control. Blacks were to be externalised from the social life of whiteness for all purposes other than menial services, demeaning labor, and sometime social entertainment, including sexual experimentation or satisfaction. The logic in the case of New Orleans is of the same order. Your presence is warranted only in so far and for as long as you service some material condition or ideological figuration of local urban or national interests, even if simply to take the edge off the charge of racism, which everyone cringes at even as they perpetuate the structure and practices of its reproduction. Racial americanisation is in the deepest sense a form of crisis creation and control, manipulation and management, personally and politically, individually and institutionally, ideologically and representationally.

In short, the state in the silently circulated name of racial americanisation is being deva-stated. Compassionate conservativism is passionate only about forcing a narrowly ideological agenda on us all, and compassionate about nothing else than the calculation of narrow self-interest. The state is in the process of being structurally transformed from a robust set of institutional apparatuses concerned above all to advance the welfare of its citizens into a structure troubled only with securing the most elevated private interests from the perceived contamination and threat of those deemed for various reasons not to belong, to have little or no standing, the welfare of whom is calculated to cost too much, economically or politically. New Orleans has simply drawn this contemporary socio-racial dynamic and its debilitating effects momentarily out of the shadows and into the blinding light of day.

This article has been reproduced thanks to the W.E.B. Du Bois Institute for African and African-American Research, Harvard University, and first appeared in the *Du Bois Review*, Volume 3, no. 1, Spring 2006.

References

Associated Press. 2005. Bush Denies Racism in Katrina Response, *chron.com.*, December 13, 2005. http://www.chron.com/disp/story.mpl/nation/3520492.html
Bennett, William. 2005. Morning in America, transcript reported on *Media Matters for America*, Wednesday, September 28, 2005.
http://mediamatters.org/items/printable/(2005).09280006
Brown, Michael, Martin Carnoy, Elliott Currie, Troy Duster, David Oppenheimer, Marjorie Schultz, and David Wellman. 2003. *Whitewashing Race: The Myth of a Colorblind Society*. Berkeley: University of California Press.
Cadenhead, Rogers. 2005. Police Trapped Thousands in New Orleans, *Workbench*, September 9, 2005. http://www.cadenhead.org/workbench/news/2748/police-trapped-thousands-new-orleans
Chronicle. 2003. The Michigan Decisions, *The Chronicle Review (of the Chronicle of Higher Education)*, July 4, 2003: 10-12.
Connerly, Ward. 2003. Murder at the Supreme Court: Meritocracy and Equal Treatment R.I.P., *National Review Online*, January 26, 2003.
http://www.nationalreview.com/comment/comment-connerly062603.asp
Crenson, Matt. 2005. Katrina Rebuild Hinges on Who Will Pay, *Associated Press*, December 4, 2005.
http://news.yahoo.com/s/ap/(2005).1204/ap_on_bi_ge/katrina_who_should_pay_1;_ylt= AqY3GYJWwSYYmKRhKdoFxWAbLisB;_ylu=X3oDMTBiMW04NW9mBHNlY wMlJVRPUCU1

Culberson, John. 2005. Transcript of Culberson's Appearance on MSNBC's The Situation with Tucker Carlson, *msnbc.com*, October 5, 2005. http://www.msnbc.msn.com/id/9610419

DeBose, Brian. 2005. HUD Chief Foresees a "Whiter" Big Easy, *The Washington Times*, September 30, 2005. http://www.washingtontimes.com/national/(2005).0929-114710-8545r.htm

Denton, Nancy. 1994. Residential Segregation: Challenge to White America, *Journal of Intergroup Relations* Vol. XXI, no. 2 (Summer): 19-35.

Dreyfuss, Robert. 2001. Grover Norquist: "Field Marshall of the Bush Plan," *The Nation*, May 14, 2001. http://www.thenation.com/doc/20010514/dreyfuss

Eaton, Leslie and Ron Eaton. 2005. Loans to Homeowners Along the Gulf Coast Lag, *New York Times*, December 15, 2005.
http://www.nytimes.com/(2005)./national/nationalspecial/15loan . .

Foucault, Michel. 2003. *Society Must Be Defended: Lectures at the College de France, 1975-1976*. New York: Picador.

Gold, Steven J. 2004. From Jim Crow to racial hegemony: Evolving explanations of racial harmony, *Ethnic and Racial Studies* 27, 6: 951:68.

Goldberg, David Theo. 2004. The End(s) of Race, *Journal of Postcolonial Studies*, 7 (2): 211-30.

Guardian Unlimited. 2005. Drowned City Cuts Its Poor, *Sunday Observer*, December 11, 2005. http://observer.gardian.co.uk/international/story/06903,1664630,00

Haines, Erinn. 2005. Black Lawmakers Vow to Repeal Ga. Voter Law, Associated Press, December 29, 2005.
http://news.yahoo.com/s/ap/(2005).1229/ap_on_el_st_lo/voter_id

Higgs, Robert. 2004. The Defense Budget Is Bigger Than You Think, *The San Francisco Chronicle,* January 18, 2004.
http://www.independent.org/newsroom/article.asp?id=1253

Kestin, Sally, Megan O'Matz, and John Maines. 2005. FEMA Reimbursements Mainly Benefit Higher Income Groups, *Sun-Sentinal.com*, December 11, 2005.
http://www.sun-sentinel.com/news/local/southflorida/sfl-fema11xdec(2005).

Pace, David. 2005. More Blacks Live with Pollution, *Associated Press*, December 13, 2005. http://news.yahoo.com/s/ap/(2005).1213/ap_on_he_me/unhealthy_air

People. 2005. The Long Shadow of Jim Crow: Voter Intimidation and Suppression in America Today: A Report by the PFAW and NAACP, *People for the American Way*. http://www.pfaw.org/pfaw/general/default.aspx?oid=16367

Post, Robert (ed.) 2001. *Prejudicial Appearances: The Logic of American Antidiscrimination Law*. Durham: Duke University Press.

Sen, Amartya. 1981. *Poverty and Famines: An Essay on Entitlement and Deprivation.* Oxford: Oxford University Press.

CHAPTER TWO

THE PROBLEM OF THE IMMIGRATION LINE: STATE RACISM AND BARE LIFE

LES BACK

W.E.B. Du Bois commented famously that "the problem of the Twentieth century is the problem of the color-line" (Du Bois 1989 [1903]: 29). Some ninety years later the renowned writer and postcolonial critique Stuart Hall remarked, mindful of Du Bois I am sure, "...Diversity is, increasingly, the fate of the modern world... The capacity to live with difference is, in my view, the coming question of the twenty-first century" (1993: 361). In the years since Stuart Hall wrote these words something else has intervened. It might be more accurate to say that the problem of the twenty first century is the problem of the "immigration line". This is certainly Europe's problem but it is a global issue the proportions of which are only just beginning to emerge.

The "immigration line" is just as vexed politically, ontologically and practically as the line of colour or race. Indeed, it is deeply implicated in the legacy of racisms past and present and of the foundational principles of citizenship and state formation. The problem of the immigration line is also the problem of the ways in which lines are drawn through and across the peoples of the world. I want to say that this is not about the ethnic or cultural qualities of so called "immigrants", rather it is with concerned the ways in which the immigrant serves as a limit figure in political life. The immigration line demarcates those lives that are endowed with the gift of citizenship and those lives that can be cut short with silent impunity. The life that is licensed by the work of the state is linked and implicated in the diminished life of people caught, often fatally, at the border.

The human population is more mobile than at any point in its history.

In mid-2000 the global population was estimated at 6.1 billion. It is growing at an incredible pace. Up until the beginning of the twentieth century the world had not doubled in population within 100 years. In the twentieth century the world's population increased fourfold. The world's population is increasing by 86 million each year More than 90 per cent of this growth is happening in the poor societies of the world. 90 million passengers pass through London's two major airports—Heathrow and Gatwick—annually. At one time flight captured the Western imagination, now air travel is banal, suburban and unremarkable (Wohl 2005). The planes also are carrying cargo like the exotic foods and flowers to our supermarkets. It is also true that we are all conducting prosaic migrations or movements all the time. Some political movements have taken this mobility and an opportunity to argue for the normality of movement claiming as their slogan that "we are all migrants."

Slavoj Žižek is more suspicious of those who lay claim to the figure of the migrant. He asks: "What do protesters who pathetically claim 'We are all immigrants' actually want?" (Žižek 1999: 230). For him this constitutes a kind of excremental identification "which imposes compassion and merciful care for the poor while endorsing the existing hierarchical order." For him this induces "a hasty claim that our own predicament is in fact the same as that of the true victims, that is, a false metaphoric universalization of the fate of the excluded" (ibid 229). Žižek touches something here but perhaps there is more at stake than this prickly critic allows for?

At the beginning of the *Sociological Imagination* C. Wright Mills characterises the experience of modern life as analogous to a series of traps. Mills suggests that people are "bounded by the private orbits in which they live; their visions and their powers are limited to the close-up scenes of job, family, neighbourhood; in other milieux, they move vicariously and remain spectators" (Mills 1959: 3). Far from being experts in our own lives Mills suggests we are spectators, caught up in the web of history, imprisoned by the expectations of others. Mills names something powerful but perhaps the scale has been transformed. In a world where there is increasing global interconnection in technology, and movement of information there are ever more complex traps.

The story of a young man who I'll call Jonathan is a profound illustration of the traps laid in our global society. Jonathan lives in Anerley in suburban south London. He is 25 years old. He was a student in Uganda studying for a degree in accounting when it started. His father, who was born in The Republic of Congo, came under suspicion in Uganda for supporting rivals of the government and of using his transport business to traffic illegal goods across the border. His mother was from Rwanda and he had a young sister. They fled to France but Jonathan stayed behind; he needed to finish his dissertation and get his degree. He was "interviewed" many times by the Ugandan police, beaten and tortured, but he stayed to collect his degree. He then joined his family in France using a passport that his father gave him. His parents later returned to the Congo and they were both murdered. Leaving his sister with friends in Paris, Jonathan came to London and he promised his 15-year-old sister he would send for her. The immigration Offices in Croydon turned down his asylum claim first time around; they claimed his passport was a forgery. All he knows is that his father got his passport for him. On arriving in Britain he spent eight months in detention centres being moved from one to another. He lives with a friend of his cousin who he barely knows; he was given her telephone number by a relative in the United States. She took him in even though he was an almost complete stranger. On his release his landlady told him that while he was in the detention centre his sister, who suffered from a kidney condition, had been taken ill and died. He sits alone in his room, he suffers from blackouts that sometimes last two or three days, haunted by feelings of guilt and trapped in an uncertain present. Some days he copes, others he does not; he has a letter that his sister wrote him before she died and can't decide whether to open it or not.

The trap is not just a product of his individual choices. This sketch of a life reveals both the increasing interconnection between people and places—what we usually refer to as globalisation—but also the thick lines drawn between people that determine who can move freely across the globe and who cannot. We can't understand these traps without understanding the wider political forces that structure the movement of people as well as the definition of citizenship and belonging. In order to make sense of this we need to develop a global sociological imagination subtle enough to prise open the public issues in these private troubles. Put simply, if asylum claims had been processed differently Jonathan would have been able to see his sister one last time.

The Labour Government under a succession of Home Secretaries has reinvigorated the idea that it is the victims that are the problems. During his tenure as Home Secretary David Blunkett claimed that the problem of integration was that South Asian communities needed to speak English to their children in order to "overcome the schizophrenia which bedevils generational relationships" (Blunkett 2002: 77). Responding to the public outcry, he disavowed being an assimilationist and professed "integration with diversity". There is little doubt on whose terms integration is defined. In this sense the language of "shared citizenship" and "mutualism" is merely a way of saying that the responsibility for "unbridled multiculturalism" is laid at the door of the Black and Asian communities. Social order, another one of the new assimilationists' favourite terms, is centred on a normative whiteness that defines the terms on which the game of assimilation is played out. What is not apprehended is the profound shift toward a banal and prosaic multiculture that has become a fact of life in British cities. In a world where multiculture is so ordinary, why does the language of assimilation retain so much power? Part of the answer is that the project of the racial state is to create particular forms of human subjecthood through the language of citizenship.

New borderlands and pariahs

In Britain and the United States the issue of race and difference is usually located in the social container of the "inner city." It is very different in Sweden and France, where it is the suburbs that are associated with "dangerous otherness." Now, in Britain there has been a shift in the geography of public concern and it is the small provincial towns on the coast like Margate, Dover and Hastings that have become the centre of concern about illegal immigration and asylum. These seaside towns occupy a special location in the national imaginary as places of saucy recreation brilliantly drawn in the essays of George Orwell (Orwell 1968). The death of 24 Chinese "cockle pickers" in Morcambe Bay, Lancashire in February, 2004 is an indication of this shift. These "illegal workers" had been brought by gangmasters to harvest shellfish and were trapped fatally by a rampaging night tide. Sister Gina Tan said during the memorial service held in Morcambe for the dead on February 15, 2004, that: "They came to this country thinking they were going to have a better life—they didn't realise that the sea would take them away" (BBC News 2004). These seaside places of recreation, where "cockles and seafood" are consumed as a quintessentially English habit, have become the new frontier for the defenders of exclusive national culture and "rights for whites."

The venom and crudeness of the public outcry revolves around the image of refugees as "beggars" and their alleged involvement in "violent crime" is a routine reference point in the media. The general context is that asylum seekers are living below the poverty line, surviving until recently on vouchers that can only be traded for goods and subject to a dispersal policy that is aimed to inhibit them from settling in particular areas together. Meanwhile, liberal or even left wing politicians try to justify these draconian measures as being "faster, firmer, fairer" on the issue of political asylum. According to the 2002 Government White Paper there is a need: "to expose the nonsense of the claim that people coming through the Channel Tunnel, or crossing in container lorries constitute an invasion when it patently demonstrates how difficult people are finding it to reach this country" (Home Office 2002: 1). So, being tough is a matter of placating the delirium of racist scare mongering. The security of those borders also creates the market of desperation that lines the pockets of smugglers and criminals who are making small fortunes out of illegal traffic.

Fig. 2-1: New Migration and the Asylum Panic

The mud of criminalisation sticks to all those seeking refuge and another layer has been added to this since the attacks on the World Trade Centre on September 11, 2001. The figure of the refugee and the asylum seeker has been transformed from political émigré to de facto criminal, and now terrorist. The levels of surveillance and monitoring have increased considerably with the introduction of electronic finger print systems and "Application Registration Cards" or identity cards. This is the product of the harmonisation of immigration policy on a European level that seeks to deter applications for asylum. The contract for the controversial "voucher scheme", now being phased out by New Labour, was awarded to a French company, Sodexho Pass International, who implemented the system in Germany.

Despite Prime Minister Tony Blair's routine references to Britain's "multcultural nature" and proud tradition of tolerance, a clear distinction is made between the "border questions" relating to new migration and the domestic settlement around the issues of race and racism. Seemingly incommensurable political commitments can be held at bay within New Labour's political formation. The relic of imperial nationalism linger and provide the touchstone for the debate on identity and citizenship, indeed at the heart of the conceptions of the state and citizenship is a distinction between a human existence that is common to all of us and a particular formation of human conduct.

Giorgio Agamben has pointed out that the Greeks had no single term for "life". Rather, they used two terms: namely, *zoe* which expressed the simple fact of living; and, *bios*, which indicated the "form of living proper to an individual or group" (Agamben 1998: 1). For Agamben the production of a "biopolitical body" is the original activity of sovereign power and is a matter of creating particular forms of life. In Agamben's analysis a stark distinction exists between the life that is created through the language of sovereignty and citizenship and what he calls *bare life*. He claimed "that the fundamental categorical pair of western politics is not that of friend and foe but that of bare life/political existence, *zoe/bios*, exclusion and inclusion" (Ibid. 8). He also introduces a figure from archaic Roman law—*homer sacer*—to characterise the quality of this bare life, that is, a person who can be killed and yet not sacrificed. There is something here that is deeply resonant with the conditions of the displaced people of the globalised world.

The named and the nameless

The desperation contained in the stories of those people trapped at the border need to be reckoned with. While we have heard much of the victims of terror since the attacks on New York and London, almost nothing is known of the thousands of people who die in desperate attempts to gain entry to freedom's province. This is often simply a matter of who is named and who is nameless. The philosopher and writer Walter Benjamin, himself an asylum seeker from Nazism who was shown a closed door with fatal consequences, once wrote that historical reconstruction should be "dedicated to the memory of the nameless".

Reckless stowaways are literally falling out of the skies along London Heathrow airport's flight path. In the summer of 2001 a young Pakistani called Mohammed Ayaz fell out of the undercarriage of the Boeing 777 descending thousands of feet only to land in a Homebase car park in suburban Richmond, West London. He had sprinted through the darkness of Bahrain airport and hauled himself up into the cavernous opening above the wheels. He was long dead before he reached British airspace. Or, seventeen old Alberto Vazquez Rodriguez and sixteen year old Michael Fonseca from Cuba who fell out of the undercarriage of an airplane to their death in a Surrey field just outside of London's Gatwick airport. Sometimes they drop without trace. In the summer of 2002 a man driving round the M25 motorway close to Gatwick airport saw a human figure fall from the sky. The body was never found. England's "green and pleasant land" ate it.

Meanwhile hospitals suffer from acute staff shortages and search the globe for nurses and doctors. One London hospital spends 17 per cent of its staff budget on non-National Health System staff. There are chronic labour shortages and the facilitation of the global movement of skilled labour is an essential priority. The British Government has introduced a Highly Skilled Migrants Programme in attempt to encourage skilled workers, particularly doctors, information technology workers and scientists to migrate to Britain.

This is happening throughout the developed world. In 2001, the United States relaxed the annual quotas reserved for professional and skilled workers by nearly 70 per cent. In August 2000 the German Government instituted a Green Card programme, which resulted in 8,600 computer and technology specialists entering Germany in 2001 (OECD 2002). Similar things are happening in Australia where there are attempts to attract skilled workers in the new technology fields.

There are huge tensions here between the necessity for global population flows in a context where the British population is ageing and not reproducing itself, and the unspeakability of the people flow debate. Indeed, the very nature of the term "immigrant" is overdetermined by the legacy of the way in which movements of labour have been coded racially. Britain faces chronic skills shortages but at the same time the legacy of racism and the discourse of immigration mean that New Labour is reluctant to have that debate. Yet the scale of such labour demand cannot be hidden.

The London Plan of 2004 produced by the Mayor of London suggests "that under different migration scenarios London's population could increase by between 690,000 to 964,000. The most plausible 'central' scenarios suggests an increase of 810,000 to 8.1 million by 2016" (Greater London Authority 2004: 25). Perhaps, the only way to open up these questions is to abandon the language of "immigrants" and "immigration" in favour of less coded terminology. One alternative would be to speak of the necessity of *global movement*, which is both fluid and not necessarily permanent, within an international pool of labour. This view is starting to be voiced in a surprisingly wide range of places on the political spectrum.

In November of 2002 *The Economist* magazine ran a cover story on the issue of migration and economic growth. It concluded that there was an economic case for relaxing immigration policies amongst the lower skilled as well as the elite global professional class: "It is impossible to separate the globalisation of trade and capital from the global movement of people" (*The Economist* 2002: 3) Economic benefits like filling vacancies in which settled communities were reluctant to work would be achieved through the recruitment of deracinated, work hungry hands. The free flow of migration even dwarfs free trade rhetoric in this version of economic liberalism; it is simply a matter of letting mobile workers earn from moving and selling their labour where it is most wanted.

The Economist conceded that opening the borders could involve a "political cost." This, it argues, is best addressed through an assimilationist approach, and if necessary unabashed and premeditated discrimination: "Winning consensus for an orderly policy may mean trying to pick the migrants most likely to bring economic and social gains [...] It may also mean (although liberal democracies detest the implications) choosing those whose education and culture have prepared them for the societies in which they will live. In Europe, that may mean giving preference to white Christian Central and Eastern Europeans over people from other religious groups and regions" (ibid. 15). It is telling that a racial logic is being admitted openly; there are certain nations and ethnicities that are close relatives to the white English and others that are not. This is ultimately about a version of whiteness that places Central and Eastern Europeans within a shared racial genealogy.

Yet, such a vision is little more than a description of the current state of play. There are literally hundreds of thousands of unnoticed economic migrants coming to Britain each year. A study conducted by Janet Dobson and Gail

McLaughlan (2001) concluded "that migrants from developed countries formed around three-quarters of the inflow from the mid eighties onwards—nearly 80% in 1995-99. Contrary to common perceptions, the biggest contributors to the increase in employed people coming from overseas were countries in the developed world, particularly the Old Commonwealth (Australia, Canada, New Zealand, republic of South Africa) and the European Union and EFTA (Iceland, Liechtenstein, Norway and Switzerland)" (Dobson and McLaughlan, 2001: 18). These mobile workers do not count as "immigrants" because the mask of whiteness renders them invisible.

There were 282,000 asylum applications between 1995 and 1999; approximately half of those will have been turned down. During the same period the inflow of workers from developed countries into the UK was 381,000. In 2001 the government published figures that asylum applications were 11 per cent lower than in 2000. Indeed, the Immigration Office in Croydon, aptly named Lunar House, decorates its interior with a board that boasts how many asylum claims have been turned down on a month-by-month basis. This trend was reversed in 2002 when published figures showed a 20 per cent increase which, in the context of the buildup to the war in the Gulf, is accounted for by the numbers of Iraqi refugees fleeing the region. However, this was not the beginning of an upward trend. Applications are falling and the number of asylum applications has halved since 2002 reaching a figure of 33,930 applications in 2004 (Refugee Council 2005). The right to asylum as a legal right was articulated in the Universal Declaration of Human Rights under Article 14: "Everyone has the right to seek and enjoy in other countries, freedom from persecution." This was elaborated upon in the 1951 Refugee Convention. This right is not universal protection for all human life. Rather, it is the gift of each state underscored by the political *bios* of citizenship and the difference between states is very wide-ranging. In 2004 90 per cent of Iraqi refugees in Jordan were given convention status and granted asylum as compared to 52 per cent in the USA and just 0.1 per cent in the United Kingdom (Sherlock 2005: 6). New Labour's strategy is making clear "how difficult (some) people are finding it to reach this country".

Recently the Blairite Journal *Prospect* opened up a debate about the limits of diversity. This debate has its origins in 1998 and was stimulated by the conservative ideologue David Goodhart who argued that at the heart of the contemporary political formation in Britain is a "progressive dilemma". Diversity in values and by extensions "culture" would mean that people— meaning white people—wouldn't be willing to pay for welfare provision. "This is America versus Sweden. You can have a Swedish welfare state provided that you are a homogeneous society with intensely shared values" (quoted in Goodhart 2004: 30). In a piece by Goodhart summing up the debate he concludes: "To put it bluntly—most of us prefer our own kind" (ibid). While he tried to hedge the issue of who exactly is included in "our own kind", this is essentially little more than a nativist or purity seeking ontology that is directly connected to the legacy of new and old forms of race thinking. He continued: "The implicit 'calculus of affinity' in media reporting of disasters is easily mocked—two dead Britons will get the same space as 200 Spaniards or 2000 Somalis. Yet every day we make similar calculations in the distribution of our own resources" (ibid: 30-31). Goodhart and his kind perform an extraordinary act of historical revisionism when they claim that diversity is the cause for concern. As Paul Gilroy has commented: "The racisms of Europe's colonial and imperial past preceded the appearance of migrants inside European citadels. It was racism not diversity that made them a problem" (Gilroy 2004: 165-166). It follows that it is the legacy of racism and not diversity that inhibits affinity and mutuality.

The "calculus of affinity" has nothing to do with a state of nature but rather a particular legacy of the creation of a racialised *bios* in which the nation is constructed as the extension of the heterosexual family. The invocation of "cultural diversity" is about the limits on what can be assimilated. The etymology of the word "integrate" is to make into "the whole". In this sense, it is about being made "the same" as the social totality. In a sense, I want to argue that there may be other ways to try and configure a politics that is agile enough to lay bare the degree to which this is not a product of nature but of history.

Globalisation has produced a tremendous movement of people. It is estimated that some 145 million people are living outside their countries of birth and that up from 85 million in 1975. The global economic and political elites are able to move across borders at will; yet, there are profound forms of anxiety about the global movement of persons. As Zygmunt Bauman has put it: "... the riches are global, the misery is local" (Bauman 1998: 74). *The Economist* is right to highlight "the line between those whose passports allow them to move and settle reasonably freely across the richer world's borders, and those who can do so only hidden in the back of a truck, and with forged papers" (*The Economist* 2002: 3). There are deadly consequences already outlined, yet, as Paul Gilroy has put it, a lingering "imperial topography" creates hierarchies between those whose lives are cherished and the bare life at the border. The three thousand dead of September 11 2001 are remembered in the exercise of patriotic *gemeinschaft* and civilised outrage. The unnamed and undocumented migrant workers who perished in the World Trade Centre on that day direct us to the development of a broader conscience which connects with the plight of today's migrants. The victims of the July 7 2005 London bombing are open to similar kinds of appropriation, but the dead of New York and London invite another kind of relationship or at least reflection.

The faces of the 53 people killed on July 7 provide a portrait of the city's ordinary multiculture. One of the most enduring images of the July 7 bombings was a dreadlocked black Londoner walking away from a blast site with his arm around a white woman. The expressions on their blood-stained faces spoke to the common human frailty that made their apparent differences only skin deep and ultimately trivial.

Fig. 2-2: Survivors of the London July 7 Bombings

On July 9 the cover of the populist right wing newspaper *The Sun* showed 29 year old Laura Webb and 20 year old Shahara Islam with the headline: "Two beautiful decent women. One Christian, One Muslim. Both missing with dozens more. Pray for them all." There was a sign of things to come inside this edition of the paper. Columnist Richard Littlejohn wrote: "Our country has become a safe haven for terrorists. Our capital is not known as Londonistan for nothing."

Fig. 2-3: Laura Webb and Shahara Islam (*The Sun*)

Commentators on the centre right rushed to use the image of the "home grown terrorist" to claim that British multiculturalism had been a big mistake, that the bombers were simply a monster of our own making. What of the three thousand and rising numbers who have died invisible, stateless deaths? What of the wretched at the border and those who are literally falling from the sky?

Fig. 2-4: The wings of Icarus and the look to the sky

Bruegel's famous masterpiece *Landscape with the Fall of Icarus* depicts a scene where a young boy falls into the sea while people are going about the business of their day—be it ploughing a field or watching a flock—indifferent to the tragedy of the boy tumbling from air. In the Greek myth, Icarus took flight from imprisonment wearing fragile wings that his father, Daedalus, made for him. Ignoring his father's warning, Icarus, full of escape's promise, flew too close to the sun which melted his wings and hurtled him downward to a watery tomb.

While the reference is to Greek antiquity, Bruegel's landscape is a sixteenth century one. He lived through violent times in which purges against Protestants were talking place all over Europe. His painting outlines a landscape that is indifferent to suffering, the ploughman keeps his head down and the herdsman looks upward as Icarus's legs disappear into the ocean. The picture, I think, is as relevant to the twenty-first century as it was when bloody orgies of religious persecution ravaged Europe almost five hundred years ago. Today's Icarus is carried skyward by steel wings that are not melted by the sun. Rather, the fall from the sky is produced under the white heat of globalisation.

Bruegel's painting has provided a contemplative image for poets to reflect on the nature of human indifference. In 1938 W.H. Auden wrote in his *Musée des Beaux Arts* of how "everything turns away" from "something amazing, a boy falling out of the sky" (Auden 2000: 29). Similarly, American poet William Carlos Williams ends his poem with the sober accusation: "a splash quite unnoticed/ this was/ Icarus drowning" (Williams 1976: 212). Both writers point to *active inaction* on the part of citizens who turn away or play deaf to Icarus. All these issues are pointedly relevant to the anonymous people who are falling out of the London skies today. As the modern Icarus hides in the undercarriages of planes and is carried toward Gatwick and Heathrow, its corpse literally passes over Lunar House in Croydon. There is a deeper and more offensive irony in the decision to name a new Asylum Seeker detention/accommodation centre located in the South of England Daedalus after Icarus's father. Yet, the stories of those who fall tragically are hidden and appear only fleetingly in the public realm like a newsflash across the screen of conscience.

Yet, it is not simply a matter of calling for compassion for those caught in this terrible fate. In fact, compassion itself can be a damaging thing. Richard Sennett, writing in a different context, has talked about the kinds of compassion that wound. Where compassion imposes a division between the magnanimity of those who give it and the compulsory gratitude demanded of those who receive it (Sennett 2003). Hannah Arendt offers a similar caution when she writes "compassion speaks only to the extent that it has to reply directly to the sheer expressionist sound and gestures through which suffering becomes audible and visible in the world" (Arendt 1963: 82). It is not, then, just a matter of taking notice of the splash made by Icarus or the sound of the jets overhead.

Indeed, we might think about the ways in which the "grid of immigration" sets up relationships of debt and gratitude. Here, at best, the "host" is always cast as being gracious and of doing the exile a favour. The "immigrant" is forced to express gratitude. One of the things that I find hard to listen to is the expression of gratitude made routinely in meetings with refugees and asylum seekers. The script is already written regardless of whether one wants to perform the role or not. Meanwhile, the words that ring in my mind are the cacophony of racist complaints about the "new strangers" that confront one at every turn in the "host's" world.

It is time to think differently about the global movement of persons, to develop a new language, or at least to try and reach beyond the "grid of immigration" that constructs the relationship between immigrant and host. Who is not an immigrant in a global world where culture, money, music and even imagination travel without the necessity of physical movement? And if everyone is an immigrant then no-one is and it is here that I have some sympathy for Žižek's complaint discussed earlier. Categories like the "illegal immigrant" and "bogus asylum seeker" retain their power and currency precisely because they provide the limit point of who belongs and who does not. As Paul Gilroy suggests: "The figure of the immigrant is part of the very intellectual mechanism that holds us—post-colonial Europeans, black and white, indeterminate and unclassifiable—hostage" (Gilroy 2004: 165).

It is time to make a case for the normality of movement; at the same time there are difficult questions to be faced. Is it simply about opening national borders and "putting people to work" as some on the Left have argued? The danger here is to create an unregulated license for capital to exploit the deracinated and desperate. It is chilling to read that economic analysts on the Right come to the same position and conclude with glee: "migration probably raises the living standards of the rich (think of all those foreign nannies and waiters) and the returns to capital (hence the enthusiasm of employers for more flexible policies)" (*Economist* 2002: 14). In the world of liquid rights and individual insecurity, the argument for the liberalisation of immigration controls may also play into the hands of unscrupulous and exploitative interests. However, it is hard to imagine a worse situation for the displaced persons of the twenty-first century than it is now. Prey to those who profit from illegal traffic, the indifference of immigration officers and hostile street racists they are at the sharp end of globalisation.

Perhaps, the argument for more liberal immigration controls couched within an economic logic is necessary. This may be an opportunity to bring further state sanctioned border killing to an end, where the bare life at the border is little more than the archaic figure of *homo sacer* identified by Agamben who can be killed without sacrifice. It is clear that economic liberalism and the Third Way agree on one thing, and that is the necessity of the project of assimilationism; put simply migration has to become like the wider society. While both can applaud a cosmetic cosmopolitanism in the urban mix of colours, sounds and flavours, neither is willing to question the interconnection of race and nation that define the terms of citizenship and belonging. This is ultimately about the legacy of racial thinking and whiteness that continues to provide a privileged passport to those who seek to move across the lines drawn around European nation states.

I mentioned earlier that the jets carrying the bodies of tragic stowaways pass over the offices of Immigration and Nationality at Lunar and Apollo House in Croydon, South London. Before they fall, these bodies pass through the "immigration line" both physically and metaphorically. It is in these austere buildings, whose names celebrate space flights, where the real pressure of the asylum system is felt. Every time a scare mongering headline appears in the *Daily Mail* or *Daily Express* it translates into political pressure and reaction inside Lunar House. The irony of the situation is that while a ferocious debate about immigration raged during the 2005 general election campaign, the government policy had been draconian and uncompromising for a long while. Removals of failed asylum seekers doubled since 1997. In 2004 12,000 people including children were deported. The backlog of asylum seekers awaiting an initial decision is under 10,000, its lowest level for a decade. Anti-asylum seeker rhetoric is clearly not about "them" but rather about the shape and the shaping of the "us", nationally and locally.

A remarkable story is partially hidden in dust raised by the public row over immigration. Lunar House is Croydon's largest employer with over 6,000 workers. It is not a happy place to work. The political pressure to process asylum claims quickly results in frequent mistakes. Independent adjudicators upheld twenty per cent of asylum appeals in 2004. The pressure to work quickly means that papers and passports are routinely lost, causing massive anxiety to those awaiting judgment. Staff in the Nationality and Immigration Directorate feel beleaguered and this part of the civil service has a reputation for the highest number of staff suicides. Even the immigration officers feel trapped in a way that C. Wright Mills would recognise. One frontline worker at Lunar House commented that this imperfect system left her feeling "anxious, frustrated and de-motivated" so that she feels disappointed in herself because she "has to act in an uncaring unsupporting way when dealing with customers." Activists and members of the community dissatisfied with how the immigration service works set up an organisation called South London Citizens. One of its early meetings was actually held at Goldsmiths College. In November 2004 they decided to conduct an inquiry into the workings of Lunar House. They took the inspired decision to take evidence from both immigration officers and asylum seekers. At a meeting there was an extraordinary moment when an immigration officer in a crowded room stood up and apologised to the users present for the misery caused by the workings of Lunar House. The cynic might say one apology does nothing to change the Kafkaesque workings of the institution but the inquiry has rattled the government and it is taking notice. Indeed, I think the South London Citizens group is the realisation of what Edward Said would call "the practice of identities other than those given by the flag or the national war of the moment" (Said 2004: 80).

Fig. 2-5: Lunar House, Nationality and Immigration Directorate, London

The enquiry suggests a kind of global sensibility but also an awareness of the sociological traps and the thicker lines drawn between people (Butler 2004). Zygmunt Bauman wrote: "All communities are imagined. The global community is no exception to that rule..." (Bauman 2003: 148). Similarly Paul Gilroy has pointed towards a way of re-imagining a sense of global community through the idea of the planetary, which captures both a sense of movement, the verb to planet, and a worldly reach (Gilroy 2000). I am appealing to a hope for the emergence of a sense of conscience of planetary belonging; this sounds very weak, I know, as I write these words. Yet, the white heat of globalisation may be forging an unforeseen antinomy in the emergence of a profoundly planetary sense of what it means to live on the earth at this moment in time. Jean Améry comments that the only universal human quality is that we all carry time in our bodies: "Time is always within us, just as space is around us" (Améry 1994:11). It is this sense of time being deposited within us at each breath and on every heartbeat that might provide the meter for a shared sense of planetary belonging.

When we look into the sky what do we see? Is it a window or a mirror? If it is a mirror does it simply reflect back the image of us and the parochial concerns of nations? "The sky that hangs over our head is no longer domestic," remarked Primo Levi (1991: 12). Raising our eyes to the sky might offer another kind of invitation to see the refracted or deflected traces of global routeways that are drawn in it like the contrail of a jet threading its way toward the horizon. Here is one place we find the scale of global sociology. It is only from the sky that a sense of the globe as a whole can be apprehended and perhaps as we contemplate the sky we will find the impression of a truly global human society.

Fig. 2-6: "The sky is no longer domestic": A jet passes over the offices of immigration in Croydon

It is not just a matter of raising our eyes skyward. The scale of global sociology is precisely this attention to the implication of our most intimate and most local experiences in planetary networks and relationships. It is about the search for remarkable things that are otherwise not remarked upon. It is about trying to understand amid the inferno of everyday life how people make a space that isn't infernal. I think our public culture is one of compressed priorities. John Berger commented recently that we live in an "instant culture" where the parameters of public discussion are limited to the not too distant past and the near future (Berger 2005). A global sociological imagination offers the possibility of refiguring the relationship between the past and the present and the near and the far. The past refuses to stay in its place, that is behind us, it is unstable. Equally, the present cannot simply explain what is past from the point of the now. Rather, as Walter Benjamin points out, past meets present and "comes together in a flash with the now to form a constellation" (Benjamin 1999: 463). Such moments of critical reckoning are like a bolt of lightning flashing across a darkened landscape in which cultural assemblages of past and present become visible.

Similarly, I am arguing for a re-thinking of the relationship between the near and the far. Georg Simmel wrote that the position of the stranger is constituted by what he called the synthesis of nearness and remoteness. I think of Jonathan riding the bus through Penge while the other passengers sitting next to him have no sense of his global story. Simmel also argued that this union of closeness and remoteness is part of every human relationship: "one who is close by is remote, but his strangeness indicates that one who is remote is also near" (Simmel 1992 [1908]: 200). This oscillation between the near and the far is to my mind the defining quality of our times.

For Hannah Arendt it is imagination that enables us to navigate our way through. Echoing both Benjamin and Simmel she wrote:

> Imagination alone enables us to see things in their proper perspective, to be strong enough to put that which is too close at a certain distance so that we can see and understand it without prejudice, to be generous enough to bridge abysses of remoteness until we can see and understand everything that is too far away from us as though it were our own affair (Arendt 1994: 323).

The task is to link individual biographies and the questions they raise with larger social and historical forces. As we zoom in from the global process to the local dispute, from the jet at 13,000 feet to the town hall meeting below, the distance spanned by the falling body of the unnamed victim of globalisation, we find the scale of global sociology.

References

Agamben, Giorgio. 1998. *Homo Sacer: Sovereign Power and Bare Life*. Stanford, CA: Stanford University Press
Améry, Jean. 1994. *On Aging: Revolt and Resignation*. Bloomington Indianapolis: Indiana University Press
Arendt, Hannah. 1963. *On Revolution*. London: Faber and Faber
Arendt, Hannah. 1994. *Essays in Understanding 1930-1954*. New York and London: Harcourt Brace and Company
Auden, Wystan. Hugh. 2000. *Selected Poems*. London: Faber and Faber
Bauman, Zygmunt. 1998. *Globalisation: The Human Consequences*. Cambridge: Polity
Bauman, Zygmunt. 2003. *Liquid Love*. Cambridge: Polity Press
Benjamin, Walter. 1999. *The Arcades Project*. Cambridge, Mass: Belknap Press of Harvard University
Berger, John. 2005. What the Hand is Holding: Writing Now, *Here is Here We Meet Season*. Queen Elizabeth Hall, South Bank Centre, SE1, April 11 2005
Butler, Judith. 2004. *Precarious Life*. London: Verso
British Broadcasting Corporation News (2004) *Cockling Death Toll 24*. http://news.bbc.co.uk/1/hi/england/lancashire/3488109.stm
Blunkett, David. 2002. Integration with Diversity: Globalisation and the Renewal of Democracy and Civil Society, in Foreign Policy Centre *Reclaiming Britishness: Living together after 11 September and the Rise of the Right*. London: Foreign Policy Centre pp. 65-77
Dobson, Janet and Gail McLaughlan. 2001. International migration to and from the United Kingdom, 1975-1999: consistency, change and implications for the labour market, *Population Trends 106* Winter, National Statistics. http://www.statistics.gov.uk/downloads/theme_population/PT106_v1.pdf
Du Bois, William Edward Burghardt 1989 [1903]. *The Souls of Black Folk*. New York: Bantam Books.
Gilroy, Paul. 2004. *After Empire: Melancholia or Convivial Culture*. London: Routledge
Gilroy, Paul. *Between Camps: Nations, Cultures and the Allure of Race*. London: Allen Lane, The Penguin Press.
Goodhart, David. 2004. Too Diverse, *Prospect*, 95: 30-37
Greater London Authority. 2004. *The London Plan: Spatial Development Strategy for Greater London*. London: Greater London Authority.
Hall, Stuart. 1993. Culture, community, nation, *Cultural Studies* 7, 1993: 349-363
Home Office. 2002. *Secure Borders, Safe Heaven: Integration with Diversity in Modern Britain*. London: The Stationery Office.
Levi, Primo. 1991. News From the Sky, in *Other People's Trades*. London: Abacus Press: 10-12.
Mills, Charles Wright. 1959. *The Sociological Imagination*. Oxford and New York: Oxford University Press.
Organisation for Economic Co-operation and Development. 2002. *International Mobility of the Highly Skilled: Policy Brief*. http://www.oecd.org/dataoecd/9/20/1950028.pdf
Orwell, George. 1968. The Art of Donald McGill, in George Orwell, *The Collected Essays, Journalism and Letters: Volume 2*. Harmondsworth: Penguin: 183-194

Refugee Council. 2005. *The Truth About Asylum*. London: The Refugee Council.
Edward Said. 2004. *Humanism and Democratic Criticism*. London: Palgrave Macmillan.
Sennett, Richard. 2003. *Respect: The Formation of Character in an Age of Inequality*. London: Allen Lane and Penguin.
Sherlock, Maeve. 2005. *Closing the door: the UK's erosion of the right to asylum*, speech given at British Institute of Human Rights, Courtold Institute. London December 8, 2005.
Simmel, Georg. 1993 [1908]. The Stranger, in Charles Lemert (ed.) *Social Theory: The Multicultural; and Classic Readings*. Boulder, San Francisco and Oxford: Westview Press: 199-204.
The Economist. 2002. The Longest Journey: A Survey of Migration, *The Economist*, November 2' 2002: 2-16.
United Nations High Commission for refugees (UNHCR). 2002. *Statistical Yearbook 2001: Refugees, Asylum Seekers and Other Persons of Concern: Trends in Displacement, protection and Solutions*. Geneva, Switzerland: UNHCR.
Williams, William Carlos. 1972. *Selected Poems*. London: Penguin Books.
Wohl, Robert. 2005. *The Spectacle of Flight: Aviation in the Western Imagination*, 1920-1950. New Haven and London: Yale University Press.
Žižek, Slavoj. 1999. *The Ticklish Subject: The Absent Centre of Political Ontology*. London: Verso.

CHAPTER III

DE-AUTHENTICATING FANON: SELF-ORGANISED ANTI-RACISM AND THE POLITICS OF EXPERIENCE

ALANA LENTIN

Introduction

The Third Worldist Fanon was an apocalyptic creature; the post-colonial Fanon worries about identity politics, and often about his own sexual identity, but he is no longer angry. And yet, if there is a truly Fanonian emotion, it is anger. His anger was a response to his experience of a black man in a world defined as white, but not to the 'fact' of blackness. It was a response to the condition and situation of those he called the wretched of the earth. The wretched of the earth are still there, but not in the seminar rooms where the talk is of post-colonial theory. They came out on the streets of Algiers in 1988, and the Algerian army shot them dead. ... Had he lived, Fanon would still be angry. His readers should be angry too (Macey 2000: 29).

The political legacy of Frantz Fanon has, today, been all but effaced from the memories of the two societies upon which it can be said that the black psychiatrist and freedom fighter had the most influence during his life-time: Algeria and France.[i] As his biographer David Macey (2000) points out, where Fanon *is* remembered is in the scholarly spaces opened by post-colonial studies in which, however, he is read as an analyst of colonised, black subjectivities and rarely, if ever, as either a radical psychiatrist or revolutionary intellectual. It appears that the memory of Fanon has always been selective and moulded to the needs of the time. Pointing out the differences between readings of Fanon in the 1960s and those of the present day, Macey (2000: 28) comments, "Third Worldist readings largely ignored the Fanon of *Peau noire, masques blancs*, post-colonial readings focus almost exclusively on that text and studiously avoid the question of violence." While Macey is right to point to the appropriation of Fanon by students of post-colonialism searching in texts for explanations of "subaltern-ness", Fanon has also been made use of in another way that connects the focus on violence of the Fanon of the 1960s to the emphasis on subjective identity that has defined interpretations of Fanon since the 1990s. Emblematically in the work of Charles Taylor on the "politics of recognition" (1994), Fanon has been taken to stand for the quest for authenticity of dominated peoples in the post-war era. This overly decisive interpretation of Fanon's grappling with negritude has been used to theorise the emergence of a so-called politics of identity that are seen as encapsulating contemporary struggles against discrimination and for equality by "minorities" in western societies. In such interpretations, a direct line is drawn between the perceived necessity of constructing authentic identities—attributed to Fanon—and current scholarly preoccupations with the inseparable pair of culture and identity as principally formative of the contemporary projects of collective action of blacks and "minority ethnic" groups in Europe and North America.

In reaction, this chapter proposes that the work of Frantz Fanon, on both the process of racialisation and the realisation of anti-colonialist self-determination, are key to a sociology of contemporary anti-racism. In particular, Fanon's ideas on the insufficiency of the visibility of the racialised without their contemporaneous freedom from colonial/racist oppression lends significant insight into the emphasis placed on representation by anti-racist organisations led by the actual or potential victims of racism. As my research on the discourse and practice of anti-racism in Western Europe has demonstrated,[ii] the importance placed on self-representation is grounded in a politicised approach to the challenge to racism. Such an approach opposes itself to the dominant discourse of culturalism that has come to replace politics both as a means of conceptualising difference in western societies and as a tool for framing collective action in a public sphere increasingly less concerned with the state. The ascription of the roots of "culturalism" to the anti-colonialist project in general, and to Fanon more specifically, is based on the failure of most scholars to historicise the emergence of the culturalist idea in the post-war world.[iii] What aspects of Fanon's writings have been misrepresented in the construction of such explanations of culturalist identity politics?

To answer this question, I examine Fanon's ambivalence towards the notion of an authentic black identity and connect his exploration of a phenomenological emphasis on lived-experience to the findings of my research on European anti-racism. This reveals the clear difference drawn in Fanon between the idea of an authentic cultural or national identity and the necessity of using the lived-experience of the racialised as a means for understanding and overcoming oppression. The fluidity of experience as opposed to the rigidity of authenticity may be shown to be a vital legacy of an anti-racist project grounded in the self-representation of the racialised. My argument is that experience today is profoundly political in that, by revealing the unavoidable ambiguity of belongingness and unveiling the sources of persistent racism, it challenges the easy classification of human difference that is facilitated by concern with "identities".

Unravelling the conceptual differences between such self-organised anti-racism and the approaches of mainstream organisations or governments and supranational institutions is also important for a discussion of the relationship of "race" to state. The study of anti-racist discourse and practice is of interest from a political sociological perspective, and not only in terms of the insight it gives into collective action. As we argue in the introduction to this volume, anti-racism is interesting because of what it tells us about racism and, therefore, about the state. Since the end of the Second World War and the discovery of the Nazi Holocaust, the official commitment in the West to the eradication of racism has been largely informed by anti-racists. Despite this, anti-racism has often been unproblematically assumed to be no more than the opposite of racism. This belies the heterogeneity of anti-racism, in particular with regard to how its various strands conceive of the role of the state in the persistence of racism. Some more mainstream anti-racisms, close to or within state institutions, tend to see racism as aberrant from the ethos of the democratic nation-state. They therefore promote state ideologies and the rule of law as the primary means for overcoming racism. On the other hand, anti-racisms that locate themselves marginally vis-à-vis the state pinpoint the institutionalisation of racism as the main reason for its persistence. They therefore deny the effective possibility of looking to the state for solutions to racism. The difference between these two extremes in anti-racist thought has a bearing on how racism itself is interpreted, because it is the positioning of each anti-racist form in relation to the state that generates different interpretations of racism. The differential power of these various forms of anti-racism to have their message heard determines whether or not explanations of racism that challenge the role of the state, and which are often uncomfortable to hear, especially when they come from those who face racism themselves in a hostile context, can be aired.

By demonstrating how the work of Frantz Fanon has influenced a self-organised anti-racism that has now been re-interpreted as a cultural politics of authenticity, this chapter intends to bring to light the origins of these chasms in anti-racist thought. As a result, we may go towards a better understanding of how racism continues to exist in a paradox of persistence and denial which hinders the ability to define it and stands in the way of developing a coherent, unified politics of anti-racism.

Mis-recognising Fanon: Taylor and the questionable roots of identity politics

The connection of the notion of authenticity with that of lived-experience, or *erlebnis*, the concept at the heart of the thoughts on experience and consciousness of Merleau-Ponty (1945) and Sartre (2001), whose writings greatly influenced Fanon, is common to many readings of his work, in particular *Black Skin, White Masks*. Macey (2000: 168) for example remarks that "*Peau noire, masques blancs* might well be described as an analysis of the author's situation or being in the world, and as a bid for black authenticity in a white world." The "truth" of the experience of the "*fellah*, the unemployed, the starving native" (Fanon, 1963: 264) is taken to lead necessarily to the attempt to construct (or return) to an identity that encapsulates that truth, a process that, within the context of colonialism, had, thanks to the work most notably of Aimé Césaire, become known as negritude. Fanon's ambivalent attitude towards negritude (Judy 1996; Kruks 1996; Goldberg 1997; Macey 2000) already points to the problematic nature of relating the outcomes of an engagement with lived-experience—or acts of consciousness in Merleau-Ponty's terms—to the espousal of an authentic, and therefore, delimited identity. Building upon the evidence of this to be found in Fanon's work itself, I propose that although, in purely philosophical terms, the "truth" of experience is arguably connected to the possibility of an authentic being in the world, the way in which this argument has been applied to the analysis of contemporary identity politics (Taylor 1992; 1994) fails to account for the very different meaning taken on by authenticity therein. The difference must be drawn between the reification to which authenticity claims are always susceptible and the reflective consciousness (Sartre, 2001) that brings lived-experience to light and makes it relevant for action.

The author whose work relies most heavily on a reading of Fanon for a theorisation of authenticity is Charles Taylor. Taylor turns to Fanon in his (1994) writings on multiculturalism and his attempt to account for the "politics of recognition" which he sees as definitive of the collective action of subjugated groups in modern societies. However, Taylor's consideration of authenticity begins previously to his specific treatment of this thorny issue: his 1992 book on authenticity reveals the sources of his misconceptualisation, to my mind, of authenticity in light of his later espousal of its importance for the achievement of minoritarian demands. In sum, Taylor separates between the notion of self-determining freedom and that of authenticity which, he claims, have been consistently confused due to their growth together in political philosophy. For Taylor, self-determination embodies a call for freedom that "pushed to its limit, does not recognise any boundaries, anything given that I *have* to respect"

(Taylor 1992: 68; emphasis in original). This drive is connected to a culture of authenticity that is narcissistic in its embracing of "self-indulgence and egoism" (Taylor 1992: 56). In contrast, the ideal of authenticity, although at the heart of modern individualism, can also propose "models of society" (Taylor 1992: 44) according to which the right to be oneself is proposed to be universal, based on the relativist dictum that "no one has the right to criticise another's values" (Taylor 1992: 45).

The problem in Taylor's rejection of self-determination as essentially narcissistic is revealed when these earlier writings are related to his later application of the ideal of authenticity to the collective politics of recognition. Taylor condemns self-determination as an individualist quest that negates the necessity of conforming to a common view of society for its better good. Instead he proposes that authenticity can only be channelled usefully if it is the objective of a group project to claim the recognition of its equality within a society perceived to be made up of a mosaic of cultural, religious, ethnic etc. groups, rather than solely of autonomous individuals. Two main problems can be identified in Taylor's argumentation. Firstly, his equation of self-determining freedom uniquely with the individualism of modern societies denies the importance of self-determination for the liberation of previously colonised peoples and, in terms of the immediate concerns of this chapter, for the construction of an anti-racist project grounded in the experiences of the actual or potential victims of racism. Therefore, it is problematic for Taylor to retain a Rousseauian definition of self-determination and apply it to a discussion of modern identity politics without taking account of the way in which the notion has taken on new meanings with the profound changes undergone by both former colonised and western societies in the latter half of the twentieth century.

Secondly, Taylor's appeal to the positive possibilities of an ideal of authenticity in the construction of a politics of recognition is based upon a misreading of Fanon's relationship to negritude. If, as I believe, Fanon's work can be usefully applied to an analysis of the contemporary sociology of self-organised anti-racism, it is important to demonstrate Taylor's misunderstanding of his grappling with authenticity. This is particularly important because the current scholarly preoccupations with "culture" and "identity", as almost the sole means of conceiving both of societal positionings and of the struggle of the racialised against persistent domination, has led to a conflation of identity politics with anti-racism that depoliticises the latter by reifying its protagonists.

Taylor (1994) bases his view of identity politics upon what he claims to be a search for authenticity in the process of throwing off domination. He attributes the concept of authenticity to two authors: Johann G. Von Herder, often known as the father of nationalism, and Frantz Fanon. For Herder, each individual has an original way of being human. This original individuality is paralleled in the

Volk which too should be true to itself and its culture. Taylor uses Herder's ideas on nationalism to explain the struggles engaged in by "minority" communities, which he terms the "politics of recognition". For Taylor, the "politics of recognition" are borne of the belief in the importance of strong identity formation for individual and group consolidation. He claims that access to such may be undermined by others' mis- or non-recognition. Being inadequately recognised is itself a form of oppression.

The attribution of the quest for authenticity and recognition in the contemporary world is made to Fanon. Fanon (1963; 1967) argues that the main weapon of colonisation was the imposition of the image of the colonisers upon the subjugated so that they were no longer recognised—even by themselves— outside of an image of them that was constructed by their oppressors. Ignoring Fanon's grappling with the ontology of the existence of black people in *Black Skin, White Masks*, Taylor concentrates specifically on Fanon's justification of violence in the process of decolonisation as he describes it in *The Wretched of the Earth*. This period in Fanon's writings emphasised the assimilation of the culture of the oppressor as a characteristic of colonisation and the creation of the "native": "it is the settler who has brought the native into existence and who perpetuates his existence" (Fanon 1963: 36). The implicit call, therefore, is to consciously reverse the effects of colonisation on the colonised, not least by shattering the self-perception of oneself as subjugated, brought about as a result of oppression: "he [the native] knows that he is not an animal; and it is precisely at the moment he realises his humanity that he begins to sharpen the weapons with which he will secure his victory" (Fanon 1963: 43).

By focusing exclusively on the first chapter of *The Wretched of the Earth*, "Concerning Violence", Taylor confuses his own version of the ideal of authenticity—as a model for society—with Fanon's advocacy of violence as a necessary stage towards the achievement of national self-determination for the colonised. He then links this artificial connection to his theorisation of contemporary identity politics. By doing so, he purposefully avoids the very strangeness of Fanon's situation: a Martinican who had elected to fight for Algerian liberation from French rule, under which his own country had elected to remain. Taylor's view that Fanon's appeal to authenticity is a foundation of present-day collective action by "minority" groups for recognition skims over the vital fact that, for Fanon, the achievement of national liberation must eschew any appeal to ethnicity or "race". Indeed, he recognises the facility with which nationalism comes to become reliant on racism when he remarks that the "racial and racist level is transcended" (Fanon, 1963: 108) in an Algerian nation that must emerge on the basis of will and consciousness and not on the grounds of shared ethnicity. Furthermore, as Macey argues, Fanon believed that, in the new de-colonised nations "there is a place for members of the European minority, provided that they 'become' negroes or Arabs in the sense of identifying with the insurgent wretched of the earth" (Macey 2000: 484). The openness of Fanon's vision of the membership of a new self-determined nation opposes the essentialism of the authentic identity that Taylor claims it is necessary to construct for the achievement of equal recognition.

If we accept that a full understanding of Fanon's interpretation of negritude cannot come about without (at least) a complementary reading of both of his most important works, Taylor's reference solely to "Concerning Violence" must be seen as insufficient. By delving further into Fanon's work and life, the simplicity of Taylor's analysis and his use of Fanon's pragmatic appeal to authenticity in the first chapter of the *Wretched of the Earth* becomes apparent. The main problem in Taylor's use of Fanon as the source of his argument about the nature of the politics of recognition as a struggle for authentic identities is his apparent neglect of Fanon's relationship to universalism. As Hesse (1999) argues, Taylor grounds his vision of a politics of recognition within a variant of universalism that would endow groups with the universal right to equal distinction. The possibility of replacing the assimilationist drive of the more accepted version of universalism, based on the equal dignity of individual citizens, with this "differentialist" equality belies the uneven spread of the universalist ideal itself. As Hesse (1999: 210) points out, by citing the civil rights movement as the greatest example of the growth in acceptance of the principle of equality, 'Taylor seems to think that historically the logic of universalism has gradually, almost inevitably, extended itself throughout the social, and as a consequence the principle of equal citizenship has become universally accepted.' On the contrary, according to Hesse, the activism triggered in the United States by civil rights and which extended itself to a host of other subjugated groups, transforms and proposes new universal principles that start out from their protagonists' particularity rather than from their discovery of pre-existing "European universals" (Hesse 1999: 211).

Secondly, for Hesse, Taylor is reluctant to let go of the idea that universalism may be disconnected from the cultural and historical situatedness that gave it its hegemonic status in the hierarchy of political ideals. Rather than slotting recognition of difference into a ready-made universalist model of politics, Hesse calls for it to be replaced by a "politics of interrogation" which "places the European hegemony of Western culture in question" (Hesse 1999: 213). In practical terms, such a politics would depart from an interrogation of the relationship of "reciprocal determination" between universalism and racism (Balibar 1994). Fanon also realises that, as Balibar (1994) would have it, the construction of universally rational man necessitates a definition in relation to an Other that also calls for a racist hierarchisation of human beings, ranked in relation to the universal ideal. It is precisely this realisation that breeds his ambiguity towards negritude. Whereas Taylor treats Fanon as existing on the "unassimilable edge of liberalism" (Hesse, 1999: 212), already in *Black Skin, White Masks* he begins to uncover the incompatibility of his existence with a universalism that up until that time, had completely taken him in. Authenticity first enters the picture as a pragmatic strategy for dealing with this deception. On reading Senghor on the beauty of "Negro art", Fanon (1967: 123) reacts:

> From the opposite end of the white world a magical Negro culture was hailing me. Negro sculpture! I began to flush with pride. Was this our salvation? I had rationalised the world and the world had rejected me on the basis of colour prejudice. Since no agreement was possible on the level of reason, I threw myself back toward unreason. It was up to the white man to be more irrational than I. Out of the necessities of my struggle I had chose the method of regression, but the fact remained that it was an unfamiliar weapon; here I am at home; I am made of the irrational; I wade in the irrational.

Ultimately however, Fanon sees negritude as a transitory stage in the process of decolonisation but not as an end in itself, as he recognises in the following:

> and sometimes these politicians speak of 'We Negroes, we Arabs', and these terms which are so profoundly ambivalent take on during the colonial epoch a sacramental signification (Fanon 1963: 68).

Such an authentic identity cannot be sustained because to do so would be to belie the extent to which the "negro" has been brought into existence by the white man. The impossibility therefore of "returning" to a pre-colonial authenticity is evident in Fanon's (1967: 132) explanation of his condition: "I wanted to be typically Negro—it was no longer possible. I wanted to be white—that was a joke." But what leads Fanon, having realised this, to affirm his negritude nonetheless in *Black Skin, White Masks*, is the rejection of its importance by Sartre on the basis of whose writing on antisemitism Fanon understood that the native, like the Jew, is "poisoned by the stereotype that others have of them" (Sartre 1960: 95, cited in Fanon 1967: 115). Sartre's writing off of negritude as a form of "anti-racist racism" (Sartre 1948: xl ff.; cited in Fanon 1967: 132) angers Fanon who sees that Sartre, a "friend of the coloured peoples" (Fanon 1967: 133) had "found no better response than to point out the relativity of what they were doing" (Fanon 1967: 133). Fanon recognises Sartre's betrayal of his true stance: within a universalist paradigm that, by describing the aims of negritude in relation to European racism, in turn proposes that the only way it may be transcended is through an acceptance of universalism. As Macey comments insightfully, Sartre's proposal that negritude is merely "intended to prepare the synthesis or realisation of the human in a society without races" (Sartre 1948: xl ff., cited in Fanon 1967: 133) connects with the specific outlook of French republicanism "that recognises—or calls into existence—abstract subjects who are French, but neither black nor white, Jewish or gentile, male or female" (Macey 2000: 187).

Fanon's negritude is bound up more with a concern for making the black visible as such, independently from the white gaze. However, it is clear that for Fanon, visibility is of little use without self-determination, not in the individualist sense given to it by Taylor, but as the process of freeing a people from colonial rule. As Goldberg (1997: 81) notes, "being recognised, whether as self-conscious or as Other, and thus being visible, requires that one be outside the Other's imposition, free of the Other's complete determination." Therefore, the recourse to authentic negritude can be a first step towards humanising the colonised by making her visible. Its necessity however can begin to be reconsidered once self-determination is established, not so as to regain the universalism that Sartre proposes is momentarily lost during this process, but to create a new politics that, as Hesse suggests, particularises that very universalism by constructing itself in opposition to it.

Problematising the authenticity of experience

Building on these observations, I propose that, in the interests of uncovering Fanon's relevance for a discussion of contemporary anti-racism, it is necessary to separate more clearly between the concept of authenticity and the use of lived-experience in Fanon's work. While lived-experience is usually taken to lead to a discovery of an authentic identity in phenomenological thought, this does not at the same time make it possible to make use of this connection for the theorisation of present day identity politics. It is necessary to recognise that, in whatever terms it may have been possible to talk philosophically of authentic experiences, the way in which the latter have become susceptible to essentialisation in their use by group-based politics of all kinds makes it urgent to disentangle the two concepts.

Joan Scott (1992) demonstrates the extent to which the use of authenticity and experience as an unproblematic conceptual couple serves to naturalise "categories such as man, woman, black, white, heterosexual, or homosexual by treating them as given characteristics of individuals" (Scott 1992: 27). In opposition to the essentialising of experiences to which their unproblematised usage gives rise, Scott advocates an historicisation of the process of experience which connects between words and things, or the way in which "concepts and identities" (Scott 1992: 33) have emerged and how they have been written about historically. Subjects have to be considered, not merely as existing "out there", but as interacting with others and as agents of their experience. This, for Scott, means that they must be "constituted discursively" (Scott 1992: 34) in a way that also recognises the conflicts and contradictions among discursive systems. To do justice to experience and to separate it from the claim to authenticity, several narratives have to be used in parallel in order to reveal the complexity of experience and to de-individualise it in a way that is aware of the multiple processes that are enacted in the construction of the historical knowledge that is later presented as "truth".

Scott's call for experience to reflect the complexity of social situations and the myriad ways in which they can be interpreted is mirrored in the existentialism of Sartre and Merleau-Ponty to whose writings Fanon turned in his discussion of the "lived-experience of the black".[iv] The nub of the contrast between the knowledge gained through an engagement with experience and the ultimate closure created by an invocation of authenticity can be found in Sartre's differentiation between reflective and pre-reflective consciousness. Pre-reflective consciousness is embodied by the individual who claims to be denied choice in what she is or what she does. This is considered to be "bad faith", a concept used by Sartre to encapsulate the notion of a lie to oneself which nonetheless "implies in fact that the liar is in complete possession of the truth which he is hiding" (Sartre 2001: 207). "Bad faith" is seen as an evasion of the responsibility that comes with freedom (Sartre 2001) because the consciousness of the self is aware of living in bad faith, or ultimately, of living a lie. Pre-reflective consciousness is inextricable from the individual's attempt to construct an identity, as in Sartre's depiction of the waiter in the café who "is playing *at being* a waiter in a café" (Sartre 2001: 219; emphasis in original). In this sense, the quest for authenticity is always built upon the search for an identity which the individual cannot find within herself, given that "pre-reflective consciousness is a *nothingness*; it has no content but is simply a relationship to what is outside" (Craib 1998: 35).

In contrast, reflective consciousness is based upon taking responsibility for one's place in the world and what one does with it (Craib 1998). This responsibility, which comes with the condemnation of persons to freedom and thus, to carrying the weight of the world on their shoulders, is borne of the "consciousness (of) being the incontestable author of an event or of an object" (Sartre, 2001: 194). The individual's responsibility is both for the world and for himself, both of which he has created in that "he is the one by whom it happens that there is a world; since he is the one who makes himself be" (Sartre 2001: 194). In this sense, it appears to me that it is only through the consciousness of experience that we live truly, according to Sartre, in full responsibility to both ourselves and to the world. As Craib notes, the lack of responsibility involved in the pre-reflective attempt to construct one's social role, and thus avoid a true engagement with experience, is evident in the fact that "identity politics are never as satisfying as they promise to be" (Craib 1998: 34).[v] The search for identity which is at the heart of the claim to authenticity is, for Sartre, ultimately impossible to achieve. This is made more concrete in Merleau-Ponty for whom consciousness becomes important in its interaction with the existing material world, a realm he calls the life-world. Consciousness, therefore in the terms proposed by Fanon, is activated in relation to lived-experience. Whereas individuals may feel the need to construct an authentic identity in order to negotiate the life-world, the interference created by experience makes it almost impossible to stick doggedly to the version of the world they have created and rely upon. Therefore, although as Craib (1998: 38) notes in relation to Merleau-Ponty, "the world continually transcends our grasp as we continually transcend the world through organising it from our specific perspective," the dissatisfaction that this process creates encourages engagement with the different experiences of both oneself and others.

Relating these theoretical considerations to the purpose of Fanon's ambivalent stance on negritude, the extent to which authenticity cannot be seen as more than a temporary stage in the transformation of black-white relations becomes clear. The radical changes undergone by Fanon in his own short life-time—from a French subject, who fought for Free France in World War II, to his choice to become Algerian, against both France and his birthplace Martinique: his own lived-experience—confronts him with the arbitrariness of fixed identities. Furthermore, the ongoing reality of white racism, which continued to deny black and Arab existence long after the adoption of negritude, was soon to lead Fanon to reject it as "no more than a 'black mirage' that was replacing 'the great white mistake'" (Macey 2000: 186).

Experience and representation in contemporary anti-racism

The issue of representation in the discourse and practice of anti-racism, as it has developed in Europe following the end of the Second World War, concerns the question "who says what, for whom and from where?" It is in this sense that lived-experience becomes the main axis around which the heterogeneity of anti-racism is constructed. Anti-racist approaches can be crudely divided, on the one hand, into those that stress the generality of the anti-racist message, the ability to raise awareness among the greatest number of people possible in a given population and, therefore, the adherence to a colour-blind attitude which emphasises anti-racist commitment over first-hand experience. On the other hand, an anti-racism emerging from the anti-colonialist legacy of the 1950s and passing via the major influences of civil rights and Black Power stresses the self-representation of the racialised as most equipped to formulate the anti-racist message. My historicisation of the development of anti-racism in Europe (Lentin 2004) revealed the emergence of a continuum of proximity-to-distance from the public political culture of the nation-state along which these varieties of anti-racism may be seen to be arranged. A so-called "generalist" anti-racism that positions itself closer to elements of public political culture important to democracies (e.g. liberty, equality, solidarity, human rights, tolerance...) disconnects its analysis of racism from the history of the racism of democratic European states themselves. State racism is reduced, in this account, to the action of individual governments, therefore reflecting the general diffusion of racism as a personal attitude in society. In contrast, the self-organised anti-racism of the racialised constructs a statist account of racism that regards its institutionalisation as the outcome of the rootedness of the "race" idea in the political structures of European states. The lived-experience of its protagonists—of persistent institutional racism—directly informs this account and, in turn, creates difficulties of alliance between "generalist" and "self-organised" tendencies.

It is this knowledge of the way in which "race", or what Gilroy (2000: 11) calls "raciology"—"the lore that brings the virtual realities of "race" to dismal and destructive life"—continues in many ways to shape the possibilities open to the racialised in western societies that Fanon recognised in his account of lived-experience. It is this experience, and more importantly, its coming to consciousness in the minds of the subjugated, that shapes Fanon's attitude on the necessity of revolt for the achievement of self-determination. This sense of urgency, of necessity, is already clearly established in Fanon's thinking by the end of *Black Skin, White Masks*. The impossibility of colonial domination continuing is felt by the "native" as a need in the present and not, as Fanon (1967: 226) comments, in relation to the "the revival of an unjustly recognised Negro civilisation." He continues,

> I will not make myself the man of the past. I do not want to exalt the past at the expense of my present and of my future. It is not because the Indo-Chinese has discovered a culture of his own that he is in revolt. It is because 'quite simply' it was, in more than one way, becoming impossible for him to breathe (Fanon 1967: 226).

A state-centred approach to anti-racism, based upon the self-organisation of blacks and "ethnic minorities" in present-day Europe, mirrors the urgency in Fanon's concluding remarks. Appeals to cultural difference or particularist identities have little to do with the demands made by organisations of this type, whose grounding in experience eschews essentialised standpoints in favour of a political project that targets the state and its policies as the main obstacles in the way of racial justice. That project bases itself in a politics of locality that creates direct links between anti-racist discourse and the lived-experience of black "communities". In many ways it reflects Fanon's understanding that "Negro experience is not a whole, for there is not merely *one* Negro, there are *Negroes*" (Fanon 1967: 136).

In the case of the Newham Monitoring Project, an anti-racist group established in East London to campaign against racist violence and police harassment, the "community" refers to the local mix of black and "minority" peoples, united by their shared experience of racism, and often poverty:

> NMP has always been at the forefront in East London and that's because we're a community-led organisation. So our work comes out of case work, our campaigns come out of case work, our case work comes out of attacks on the ground (Newham Monitoring Project, cited in Lentin 2004: 270).

Similarly, the spontaneity with which the *Sans-papiers* movement created itself in France, through the decision to occupy the Saint Ambroise church in 1996, is emblematic both of the extent of the desperation that enabled such radical action to be taken and the strength to do so, emerging from the shared experience of precariousness. The movement produced a blurring of the boundaries between the experience of daily living (in the churches) and strategic politics:

> It's spontaneous. It was born in fact outside of any type of political or anti-racist organisation, it was born rather in the hostels for African workers, in particular in a hostel at Montreuil in the East of Paris where there are many Africans. And it's above all in these hostels that the idea of holding this sort of event was born, an event which was a little bit spectacular because as soon as you put 300 Africans with women, children and all that in a church in Paris, well, immediately everyone looks and asks questions. So it's that which is really particular to the Sans-papiers (Sans-papiers Movement, cited in Lentin 2004: 271).[vi]

The importance of experience as central to disseminating the knowledge of racism that is necessary in order to challenge it has also been emphasised by organisations involved in the more recent campaign against the detention and deportation of migrants, refugees and asylum seekers. The invisibility of many of these individuals in European societies, due to policies of dispersal or detention, increases the importance of their playing a role in raising public awareness of their treatment. The involvement of this new target of racism in its own defence against consolidated European anti-immigrationism is seen as a central tool of empowerment by the British National Coalition of Anti-Deportation Campaigns:

> They [asylum seekers] have to be involved; we cannot run a campaign for somebody. If they do not want to be involved, we don't have power of persuasion of another people. If you personally are affected and you don't want to do

anything for yourself then how can you expect anybody else. That's one point of view. The other point is that it's important for them to get involved because it's very empowering. It's very healthy in terms of the state in which they are so they should break... And I know it's very difficult because people are very scared, they're being increasingly criminalised through the right-wing press in this country so it's very difficult for them but it's very important. Once when they face deportation many of them actually do get involved and prior to that they wouldn't because they have nothing to lose (NCADC, cited in Lentin 2004: 261).

The prioritisation of lived-experience as a means both of formulating anti-racist discourse and of empowering those targeted by racism is added to, furthermore, by the self-definition that is central to an anti-racism led by and represented by the racialised. In his discussion of the relatedness of visibility and self-determination in Fanon's vision of de-colonisation Goldberg (1997) comments in this regard that "denied self-determination, denied the freedom to choose one's principles, one is denied self-definition and so the visibility self-definition makes possible and marks' (Goldberg 1997: 101). The importance of being able to make such choices demonstrates the weakness of Taylor's interpretation of Fanon's argument in terms of recognition alone: the achievement of a status of mere visibility that implies neither freedom nor a transformation of the status quo. The importance of choosing one's own principles is stressed by Madjiguène Cissé (1999), spokesperson of the *Sans-papiers* movement. She emphasises the movement's choice of arguments and their presentation as itself an act of self-determination that is cognisantly unreflective of the pre-determined discourses of established French anti-racist organisations:

We chose this form of collective protest, we designated ourselves sans-papiers and not clandestine. We denounced illegitimate laws. Some of us recalled France's historical relations with their countries. On French territory, we posed the question of the relations between "rich" countries and "poor" countries (Cissé 1999: 180).

Conclusion

The importance of self-representation, both for setting the agenda of anti-racism and for the empowerment of the actual or potential victims of racism, particularly in today's current climate of intense racism against non-whites, non-Christians and non-westerners, may be glimpsed in these examples from contemporary self-organised anti-racists. Their insistence on the right to self-organisation is based neither on a belief in the authenticity of their claims nor on an essentialism that excludes the possibility of alliance building. On the contrary, self-organisation insists on listening to and being informed by the experiences of

Race and State 67

the racialised in the interests of constructing a viable politics of anti-racism to which both black and white can subscribe. The difficulty of acceptance with which such openness has often been met explains the continued disunity of anti-racist movements throughout Europe. The experiences of racism are often neglected in the belief that they bear no relevance for the construction of anti-racist arguments. For example,

> I think that through the '70s and most of the '80s there was blacks of organisations on the one hand and there were black people of black communities organising and sometimes in alliance with other organisations around specific issues. But, the anti-racist organisations that existed, of which there were a number, did not have as part of the principles of their organisation or even as a very conscious fact that the black communities and the people who suffered racism had a very... had a predominant role to play in how it was confronted. And that was sometimes consciously rejected as in the case, for example, of the Anti Nazi League or in some cases just hadn't been really thought about and so, although it's not that the black communities weren't organised and didn't fight racism, the majority white organisations of the society that was concerned about racism did not give priority to those black organisations and didn't bend over backwards to involve them and certainly didn't see them as playing the leading role in the fight against racism (National Assembly Against Racism, cited in Lentin 2004: 242).

The need to redress this lack of concern with the lives of black people in Europe and the preference for a discourse which, rather, does little more than symbolise their existence is at the core of self-organised anti-racism.[vii] The call to place lived-experience at the centre of the construction of the anti-racist project, and in so doing, to politicise it by historicising the roots of the racism experienced as a result of ongoing institutionalised practices, epitomises activists' struggle. The engagement with experience has generally been the catalyst for the creation of anti-racist organisations, as the case of the Newham Monitoring Project demonstrates:

> Horror and outrage—and above all the feeling that no such murder should ever again be tolerated on the streets of Newham—led to a spontaneous eruption of anger, particularly among young Asians who formed the Newham Youth Movement. ... From out of the Akhtar Ali Baig Committee and the Newham Youth Movement came the Newham Monitoring Project—a concrete and durable expression of black self-organisation (NMP 1989: 3).

The direct encounter with the experience of racial violence or institutionalised discrimination creates the foundations for a political project which, in contrast to "identity politics", organises around a target—racism—rather than around a pre-constructed ideal of authentic we-ness. These struggles are most often local rather than transnational, political rather than cultural and autonomous as opposed to those that are

> ...manipulated, either by the local collectivities where they are based or by the relationship with the consulates of their countries of origin. So, they don't have the right, the liberty to say what they want and to say what they think (Association des Travailleurs Maghrébins en France, cited in Lentin 2004: 277).

In the work of Frantz Fanon, the instigators of many self-organised anti-racist organisations could find many more parallels with their ideals than in the "politics of recognition" theorised by Charles Taylor. They are the ideals of those who recognise that a responsible engagement with experience makes the construction and maintenance of authentic identities, as the basis for a political project, a near impossibility. By stressing lived-experience and a rootedness in the local they recognize—because they see it first—the inevitability of change. Little could attest to this more strongly than the current necessity of locally-based anti-racist organisations to enlarge their activities to incorporate the interests of new migrants, refugees and asylum seekers alongside established black and "minority ethnic" communities. Their approach to the notion of the collective surpasses the adherence to particularity that others—most often academics—seek to endow them with. This could be summed up no better than by returning to Fanon in the final passages of *Black Skin, White Masks*:

> If the question of practical solidarity with a given past ever arose for me, it did so only to the extent to which I was committed to myself and to my neighbour to fight for all my life and with all my strength so that never again would a people on the earth be subjugated. It was not the black world that laid down my course of conduct. My black skin is not the wrapping of specific values (Fanon 1967: 227).

Notes

[i] As Macey rightly points out, the failure to remember Fanon as a leading figure of the revolution in Algeria is due to political and ideological reasons that elevated the "people" above any individual in the struggle for national independence. In France, the memory of Fanon has almost been effaced together with that of the Algerian war itself which France recognised officially only in 1999 (Macey 2000). More personally, Fanon, a French citizen of what had become a *département de l'outre mer* (overseas district) of the Republic, epitomised the rejection of French values which, it was undoubtedly felt in France, he had been lucky to receive through his education in the metropolitan mother land.

[ii] The research was carried out for my book *Racism and Anti-Racism in Europe* (2004). The research was carried out in Britain, France, Ireland and Italy.

[iii] Such a process of historicisation reveals that the establishment of the concept of culture as the principal means for explaining human difference and conceiving of group belonging emerges, following the *Shoah*, with the UNESCO project against "race and racial prejudice" (UNESCO 1968). This was an institutional project, grounded in the academic production most notably of anthropologists and geneticists, that received widespread support from western governments. The key role it gave to culture, which in turn informed the emergence of European anti-racist discourse in the post-war era, demonstrates the difficulty of attributing the current culture-identity nexus solely to the self-organisation of blacks and "ethnic minorities" and connecting it to the legacy of anti-colonial struggle.

[iv] Judy (1996) usefully shows that the English translation of Chapter Five of Fanon's *Black Skin, White Masks* as "The Fact of Blackness" misrepresents his meaning in the French "L'expérience vécue du noir". As Judy (1996: 53-4) reminds us, "Even idiomatically *l'expérience vécue* is not "the fact" but the "lived-experience"; it is not the objectively given or an event, but the process in which objects acquire their status as such for-consciousness. It is also in this sense that it is reality." Therefore, for Judy, the chapter's title should be translated as "The Lived-Experience of the Black". The centrality of experience is vital for the interpretation of Fanon's relationship to the concept of negritude.

[v] A useful analogy may be found in the case of the numerous individuals for whom a religious or ethnic identity takes precedence over all other social ties. The primacy the individual places upon his involvement in, for instance, the Jewish community allows her to reject as unimportant, or even negative, the friendships she made in the world beyond the identity with the rites of Judaism. In this sense, alliances which may have otherwise become central to the individual's life are never embarked upon due to the explicit rejection of experiences in favour of the construction of a specific, purportedly authentic, social role.

[vi] All translations from either interviews or texts in French or Italian are my own.

[vii] An example of such a process of symbol-construction is embodied in the contemporary scholarly discourse on immigration and racism in Italy. For example, Dal Lago and Mezzadra (2002: 153) point to the new migratory movement into Europe as symbolic of the universalism of the migrant as against "western 'racism', understood to be the politico-cultural expression of the material predominance of the more developed countries." For these writers, the "migrant" represents a new figure of the universal that poses a fundamental critique to the "modern political project" (Dal Lago and Mezzadra 2002: 153) and which resists its multiculturalisation in favour of an equality that supersedes "difference".

References

Balibar, Etienne. 1994. *Masses, Classes, Ideas: Studies on politics and philosophy before and after* Marx. New York: Routledge.

Cissé, Madjiguène. 1999. *Parole de sans-papiers*. Paris: La Dispute.

Craib, Ian. 1998. *Experiencing Identity*. London: Sage.

Dal Lago, Alessandro and Sandro Mezzadra. 2002. I confini impensati dell'Europa, in Heidrun Friese, Antonio Negri and Peter Wagner (eds.), *Europa politica: ragioni di una necessità*. Roma: Manifestolibri.
Fanon, Frantz. 1963. *The Wretched of the Earth*. New York: Grove Press.
Fanon, Frantz. 1967. *Black Skins, White Masks*. London: Pluto Press.
Gilroy, Paul. 2000. *Between Camps: Nations, cultures and the allure of race*. London: Allen Lane.
Goldberg, David Theo. 1997. *Racial Subjects: Writing on Race in America*. New York and London: Routledge.
Hesse, Barnor. 1999. "It's Your World": Discrepant M/multiculturalisms, in Phil Cohen (Ed.), *New Ethnicities, Old Racisms*. London : Zed Books.
Judy, Ronald A.T. 1996. Fanon's Body of Black Experience, in Lewis R. Gordon, Renee T. White and T. Denean Sharpley-Whiting (eds.). *Fanon: A Critical Reader*. Oxford: Blackwell.
Kruks, Sonia. 1996. Fanon, Sartre and Identity Politics, in T. Denean Sharpley-Whiting, Renee T. White and L.R. Gordon (eds.) *Fanon: A critical reader*. Oxford: Blackwell.
Lentin, Alana. 2004. *Racism and Anti-Racism in Europe*. London: Pluto Press.
Macey, David. 2000. *Frantz Fanon: A Life*. London: Granta Books.
Merleau-Ponty, Maurice. 1945. *La Phénoménologie de la perception*. Paris: Gallimard.
Newham Monitoring Project. 1989. *Into the 1990s From Strength to Strength: Annual report 1989*. London: NMP Publications.
Sartre, Jean-Paul. 1948. *Orphée Noir*, preface to *Anthologie de la nouvelle poésie nègre et malgache*. Paris: Presses Universitaires de France.
Sartre, Jean-Paul. 1960. *Anti-Semite and Jew*. New York: Grove Press.
Sartre, Jean-Paul [Stephen Priest. (ed.)]. 2001. *Jean-Paul Sartre: Basic writings*. London and New York: Routledge.
Scott, Joan Wallach. 1992. Experience, in Judith Butler and Joan W. Scott (eds.), *Feminists Theorize the Political*. New York and London: Routledge.
Taylor, Charles. 1992. *The Ethics of Authenticity*. Cambridge Mass. and London: Harvard University Press.
Taylor, Charles. 1994. *Multiculturalism*. Princeton, NJ: Princeton University Press.
UNESCO. 1968. UNESCO Statement on Race and Racial Prejudice, *Current Anthropology* 9 (4): 279-2.

CHAPTER FOUR

THE LEVIATHAN BLACK HOLE AND THE HYDRA IT
BEHOLDS: STATE, RACISM AND THE
MODERN/COLONIAL HABITUS

FESTUS IKEOTUONYE

> Art goes yet further, imitating that rational and most excellent work of Nature, man. For by art is created that great LEVIATHAN called a COMMONWEALTH, or STATE (in Latin, CIVITAS), which is but an artificial man, though of greater stature and strength than the natural, for whose protection and defence it was intended... (Thomas Hobbes, Leviathan 1651)

> The threat to man does not come in the first instance from the potentially lethal machines and apparatus of technology. The actual threat has already affected man in his essence. The rule of Enframing threatens man with the possibility that it could be denied to him to enter into a more original revealing and hence to experience the call of a more primal truth. (Heidegger 1961: 28)

Introduction

Quite recently, I attended the 37th World Congress of The International Institute of Sociology conference in Stockholm Sweden. The title of the session where I presented my paper, "Racism and Xenophobia: A European Dilemma", regurgitates a perennial problem at the kernel of modern imagination. What is important is that this "dilemma" was the recurring theme in many of the sessions I attended. Renford Reese's paper, "Noble Principle, Ignoble Practices" not only echoed his book *American Paradox* (2004), but summed up this dilemma that underlines the conference as a whole. But, there is nothing really new here since the "gift and curse" paradox is a defining feature of modernity and modern discourses. We only have to look at the proliferation of the prefixes of "post" and "beyond" that precede the word "modern" in academic and popular literature. The social sciences in particular have been churning out theories of the "gift and the curse" since the rise of methodological individualism/nationalism until today's reformistic mixes anchored on a contradictory fluidism. In this chapter my aim is to offer a way of looking at this perennial problem by moving away from the Eurocentric triumphalism and collective dissimulation that is rife in modern "complex" societies and their disciplinary discourses.

To do this also means to fundamentally question the truth that modern "complex" societies are heterogeneous. "Heterogeneity" in this sense refers to the multiplication of individuated units locked in the horizon of a cybernetic lengthening chain of interdependency. The truth about this "heterogeneity" is that it is based on a vanishing "biodiversity"; a depleting array of human cosmology, alternative social formations, and language variety. What we have here then is a fundamental contradiction which the cunning language of fluid mechanics cannot solve. But as is the case with all mechanistic thought, rigid or dynamic, it is predicated on enclosure, negation or what Enrique Dussel (1988) described as "con-ceal". I take this incongruous con-cealment as my point of departure in looking at race and the state as manifestations of a base modern paradox. This modern paradox is easily recognisable when the same modern states that David Theo Goldberg (2002) credited with "racial distinction" are seen as mechanisms of social membership, solidarity, and integration. What then is this modern paradox with a propensity for differentiation, integration, and con-cealment? The easiest way to simplify this paradox is to reduce it to what I crudely call the "connnexus", or nexus of contradictions and con-cealments, that sustains the modern process. At the crux of this connexus[i] is what I call the eugenic agonistic binary, whose paradoxical spirals we are very familiar with in modern self representation. Many examples will be used to illustrate this contradictory antagonistic binary. But I will be using Nicolas Veroli's take on modernity and Descartes as the main basis of my arguments.

To put things in perspective, this agonistic binary is fundamental in the sense that the emergence and existence of one side of the binary is predicated on the colonisation and negation of the other side. What is unique here, as Bauman (1989) points out, is the linking of destruction with creation; the grand vision of the perfect society built on the pyramids of the subjugated imperfect. Modern destruction and cruelty differ from other forms because they orbit the goal of destruction as the starting point of creation; negation for the sake of affirmation; subordination in the pursuit of ordination; and coloniality as a basis of self/social constitution. It is not simply a case of the colonising half being cruel or unjust, but that the coloniser's very emergence and sustenance is based on coloniality. We can use this background as a way of looking at other modern agonistic binaries of mind and body, nurture and nature, master and slave, industry and raw materials, capital and labour etc. Zygmunt Bauman's metaphor of "gardening", where the "plants" that fit the gardener's design are propagated and the "weeds" are segregated, contained, prevented from spreading or exterminated is also a useful way of looking at this binary.

Within the domain of most mechanistic thinking, formal or substantive, the passive primitive "nature" is simply seen as a "raw material"; a blank object subjected to "design", "cultivation" and "weed poisoning" (Beilharz 2001). This natural image is evoked when dealing with humans. In fact the modern world view is so hostile to "nature" that it sees the growing distance from nature and the "image of its origin" as "progress" and development. This eugenic antagonistic image and representation of "nature" stem from the view of nature as an embodiment of uncertainty and alterity. Both "nature" and others, as Georg Simmel put it, represent the personification of "those irrational, instinctive, sovereign traits and impulses which aim at determining the mode of life from within" (Simmel 1964: 413). Why is this uncertainty so problematic for the modern? Uncertainty became a problem when modern mechanistic self/social constitution and systemic maintenance became based on the elimination or subordination of all traces of alterity in the quest for certainty. This quest for objective and subjective certainty as a basis of "order", "knowledge" and "power" became a new tool, "a new machine for the mind" that would "establish and extend the power and domination of the human race over the universe" (Francis Bacon's Novus Organum cited in Merchant 1980: 169-172). Nature is then constrained and put into service as a "slave" moulded into shape by its human masters and "possessors". This image of "nature" is easily interchangeable with the historical image of ancients, vagabonds, Africans, Native Americans and other indigenous peoples. At the other end of the extreme, the super human master's image easily corresponds to the social formation and self representation of whiteness. "Whiteness" in other words, is a signifier for "certainty's colonisation of its own condition of possibility." Such a mechanistic "cultural identity of superhuman dimensions," as noted by Roszak (1972: 211), characterises the dominant trajectories of modernity, despite the recent overemphasis on exceptions within modernity. It is true that many in the modern world, from E.A. Burtt to Edmund Husserl have mounted strong critiques of this mechanistic ethic, but fundamentally we still live in a "Newtonian/Cartesian" world (Koestler 1959; Wallerstein 1997). To demonstrate this, we only have to look at the dynamics of what we call the "digital age", built on an agonistic binary between "hard" and "software" and the even more telling, "ones" and, of course, "zeros".

We also live in a world where mechanistic organisational forms of social management like bureaucracies dominate even so-called "sub-politics" and private spheres. Mechanistic systems and their habituated personalities, as Wallerstein, Bauman and others have argued, are loaded dice within a total cultural environment that reinforces that loaded dice. For example, why is it that "racism" is so entrenched in the modern world, even in supposedly "neutral" processes like development aid (Goudge 2003)? It is important to understand that the category of the "third world", the logic of "development" and the seemingly deviant practice of "racism" are all manifestations of a mechanistic historical formation that endows "whiteness" with power. The power of whiteness is inseparable from the quest for certainty that characterises the dominant local histories commonly associated with whiteness and its relations with non-white people, seen as devoid of history. Therefore, "race" (in both its competitive and classificatory connotation) is integral to the modern episteme and therefore central to the modern state and habitus. And, since the personalities that inhabit this habitus draw on its cumulative "reservoir" of images, techniques, knowledge and common sense to respond to new challenges and situations, racism becomes deeply installed as a condition of social interaction.

In a nutshell, the story of modernity/coloniality is also the story of how the modern occident became "white": "white", that is, not in terms of the mythical biological category, but as the "unitary and sovereign" Cartesian umpire, one of the defining features of modernity. My argument in this chapter is that racism is a manifestation of this antagonistic binary at the core of modern self/social constitution. This binary manifests itself in the mechanistic quest to dominate or eliminate nature as an embodiment of uncertainty. Therefore, all those who are seen as sharing this quality of uncertainty receive the same treatment. Using this as the pivot of my argument, it becomes easy to see correlations within the "global design" engendered by this agonistic binary. It equally becomes easier to link the conditions that prompted Queen Elizabeth to cry "Pauper ubique jacet" in England with the "scramble and partition" of Africa. Both the former and latter led to what Marx described as the "expropriated vagabonds" whipped and tortured by "terrorist laws" into accepting the discipline necessary for the wage-labour system (Marx 1979). This *encomienda* process, repeated across the world, described by Marx as the "enclosure" of the "commons" is generally seen as a necessary part of state, inter-state and empire formation. The "disciplining" or internal pacification of the vagabond represents not only social or spatial enclosure, but also a mental enclosure parallel to the social and spatial one. This mechanistic eugenic quest to put uncertain nature within and without "in constraint" and "mould" it into the "service" of its master characterises the production of the social formation of "whiteness" that signifies the war on alterity.

Colouring the world with imperial reason

In countries where the educational regime was largely established and maintained by colonial administrations, education and research can continue to have colonising functions, long after imperial rule. Even with the rise of nationalism, in each venue, the production of knowledge in these nation-states are based on Western epistemological schema and theories, deeply rooted in and informed by colonial thought (Kwek 2003: 1).

I've got a new division of history. In my division into periods we are now in the late middle ages...and then you ask; 'so when does the modern period begin?' I have no clear answer to that (Elias 1984: 10-11).

Although my focus is on what some might consider being the "big picture", I do not doubt the usefulness of micro analysis. I am not by any means pretending that the entire history of "modernity", "modernities"[ii] or the modern state can be completely encapsulated by a single term, wretched phrase or chapter in a book. The argument I am trying to put forward here only aims to move away from the dominant binary and nationalistic debates between an oscillating liberalism and a quasi reformist "Marxism". I am also aiming to avoid the constant reference to the "complexity" of pluralism, citizenship or other compartmentalized discourses of a disciplinary body politic. On the one hand, I hope to eschew the occidentalist[iii] tendency to begin every story of modern social formations in Ancient Greece, Rome or the "middle" ages. My goal is not to bemoan the "incompleteness" of the modern project, vested in the nation state model: Nicolas Veroli (2002) has shown that this incompleteness is built into the modern framework. On the other hand, I am not out to simply affirm a Rousseau-inspired location of "evil" in what Jacques Ellul (1964) described as "Technique",[iv] "nurture" or "second nature".[v] My ultimate aim is not simply to catalogue the sins of the state (and there are many), but to attempt an extrinsic description of the modern/colonial process exercising itself in modern states and personalities.

While on this point, it is important to bear in mind that the world we live in today would not be possible without what we call "colonialism" and "imperialism". Michael Parenti, in the introduction of his book *Against the Empire*, makes the case that,

Imperialism has been the most powerful force in world history over the last four or five centuries, carving up whole continents while oppressing indigenous peoples and obliterating entire civilisations. Yet, it is seldom accorded any serious attention by our academics, media commentators, and political leaders (Parenti 1995: 1).

While of course the experiences of this individuating "imperialism" vary greatly, these variations hide and compound the insidious continuities and designs within the total cultural environment engendered by imperialist intervention and pre-emption. According to Nak-chung Paike,

> ...rudimentary facts remind us that coloniality in East Asia—even in Korea with its colonial past—would exhibit a different aspect from what one would find in Latin America, Africa, or some other parts of Asia. They may also serve to conceal the fact that coloniality with all its accompanying features of Eurocentrism, racism/ethnicity, lack of democratic rights, etc., has been and still is not the less real in East Asia... Japan's success in emulating Western industrial (and colonial) powers (datsua nyuo) did pose a challenge to the simpler variants of Eurocentrism, but in a deeper sense it reinforced the 'universality' of the reigning world-system and its ideologies (Paike 2000: 73-74).

One good example of this collective dissimulation can be seen in the very use of words. The word "imperialism" is often used to describe a form of indirect domination, while colonialism is generally seen as direct domination. The problem though is that Britain, a giant in "state building", "imperialism" and "colonialism", practiced a colonial technique it referred to as "indirect rule". Colonial conquests are always accompanied by native "pacification" or winning the "hearts and minds" of the conquered people. This simply implies an epistemological conquest through social engineering and institution building (Kwek 2003) that is designed to legitimize the conqueror's cosmology. While of course no word or phrase can encapsulate all the contours and nuances of large historical processes, "compartmentalizing" these processes in ideal types is not the right way to respond to this problem. "Global designs" and cosmopolitan projects (Mignolo 2000a) must be analysed globally, for the simple fact that what we describe as "empires" or "imperial" powers overlap and can act in many synchronic contexts simultaneously. Are the main modern "empires" not enactments of modern states within an inter-state system? The point one is making is that coloniality is not simply an event, a "vector", or an instance of the exercise of modern power, but that it is integral to the very emergence and existence of the modern/colonial world as a cosmo-polis of modern states. An understanding of the coloniality/modernity couplet, the dark, or underside of modernity (Dussel 1996), is vital to understanding why race is entrenched in the modern/colonial state. Using this dark or underside of modernity as a basis of my contention, I will again define racism as a signifier of the eugenic agonistic binary that drives the dialectic of modern state/self constitution. This agonistic binary ingrained in the modern process cannot be reduced to a simple inversion of "Orientalism" (Said 1978), conceptual circularity or the idea that universalisms simply pave the way for the numerous insurgencies against them.

The root of the problem remains the colonising half of the binary whose basis of self constitution is the ceaseless colonisation of its own condition of possibility and the "rupturing" of its own biological continuities. With this split as its basis, the relational dynamics of the whole system and its "life worlds" became predicated on the "struggle". This is not because the "struggle" is inevitable or a natural "creative destruction" (the key is in the oxymoron) of geometric progression, but because it is the basis of modern self constitution. Without the agonistic element, the modern ceases to exist since the vital combustive ingredient at the roots of all things modern is missing. The modern order must be about ridding the world of all heterogeneity in the quest for the indubitable. Any process that is predicated on the colonisation of the image of its origin or its own condition of possibility is, as Veroli argued, a process or concept of "crisis".

We see this same hostile contradiction in most of the inherited historical appearances of this Cartesian social formation whatever the specific context. Psychoanalyst Erik Erikson reaffirmed this recurrent modern contradiction when he characterised the "functioning American" as heir of a historical struggle and "antithesis"

> Thus the functioning American, as the heir of a history of extreme contrasts and abrupt changes, bases his final ego identity on some tentative combination of dynamic polarities (cited in Luther 1988: 25).

This agonistic history of extreme contrasts, ruptures and great divides distinguishes the Cartesian programme of modernity from most other local histories. In recent years there have been loud protests against certitude from within the core regions of modernity. But this age old rage against the modern machine does not mean the end of the modern. Just as "God" defied Nietchzsche's obituary, modernity persists in more ways than one. Physics Nobel Laureate Ilya Prigogine summarised this problem in these words,

> As is well known, Newton's law has been has been superseded in the twentieth century by quantum mechanics and relativity. Still, the basic characteristics of his laws—determinism and time symmetry—have survived... By way of such equations, laws of nature lead to certitudes. Once the initial conditions are given, everything is determined. Nature is an automaton, which we can control, at least in principle. Novelty, choice, and spontaneous action are real only from our human point of view...The concept of a passive nature subject to deterministic and time irreversible laws is quite specific to the Western world. In China and Japan, nature means 'what is by itself' (Prigogine 1997:11-12).

Given such fundamental differences in the basic frame of reference, it is one thing to put a slash between knowledge and power, discourse and society, while located at the centre of a universalistic production of knowledge, and quite another to criticise the universalistic bents of dominant knowledge from a historical exteriority to the overarching notion of immanent modern order and knowledge. This acute awareness of power relations, location or the uneven locus of enunciation is what distinguishes the internal critics of modernity and the state (such as Marxists, Kantian universalists, postmodernists, poststructuralists, feminists, relativists, deconstructionists, reflexivists, neo-Nietzcheanists etc.) from those that critique modernity and its vestiges from the margins of modern metaphysics; that is, from those dispirited and fractured places silenced by the spatial, epistemological and ontological conquest and tyranny of the dominating cosmology (Mignolo 2000a; Outlaw 1997; Bernasconi 1997).

Black hole and hydra dialectic

> No doubt, the body politik is a monster—so much so that it is not even a body (Latour, 2005)[vi]

What is a black hole in "plain English"?

A Black Hole according to Microsoft's Encarta Encyclopaedia (1998) is a theoretical cosmic mass with a gravitational field so dense that nothing, including electromagnetic radiation, can escape its vicinity. The body is surrounded by a spherical boundary, called a horizon, through which light can penetrate but not escape. Black holes are thought to form during the course of stellar evolutionary process. As nuclear gases are exhausted in the core of a star, the pressure associated with the high temperature they produce is no longer able to withstand the convulsion of the crux to ever higher concentration, thus causing the centre or core that holds the mass to collapse into a "black hole". According to Karl Schwarzschild's reformulation of Albert Einstein's theory of general relativity something called an "ergosphere" comes into being outside the "horizon" of the "black hole". Matter is cut up and locked in the swirl of the black hole giving it form as it rotates and grabs more matter. It is believed that gravitation severely alters "space and time" in close proximity to a black hole. As the pull of the horizon is approached from the outside,

> time slows down relative to that of distant observers, stopping completely on the horizon. Once a body has contracted within its 'Schwarzschild radius', it would theoretically collapse to a singularity, that is, a dimensionless object of infinite density. vii

The Hydra in Greek mythology is a many-headed monster that lived in a swamp or marsh near Lerna, in Greece. A "terrorist" to all of Árgos, the Hydra is thought to have poisonous breath, a "dirty bomb" or venom that can kill anything within its range. The Hydra is incredibly difficult to kill because when one head is severed, two grow in its place. In addition to this salamander-like ability, the Hydra's main head is immortal. Hence, the Hydra cannot be killed, only subdued. In other words, the term hydra is commonly used to describe any complicated condition or problem that incessantly creates difficulties.

There are a few quite astonishing similarities between the theoretical cosmic mass known as a "black hole" and the theories and empirical expositions on a social historical planetary mass we describe as the modern state. We can for example choose to ignore the textual parallels between the black hole's "ergosphere" of "cut up" "matter" "locked in the swirl…" and the planetary spatial transformation via the modern state's social engineering in the constitution of the "egosphere".[viii] But the idea of an alteration of time and space by "gravitational" time-space distanciation, to paraphrase Anthony Giddens, or time-space convergence in the words of geographer Donald Janelle, ties in with the theories and experiences of today's modern states and the state of modernity in most of social theory. Discourses on time and spatial transformation form the crux of the analysis of modernity by Bauman, Beck, Giddens and most of the classical texts in the social sciences.

Paraphrasing Hegel and to an extent Marx, Bauman (2000) for example theorises the move from a "heavy modernity" that expands its spherical boundaries through conquest and territorial acquisition, thereby transforming space and time to a "liquid" or light "modernity" that constricts experiences of this same time/space to that "of a distant observer". Since "black holes" grab matter, squash, homogenise or "digest" it into a cosmopolitan paste and then push it down towards the "singularity", the similarity by analogy to the tendency in modernity, the state and empires to force hitherto "independent particles" to "cohere" can not be overemphasised. Max Weber defined the modern state on the basis of its successful claim over rule-making through monopolising the "legitimate" use of violence. This monopoly over rule making and the "legitimate" use of violence is not for its own sake. The modern state's propensity for monopoly of social management mechanisms is a means whose end is the "singularity" of certainty embodied by "order", understood here as a "row of grades".

The quest for, or pursuit of, certainty is a quality the modern state shares not just with modernity, as the broader social historical construct inside of which the state is located, but also the modern "private" persons produced in the process of larger socio-historical formation. The social/personality formation idea is so popular, both in social theory and in general, that it needs no further elaboration here. Hegel, Marx, Freud, Elias, The Frankfurt School, Foucault, and many others linked the modern cognate ego to its artificial extension—the superego.

As is well known, this ego is seen as the embodiment of the dividing line between reason and unreason. Such a dividing line authorises a vision of a perfect society produced through a specialised and routinised process of elimination or subordination of all things outside the boundaries of reason. It is crucial to understand that it is against such agonistic binary background expressed in the numerous wars with "impurity", "imagination", "ancients", "strangeness", "barbarians", "foreigners", "disease" as embodiments of uncertainty, chaos or evil that the modern ego and its leviathan order is constituted.

This particular modern conception of order was constituted as an intervention, or perhaps according to Eric Voegelin, as a gnostic escape, solution or "pre-emptive" strike on this default of uncertainty or evil. It is also upon such order and its associated precepts, categories and global classifications that the "in" and "out" group differentiation and subsequently the "civilised" and "barbarian" or perhaps "order" and the "other" binaries of the "integration struggle" are based. If we take a look at any manifestation of the modern binary between mind and nature, nurture and nature, rational and irrational, civilised and barbarian we will see that they are always presented in the form of contradictory oppositions. Eric Voegelin attributed such agonistic binary thinking to the influence of Gnostic dualism. According to Voegelin, Gnostics see the world as it "is" as evil (evil being the default), thereby making its transformation or eugenic "correction" through secret but transmittable knowledge (gnosis) available to the "elect" few. The crux of Gnostic belief is that the "cosmic ordering" is the work of an evil Demiurge, so the ultimate destination of the human soul is outside of this default world. Hence,

> The Gnosis, the knowledge which ensures salvation, is the realisation by man that he contains a spark of God, and the necessity of awaking from the half-life he leads on earth—described variously as 'numbness', 'sleep', or 'intoxication—to a full consciousness of his divinity... (Webb 1971: 126).[ix]

The move from this inferior and underdeveloped state of darkness, "sleep", "intoxication" and "numbness" to the full consciousness of the ego's divinity through secret transformative knowledge characterises most domains of mechanistic thinking. Francis Bacon's drive to engineer humanity back to the "paradise lost" does not deviate significantly from the above Gnostic orientation. The usual attempt to locate the genesis of modernity in the gulf between "is" and "ought" or between the real and ideal can be seen as similar to Webb and Voegelin's insight. The object-avoiding (Latour and Weibel 2005) propensity to succeed, escape, transform, silence or negate the world as it is, for Voegelin, serves as a relevant platform for understanding the contradictions of the "body ideals" of racism, modernity and modern ideologies (Voegelin 1999).

This platform may also help us understand the inherent "eugenic" propensity in the mechanistic quest for certitude finding expression in the debates on "utility embryos" and genetic "abortion". It is interesting to note that the term "eugenics" and the agonistic binary "nature" and "nurture" were supposedly coined by Charles Darwin's racist cousin Francis Galton (Gosset 1965). The scientific mission of the Eugenic movement is to root out the weeds or "inferior races", representing uncertainty, irrationality, and impurity, while propagating the useful "superior races", representing certainty and rationality (Ifekwunigwe 1997).

The choice tool of probing and determining who fits into the category of uselessness or inferiority, or the superior rank of usefulness is of course the same quantitative measurement of rational "intelligence" that seeks to master "nature". This is the choice tool employed historically to map and classify the world as a "row of grades" from which, etymologically, the word "order" is derived. To be sure, this calculus quality of rationality is mainly attributed to the social formation described as "white", male, rational, heterosexual, and "well-adjusted" (well-adjusted to what? "technique"?). The "others" dragged or "shanghai-ed" into this self-referencing eugenic schema are then graded according to their ability to approximate this calculable "whiteness" as a dense signifier of an exclusive social membership. Since reason or rational "thinking" and its extensions define "man" or social membership, those seen as outside the strictly policed boundaries and horizons of reason become lower than human (sub-human) and thus enter the eugenic framework as a "problem" to classify, mystify, overcome, negate, silence, correct, number, regulate, enrol, indoctrinate, preach at, control, check, estimate, value, censure and command.

Racial Darwinism,[x] the thinking intrinsic to this world view, came to represent the motivating force both for the private persons within each row of grades and the inter-social body enmity that exemplifies the many manifestations of this conception of a will-to-struggle order. This fierce struggle is not only evident in notions of competitive "free markets", private property, private interests, national interests or "sperm wars", but also the selfish gene biologism that underscores primary self understanding within the modern row of grades. The underlining logic is simply that "...the world is like an oilpress: under pressure. If you are the dreg of the oil you are carried away through the sewer; if you are genuine oil you will remain in the vessel. But to be under pressure is inevitable" (cited in Lowith 1949: iv).

The "hawks" and the "doves" of the usual politico-economic divide both buy into the fundamental logic of the oilpress theory. The difference may be that the "doves" want those dregs who are "carried away" to be carried away "gently". This oilpress row of grades *univers de discours* was also intrinsic in the views of the major European Enlightenment thinkers like David Hume, Kant etc, a thinking that still hangs on the Cartesian model, whatever the protest against "pure reason". Emmanuel Chukwudi Eze writes,

> As in Hume, the assumption behind this arrangement and this order is precisely skin colour: white, black, red, yellow; and the ideal skin tone is the 'white'...to which others are superior or inferior as they approximate the 'white'. It is therefore not unfair to point once again to Kant's statement: 'This man was black from head to toe, a clear proof that what he said was stupid' as clear proof that Kant ascribed to skin colour (white or black) the evidence of rational (and therefore, human) capacity—or lack of it (Eze 1994: 201-41).

The problem with the "black" or "uncertain" man is his distance from rationality, not just his skin colour or his Tarzan habitat. Thomas Jefferson wrote in his book *Notes on the State of Virginia* (1781) that in the faculties of memory and imagination the "Negro" appears to be equal to "whites". But that when it comes to reason and rationality they (Negroes) are inferior since none can be found capable of "tracing" or "comprehending the investigations of Euclid". However, these reason-challenged Negroes "are more generally gifted than whites with accurate ears for tune and time" (Levine 1978: 4).

Therefore, central to this agonistic split or great divide is the difference based on the distribution of reason. This reason is also the defining quality of rational "man", the protection of whom the leviathan was intended. Finally, the whole order was constituted as an artificial extension of this reason-enabled man with deficient ears for tune and time. This calculus man who comprehends Euclidean geometry shares in this defining quality of rationality which does not only measure and determine to which side of the divide he belongs, but also what everyone or everything must be the embodiment of to qualify for social membership.

The modern order is fundamentally object-avoiding and transformative since its whole essence is tied to this binary "other", constituted from the beginning as a problem to overcome (Bauman 1991). We see this same binary in different guises in almost all of social theory. Bruno Latour (1993) described it as the "great divide" while Ernst Gellner (1979; 1982) saw it as a "big ditch". In other words, this agonistic binary between certainty or "order" and uncertainty is crucial if we are to understand, not just modernity, but the modern/colonial state/personality and the racism constitutive of the modern habitus as sturdily installed generative principles (Bourdieu 1977; 1984).

My primary focus in this chapter then is not simply to duplicate these already stated arguments but to unite elements within these compartments scattered in the "disciplinary" divide of the academy to account for the appearances and persistence of what we call "racism" within modernity's cosmopolis of nation-states. Using the "monstrous" analogies of the black hole and hydra binary, this chapter hopes to illuminate the underpinnings of "race" and the state by drawing from Nicolas Veroli's attempt to take Rene Descartes seriously.

Coloniality as the motions of modern self constitution

My story begins then with the emergence of the modern/colonial world and of modernity/coloniality, as well as with the assumption that cosmopolitan narratives have been performed from the perspective of modernity. That coloniality remains difficult to understand as the darker side of modernity is due to the fact that most stories of modernity have been told from the perspective of modernity itself, including of course those told by its internal critics (Mignolo 2000b: 723)

Before proceeding any further it is important to clarify a few crucial points. The basic assumption one is working with is that "racism" is a signifier of the agonistic binary relation that is constitutive of modernity and therefore the modern state. This agonistic binary forms the base upon which the whole discursive edifice of modernity, including the internal criticisms or intrinsic descriptions of this modern historical edifice rests. All these, according to Lewis Mumford, paralleled Western societies' yield to the "machine" (Mumford 1946). "Racism" and coloniality as signifiers of modern classificatory schemes are necessary and integral parts of the programme of modernity, both as a project and a particular historical orientation to reality. William H. Goetzmann (1988: 320) reminds us how design and the "open-endedness" of the "American dream" can be combined and coexist in a milieu where "Spencerian teleological Darwinism merely reinforces ideas of racial and industrial progress in a competitive world".

As Wallerstein (1995: 86) knows so well, within any inegalitarian historical system there must be an underclass. Thus, within an inegalitarian historical order, an under-race is inevitable. Order is constituted and therefore implies the problemitisation of the "other" who naturally occupies the under-strata of the system or, as Bauman (1991) put it, one who enters the picture as a "resistance to overcome". Was this not why W.E.B Du Bois (1905) told us what it was like to be a "problem" within such colonial order of things?

Over the years many, including Eric Voegelin (1987), Zygmunt Bauman (1989) Howard Winant (2001), David Theo Goldberg (2002) and Alana Lentin (2004) have made similar arguments about the embeddedness of racialism and racism within the institutional structures of the modern state. The corresponding argument that coloniality is also constitutive of both modernity and consequently the modern state has already been made by Enrique Dussel, Nicolas Veroli, Anibal Quijano and Walter Mignolo, to mention only a few.

Foucault, in his lectures on bio-power (2003), characterised racism as entwined in the underlying modern mechanism of power that "exercises itself in modern states" (Stoler 1995; Gordon 1980).

Foucault is not arguing that this disciplinary and regulatory power is bound up in the boundaries of a single state. Rather, he argues that they are all part of a larger modern episteme that introduces "ruptures" and "great divides" into the biological "continuum of the human species". Peruvian Sociologist Anibal Quijano (2000) describes this rupturing universal mechanism of power as the "coloniality of power". Quijano theorises this world system of classification or "race", un-known before modernity, as the bedrock of the entire history of what Edge (1994) called dominionism. Most previous forms of domination and prejudices became reconfigured in accord with this brand-new-good-for-you sixteenth century European historical formation. For Anibal Quijano "coloniality of power" is fundamentally based on, firstly, the classification and reclassification of the planet population. The concept of "culture" becomes crucial in this task of classifying and reclassifying (this includes the so called "culture" or "science" wars and identity politics). Secondly, "an institutional structure functioning to articulate and manage such classification (state apparatus, universities, church, etc)" is necessary. Thirdly, there is "the definition of spaces appropriate to such goals and an epistemological perspective from which to articulate the meaning and profile of the new matrix of power and from which the new production of knowledge could be channelled" (See Mignolo 2000a: 17). It is on the basis of this inherent coloniality within modernity that Mignolo chooses to make visible the hidden face of modernity by introducing the term "modern/colonial world". Since the modern nation-state is a defining feature of modernity, the term "modern/colonial" state serves the same purpose by bring into view the kernel code or hidden condition of possibility of both modernity and the state. Global and cosmopolitan projects are not incompatible with nationalism. "Globalisation" as many erroneously assumed does not mean the end of the nation-state model. Chomsky (2005) argued that both are inseparable because the so called "forces" of globalisation are the "tools and tyrants" of modern states.

It is then not surprising to note that the reason why coloniality appears hidden to most of us is the bias now recognised as "methodological nationalism" (see Wimmer and Schiller 2002). This bias ensured that the modern state is seen as the natural embodiment of histories and societies and therefore the "indubitable" unit of analysis. This deference to the compartmentalising logic of the modern episteme makes every local history "post traditional" in the linear time symmetry of modern/colonial global designs. Of course such reasoning conforms to the colonising heaped up "avant-garde of the avant-garde" (Latour 1993: 47) self image of modernity as a succession in a natural and inevitable logical order or arrangement. This tendency for the modern to assume the "other" is a blank slate awaiting the rational scriptures of the modern episteme reflects this base agonistic binary and its inherent contradiction pulsating within all things modern.

In the course of this chapter, I hope to clarify a key point, which is that this agonistic binary is not just based on the usual "negation of the "other" as a basis of the constitution of self thesis, but a permanent crisis or base contradiction that drives the binary dialectic of "order" and "other". The paradoxical phrase "leviathan black hole" (beholding a Hydra) seeks to convey this crisis and convolution at the crux of the modern episteme that manifests and exercises itself in modern states and personalities. Foucault's identification of the process of subjectification with more rigorously policed lines between reason and its inverse can help us understand the intricacies of this binary to a point. But Nicolas Veroli's (2002) five theses on Descartes give us a clearer perspective on the contradictory intricacies of the modern/colonial condition. Grasping the intricacies of this binary not only gives us a useful insight into the dynamics of race, but also the state-centred debates on the "environment", "resource efficiency ecology", "multiple modernities", even "carbon emissions trading" and the body/machine complex of the "market" (Seltzer 1992).

The modern state as empire in brief

> To be GOVERNED is to be watched, inspected, spied upon, directed, law-driven, numbered, regulated, enrolled, indoctrinated, preached at, controlled, checked, estimated, valued, censured, commanded, by creatures who have neither the right nor the wisdom nor the virtue to do so (Proudhon, 1923: 293-294).

The modern state, a defining feature of the historical period generally known as modernity, emerged as a specific social management model conceived as a solution to what Thomas Hobbes saw as the problem of order. The state as it is well known became formalised through the French revolution and the peace of Westphalia before it. The collapse of the Habsburg regime coupled with the rise of diplomacy after the thirty years war made Europe "safe" for the development of the modern state alongside the "axial" division of labour crucial to the development of the capitalist world economy (Wallerstein 1997). However, the fundamental value upon which the state and its accompanying apparatuses were built can be encapsulated in the Hobbesian idea of the leviathan. The fact that all humans and non-humans now live within the shifting boundaries and "horizons" of the planetary cosmopolis of modern states makes Karl Marx's claim that Hobbes is "the father of us all" much more credible.

Thomas Hobbes's take on the core logic of the modern state provides two pivotal points that are central to the aim of this chapter. On the one hand is Hobbes's idea that the "great leviathan", or the all-powerful modern state or social body, was necessary to solve the problem of "order" which incidentally is also the problem of the "other" as an incarnation of uncertainty, strangeness or the "outsider". On the other hand, Hobbes argued that this unitary leviathan or the modern state is a reflection of that "rational" and most "excellent" work of nature, "man". In addition, Hobbes's cybernetic metaphor tells us that the modern state's raison d'etat is to protect and defend the very thing it artificially extends and reflects—this same rational "man" it was constituted to protect and defend. We need to bear in mind that the backdrop of Hobbes's conceptualisation of order is the so-called chaos embodied in the appearance of "strange behaviour" (Foucault 1961) and the thirty years war in Europe. As previously stated, the Hobbesian word "man" must be understood as that whose defining quality is "rationality" and "excellence". To put this into perspective, rationality or the associated word "reason" in this case refers to the logico-deductive capacity or the faculty that forms the grounds for calculation. In other words, those that possess this capacity can grasp not only "first principles" but also the laws of force, mass, motion and displacements. It is not surprising that in the modern West, logico-deductive reasoning associated with what Ellul described as technique is valued so greatly. "Technique" and calculus in this Cartesian "mathematicalisation of reality" sense becomes the modern equivalent of the great psychological leap or historical moment that produced monotheism (Berlinski 1995). The aim of this calculus man and his extension then is to introduce "order" into what Oxford University history professor Egerton described as "blank uninteresting brutal barbarism" (Davidson 1993). The modern framework is an artificial rational order inaugurated to solve, discipline, and render decidable a natural state of chaos, undecidability, tragedy and uncertainty. This agonistic but dialectical binary[xi] contains an inherent contradiction and, therefore, a perennial paradox experienced as the ceaseless epochal crises or "permanent liminalities" popular in both natural and social theory.

It is in fact fair to claim that this perennial paradox of "differentiation" and "integration", to borrow the metaphors of calculus, has been the pivotal idea running through most classical and contemporary social theory from The Saint Simonians, Simonde de Sismondi, to Durkheim, Marx, Weber etc. It provided the backdrop to the expositions of the apostles of the modern dilemma like Louis Mumford (1946) Georg Simmel (1964), the Frankfurt School, especially Horkheimer (1982), Fromm (1978), Marcuse (1969), and Adorno and Horkheimer's *Dialectic of Enlightenment* (1944; 1993). More recent efforts have in some way thrown new light on what is a perennial debate on the spatial and mental coloniality characteristic of the ethic of rationality and the mainly Western programme of modernity. This Western eugenic "tech ethic" mainly manifests itself in what the sociologist Jacques Ellul described as "technique". "Technique" in all its intended and unintended ramifications is ultimately indissociable from calculus since both are involved in the overarching Cartesian quest for certainty. Darrell Fasching (1981) wrote in his expositions of the thoughts of Jacques Ellul that,

> The characteristics of technique which serve to make efficiency a necessity are rationality, artificiality, automatism of technical choice, self-augmentation, monism, universalism, and autonomy. The rationality of technique enforces logical and mechanical organisation through division of labour, the setting of production standards, etc. And it creates an artificial system which 'eliminates or subordinates the natural world' (Fasching 1981: 17).

Here again we see not only the danger Voegelin (1987) identified in the enclosure of knowledge or what counts as science, but also a struggle where an affirmation of one half of the binary is predicated on the subordination or elimination of the colonising half's own condition of possibility. The dilemma of course is the same as that which forever confronts the Cartesian ego in all its incarnations. These incarnations include the many faces of modernity and the modern subject enumerated by Matei Calinescu (1987). It also includes the modern rational forms exercising themselves in Nietzsche's will to power as "societies and individual; Locke's idea of private property, Adam Smith and Hobbes's notion of private interest, John Stuart Mill's exposition on privacy, Kierkegaard's idea of loneliness, or the early Sartre's insight on freedom" (Tu Wei-ming 1996: 76, cited in Mignolo 2000a: 6). Nicolas Veroli (2002) offers an interesting explanation not only for this reoccurring base dilemma and its under girding agonistic binary but also the connecting dialectic that maintain the nexus of contradictions that sustains the process. According to Veroli,

> Descartes extirpates from his system precisely what he must invoke in order to constitute it: the imagination. Furthermore, this imagination which he extirpates (or attempts to extirpate), he characterises as what could never produce his system of 'clear and distinct ideas' under any conditions, even though it is the condition of possibility of his thought (Veroli 2002: 2).

For Veroli, the foundation of Cartesianism lies in the thinking "I" which doubted itself into existence by negating everything else which is not it. Veroli sums this up with the statement

> 'After the rain there must come the sun' goes the old French proverb. Similarly, after doubt there comes certainty in the Cartesian epic: I have doubted everything

that could be doubted, and must thus come to the conclusion that the only thing I cannot doubt is my own existence as the one who doubts. But who am I? The inquiry must turn from the question of existence to that of identity: what is this 'I' that doubts? The theoretical task, henceforth, is that of constituting the cogito, the subject, as a purely homogeneous substance that will contain no trace of alterity. 'I' must be 'I' and not another. Since, as it turns out, I can only be (with absolute certainty) a thing that thinks, a thinking thing, that is, the opposite of a material or extended thing, corporeality will be the stand-in for alterity, for the threat of heterogeneity (ibid: 5).

In the first paragraph (part four) of the Discourse, Descartes wrote,

But because I wished to occupy myself only with the pursuit of truth, it occurred to me that I should do exactly the contrary, and that I should reject as absolutely false all that I could imagine having the least doubt in [*tout ce en quoi je pouvais imaginer le moindre doute*] so as to see if there would not remain, after that, something in my beliefs that were entirely indubitable (cited in Veroli 2002: 4).

Veroli cites Kai Lundgren-Williams (2001) who seems to be paraphrasing Bernard of Charters when he notes the exuberant moment when the cogito doubted itself into existence by freely hoisting itself onto the shoulders of the imagination or the "other" it has to colonise to constitute itself. The interesting question then is, how can "technique", the Cartesian calculus subject, or cogito, simultaneously subsume or colonise its own condition of possibility or alterity that propels it ontologically without completely destroying this crucial "other" and consequently itself? We have to bear in mind that, on the one hand, if the modern ego ceases splitting and rupturing it cannot secure the eugenic homogeneity necessary for its self-constitution so it will die. On the other hand, if the cogito completes its mission of killing off the inefficient and uncertain alterity by becoming the "perfect" autopoitic[xii] machine (of its sentimental imagination!), the contradictory ego also dies. This is because the Cartesian reason-enabled subject not only loses what propels it ontologically but also what its very existence depends on. For Veroli, the key to this problem requires an exploration beyond the formal limits of epistemology and once we do this, the answer becomes quite simple. The unitary and sovereign cogito must colonise alterity in order to attempt to secure the homogeneity of its essence embodied in its concept of "order" because only on such a basis can the antagonistic separation of mind/body, reason/imagination, coloniser/colonised or ones and zeros be maintained. But equally, this violent homogeneity-based identity of the cogito has to be constantly steered, watched, pursued, accomplished and secured by force, because it is constantly resisted.

The cogito constitutes itself with the exuberance of a pure act that will transform it into the paradigmatic spectator. Its problem, henceforth, will be that of managing the imagination—that is, the image of its origin—in order to protect its own integrity from this other that is itself, to 'cement it forever after into a foundational principle'. Whatever it does, however, the cogito cannot destroy the imagination: it must preserve it in order to preserve itself. And yet, it must contain it so as to assert its self-identity. At heart then, the cogito is a concept of crisis (Veroli 2002: 7).

The cogito also converts the surplus energy gained through this interior colonialism into an external one—an external and spatial projection of reforming energy aimed at getting the world within and without to conform to or perhaps be "pacified" into the cogito's self image of instrumental rationality or reason. As Hobbes stated, the leviathan empire without is an augmented consciousness of the distinctively modern leviathan umpire within. Hence coloniality and its consequent hang-over described as "racism" is an inherent tendency of both the modern/colonial world and the modern/colonial state.

> But I discovered that the couple is not an isolated entity, a forgotten oasis of light in the middle of the world; on the contrary, the whole world is within the couple. For my unfortunate protagonists, the world was that of colonisation (Memmi 1965: vii).

With Memmi's solemn words in mind, Thomas Hobbes's characterisation of the Leviathan as an artificial but larger extension of the "rational" man whose defence the leviathan is intended to serve provides us then with a clear basis to organise the complicated threads of this chapter. This is because Hobbes's problem of "order" is also a specific problematisation of alterity and therefore it is a re-enactment of the Cartesian agonistic binary many see at the roots of modernity. In fact Veroli using Habermas's (1991) concepts went even further to claim that

> My argument is that the theoretico-historical constitution of the bourgeois subject-form on the basis of its conflictual relationship with the imagination (grasped both as conceptual category and as social-historical content) is the building block on the basis of which the sphere of private persons gathered together in a public is politically instituted (Veroli 2002: 1).

The connection between the emergence of the mechanistic world view in France associated with Descartes, and Thomas Hobbes's "will to order" is not simply limited to their common preoccupation with natural "laws", Euclidean geometry and the common ultimate aim of certitude. It is well known that Hobbes lived in France and also engaged in intellectual exchanges with both

Descartes and Robert Boyle (Shapin and Schaffer 1985). Rene Descartes who perhaps, can be described as "the grandfather of the modern episteme in all its varieties" remains the most convenient tool in conceptualising this foundational agonistic binary as Nicholas Veroli (2002) argued above. Michael Hardt and Antonio Negri (2000: 80) remind us that

> With Descartes we are at the beginning of the history of the Enlightenment, or rather bourgeois ideology. The transcendental apparatus he proposes is the distinctive trademark of European Enlightenment thought. In both the empiricist and the idealist currents, transcendentalism was the exclusive horizon of ideology, and in the successive centuries nearly all the major currents of philosophy would be drawn into this project.

It can be argued that Hardt and Negri are understating the case because with reference to Descartes, Heidegger went even further:

> ...when it (the Cartesian cogito) is nonetheless thought through in its metaphysical import and measured according to the breath of its metaphysical project, then it is the first resolute step through which modern machine technology, and along with it the modern world and modern mankind, became metaphysically possible for the first time (Heidegger 1982: 116).

Carolyn Merchant wrote in *The Death of Nature: Women, Ecology and the Scientific Revolution* (1980: xxi) that her mission in the book was to "re-examine the formation of a world view and a science that, by reconceptualising reality as a machine rather than a living organism, sanctioned the domination of both nature and women." She singled out the values of calculation and quantification, both essential to bourgeois thinking and the goal of sequestrating non-human nature, as a necessary ingredient of human domination. According to Merchant, "In France, the rise of the mechanical world view was coincident with a general tendency towards central governmental control and the concentration of power in the hands of the royal ministers" (ibid: 205).

The connection between the emergence of the mechanistic world view and the particular kind of eugenic and hierarchical social order we are used to in modernity is evident not only within the sophisticated discourses of modern self image, but also in the "machine civilisation" descriptions of the outside enemies of modernity (Buruma and Margalit 2004). This paradoxical Cartesian mechanical model and the inevitable agonistic binary that forms its basis can give us valuable insight into the relationship between "race" and "state" as tentacles of the modern episteme "exercising itself" in the world.

As we shall see in the case of Spain, the quest for internal homogenisation or "pacification" through "civil" wars is connected to the external projection of the transforming and reconfiguring energy we call empire. In Spain, France, Britain, and to a lesser extent Ireland for example, the violent homogenisation of the population within by devouring natives, difference, heresy, vernacular, madness, witchcraft and "fools" etc was not only the basis for the establishment of internal boundaries but the springboard for the colonisation of the exterior "other". In other words, the technology of power of the Inquisition, within which was created the normalising modern state and the disciplined modern subject form, became the basis for the external colonial inquisition that created both "racism" and the shifting configurations or order of "things" within the cosmopolis of the modern/colonial world. To put the above analogies in perspective, let us consider a few events in the processes of state formation using a few examples mainly from Spain and, to a lesser extent, France.

The problem of order and "other" in state formation

The technical revolution meant the emergence of a state that was truly conscious of itself and was autonomous in relation to anything that did not serve its interests: a product of the French Revolution (Ellul 1964: 43).

The international system built-up by the West since the Treaty of Westphalia will collapse; and a new international system will rise under the leadership of a mighty Islamic state (The terrorist network al-Qaida, March 2004 after the Madrid attacks).

Thomas Pownall, the Governor of Massachusetts in 1772, defines the word "empire" as

This modelling of the people into various orders and subordinations of orders, so that it be capable of receiving and communicating any political motion, and acting under that direction as a whole is one which the Romans called by the peculiar word 'Imperium'...by this system only that a people become political body; tis the chain, the bonds of union which very vague and independent particles cohere (Quoted in Pagden 1995: 13).

One instrument of this interdependent "chain" or "bond" is language because language has always been the perfect instrument of empire. Language was generally seen to be the social glue of modern state formation and the administrative attempt to make vague and independent entities "cohere". As noted by Walter Mignolo (2000b), it first began as a religious project with a global vision under the Paulian banner of "Orbis Universalis Christianum" bringing with it not only the inquisitional discourses of anthropoghagic negation, conquest and "assimilation" but also the soft imperialist discourses of the "rights of the people". This was later displaced (not replaced) by another global design and "emancipatory" cosmopolitan project, this time secular but still inquisitional, that ushered in a "cosmo-polis of nation-state". The third project following colonialism and nation building corresponds to national modernisation missions that entrenched internal colonialisms within the nations of the early twentieth century. Today, this has been displaced by another transnational mission anchored on the neoclassical body/machine complex of the "market". For Mignolo all of these global designs and cosmopolitan projects are linked to coloniality, which is the hidden face of modernity and its very condition of possibility. In order not to regurgitate well known historical events, the focus here will have to be highly selective; my radar then will be on those historical moments and events that help to illuminate the agonistic binary of order and other, central to the thesis of this chapter.

The year 1492 was not just the year that Columbus "sailed the ocean blue" or the opening of the transatlantic trade and commercial circuit. It was also the year that Nebrija published his book *Granidtica Castellana*. 1492 was also the year that Spain as an imagined entity of singularity emerged piggybacking *La Reconquista*, or reconquest. *Reconquista* heralded in not only the forerunner of modern racist ideology of *limpieza de sangre* or cleanliness or purity of blood, but also the colonial practice of *encomienda* associated with the conquistador and the noble title of *hidalgo*. It was against this evolving local Iberian historical backdrop that the global meeting of Spanish conquistador Pizarror and the Inca Atahuallpa in 1532 must be understood. Henry Kamen (1965) reminds us that,

> The Reconquest meant the slow and systematic extension of Christian power all over those lands that has been Muslim since the eighth century... What the Reconquest destroyed, however, was the racial and religious coexistence, which despite incessant armed conflict had distinguished the society of mediaeval Spain (ibid: 2).

Within Spain the Reconquest also meant the systematic persecution and mass deportations of the *conversos* (Jews who converted to Christianity) and *moriscos* (Muslims who converted to Christianity) (Ali 2002; Dunbar-Ortiz 2003). It has been claimed that Columbus watched one of these "deportations" as he set sail to the Americas to inaugurate the external version of this violent internal homogenisation. Historian David Stannard's (1992) and Howard Zinn's (1995) accounts of the "American Holocaust" show clearly that the road to Auschwitz and the Herero holocaust before it was paved on this nascent colonial process of forcing "independent particles" into the certainties of identity singularity. The attempt to homogenise does not always produce the homogenised identities envisioned by the homogenising power as we can see in the modern states of Spain and Bolivia today. Global designs and programmes do not produce "complete" realities of their design because the world is not a blank slate, so to speak. But their power to transform, alter, displace, kill, maim, silence and dominate is not in any doubt. The counter claims within the dominant Castilian arrangement by the Basques, Catalans etc. can be seen as perennial challenges to the dominant discourse. There is no doubt, however, as to where the "legitimate" power of "political motion" lies.

In 1479, prior to the stated external projection of reforming energy, the regions of Aragon and Castel united in the persons of Isabella and Ferdinand under one religion, crown and language. The challenge after the violent homogenisation of the diverse population within the emerging boundaries of this imagined single entity of Spain was how to transform this imagined construct into the only reality of belonging available. Nebrija's "will to grammar" (Veroli 2002) seemed to provide the "social glue through which...governments seek to bond these human fissures into a stable political and social whole" (Baer and Jacob 1985: 1). In other words, language becomes a chain to bond "very vague and independent particles to cohere". But, as Nebrija (1946) pointed out to the queen, this "chain" or "yoke" is not simply an instrument of "civilising" the barbarians within, it is also necessary to extend the yoke to those conquered "towns and nations with strange tongues" outside the expanding boundaries of the emerging state/empire.

> Soon Your Majesty will have placed her yoke upon many barbarians who speak outlandish tongues. By this, your victory, these people will stand in a new need; the need for the laws the victor owes to the vanquished, and the need for the language we shall bring with us. My grammar shall serve to impart to them the Castilian tongue, as we have used grammar to teach Latin to our young (cited in Illich 1981: 49).

The surprising irony in the quotation above is Nebrija's reference to the older colonial technique of teaching "Latin to our young". Nebrija was not only evoking the usual colonial childlike image of the vanquished other but also how imperial socialisation is an instrument of intergenerational transmission of colonial knowledge. It was in the Roman province of Spain that Julius Caesar supposedly encountered the statue of Alexander the Great that inspired his "barbarian" conquests and reconquest of Rome itself? This reconquest transformed Rome into an empire ruled by an emperor rather than a plutocracy of nobility and land owners. This brings to mind Mignolo's (2000a) characterisation of "Occidentalism" as a Western affirmation of Greco-Roman culture. However, Veroli (2002) argues that it is the same impulse that moved the European bourgeoisie to enclose "the common" that also propelled Columbus to stick a flag in Cuban soil and Nebrija to propose colonisation through a language "...wielded by a new kind of mercenary, the *letrado*" (Illich 1981: 28).

"Grammar" as Veroli sees it, is crucial in spatial and mental transformation or "civilising missions", playing out within the embryonic empire that Spain was at the time. Grammar, as Nebrija confirmed, is also a vital tool in the colonisation of the "others" as a basis for the constitution of the modern state, self or empire. In France, during the same period, Cardinal Richelieu, a prominent politician of his time, established the Academie Francaise (1635), to purify French language and make it more amenable to the demands of "technique" and its inherent tendency towards centralisation under the authority of the literati.

In Britain, a "united" kingdom where Francis Bacon epitomised a yearning to engineer humanity back to the "paradise" or "enclosed space" from where humans were expelled, we can see the same agonistic binary impulse at work. Britain was also the place where Isaac Newton praised Descartes and Thomas Hobbes left us with a binary between the engineered "enclosed space" of certainty, and what Norbet Elias described as "cold, wild, deserted chaos".

Veroli points our attention to the fact that,

> Descartes (along with Bacon in England) opens the door to the enclosure of knowledge. Madness, but also witchcraft and magic become crime, violence, anarchy, and superstition impinging upon the onto-epistemological territory of Reason. All of these phenomena are considered threats that must permanently be confined to the hospitals and prisons of Europe that start to emerge in the mid-17th century. The 'great confinement' that Foucault so memorably described in the chapter by that name of his Madness and Civilisation is but the other side of the enclosure of the commons Marx had denounced in Capital (Veroli 2002: 17).

In the views of Nicolas Veroli, the emergence and institutionalisation of "confinement" and "surveillance" is not just a parallel process to the enclosure of the commons or perhaps knowledge, it is also a process through which subjectivity becomes transfigured in order to validate the agonistic binary between reason and imagination.

> Thought and extension must both come under the compass of central authority. Simultaneously, and in a complementary manner, the chaff must be separated from the wheat and brought under the control of the state-machine. The political imperative defined by the institution of the philosophical subject is the colonisationof its interior, the purification of both thought and society from swerving elements, from everything that threatens the fledgling rational order of the absolutist state (Ibid: 18).

In the United States, a "settler colony", the extension of the vestiges of European local histories by the Spanish conquistadors in America, continued through the reformulation of the "purity of blood" doctrine. In the words of Walter Mignolo,

> 'Purity of blood' was no longer measured in terms of religion but of the color of people's skin, and began to be used to distinguish the Aryan 'race' from other 'races' and, more and more, to justify the superiority of the Anglo-Saxon 'race' above all the rest (Mignolo 2000a: 31).

Arthur Mann linked the emergence of Anglo-Saxon superiority with the founding history and emergence of the social sciences in the United States. The popular and specialist view of the day, influenced by the mixture of social Darwinism and Darwin's theory of evolution, "...sanctioned the classification of mankind into races according to their fitness" (cited in Luther 1988: 73). While this powerful idea of "beaten men of beaten races" is said to be "discredited", it is nevertheless evoked in more politically correct terminology whenever the issue of progress and underdevelopment is on the table. We have to remember that the whole point of this distinction is to separate those ascribed with "rationality" from those savage embodiments of "chaos" that threatens the rational *Novus Ordo Seclorum* through contamination. Based on this binary the Native American culture and population became subject to the same violence, although with some differences, visited on the "blank slates" of state formation in the Iberian Peninsula and the South of America. Thomas Jefferson's *encomienda* "empire of liberty" arose to "extend the area of freedom", as Andrew Jackson famously put it. This triumphalism was uttered alongside the slave economy that supported it. Just as the "elevator operators" of the Roman Coliseum were "parts" in the elevation mechanism that brings participants into the bloody arena. These interchangeable words deployable in a different context may be criticized on the basis of insensitivity to the pluralities of contextual variation. But as Warren Zimmermann (2002: 17) wrote,

> Americans like to pretend that they have no imperial past. Yet they have shown expantionist tendencies since colonial times...Overland expansion, often at the expense of Mexicans and Indians, was a marked feature of American history...The War for American Independence, which created most of the founding myths of the republic, was itself a war for expansion.

The American "civil" war which marked the official end of slavery was not just a war against the "confederates", it was also a war of internal homogenisation linked to the establishment of order under a single mechanism of belonging subsumed in the ideological rationalisation of coloniality. It was also during this period, described as the "first reconstruction" by African American historians, that the ghost of Jim Crow paved the way for the great "confinement" of African Americans first in the "plantations" and subsequently, in the deadly symbiosis (Wacquant 2002) of the "black belts" and "correctional facilities" of the twenty-first century (Marable 1991). To a large extent even colonised Ireland did not deviate significantly from the core binary of order and the other apparent in the formation of the modern state in Spain, France, Britain and the United States. As Bertrand De Jouvenel (1993: 253) observed,

> The interests and memories which spring from local customs contain a germ of resistance which is so distasteful to authority that it hastens to uproot it. Authority finds private individuals easier game; its enormous weight can flatten them out effortlessly as if they were so much sand.

A specific illustration of this is the change in orientation with regards to what the "ancients" in Ireland referred to as "Duine Le Dia". The Irish state from its inception absorbed the typical European discourses of statecraft and nation building. Secularisation, modernisation and the "industrialisation thesis" may have been late in coming into the Republic of Ireland but the enthusiasm to bring Ireland into "line" with its European "neighbours" is clearly evident even today. While the root of the modern state in Ireland lies in, and was constituted against, its colonising neighbour Britain, the Irish state (like the Japanese "datsua nyuo") nevertheless internalised the base binary and colonial template deployed in the British colonisation of Ireland. Ireland became a typical British/European state with Irish "characteristics". This in some way reflects the same dominance of "colonial knowledge" in that region of the world from where the "tiger" before the Celtic was borrowed. Like we have seen elsewhere, the attempt to homogenise a heterogeneous population seems to always replicate the "order", "other" binary as a basis for self constitution.

Greenslade (1992), Fanning (2002) and Lentin and McVeigh (2002) have shown how the "social control" of Travellers reflects an internalisation of the colonial obsession with "race" and "hygiene". Fanning (2002) has argued that even the philanthropic image of the Irish "underclass" is still subsumed by the colonial lens of exclusion from "social membership" and the Victorian notions of the poor as a "race" apart. Catholic welfare institutions such as the Magdalene Laundries evoked this perennial image of the "other" as depraved and lazy. The depiction of the "Traveller" other is interchangeable with both President Truman's dehumanisation of the Japanese prior to dropping the Atom bomb on Japan and David Hume's depiction of Africans more than a century ago

> I am apt to suspect the Negroes ... to be naturally inferior to the white. There never was a civilised nation of any other complexion than white, nor even any

individual eminent in action or speculation. No ingenious manufacturers amongst them, no arts, no science (cited in Fryer 1984: 152).

Why is there this quest or need to show or prove European superiority throughout modern history? What is the point of all the intellectual and material investment on this notion of superiority centred on reason or its material manifestations? If we ask why this absence of "reason" and "science" should constitute inferiority or even why this "inferiority" should matter in the conduct of human affairs, we begin to see that the categories of inferiority and superiority are vital not only to the constitution of self but also the distribution of entitlements within the modern row of grades. It is crucial to remember that after Count Joseph de Gobineau's *Essai sur l'inégalité des races humaines* (1835), G. Vacher de Lapouge (1897) used Gobineau's theories to formulate the "laws of the distribution of wealth" (see Diop 1981).

In conclusion the important point made here is that instead of focusing on the synchronic loops, snapshots, or mutilated discourses of race, state or class bound together in one context, we should focus on the diachronic contradictions of the modern/colonial process producing these eugenic binary discourses and the "private persons" (gathered in Walter Lippmann's (1925) phantom public) made in its image. This is because,

…racism…sinks deeply and imperceptibly into the individual's sub-conscious; in the traditions, values, and even aesthetics of the cultural environment- an environment evolved over centuries during which self-designated 'superior' cultures assume the right to penetrate and dominate 'inferior' cultures. These roots are also buried in the sophisticated theorems of both liberal and conservative economics, sociology, political science, anthropology, and history. For these reasons, citizens… must first emancipate themselves from the seemingly endless web of threads that bind them emotionally and intellectually to the imperialist condition (Jalée 1973: xvii-xviii).

The "citizen", as Ernest Renan realised more than most, is fundamentally linked to the specifically modern distribution of power (Elias 1978) within the overarching cultural environment that produced race and racism. Therefore the crucial issue here is the rupturing "cultural environment" and the agonistic binary ethic exercising itself in social formations and individual egos cleaved from their own condition of possibility. This "race" inducing cleaving is part of the coloniality of the modern historical process which, as Jacques Ellul (1964: 125) reminds us, "…cannot be otherwise than totalitarian… because … everything is its concern".

Notes

[i] "Connexus" can be defined as the nexus or spirals of contradictions that came out of the modern violent split between mind and body/nature. The "modern" is fundamentally constituted on this contradictory split but its authority is based on a claim or intolerance of contradiction.

[ii] Modernities suggesting the many variation of the same cluster of "things" though this is denied vehemently by people like geographer Peter Taylor (1999) whose geohistorical framework of multiple modernities include the mercantile, industrial and consumer "modernities". See also Eisenstadt (2000)

[iii] Mignolo (2000a) defined "Occidentalism" as a Western affirmation of Greco-Roman (and if I may add the word "empire" to culture) culture.

[iv] According to Ellul, technique is "the totality of methods rationally arrived at and having absolute efficiency in every field of human activity" (1964: xxv). "Technique" for Ellul is not simply a way or process of doing things but a "…means of apprehending reality, of acting on the world" (131), which "…cannot be otherwise than totalitarian" because "everything is its concern" (ibid: 125).

[v] See a summary of the Dialogue between Voltaire and Rousseau on the Earthquake of Lisbon by Russell R. Dynes, published in International Journal of Mass Emergencies and Disasters in 2000.

[vi] See Bruno Latour and Peter Weibel (2005) "From Realpolitik to Dingpolitik — or How to Make Things Public" http://www.ensmp.fr/~latour/articles/article/96-DINGPOLITIK2.html.

[vii] http://encarta.msn.com/encyclopedia_761558067/Black_Hole.html

[viii] The Enlightenment inspired anthropocentric term "anthroposphere" assumes a universal human involvement (even those Shangai-ed) and a Kantian "happy synthesis" in the constitution of a sphere with vanishing "bio-diversity". Let us not forget that this "…happy synthesis... will lead us to a mutual reproduction of Western epistemology" (Mignolo 2000a: 67-68). Lacan I believe used the term "ego era" for the same age Beck described as the "eugenic age" and Burke labelled the age of calculators, economists and sophists.

[ix] See also Jones, 1963.

[x] Racial Darwinism, according to Paul Gordon meant that "nations and races progressed only through fierce competition" (See Fredrickson, 2002, p, 108)

[xi] In terms of the Hegelian reason enabled but fractured "Entfremdungen" ego working itself out in the world.

[xii] Milan Zeleny defined Autopoiesis as "A unity realised through a closed organisation of production processes such that (a) The same organisation of processes is generated through the interaction of their own products and (b) a topological boundary emerges as a result of the same constitutive process" (Zeleny 1981: 6).

References

Adorno, Theodor and Max Horckheimer, Max. 1993 [1944]. *Dialectic of Enlightenment*. New York: Continuum.

Ali, Tariq. 2002 *Clash of Fundamentalisms; Crusades, Jihads and Modernity.* Verso, London.
Baer, William and James Jacob (ed.). 1985. *Language Policy and National Unity.* New Jersey: Rowman and Allanheld Publishers.
Bauman, Zygmunt. 1989. *Modernity and Holocaust.* Cambridge: Polity Press.
Bauman, Zygmunt. 1991. *Modernity and Ambivalence.* New York: Cornell University Press
Bauman, Zygmunt. 2000. *Liquid Modernity.*, Cambridge: Polity Press, Cambridge.
Beilharz, Peter. 2000. *The Dialectic of Modernity: The Holocaust and the Perfect Order.* Sage, London.
Berlinski, D. 1995. *A Tour of The Calculus.* New York: Vintage Books.
Berlinski, D. 1995. *A Tour of The Calculus.* New York: Vintage Books.
Bernasconi, Robert. 1997. African Philosophy's challenge to Continental Philosophy, in *Postcoloial African Philosophy. A Critical Reader.* Emmanuel Chukwudi Eze (ed.). London: Blackwell: 183-196.
Buruma, Ian and Avishai Margalit. 2004. *Occidentalism: The West in the Eyes of Its Enemies.* Penguin Press
Carlinescu, Matei. 1987. *Five Faces of Modernity: Modernism, Avant-Garde, Decadence, Kitsch, Postmodernism.* Durham: Duke University Press.
Davidson, Basil. 1993 The Ancient World and Africa: Whose Roots, in Van Sertima, Ivan (ed.), *Egypt Revisited.* New Brunswick: Transaction Press.
De Jouvenel, Bertrand 1993. *On Power.* Indianapolis: Liberty classics.
Delanty, Gerard. (ed.). 2000. *Modernity and Post Modernity: Knowledge, Power and Self.* London: Sage.
Diop, Cheikh Anta. 1981. *Civilization or Barbarism: An Authentic Anthropology.* New York: Lawrence Hill Books.
Du Bois, W.E.B. 1905 [1990]. *The Souls of Black Folk.* New York: Vintage Books.
Dunbar-Ortiz, Roxanne. 2003. The Grid of History: Cowboys and Indians, *Monthly Review* Volume 55, Number 3. http://www.monthlyreview.org/0703dunbarortiz.htm.
Dussel, Enrique. 1988. "Was America Discovered or Invaded?" In *Concilium* 220: 126-134.
Edge, Hoyt. 1994. *A Constructive Postmodern Perspective on Self and Community: From Atomism to Holism.* New York: Edwin Mellen Press.
Ellul, Jacques. 1964. *The Technological Society.* New York: Vintage Books.
Eze, Emmanuel Chukwudi. 1997. The Color of Reason: The idea of "race" in Kant's anthropology I, in E. C. Eze (ed.) *Postcolonial African Philosophy: A Critical Reader.* Cambridge: Blackwell.
Fanning, Bryan. 2002. *Racism and Social Change in the Republic of Ireland.* Manchester: Manchester University Press.
Fasching, Darrel J. 1981. *The Thought of Jacques Ellul.* New York: Edwin Mellen Press.
Foster, John Bellamy. 2003. The New Age of Imperialism, Monthly Review 55 (3) http://www.monthlyreview.org/0703jbf.htm.
Foucault, Michel . 1965. *Madness and Civilization.* New York: Vintage Books.
Foucault, Michel. 1961. *Folie et deraison: histoire de la folie a l'age classique.* Paris: Plon.

Foucault, Michel [Trans. David Macey]. 2003. *Society Must Be Defended: Lectures at the Collège de France, 1975-76.*. London: Penguin Books.
Fromm, Erich. 1978. *To Have or To Be?* London: J. Cape.
Fryer, Peter. 1984. *Staying Power*. New York: Pluto Press.
Gobineau, Arthur Comte de. 1835. *Essai sur l'inegalité des races humaines*. Philadelphia: Lippincott.
Goldberg, David Theo. 2002. *The Racial State*. Oxford: Blackwell.
Gordon, Colin (ed.). 1980. *Power and Knowledge: Selected Interviews and Other Writings, 1972-1977*. New York: Pantheon Books.
Gossett, Thomas F. 1963. *Race: The History of an Idea in America*. Dallas: Southern Methodist
Greenslade, Liam. 1992. White skin, white masks: Psychological Distress among the Irish in Britain, in Patrick O'Sullivan (ed.) *The Irish in the New Communities*. Leicester: Leicester University Press.
Habermas, Jurgen. 1991. *The Structural Transformation of the Bourgeois Public Sphere*. Cambridge Mass.: MIT Press.
Hardt, Michael and Antonio Negri. 2000. *Empire*. Cambridge Mass.: Harvard University Press.
Horkheimer, Max [Trans. Matthew J. O'Connell]. 1995 [1982]. *Critical Theory*. New York: Continuum,.
Ifekwunigwe, Jayne O. 1997. Diaspora's Daughters, Africa's Orphans?: On Authenticity, Lineage and "Mixed Race" Identity, in Heidi Mirza (ed.) *Black British Feminism*. London: Routledge: 127-52.
Illich, Ivan. 1981. *Shadow Work*. Salem NH: Marion Boyars inc.
Jalée, Pierre. 1973. *Imperialism in the Seventies*. New York: Third World Press.
Jefferson, Thomas. 1984 [1781]. *Writings*. New York: Library of America.
Jonas, Hans. 1963. *The Gnostic Religion*. Boston: Beacon Press.
Kamen, Henry. 1965. *The Spanish Inquisition*. New York: NAL.
Koestler, Arthur. 1959. *The Sleepwalkers: A History of Man's Changing Vision of the Universe*. Harmondsworth: Penguin.
Latour, Bruno [Trans. Catherine Porter]. 1993. *We Have Never Been Modern*. Cambridge, Mass: Harvard University Press.
Latour, Bruno and Peter Weibel. 2005 (eds). *Making Things Public. Atmospheres of Democracy*. Cambridge Mass.: MIT Press
Lentin, Alana. 2004. *Racism and Anti-racism in Europe*. London: Pluto Press.
Lentin, Ronit and Robbie McVeigh (eds.). 2002. *Racism and Anti-racism in Ireland*. Belfast: Beyond the Pale Publications.
Levine, Lawrence. 1978. *Black Culture and Black Consciousness: Afro American Folk Thought From Slavery to Freedom*. Oxford: Oxford University Press.
Lippmann, Walter. 1993 [1925]. *The Phantom Public*. Brunswick: Transaction Publishers.
Löwith, Karl. 1949. *Meaning in History*. Chicago: University of Chicago Press.
Luedtke, Luther (ed.). 1988. *Making America: The Society and Culture of the United States*. Washington: USIA.
Marable, Manning. 1991. *Race, Reform and Rebellion: The Second Reconstruction in Black America, 1945-1990*. Jackson and London: University of Mississippi Press.

Marcuse, Herbert. 1969. *An Essay on Liberation*. Boston: Beacon Press.
Memmi, Albert. 1965. *The Colonizer and the Colonized*. Boston: Beacon Press.
Merchant, Carolyne. 1980. *The Death of Nature*. New York: Harper & Row.
Mignolo D. Walter. 2000a. *Local Histories/Global Designs: Coloniality, Subaltern knowledge and Border Thinking*. Princeton NJ: Princeton University Press.
Mignolo D. Walter. 2000b. The Many Faces of Cosmo-polis: Border Thinking and Critical Cosmopolitanism, *Public Culture*, 12 (Fall 2000): 721-748?.
Morton, Eric. 2002. Race and Racism in the Works of David Hume, *Journal on African Philosophy* 1 (1). http://www.africanphilosophy.com/afphil/vol1.1/morton.html.
Nebrija, Antonio de. 1946. *Gramatica Castellana*. Madrid: Junta del Centenario.
Padgen, Anthony. 1995. *Lords of All the World—Ideologies of Empire in Spain, Britain, and France (1500-1800)*. New Haven: Yale University Press.
Paik, Nak-Chung. 2000. Coloniality in Korea and a South Korean Project for Overcoming Modernity, *Interventions* 2 (1): 73-86.
Parenti, Michael. 1995. *Against Empire: The Brutal Realities of U.S. Global Domination*. San Franscisco: City Lights Books.
Quijano, Anibal. 2000. Coloniality of Power, Eurocentrism, and Latin America. *Nepantla: Views from South* 1 (3): 533-580.
Said, Edward W. 1978. *Orientalsim*. New York: Pantheon Books.
Seltzer, Mark. 1992. *Bodies and Machines*. London: Routledge.
Shappin, Steven and Simon Schaffer. 1985. *Leviathan and the Air-Pump: Hobbes, Boyle, and the Experimental Life*. Princeton NJ: Princeton University Press.
Stannard, David E. 1992. *American Holocaust: The Conquest of the New World*. New York: Oxford University Press.
Stoler, Ann Laura. 1995. *Race and the Education of Desire: Foucault's History of Sexuality and the Colonial Order of Things*. Durham: Duke University Press.
Tu Wei-mMing. 19966. *Confusian Thoughts: Selfhood as Creative Transformation*. Albany: State University of New York Press.
van Krieken, Robert. 1984. We have not learnt to control nature and ourselves enough: an interview with Norbert Elias, *De Groene Amsterdammer* 16 May, 1984: 10-11. http://www.usyd.edu.au/su/social/elias/intervie.htm.
van Krieken, Robert. 1990. The Organisation of the Soul: Elias and Foucault on discipline and the self, *Archives Européennes de Sociologie* 31(2): 353-71.
Veroli, Nicolas. 2002. *How a Fiction became the Truth: Five Thesis on Cogito, Imagination and Modernity.* Ijele: Art eJournal of the African World 2 (1): 1-55. http://www.ijele.com/issue4/veroli.html.
Voegelin, Eric. 1987. *The New Science of Politics*. Chicago: University of Chicago Press.
Voegelin, Eric. 1999. *The Collected Works*. Columbia: University of Missouri Press.
Wacquant, Loïc. 2002. Deadly Symbiosis: Rethinking race and imprisonment in twenty-first-century America. *Boston Review* (April/May). http://www.bostonreview.net/BR27.2/wacquant.html.
Wallerstein, Immanuel. 1995. *Unthinking Social Science:The Limits of Nineteenth-Century Paradigms*. Cambridge: Polity Press.
Wallerstein, Immanuel. 1996. Eurocentrism and its Avatars: The Dilemmas of Social Science, paper presented to the *Korean Sociological Association—International*

Sociological Association East Asian Regional Colloquium on The Future of Sociology in East Asia, Seoul, 22-23 November, 1996.

Webb, James. 1971. *The Flight From Reason: Volume 1 of the Age of the Irrational.* London: Macdonald and Co.

Williams, Kai. 2001. The Politics of Exuberance. Ph.D. Dissertation. Binghamton: State University of New York.

Wimmer, Andreas and Glick Schiller, Nina. 2002. Methodological Nationalism and Beyond: Nation-state building, migration and the social sciences, *Global Networks* 2 (4): 301-334.

Winant, Howard. 2001. *The World Is a Ghetto: Race and Democracy Since World War II*. New York: Basic Books.

Zeleny, Milan. (ed.). 1981. *Autopoiesis: A Theory of Living Organization*. New York: North Holland.

Zimmermann, Warren. 2002. *First Great Triumph*. New York: Farra Straus and Giroux.

Zinn, Howard. 1985. *A People's History of the United States: 1492—Present*. New York: Harper.

CHAPTER FIVE

ASYLUM SEEKERS AND THE NATION-STATE: PUTTING THE "ORDER" BACK INTO "BORDERS" IN AUSTRALIA AND THE REPUBLIC OF IRELAND

STEVE GARNER AND ANTHONY MORAN

Introduction

Large-scale movements of people, and the increasingly global nature of such flows (Castles and Miller 1998), are major issues faced by nation-states in the contemporary world. One portion of these flows is represented by asylum seekers.[1] While neo-liberals and many governments of wealthy countries advocate the free movement of goods, services and capital across borders, asylum seekers are frequently met with the politics of fear, resistance and resentment.

Since the early 1990s, both the Republic of Ireland and Australia have significantly tightened their regimes for controlling asylum seekers. While it is important to situate these actions within a more general trend among wealthy western countries—and as part of a globally coordinated crackdown on asylum seekers—this should not obscure the ways that specific reactions to asylum seekers have been shaped by the history, traditions, and domestic politics of these two countries.

In this chapter we compare recent governmental and public responses to asylum seekers in the Republic of Ireland and Australia, arguing that: borders can be adjusted as policy outcomes; the state thus produces nationals and non-nationals; asylum seekers are particular exemplars of non-nationals, and can be deployed as devices elucidating the state's role in defending territory; yet there has to be a bi-directional process of intent (between state and citizens). Through the example of control of asylum seekers we also provide a counter-argument to those boosters of globalisation who claim that the nation-state is becoming increasingly powerless and irrelevant in a "borderless" world (Ohmae 1990).

The nation-state and asylum seekers

Transnational capital flows, the power of transnational corporations, new forms of communication and transport, and new modes of and sites for regional and global governance, all constrain the capacities of governments to control what goes on within their national territories. However, these constraints can be exaggerated (Hirst and Thompson, 1999). Dittgen (1999) argues that nation-states have experienced a loss of *autonomy* rather than *sovereignty*, and that some functions of borders remain, especially those concerning defence and nationalist ideology. EU experience indicates the ongoing importance of borders, albeit in transformed geopolitical conditions. In ancient times the *limes* marked the point up to which civilisation was guaranteed in the Roman Empire (Rufin 1991). Both King (1998) and Dittgen (1999) suggest that the contemporary *limes* is effectively the Southern border of the EU. If the Republic of Ireland can be included as a "southern border", then we might use this image for our purposes here. Similarly, Australia's recent and spectacular repulsion of refugee boats was justified under a policy of "border protection".

Hindess (2003) contends that the asylum seeker is a product of the international system of nation-states with its origins in the 1648 Treaty of Westphalia. The existence of this system means that each state is responsible for the welfare of its own citizens, and this stifles feelings of sympathy for those who, in desperation, flee their own country and seek refuge in another (2003: 28). If, as Balibar (1991) argues, nationals are the result of strategies and politico-cultural regimes aimed at "producing the people", then the asylum seeker, like all "non-nationals", is therefore produced by the same process.

Yet the asylum seeker or refugee is somehow *more* non-national than others. Agamben (1995, 1998) argues that the refugee, like other denizens or stateless people, is disturbing because he or she disrupts the certainty of all the categories important to the nation-state as components of a stable system for the classification of peoples:

> ....The refugee should be considered for what he is, that is, nothing less than a border concept that radically calls into question the principles of the nation-state and, at the same time, helps clear the field for a no-longer-delayable renewal of categories (Agamben 1995: 118).

But rather than clearing the field for a "renewal of categories", we argue that asylum seekers often have the opposite effect, helping to strengthen the resolve to "act like a sovereign nation-state". Through increased policing and surveillance of borders, and by acting swiftly and decisively against asylum seekers, a government can be perceived by its people as a *national* government serving the interests of the nation by exercising a form of control over the global environment.

Here, bi-directional processes become apparent, involving both top-down stimulation of fears, and bottom-up feelings about dangers to the national "body". As borders have become in many ways increasingly porous (for certain groups), the asylum seeker has become a symbol of loss of control. Anxieties about globalisation have been condensed in the image of the asylum seeker trying to penetrate actual and symbolic national boundaries (Bauman 2002: 112-15; 2004: 66). In this way, the asylum seeker crystallises anxieties about the disruption or undermining of local, regional and national economies, cultures and ways of life attributable to the flow of capital, goods and ideas over borders. While it has become increasingly difficult to control *those* flows, the movement of people can still be controlled, and in some cases even more effectively than in the past because of sophisticated surveillance technologies and procedures.

Moreover, asylum seekers constitute such a threat because they represent a projection of fears about diminishing welfare being absorbed by the undeserving poor. Some categories of asylum seeker in Australia and most in Europe are not allowed work permits, instead receiving minimal social security (Department of Immigration and Multicultural and Indigenous Affairs 2003a). They are structurally excluded from productive activities and thus inevitably become welfare recipients or are funded by charities. In cultures where such a premium is placed on narrowly-defined productivity, the unproductive national, as opposed to the more useful labour migrant, is increasingly viewed as a drain on resources. When this drain is generated by non-nationals, an intense border reaffirmation reaction is triggered.

Republic of Ireland

The example of the Republic of Ireland demonstrates the state's pro-active role in modifying the symbolic borders of nation at a moment when that nation is constructed as being under threat from asylum seekers. Since 1996, Ireland has been a net importer of people. The surplus of immigrants over emigrants is supplied principally by labour migrants and their children.[ii] In fact the number of work permits granted to non-EU labour migrants outnumbers asylum applications by around 7:1 (although it was 4:1 in the 2000-03 period). This is of paramount importance when we focus on the two key state-led amendments to the country's immigration regulations identified below: the Supreme Court ruling of January 2003 in relation to children-citizens of migrant parents, and particularly the Referendum on Citizenship in June 2004. In both these cases, though not directly focusing on asylum seekers, the explicit references have been toward the threat to the "integrity" of the immigration process posed by asylum seekers alone.

The Republic of Ireland government actions have from the outset been *ad hoc* and short-term, constructing immigration as a set of administrative problems and minimising its human and social dimensions, which have been left to NGOs (like the Irish Refugee Council, Amnesty International and local support groups) to emphasise. The legislative inertia and the focus on asylum-seeking as a drain on the country's resources have been major contributions to the discourse on immigration of all kinds and to the racism flourishing in the Republic of Ireland since the mid-1990s (Garner 2003; Lentin and McVeigh 2002). A set of contradictory arguments has emerged, involving one that identifies asylum seekers as threats to welfare, national culture and cohesion, and another that draws a parallel with Irish historical experience, positing a fair and liberal welcome to outsiders as the necessary response. Attitudes toward minorities and immigration (as measured by opinion polls) have hardened since the late 1990s (Garner and White 2001). People have become less inclined to view immigration as positive and more likely to see non-nationals as absorbing scarce resources. This can be interpreted as a complex response to the messages conveyed by the media and the government, growing local awareness of the presence of 'non-nationals', and a reaction to sets of striking and contradictory changes in the country's economy. The "Celtic Tiger" economic boom has actually been relatively patchy and has exacerbated inequalities of wealth (Garner 2003).

While enacting equality legislation,[iii] the key state actions have sought to limit access to the country and reduce asylum seekers' freedom of manoeuvre. This process has accelerated since the elections of May 2002, after which Michael McDowell became Minister for Justice. McDowell had previously gone on record as seeing asylum, or more precisely, "abuse" of the asylum system as a serious issue (Coulter, 2002). He then implemented a crackdown, a series of police raids code named "Operation Hyphen", aimed at removing asylum seekers having exhausted the appeals procedure. It cost over €100,000, and its ineffectiveness drew criticism from other parliamentarians and NGOs. Amnesty International Ireland's development manager Jim Loughran, warned that "this kind of manhunt, with hundreds of *gardaí* [police] and the holding of those arrested in undisclosed detention centres" was "dangerously close to the hard line approach taken by countries such as Australia" (Fekete 2002).

The state has endeavoured to alter or at least narrowly re-interpret the 1937 constitution's founding principles in relation to nationality, according to which all persons born in Ireland were automatically entitled to Irish citizenship (see Lentin, R. in this volume). Paradoxically, the defence of bloodline borders surfaced when the political border between the Republic and Northern Ireland had just assumed a more porous nature. The Good Friday/Belfast Agreement of 1998 involved a series of trade-offs to bring nationalist and unionist politicians on board. One of these was to allow people born in Northern Ireland to claim Irish citizenship as of right.[iv] As a result of the subsequent legislation, the 2001 Citizenship Act, any child born *on the island of Ireland* acquires citizenship as of right. The two latest developments initiated by the state in terms of Irish nationality reversing this automatic right are analysed below.

a) The Supreme Court ruling on the residence rights of "Irish-born children", 2003

The degree of *ius soli* enacted in the 2001 Act constituted the "loophole" that Minister McDowell maintained had to be closed. The 1989 Supreme Court 'Fajujonu' ruling had granted the eponymous Nigerian father of three "Irish-born children" (i.e. Irish citizens) the right to residence in Ireland due to the Constitution's Articles 41 and 42. These enshrine the family as the basic unit of society, and granting children the right to enjoy the "company, society and protection" of their family. The Court viewed this right as taking precedence over the Minister's right, granted under the 1935 Aliens Act and the 1946 Aliens Order, to remove foreign nationals from Irish territory (Annual Review of Population Law 1989).

McDowell challenged this ruling within months of taking office as Justice Minister, bringing a case against two asylum-seeking families who had appealed decisions to deport them, on the grounds of having "Irish-born children". In January 2003, the Supreme Court ruled by 5-2 to uphold the Department of Justice's decision that the "Fajujonu ruling" could not be applied systematically. 7,000 to 10,000 foreign nationals had been granted residence on that basis, and around 10,000 more applications were already in the system (Haughey 2003). The Minister for Justice argued that granting residence to every foreign parent of "Irish-born children" would lead to widespread abuse of the asylum and immigration systems, thus threatening their "integrity".

However, the Supreme Court's interpretation constitutes an implicitly racialised imaginative geography of Irishness, surpassing the isolated cases of what became labelled "citizenship tourism" (i.e. women coming to Ireland just to give birth, and obtain nationality for their child, and the ensuing residence rights for parents) (*The Economist* 2004). The legal arguments of the case revolved around the question of whose rights should take precedence; a child's constitutional right to unqualified citizenship and thus family protection in his/her country of birth, or the state's right to control the movement of non-nationals across and within its borders. Yet as the two dissenting judges (Fennelly and McGuiness) pointed out in their rulings, the Minister had focused his argument on the rights of the *parents* rather than those of the *child*. Neither judge felt that the Minister's rights should usurp those of the child (guaranteed by Articles 41-42 of the Constitution), which was, in effect, the substance of the majority ruling.

The 2003 ruling still had to be legislated on and tested in the courts, but it opened a revealing line of reasoning, underlying the development of a *de facto* two-tier Irish citizenship. Another constitutional principle that survived the Good Friday Agreement and the 2001 Citizenship Act recognises Ireland's heritage as a diaspora nation. Proof of only one grandparent born in Ireland still suffices for citizenship. So people of Irish descent whose bloodlines run through Boston, Sydney or London for example, can obtain the full array of rights open to citizens and bring family to settle permanently in Ireland with no questions asked. Yet children born in Ireland but whose direct ancestry is "non-EU" (i.e. beyond the new *limes*) are to have their constitutional right weighed on a case-by-case basis.

Moreover, the term "Irish-born child" or "IBC" is an administrative construct, with "Irish-born" rather than "Irish" used only in the case of parents who are not nationals. Yet the vision of citizenship and membership explicit in the Citizenship Act, 2001 (and in the 1916 Proclamation of the Republic) states the opposite: i.e. that birth on the island of Ireland confers Irish citizenship, regardless of parentage.

b) Referendum on Citizenship, 2004

The outstanding ambiguity surrounding the Supreme Court ruling did not satisfy the Minister, who persuaded his Cabinet colleagues to call a referendum to resolve it, to be held on 11 June 2004, coinciding with the European elections. The referendum sought approval to put to the vote an amendment to the wording of Article 9 of the constitution: citizenship would henceforth be granted to children of non-national parents only if the latter had resided legally in the state for three of the four years prior to the child's birth.[v]

The justifications given for amendment to the 2001 Act were threefold. Revealingly, McDowell first contextualised the need for change by announcing that 60,000 children had been born to non-national women in Irish hospitals in 2003. He argued that the Masters (maternity hospital managers) of Dublin hospitals had requested a change to the law because of the stretched resources entailed in dealing with this wave of foreign-derived births, with many women arriving very late in their pregnancies without medical notes. These health officials soon distanced themselves from this claim, although it was often repeated by key players in the debate (RTÉ 2004).

The second stream of justification was a putative necessity to comply with general EU norms on citizenship, in respect of which Ireland, through its *ius soli* element of citizenship, allegedly appeared anomalous. This procedure was posited as merely an act of harmonisation, a purely administrative operation.

The last argument links the previous two: Ireland (and by extension the EU) had to be protected against "citizenship tourism". The references made to the "Chen case" by the Minister underlined the need to plug what was termed a "loophole", abused by non-nationals. Chen, a Chinese national seeking residence rights in the UK, travelled to Belfast to give birth. She thus obtained Irish nationality for her child and bolstered her case to remain in the UK. The British government's decision to refuse her residence was overturned by the European Court of Justice in 2004.[vi] The thrust of the Minister's argument was that citizenship acquired by people with "insufficient" links to Ireland was an abuse. Senator John Minihan argued for example that:

> People with no social, historic or cultural links to Ireland should not be able to freely confer Irish citizenship on their children. Those children currently born in Ireland will, in turn, be able to confer Irish citizenship on their own children and grandchildren even if they never reside in Ireland.[vii]

What the objective nature of these links could be was not discussed in the campaign. We can only speculate (as we do below) about what they actually mean. The result of the Referendum on Citizenship was a resounding "Yes" to change, with 80 per cent nationwide approval on a 62 per cent turnout. The amendment was introduced in autumn 2004, and became law on 1 January 2005.

The justifications for the referendum were pretexts for renewing a project of defending the borders of Irish nationhood in a context where its actual borders are arguably more open than ever before. Moreover, the Minister's "60,000" foreign births included those to women who were legally resident. The context is one of a demographic increase that has returned Ireland's population to above its 1871 levels for the first time in a century, a health service that has been steadily recruiting non-EU personnel to work in it for the last seven years, and reducing maternity facilities over the last twenty (Kennedy and Murphy-Lawless 2003).

The argument that there is a requirement to harmonise laws with other EU member-states is supported by neither EC directives nor recent practice on the part of the Irish state. Ireland was the last EU state to sign the UN Charter on the Elimination of Racial Discrimination for example, and is still the only one without comprehensive immigration legislation. Indeed, there is as cogent an argument for maintaining *ius soli* derived from the fact that around 40 other republics including the USA and India, as well as New Zealand and Canada, include it as a criterion for citizenship. Moreover, the "bloodlines" pathway to citizenship (through at least one Irish-born grandparent) remains unaltered, enabling people with no engagement with Ireland except through family history to travel, settle and transmit citizenship unfettered.

Lastly, the question of "citizenship tourism" is hardly pressing. No figures were provided by the state on the precise number of alleged abusers of this "loophole", namely non-national women arriving in late stages of pregnancy, giving birth and then claiming residence. The European Court of Justice 'Chen' ruling stated that one: "Member State cannot restrict the effects of the granting of the nationality of another Member State." Yet what is the substantial distinction between Mrs. Chen's child and a US citizen whose grandmother happened to be born in Ireland in the 1920s? Why should the former *a priori* enjoy fewer rights than the latter? Surely both have just as slim a "social, cultural and historical" bond with Ireland.

The State has been remarkably pro-active in this crisis-creation process, setting out parameters, generating legislation and calling a referendum to alter the constitution. Although attributing personal responsibility is a problematic area, the role of Minister McDowell has been extraordinary.[viii] The contrast between his leadership and his predecessor's is stark: the 1997-2002 period is characterised by reactive and ad hoc measures, while since 2002 there has been a deliberate project to "tighten up" asylum regulations, and make obtaining a work permit, and residency more difficult. The outcomes of this process are firstly, for Irish nationality to have become more racialised, and secondly, for rights of children guaranteed under the 1937 Constitution to have been sacrificed in return for making non-national parents' status in Ireland more insecure. The constitution has thus been manipulated for short-term policy objectives. Irish citizenship regulations have been amended as part of a process of redrawing the border as a defence against the Third World: only non-EU national parents are adversely affected by this legislation, as well as children who would formerly have been Irish citizens as of right. Now, the routes to citizenship favour bloodlines over residency, biology over material engagement. Using a combination of appeals to administrative rationality, defence of resources and blood and soil nationalism, the Irish nation was constituted in the referendum as "a political community of fate," as Benhabib (2004: 206) argues in the case of Germany in 1990. The Irish nation is thus reconfigured primarily as ethnos rather than demos.

Australia

Australia's history and context differ from Ireland's, yet it has also cracked down on asylum seekers in the same period. Part of the reason for the similar response is that asylum and refugee policies among western nations have been subject to processes of intergovernmental discussion and collaboration (Humphrey 2003: 34-36). On the other hand, Australia has not altered its constitution or "racialised" its nationality in order to deal with this situation. This illustrates quite powerfully how "outsiders" can be treated just as, or even more, poorly under civic forms of nationalism as under ethnic forms of nationalism.

With the exception of its small indigenous population, Australia is an immigrant nation built first upon European and, since the 1970s, increasingly upon Asian and other non-European migration. Officially abandoning its "White Australia Policy" in 1973, Australia now defines itself as a multicultural nation. Debate about unauthorised asylum seekers, at least at government level, is mainly about the disruption and dangers represented by their so-called illegal entry into Australia.

Australia has a history of integrating refugees since the end of the Second World War when it attracted hundreds of thousands of displaced people from Europe (United Nations High Commissioner for Refugees 2000: 13; Jordens 2001). It sought these refugees mainly in order to build its population and economy. From the late 1970s, it accepted more than 185,000 refugees from Indochina, the largest number after the United States and Canada (United Nations High Commissioner for Refugees 2000: 181-82). While about 2,000 Vietnamese refugees arrived as boatpeople in the late 1970s, the vast majority entered Australia via official channels under government programmes of resettlement.

Historically, therefore, Australia has actively selected refugees rather than dealt with asylum seekers who arrive at its doorstep (Howard 2003), with geographical isolation and lack of land borders being the determining factors. Like only a handful of countries, Australia maintains an active refugee resettlement programme, accepting about 12,000 refugees each year under various categories (Howard 2003: 36, 47; Crock and Saul 2002: 12; McMaster 2001: 63). Two thirds of these, described by government officials as those refugees with "the most pressing need", are selected from refugee camps and other places outside Australia. The existence of this small refugee programme is used as an ideological weapon against asylum seekers who arrive by boat or plane without a valid visa. Unauthorised asylum seekers are described as "queue jumpers" and contrasted with "legitimate refugees".[ix] It is also claimed that defending the country against unauthorised asylum seekers protects "legitimate" refugees and maintains public support for the refugee programme. More importantly, and paralleling Irish political discourse, it is argued that strict border control against asylum seekers is crucial to the public's acceptance of the entire immigration programme as well (Betts 2003; Department of Immigration and Multicultural and Indigenous Affairs 2004; Ruddock 2003), which is seen as essential to the Australian nation's ongoing development. Here, as Stevens (2002: 890) points out, the "system is geared to provide protection primarily to the state and only secondarily to asylum seekers or refugees."

Increased capacities for communication and transport over vast distances have made Australia's isolation and lack of land borders less relevant than in the past. Since the mid-1970s Australia has experienced four small waves of asylum seeker boats (Brennan 2003; Manne and Corlett 2004; Stevens 2002). The first three waves involved asylum seekers from Australia's region, especially as a result of instability in Indochina. The fourth wave involved asylum seekers from the Middle East, mainly Iraqis and Afghans, and some Iranians, from about 1999 to early 2002. Though they represented a significant increase on the numbers from the late 1980s through the 1990s, by world or European standards, and even as a ratio of Australia's population, the numbers were nevertheless still small: 921 in 1998-99, 4,175 in 1999-2000, and 4,137 in 2000-2001 (Senate Select Committee on a Certain Maritime Incident 2002: 291).

In the late 1980s, the Hawke and Keating Labour governments set up detention centres to hold boat arrivals, many of whom were repatriated, some after long years in detention (Stevens 2002: 868-9). In order to prevent the interference of Australian courts, the Keating government introduced legislation in 1992 requiring mandatory detention of anyone who arrived in Australia without a visa (Crock and Saul, 2002). After its election in 1996, the Liberal-National Howard government expanded Australia's detention system, employed a private security firm to run the centres, and applied more punitive measures against those who had entered Australia without a visa, even after refugee status had been established. In the late 1990s, it focused public attention on the asylum seeker "threat" (Moran 2005).

The context of the reaction to the fourth wave of asylum seekers includes two important interrelated features. First, some sections of the Australian public were disoriented, nervous and angry after almost twenty years of dramatic changes. These included the ways that government manages the economy and social welfare, including major privatisations of government services and utilities; the perceived and actual decline of some manufacturing and rural industries, partly as a result of the restructuring and internationalising of the economy since the 1980s; and changes to the ethnic composition of the population and in relations between settler and Aboriginal Australians (Moran 2005). The second factor was the rise of a right wing populist-nationalist movement after 1996, around MP Pauline Hanson. Her One Nation Party advocated a return to a protectionist, economically nationalist Australia, and attacked Aborigines, Aboriginal policies, Asians, multicultural policy and asylum seekers. Both the Liberal-National coalition government, and the Labour

Party were concerned to recapture the million or so voters attracted to the One Nation Party in the 1998 election, and dealing harshly with asylum seekers was one way to reconnect with these voters (Manne 2002).

During the late 1990s, Minister for Immigration Phillip Ruddock was prominent in the media, defending and advocating his government's approach. Behind the few thousand who had arrived, Ruddock and others claimed, there was a human tide waiting to flood Australia.[x] These actions created a sense of crisis that the Howard government "resolved" through its actions in preventing the landing on Australian territory in August 2001 of the Norwegian cargo vessel *MV Tampa*, carrying more than 400 asylum seekers. When the *Tampa* came onto the horizon in the run-up to the 2001 federal election, the Howard government seized the opportunity to declare itself as a government that would protect Australia's borders and sovereignty before anything else, including humanitarian and internationalist values. This stance proved very popular with the Australian public (Roy Morgan Research 2001), and after trailing in the polls earlier in the year, the Howard government was comfortably re-elected.[xi] From this government-manufactured crisis emerged the invention of the "Pacific solution", whereby the Australian state made arrangements with poor Pacific nations (Nauru and Papua New Guinea) to set up detention camps to receive boatpeople trying to reach Australia. Pursuing this new policy, the Howard government set up a "People Smuggling Taskforce" and engaged the Australian armed forces in "Operation Relex"—navy boats sought out any suspected unauthorised vessel headed for Australia, warned it off or, as a last resort, took control of the passengers and delivered them to an off-shore detention centre (Senate Select Committee 2002: Ch. 2; Mares 2002; Marr and Wilkinson 2003; and Howard 2003). Many of these people were subsequently found to be legitimate refugees and some were allowed into Australia, while others were accepted by other countries. From late 2001 onwards, the Howard government also legislatively altered Australia's migration zone, removing places like Christmas Island and Ashmore Reef, thus ensuring that asylum seekers on boats landing there could not make asylum claims on the Australian state (Department of Immigration and Multicultural and Indigenous Affairs 2004).

The management of the asylum seeker shows how the national border can become a zone of violation, and unauthorized attempts to cross it give rise to punitive responses. This is evident in the lack of sympathy shown by most political leaders on both sides of the political fence for those, including children, languishing in isolated detention centres, sometimes for years. Government language oscillates between the blandly bureaucratic to the openly hostile, from talk of the management of a global problem to the vilification of asylum seekers as "potential terrorists" (Mares 2002: 134; Marr and Wilkinson 2003: 151, 198, 280-281); people who "throw their own children overboard" in an attempt to reach Australian soil, who partake in "barbaric acts" like sewing up their own lips, self-mutilating, rioting and setting things alight when they are held in detention. Government ministers like Ruddock responded to these acts of desperation by repeatedly declaring that Australians would not be blackmailed, and that such actions were alien to ordinary Australians.[xii] When, in October 2001, his government falsely claimed that asylum seekers had thrown their own children overboard in an attempt to gain access to a navy boat and thus to Australia's refugee processes, Howard declared that:

> I don't want in this country people who are prepared... to throw their own children overboard... I don't know their backgrounds but I do know this, it's a matter of common humanity. Genuine refugees don't throw their children overboard into the sea.[xiii]

Though Howard was referring to particular individuals and groups, his comments, like those of other government ministers, were no doubt read by some members of the public to mean "barbaric" or racially different people who could never fit into Australia and who would, moreover, be a physical threat to other "decent" Australians.

Judging from the results of a recent qualitative research project (Brett and Moran 2004) interviewing Australians from various ages, occupations and ethnic backgrounds, the public rejection of unauthorised asylum seekers is comprised of a complex amalgam of ideas and beliefs about the law, illegitimacy of claims, national sovereignty, containing the Muslim presence in Australia, and maintaining Australia's living standards. Some people equated controlling asylum seekers with controlling the impact of Muslim fundamentalism in Australia and helping to protect Australia from terrorism. The government's use of military forces to "defend" Australia's coastline from asylum seekers during "Operation Relex", and indeed some of its public statements, tended to reinforce this perception and to give it legitimacy. As in Ireland, it is also claimed by some people that, as public resources are scarce, Australia cannot afford to accommodate the needs of asylum seekers. The irony is that the federal government has been spending vast amounts of money on keeping people in detention, and implementing the border protection plan. The lack of a public outcry about this suggests that people feel strongly enough about the issue to allow whatever is deemed necessary by government to be spent. Also apparent was the way that concentrating on rules and legalities mediated the moral claims of non-citizens on Australian "generosity". A strict interpretation of legality, focused upon the way that people try to enter the country—lacking or having destroyed documents and identification, without visas, using "criminal people smugglers"—is one kind of defensive strategy. Equally important is the way that the principle of nationality, as explained earlier, is brought into play. Sympathy for non-national others is defended against by claiming that their plight is not "our" moral duty to rectify, but that of their own governments and nations.

One important finding from this qualitative research is that it was not only non-immigrant or Anglo-Celtic Australians who rejected the claims of asylum seekers, but also many people from non-English speaking immigrant backgrounds. This raises important questions about the interaction between multiculturalism and the asylum seeker issue. While many of the same people supported concepts of multiculturalism and saw benefits accruing to Australia from the increased cultural diversity of its population, they rejected asylum seekers, not because of their ethnic difference, but for other reasons including illegitimacy of claims, welfare concerns, and for not entering Australia by the right processes. Multiculturalism was not necessarily an internationalist ethic, extending solidarity to the different peoples of the world, but rather a nationalist ethic bounded by the nation-state.

The border is now being drawn between "good", "deserving" refugees and "bad", "undeserving" refugees. In effect the "good" refugees, like other immigrants, are being invited into the national community by government. However, these numbers are made palatable to the public by use of a strict yearly quota, and by their selection according to government rules. Even this category is unstable for a public wary of Middle Eastern refugees (McAllister 2003), and which feels that jobs and welfare are being taken from Australian citizens. "Bad" refugees live within the territory of Australia but are excluded from the nation. They are now granted Temporary Protection Visas (TPVs) instead of permanent visas as punishment for the unauthorised way they originally entered the country (Department of Immigration and Multicultural and Indigenous Affairs 2003b). TPV holders have restrictions on their capacity to travel overseas; receive social security benefits; access English classes available to other refugees and recent immigrants; seek family reunion, or ever achieve a more permanent residency status or citizenship. There is no guarantee that TPVs will be renewed after they expire, leaving such refugees in a state of permanent uncertainty about the future, and unable to establish themselves in Australian society. Permanent residence status, citizenship and family reunion are available however, for refugees who enter Australia with some kind of visa (Crock and Saul 2002: Ch. 7).

Like Ireland and the EU, Australia has developed strategies to keep the Third World at bay. It is using its fortuitous geography and lack of land borders to insulate itself from the need to deal with unauthorised asylum seekers *at all*. The Howard government has been explicit about this, arguing that it is far better for asylum seekers to be managed within the countries where they first arrive after fleeing their own, even if it means providing aid to enable this desired outcome. Unstable and poor countries like Pakistan or Indonesia must therefore bear the primary responsibility for such flows.[xiv]

Conclusion

As part of the process explained in the first part of this chapter, nation-states, through which the EU also operates, move toward *ad hoc* and concerted consensuses on asylum seekers and refugees. Ireland sees itself as plugging a "loophole" through which the South penetrates the *limes*, for example. "We in Ireland," argued parliamentarian Tom O'Malley, "should not allow a hole in our back fence to create problems for our next-door neighbours in Britain or for our European neighbours. We should fix the hole in the fence for our own good and for the good of our neighbours."[xv] Such potential access points can only be seen as a threat *per se* if the idea of the Irish nation is based primarily on blood and kinship rather than residence. It also assumes an international order of self-protecting states. In Australia, "mending the hole in the fence" is pursued strictly in the service of national sovereignty and in ensuring the best interests of the Australian nation, construed narrowly as public support for the immigration programme, and erroneously (in our view) in terms of national security through confounding asylum seeker flows with defence issues. Other considerations, like being a good global citizen, and humanitarianism, are secondary.

In both cases the state played a leading role in setting agendas, bringing forward legislation and presenting itself as the institution most capable of defending borders and territory in a world of instability and disorder. Important strands of information fuelling public debates have been distorted and spun to provide particular versions of the national interest. Recognising the state's leading role in framing the debate about asylum seekers and giving shape to amorphous feelings of public insecurity, including doubts about globalising processes and the fate of nationality, we conclude with a caveat about the recent experiences of the two countries.

While polls in Australia showed strong support for the Howard government's tough stance, public sympathy for individual asylum seekers was sometimes aroused. It is perhaps because of the ways that ordinary people have shown the capacity to actually work alongside and accept people from so many different backgrounds that government has felt it necessary to physically and symbolically isolate asylum seekers from mainstream Australian life. By locking them away from people they cannot forge the local links that might make their future deportation an even greater problem. Government officials have been careful not to humanise asylum seekers. During the period of "Operation Relex" when the Australian navy was sent out to commandeer and repel asylum seeker boats, personnel dealing with media images of the operation were directly told not to produce images that would "personalise" asylum seekers (Senate Select Committee 2002: 22-25). Despite these attempts to isolate asylum seekers there has been a steady movement of resistance and protest that draws its support from citizen action and community groups, trade unions, schools, churches and refugee support groups.

In Ireland, the not-for-profit sector has thrown up a host of small organisations aimed at supporting asylum seekers and refugees. The dispersal programme of April 2000, sending asylum seekers to "direct provision" centres throughout the country, while creating initial tensions, also brought provincial Ireland into contact with asylum seekers. Not all the responses have been positive, but supportive relationships have developed. In April 2005, a Nigerian 'aged out' unaccompanied asylum seeker who had been attending a school near Dublin and was deported after failing to gain asylum seeker status, was brought back into the country after a national campaign instigated by his classmates had convinced the Minister for Justice to rescind his initial decision (see Moriarty in this volume).

In the examples from both countries, suggesting contradictory responses of rejection and sympathy and support for asylum seekers, we witness the difference between institutional and individual agencies, and more precisely the difference in perception of "masses" of disorderly threatening non-people as opposed to individuals who make you realise they are not so different from you after all. Clearly, picturing asylum seekers as an undifferentiated mass, and sharing space on equal terms may produce quite different outcomes in terms of political action. The state's interest in both countries has thus been best served by painting the picture of asylum seekers as masses rather than people.

Notes

[i] 19.2 million displaced persons as of early 2005, according to the UNHCR.
[ii] In the 1996-2002 period, 45.4% of immigrants were "Returning Irish emigrants", 17% were non-EU nationals, 16.7% were UK nationals and 13.5% other EU nationals (Garner 2003: 51).
[iii] Equal Employment Act 1998; Equal Status Act 2000.
[iv] According to the Citizenship Act, 1986, they had to do so through the birth of a grandparent before 1921 (when Northern Ireland came into existence).
[v] Time waiting for asylum applications to be dealt with does not count, although asylum seekers are legally resident. Perhaps "legally" in this case could be read as "productively".
[vi] European Court of Justice. Press release 84/04, 19 October 2004: Judgment of the Court of Justice in Case C-200/02, *Kunquian Catherine Zhu and Man Lavette Chen v Secretary of State for the Home Department*
[vii] Speech at the Smurfit Business School Debate on the Citizenship Referendum, May 31, 2004.

[viii] Beginning with calls for an end to what he termed the abuse of the asylum and immigration system for years prior to his accession to office as Minister, while he was Attorney-General.
[ix] See PM Howard's interview with talkback radio announcer Neil Mitchell on Radio 3AW on 17 August 2001, http://www.pm.gov.au/news/interviews/2001/interview1177.htm, and joint press conference of Howard and Ruddock defending the tough stance on *Tampa*, 27 August 2000. http://www.pm.gov.au/news/interviews/2001/interview1187.htm.
[x] See Ruddock's claim on national radio that 10,000 asylum seekers were ready to leave from the Middle East for Australia (ABC Online 1999).
[xi] In an analysis of the 2001 Australian Election Study, McAllister (2003) has shown that the issue of "border protection" coupled with terrorism won the election for the Howard government.
[xii] As reported on the AM program, ABC Radio, "Woomera Politics", 21 June, 2002. http://www.abc.net.au/am/stories/s462492.htm.
[xiii] PM Howard interviewed by Alan Jones, Radio 2UE, October 8, 2001 http://www.pm.gov.au/news/interviews/2001/interview1369.htm.
[xiv] In a radio interview Howard argued this point, initially in the context of Pakistan having to deal with Afghan refugees from the 2001 war in Afghanistan, but he generalised the claim to all such asylum seeker flows http://www.pm.gov.au/news/interviews/2001/interview1177.htm.
[xv] Daíl (Irish parliament) debates, April 21, 2004.

References

ABC Online. 1999. Government Struggles to Stop Flow of refugees, *PM Program*, November 15, 1999. http://www.abc.net.au/pm/s66365.htm
Agamben, Giorgio. 1995. We Refugees, *Symposium* 49 (2): 114-119.
Agamben, Giorgio [Trans. Danile Heller-Roazen]. 1998. *Homo Sacer: Sovereign Power and Bare Life*. Stanford: Stanford University Press.
Annual Review of Population Law. 1989. (16):168. Fajujonu v. Minister for Justice [December 8, 1989].
Balibar, Etienne. 1991. Racism and nationalism, in Etienne Balibar and Immanuel Wallerstein, *Race, Class, Nation: Ambiguous Identities*. London: Verso: 37-67.
Bauman, Zygmunt. 2002. *Society Under Siege*. Cambridge: Polity.
Bauman, Zygmunt. 2004. *Wasted Lives: Modernity and its Outcasts*. Cambridge: Polity.
Benhabib, Seyla. 2004. *The Rights of Others: Aliens, Residents and Citizens*. Cambridge: Cambridge University Press.
Betts, Katharine. 2003. Immigration Policy under the Howard Government, *Australian Journal of Social Issues* 38 (2): 169-92.
Brennan, Frank. 2003. *Tampering With Asylum: A Universal Humanitarian Problem*. St. Lucia, Qld: University of Queensland Press.
Brett, Judith and Anthony Moran. 2004. Understanding a Changing Australia: Ordinary People's Politics, *Australian Research Council Discovery Grant Project* (DP0343870203).

Castles, Stephen and Mark J. Miller. 1998. *The Age of Migration: International Population Movements in the Modern World.* London: Macmillan Press.
Coulter, Carol. 2002. Minister with a mission to push through reform of the system, *The Irish Times,* 13 July, 2002.
Crock, Mary, and Saul Ben. 2002. *Future Seekers: Refugees and the Law in Australia.* Sydney: The Federation Press.
Department of Immigration and Multicultural and Indigenous Affairs. 2003a. *Fact Sheet 62. Assistance to Asylum Seekers* (revised 20 November 2003). http://www.immi.gov.au
Department of Immigration and Multicultural and Indigenous Affairs. 2003b. *Fact Sheet 64. Temporary Protection Visas* (revised 20 November 2003). http://www.immi.gov.au
Department of Immigration and Multicultural and Indigenous Affairs. 2004. "Excision" Legislative Changes. http://www.immi.gov.au/legislation/refugee/01.htm. Accessed 9/14/2004.
Dittgen, Herbert. 1999. World without Borders? Reflections on the Future of the Nation-State. *Government and Opposition* 34 (2): 161-179.
Economist. 2004. Ireland's referendum on citizenship rules: Harder to be Irish, *Economist,* June 3, 2004.
Fekete, Liz. 2002. Minister defends deportation drive, *Institute of Race Relations, IRR News,* 1 September.
Garner, Steve. 2003. *Racism in the Irish Experience.* London: Pluto.
Garner, Steve and Allen White. 2001. *Racism in Ireland: Baseline report for the "Know Racism" Campaign.* Dublin: Department of Justice, Equality and Law Reform.
Haughey, Nuala. 2003. Residents of Limbo, *Irish Times Weekend,* June 7, 2003.
Hindess, Barry. 2003. Responsibility for Others in the Modern System of States, *Journal of Sociology* 39 (1): 23-30.
Hirst, Paul and Grahame Thompson. 1999. *Globalisation in Question: The International Economy and the Possibilities of Governance.* Cambridge: Policy Press.
Howard, Jessica. 2003. To Deter and Deny: Australia and the Interdiction of Asylum Seekers, *Refuge* 21 (4): 35-50.
Humphrey, Michael. 2003. Refugees: An Endangered Species? *Journal of Sociology* 39 (1): 31-43.
Jordens, Ann-Mari. 2001. Post-war non-British Migration, in James Jupp (ed.) *The Australian People: An Encyclopedia of the Nation, its People and Their Origins.* Cambridge: Cambridge University Press: 65-70.
Kennedy, Patricia, and Jo Murphy-Lawless. 2003. The Maternity Care Needs of Refugee and Asylum Seeking Women in Ireland, *Feminist Review* 73: 39-53.
King, Russell 1998. The Mediterranean: Europe's Río Grande, in Malcolm Anderson and Eberhard Bort (eds.) *The Frontiers of Europe.* London: Pinter: 133-147.
Lentin, Ronit, and Robbie McVeigh (eds.). 2002. *Racism and Anti-Racism in Ireland.* Belfast: Beyond the Pale Publications.
McAllister, Ian. 2003. Border Protection, the 2001 Australian Election and the Coalition Victory, *Australian Journal of Political Science* 38 (3): 445-463.
McMaster, Don. 2001. *Asylum Seekers: Australia's Response to Refugees.* Melbourne: Melbourne University Press.

Manne, Robert. 2002. Reflections on the Tampa "crisis", *Postcolonial Studies* 5 (1): 29-36.
Manne, Robert with David Corlett. 2004. *Sending Them Home: Refugees and the New Politics of Indifference, Quarterly Essay, Issue 13*. Melbourne: Black Inc.
Mares, Peter. 2002. *Borderline: Australia's Response to Refugees and Asylum Seekers in the Wake of the Tampa*. Sydney: UNSW Press.
Marr, David, and Marian Wilkinson. 2003. *Dark Victory*. Crows Nest, NSW: Allen and Unwin.
Moran, Anthony. 2005. *Australia: Nation, Belonging and Globalisation*. New York: Routledge.
Ohmae, Kenichi. 1990. *The Borderless World*. New York: Harper Business.
RTÉ. 2004. Hospital masters deny citizenship law call, *RTE News*, March 13, 2004. http://www.rte.ie/news/2004/0313/citizenship.html.
Roy Morgan Research. 2001. "Refugees Not Welcome," Australians Say, Roy Morgan International Poll, Finding No. 3446. *The Bulletin*, September 25, 2001. http//:www.roymorgan.com/news/polls/2001/3446/index.cfm.
Ruddock, Phillip. 2003. The principles of Australian Migration, *New Zealand International Review*, January 1: 12-14.
Rufin, Jean-Christophe. 1991. *L'empire et les nouveuax barbares*. Paris: Lattès.
Senate Select Committee on a Certain Maritime Incident. 2002. *Report of the Senate Select Committee on a Certain Maritime Incident*. Canberra: Commonwealth of Australia.
Stevens, Christine A. 2002. Asylum seeking in Australia, *International Migration Review* 36 (3): 864-893.
United Nations High Commissioner for Refugees. 2000. *The State of the World's Refugees: Fifty Years of Humanitarian Action*. Oxford: Oxford University Press.

CHAPTER SIX

CONTINGENT REGULATIONS: NAZI SEXUAL POLITICS OF RACE IN THE OCCUPIED TERRITORIES OF THE SOVIET UNION, 1941—1945

REGINA MÜHLHÄUSER

"Racial restructuring of Europe" (*Rassische Neuordnung Europas*). This was the term under which the Germans envisioned the creation of a new social order in Europe based on racial criteria. The territory upon which this concept was to be realised in its most radical form was occupied Eastern Europe. The German politics of colonisation, extermination, and "germanisation" in Poland and the occupied territories of the Soviet Union were extremely violent. "Racial selection" became the basic principle of the German efforts to control and organise the populations in these countries: all that was defined "useful" was to be separated from the "useless", "Aryan" or "Germanic" from "alien" or "foreign", and "germanisable" from "non-germanisable" (Harvey 2003: 78; Heinemann 2003: 417).

Central to this new racial order in Eastern Europe was the discursive management of sexual encounters between occupiers and occupied. From the outset of the German invasion of the Soviet Union, various Nazi authorities were deeply concerned with the control and regulation of rape, military and civil prostitution, sexual affairs, and romantic relationships.[i] According to the logic of Nazi racial hygiene, they feared that associations between German men and "ethnically alien women" (*fremdvölkische Frauen*) would endanger national health and vitality.[ii] On 16 September 1942, the Reich Commissioner for the Strengthening of Germandom (*Reichskommissar zur Festigung des Deutschen Volkstums*), Heinrich Himmler, asserted that "undesirable intercourse" in the "occupied Eastern territories"[iii] must be "prevented if possible". At the same time, however, Himmler conceded the impossibility of gaining complete control over the desire of the individual man—the soldier as well as the member of SS, police and civil occupation authorities. At a conference in the Ukraine, he advised leaders of the SS and the police, if [...] the necessities of the blood, the being, and the man are different, and cannot be avoided during war, then you are bound to tell your men that they may only be responsive to a liaison that they can account for to Germany, to their own blood, and to their future child.[iv]

Himmler's elaborations show that images of male sexuality and militaristic masculinity contradicted Nazi ideas on the purity of the Aryan Race. Different Nazi authorities did indeed emphasise the soldiers' need for regular heterosexual activity in order to improve their military performance (Beck 2004: 272; Timm 2002: 253; Meinen 2003: 72). Furthermore, the "sexual surrender" of a non-German woman to a German man was generally considered to be one form of conquest of the enemy nation (Kundrus 2002: 204, 221). Consequently, the Nazi authorities did not exercise a strict ban on sexual encounters between German men and "ethnically alien women" in the occupied territories of the Soviet Union. On the contrary, the directives issued in order to control interracial sexuality were often contradictory and open to interpretation.

Moreover, the regulations on "undesirable intercourse" were subject to change according to different concepts of military strategy and occupation politics at different stages of the war. From the beginning of the War of Annihilation, Nazi authorities had to deal with rape (Beck 2004), sexual slavery, and military and civil prostitution (Gertjejanssen 2004). In some regions, German soldiers were also known to get engaged with non-German women. They increasingly applied for marriage permits, and "racially mixed children" were born (Müller 2003; Kaminski 2002). In response, the Nazi authorities sometimes changed sexual policies in specific territories. Regional military commanders and occupation authorities, however, often failed to keep pace with these regulatory alterations. Furthermore, they had a certain amount of autonomy, which allowed them to create their own dynamic scope for interpretation and action (Hamburger Institut für Sozialforschung 2002: 579; Reemtsma 2002).

The following analysis will explore Nazi sexual policies in the "occupied Eastern territories" in light of conflicting racial, sexual, and military aims. The first section will focus on different Nazi concepts of "racial mixing" (*Rassenmischung*) and "racial purity" (*Rassereinheit*) in order to analyse the ideological precepts that established the bases for the avowed aim to control and regulate the sexuality of German men. The second section will turn to the sexual assumptions of different Nazi authorities in order to investigate the images of soldierly masculinity and sexual conquest that shaped the directives that were issued to control "undesirable intercourse". The third section will outline the impact of the everyday situation of war and occupation in order to demonstrate how the conditions and demands of warfare influenced and modified the initial declarations on "racial mixing" and "racial purity".

In conclusion, Himmler's elaborations on the responsibility of the individual German man "towards Germany, his blood, and his future child" will be reconsidered in order to highlight the ambiguities of the National Socialist categories of Race and Ethnicity in relation to Nazi Sexual Politics of Race. These ambiguities, however, did not cause visible confusion among German men stationed in "the East". On the contrary, this chapter argues that it was precisely the combination of strict orders, practical ambivalence and contradictions that contributed to the maintenance of state power in a rather uncontrollable territory.

Different concepts of "Racial Purity" and "Racial Mixing"

Nazi Sexual Politics, aimed at ensuring the purity of the Aryan Race, focused primarily on the prevention of sexually transmitted diseases, the disciplining of desire and the control of "racially mixed offspring" (Heineman 2002: 42). According to Adolf Hitler's elaborations on "racial hygiene" in *Mein Kampf* in 1925, the "mixing of races" would necessarily lead to infertility and the deterioration of a race:

[T]he result of every racial crossbreeding [is] as follows:
(a) Lowering of the level of the higher race,
(b) Physical and mental regression and thus the beginning of an, although slow, nonetheless surely advancing degeneration.^{v}

From a scientific point of view, the polygenic concept of races as separate species, which could not produce offspring at all, had been outdated at least since the end of the nineteenth century. Still, the belief that "mixed race people" would be infertile and lead to biological decay was widespread in German media and propaganda during the Third Reich (Essner 2002: 40). According to this logic, sexual encounters between Germans and non-Germans were to be subject to strict penalties. The children who were the products of such encounters served as symbols and evidence for a lack of "racial awareness" (*Rassebewußtsein*) among Aryan men, and were generally perceived as a direct threat to the purity of the Aryan Race and to national vitality.

Nazi "ethnic politics" (*Volkstumspolitik*) in the "occupied Eastern territories", however, reveal a different concept of the "mixing of races". In September 1942, Himmler delivered a speech on the "ethnic goals" in Eastern Europe, which painted a rather vampire-like portrait of these ideological differences:

In all these peoples we are dealing with, anything in this hotchpotch—be they Pole, Ukrainian, Belarusian etc.—anything of good blood in this giant organism, if I take the people as a an entire organism, each extracted drop of pure blood is going to be assimilated or, if it cannot be assimilated any longer, extinguished.[vi]

According to Himmler's logic, the blood of people of "different races" would not mix entirely. Rather, different "streams of blood" (*Blutströme*) could be detected within its carriers and isolated from each other. Himmler believed that the "share of Germanic blood in a mixed race person" would exist within his or her body, and eventually appear again "in the third, fourth, fifth, sixth, and even later generations if it is combined once again with a share of blood of equal value."[vii] Consequently, he did not generally regard the "soldier's children" as "inferior". Rather, he feared that the "Eastern peoples" (*Ostvölker*) would profit from the "share of Germanic blood" of the German fathers. In order to prevent strengthening the enemy, he reasoned, the "racially mixed children" needed to be claimed for the "German *Volk* community" (*Deutsche Volksgemeinschaft*). Furthermore, the supporters of this line of reasoning saw these children as a human resource. Various Nazi officials harboured interests to "render the children useful" (*nutzbar machen*) in order to balance the relatively low birth rate in the "old Reich",[viii] and strengthen future military campaigns (Mühlhäuser 2005). As Cornelia Essner has pointed out, the same logic is displayed in Himmler's plan for a "comprehensive new blood protection law after the war" (*umfassendes neues Blutschutzgesetz nach dem Kriege*). In favour of the aims of Germanisation politics, Himmler planned to distinguish "germanisable persons or families" (*eindeutschbare Personen oder Sippen*) among the "ethnically alien people" (Essner 2002: 421).

In short, Hitler's idea of the alleged infertility of "bastards" and the decay of the race as a necessary consequence of "the mixing of races" presented a logical contradiction to Himmler's concept of the Predominance of Germanic Blood, which tried to single out "valuable shares of blood" in "mixed race persons" or "ethnically alien people". These obvious inconsistencies, however, did not cause visible irritation or protest within the Germans stationed at the Eastern Front or in the "occupied Eastern territories". Indeed, despite the contradictions, both concepts had identical goals: both were based on the naturalist conception of Aryan or Germanic Supremacy; both valued the purity of race as the highest virtue; and both feared a specific, uncontrollable power of "mixed race people". In conclusion, the different versions of Nazi racial ideology complemented one another. Their coexistence gave the Nazi regime the flexibility to react varyingly in different situations, and to adjust policies and actions according to its current goals.

Dominant images of soldierly masculinity and sexual conquest

Despite the fear of the deterioration of the Aryan Race, a strict ban on sexual relations between German men and non-German women in the occupied territories of the Soviet Union was not in the interest of the German army. In September 1939, Hitler himself emphasised the soldiers' need for regular (hetero)sexual acts in order to improve their military performance:

> If the German man as soldier shall be prepared to die unconditionally, then he must also have the freedom to love unconditionally. Combat and love do belong to each other. [...] One may not approach the soldier with the churchly doctrine of abjuration in the field of love if one wants to keep him capable of fighting.[ix]

Hitler's use of the term love rather than sexual drive is revealing. His explication of the connection between "love" and combat as an anthropological constant, a condition of the existence of men, drew on common cultural codes in Western European countries. Love and killing symbolised the two eternal experiences of men, and male sexual lust figured as sublimation for the endurance of the possibility to be killed (Pohl 2004; Zipfel 2001; Bourke 1999).

Correspondingly, the ideal of the soldier that Hitler depicted was shaped by aggression, physical force, and a strong sexual urge. Following this logic, the allegedly natural drive needed an outlet in order to maintain the soldier's capability to fight. If his sexual urge was left unsatisfied, the presumption was that the soldier's spirits would be dampened. Furthermore, such abstinence would lead to a drastic increase of homosexuality in the military. This view was generally shared by the military authorities (Timm 2002; Kühne 1996). In this vein, the medical corps of the Wehrmacht coined the term "sexual desperation" (*Geschlechtsnot*) in order to explain the soldier's presumed need for heterosexual activity (Beck 2004: 272).

"Unconditional love", however, was not intended to be interpreted as uncontrolled sexuality. In order to deal with the sexual "tensions and necessities [...] here and there," as supreme commander Walther von Brauchitsch explained in July 1940,[x] the Wehrmacht had already established military brothels or organised controlled access to local brothels in occupied France and Poland (Gertjejanssen 2004: 169; Meinen 2002: 17). Correspondingly, Field Marshal Wilhelm Keitel from the Wehrmacht High Command [*Oberkommando der Wehrmacht*; OKW] supported the establishment of brothels in the "occupied Eastern territories" in September 1942. The controlled access to heterosexual services was aimed at ensuring military discipline and preventing sexually transmitted diseases and the "siring of racially mixed bastards that are of no interest to Germany".[xi]

Hitler's line of reasoning on the connection of love and conquest reappeared in the "occupied Eastern territories" when an adjutant of the "Eastern battalion" (Ostbatallion) claimed, "the man who is prepared to die for Germany must also be granted access to the brothels".[xii] This idea that the soldiers needed an outlet for their sexual drive was, however, disputed. Others envisioned the strong soldier to be in control of his sexual urge, as a letter with reference to "Party and Wehrmacht in the General Government and their Executive Functions" from August 1944 illustrates:

> The present conditions, in which man and woman believe to possess complete sexual freedom, have a highly embittering effect upon the front fighters, who have to live ascetically. Furthermore, from my point of view, brothels have no right of existence. They are feeble concessions to impulse-driven human beings, and typical of the spirit of the rear [*Etappengeist*].[xiii]

Images of the "racially aware Aryan master", which were shaped by conceptions of aristocratic manhood (Diehl 2005: 162), focusing on a mature character, a controlled will, and sexual self-restraint, obviously contradicted the idea of soldierly masculinity as aggressive and sexually active. As Insa Meinen has pointed out, this point of view could have prohibited the establishment of military brothels (Meinen 2002: 72). Hitler himself had originally opposed prostitution as a major cause for Germany's decline (Roos 2002: 67). In the course of the war, however, sex was increasingly considered to be "the underlying fuel of the military machine" (Timm 2002: 254), and the Nazis established a system of sexual gratification as reward for military service. As Anette Timm has argued, "the expression of male sexuality was not a matter of individual pleasure but of the nation's military strength" (Timm 2002: 253).

The fact that most of the women working in the brothels in the "occupied Eastern territories" were not what the Nazis themselves would have considered Aryan was at least condoned. Indeed, Himmler had explicitly approved of this kind of "racial mixing" in 1942, because it was allegedly outside the context of personal attachment and reproduction.[xiv] In a similar manner, military judges did not assess the rape of a Soviet woman in accordance with considerations of "undesirable intercourse" or "race defilement". As Birgit Beck has shown, they rather sentenced a rapist for harming the reputation of the Wehrmacht, and lacking the necessary military discipline (Beck 2004: 277, 247). At any rate, the establishment of brothels and the raping of foreign women could be viewed as a kind of sexual occupation of the body of the enemy nation. It symbolised both the military defeat of the enemy nation and the humiliation of its male population.[xv]

In short, the Wehrmacht authorities had different images of militaristic masculinity and soldierly sexuality. Some military commanders created the image of the "racially aware Aryan master", shaped by a mature character, a controlled will, and sexual self-restraint. The dominant idea, however, was that of a combat-ready soldier, shaped by aggression, physical force, and a virile sexual drive. At any rate, the Wehrmacht High Command acted on the assumption that men could only become effective soldiers if they were provided with an outlet for their allegedly natural heterosexual needs. Military commanders established brothels and condoned various forms of "undesirable intercourse". As a result, the belief about the soldiers' need for heterosexual satisfaction, and, furthermore, the idea that the conquest of an enemy nation was accompanied by its "sexual surrender" contradicted the idea of the "racial awareness" of Aryan men. In general, the soldiers' fulfilment of their alleged heterosexual drives surpassed the "ethnic aim" *(volkstumspolitische Ziel)* of "racial purity".

Changing demands in the everyday situation of war and occupation

German men in the "occupied Eastern territories"—mainly soldiers, but also members of the police, the SS, and the civilian occupation authorities—did not always choose the objects of their desire in accordance with Nazi criteria. Indeed, directly after the German Wehrmacht invaded the Soviet Union, soldiers were involved in incidents of rape, civil and military prostitution, sexual affairs, and romantic relationships. In response, the military and civil occupation authorities revised strategies and issued new directives.[xvi]

Similar to other armies in World War II, the Wehrmacht maintained conflicting interests concerning rape, prostitution, and "fraternisation" (Seidler 1977; Yoshimi 2000). While the main interest of the military was to ensure the sexual satisfaction of its soldiers in order to raise their spirits and improve their strength, the authorities did indeed fear an increasing lack of military discipline, the loss of soldiers due to venereal diseases and other infectious illnesses, and the transfer of military secrets. On 17 November 1941, a senior officer of the 18th armoured division elaborated:

> Lately venereal diseases have been discovered for the first time as a result of contacts with the female Russian population. Instruction to the troops should stress that intercourse with female civilians is not only unworthy of the German soldier, but also carries with it the danger of being exploited or harmed by a spy, of falling into the hands of a female partisan and of being terribly mutilated or infected with VD or other infectious diseases.[xvii]

In order to raise the soldiers' vigilance and willingness to murder women, the picture of the "racially inferior" female enemy spy was conjured up. In some cases, the expression of military orders reveals that the commanders were trying to prevent any sympathy for the population, and, in particular, to dissuade the troops from seeking sexual encounters with Soviet women. As Omer Bartov has demonstrated, the GD Division in Russia tried to solve "the problem of fraternisation by evicting all the inhabitants of houses used for accommodation by the soldiers." Nevertheless, this measure did not prevent intimate encounters, particularly because the German army employed growing numbers of local women in various service duties, and in direct contact with German men (Bartov 1985: 126).

Not only did the Wehrmacht harbour conflicting interests concerning the sexuality of German men, but the sexual policies of the civil authorities were not uniformly enforced either. Above all, the Nazi term "occupied Eastern territories" comprised a variety of countries, geographical settings, internal political situations, societies, languages, cultures, and historical experiences. The degrees of collaboration with and resistance against the Nazis varied; and, correspondingly, varying political attitudes towards the Soviet Union and the Red Army existed (Ueberschär and Wette 1984: 312). In this context, local bureaucrats often found it difficult to assess the situation and establish standard measures.

In general, the civil authorities accepted or even encouraged relations of "Reich German" (*reichsdeutsch*) men with women regarded as "Ethnic German" (*volksdeutsch*)[xviii] as long as the women passed the "racial inspection".[xix] On the other hand, relations of Reich German men with women who were identified as foreigners were generally considered "inappropriate" and "unwanted". They symbolised the lack of "racial awareness" of the German men and were likely to endanger the "mastery of the Aryan Race". At the same time, however, the civil authorities sought to promote and stimulate relations between Reich Germans and non-Germans who were considered to be "racially valuable". On 27 July 1941, the Reich Commissioner for the Ostland (*Reichskommissar für das Ostland*, RKO) observed:

> Ever since the liberation [of the Soviet rule, RM], the local female population of the Baltic General Districts has exceedingly accommodated the German soldier in such a way that extramarital intercourse could not be controlled anymore.[xx]

In the same letter, the RKO opposed the marriage ban for Reich Germans, which the Nazi Party (NSDAP) had issued in 1941. This measure, according to his reasoning, would destroy the opportunity "to lead these people towards the German Volk" (*diese Völker an das deutsche Volk heranzuführen*). Similarly, he found it problematic, on the one hand, to decorate local men volunteering for the Wehrmacht with the "iron cross" (*eisernes Kreuz*) in order to acknowledge that they had risked their lives for Germany, and, at the same time, to discriminate against their sisters by deeming them unworthy of marrying a German (Müller 2003, 250). Furthermore, various forms of relationships—despite state efforts to control them—had already developed: German soldiers were known to get engaged to non-German women, they increasingly applied for marriage permits, and "racially mixed children" were born. Different bureaucrats accommodated to this new situation by planning a marriage-law for German men in the "Ostland" in July 1942. The Reich Commissioner for the Strengthening of Germandom, Heinrich Himmler, however, opposed this plan by arguing that there should not yet, "after only one year of experience", be any legal writings. Still, he conceded that there could be individual exceptions to the marriage ban in Estonia and Latvia. "Reich German" men should hence be able to marry local women after the procedures of "racial inspection".[xxi]

Nazi Sexual Politics in the "occupied Eastern territories" did not only apply to soldiers. Members of the SS and the police were also known to seek sexual encounters with women regarded as "racially inferior" (Mallmann et al. 2003: 93; Wilhelm 1981: 480). At a conference of Supreme judges of the SS and Police courts in Poland and the "occupied Eastern territories" in May 1943, the most lengthily discussed item on the agenda was entitled "undesirable intercourse". According to the minutes of this meeting, SS-Sturmbannführer Heinz from the SS and Police Court in Kiev assumed that at least 50 per cent of all members of the SS and the police violated the "ban on undesirable intercourse with ethnically alien women". Since it was not in the interest of the judges to sentence more than half of the SS and policemen in "the East", all participants finally agreed to advise Reichsführer-SS Heinrich Himmler to abolish the order.[xxii]

In short, neither the ideological declarations on the purity of the Aryan Race nor the various regulations led all German men to choose the objects of their desire according to Nazi criteria. Indeed, following the logic in Michel Foucault's lectures on governmentality, one could argue that individual desire and social regulation can never be congruent (Foucault 2004; Lemke 1997: 134). Furthermore, not all incidents of "undesirable intercourse" were handled according to fixed policies. After balancing interests and benefits, individual cases could easily be handled differently. The ways in which "undesirable intercourse" was dealt with, and the decisions that were ultimately reached depended on different rationales and knowledge. Sexual Politics of Race varied according to interests, territories, concepts of military strategy and occupation politics at different stages of the war and the occupation.

Conclusion

Nazi Sexual Politics of Race in the occupied territories of the Soviet Union between 1941 and 1945 were the outcome of complex and often contradictory ideas about racial purity and the health of the nation, concepts of male sexuality and sexual conquest in wartime, and demands of everyday warfare and occupation in different territories. When Heinrich Himmler insisted, on 16 September 1942, that the individual man in "the East" must only "be responsive to a liaison that he can account for to Germany, to his blood, and to his future child", he knew that the Nazi categories for assessing the "racial value" of a woman were contingent. In the very same speech he expressed his concern that "it is pure coincidence if the girl a soldier gets attached to is racially valuable or not". If the woman became pregnant, according to his logic, she would have to undergo a "racial inspection". If she was to be considered "racially valuable", "there [was] no harm done: The soldier behaved like a real man". On the other hand, if the woman was to be considered "racially inferior", the man was to be severely punished.[xxiii]

Himmler's elaborations were not shared by all parties concerned about the German war and occupation in Poland and the Soviet Union. Still, they indicate a variety of aspects that can safely be generalised. First, soldiers as well as members of the SS, the police and the civil occupation authorities were involved in incidents which Nazi racial hygiene designated as "undesirable intercourse". They committed rape and forced women into sexual slavery, they visited civilian prostitutes and military brothels, they engaged in sexual affairs and romantic relationships, and they planned future engagements and marriages. The extent of these practices has not yet been the subject of in-depth research. Still, Nazi sources document these forms of sexual encounters and the concern of the authorities to control them. Second, while the military and civil occupation authorities worried that their men lacked "racial awareness", they had to concede that "racial value" was a highly ambiguous and contested category. It was not only about a biological inspection, but also about the character, the intelligence, the soul and, in the case of a woman, about her sexual history. Third, the ambiguity of the categories facilitated the individual soldier with the possibility to despise and kill Russian women because of their alleged "racial inferiority" and at the same time consider the object of his desire to be "racially valuable". Indeed, a German man could justify an affair with an "ethnically alien woman" without questioning his racial and racist ideas. Fourth, most Nazi authorities believed that soldiers needed to fulfil their allegedly natural heterosexual drives in order to maintain their military performance. As a result, they did not enforce a general ban on interracial sexual encounters in "the East". On the contrary, the way, in which "undesirable intercourse" was dealt with, and the decisions that were ultimately reached depended on different rationales and knowledges. Sexual Politics of Race varied according to interests, territories, concepts of military strategy and occupation politics at different stages of the war and the occupation. Finally, even though the Nazi authorities did not punish every man who violated Nazi rules, the regulating technologies existed in order to have the possibility to do so and the threat of potential punishment. Furthermore, the assessment of a penalty was not regulatory according to the initial transgression of "undesirable intercourse". On the contrary, the punishment could be disciplinatory according to the result of the sexual encounter.

Nazi Sexual Politics of Race in the occupied territories of the Soviet Union were characterised by ambivalences and contradictions. As a result, initial ideological declarations on the "purity of race" appeared to be permeable and the megalomaniac Nazi vision of a "racial restructuring of Europe" was fundamentally challenged. These contradictions, however, did not obstruct the brutality of the German politics of colonisation, extermination, and "germanisation". On the contrary, the complex combination of strict rules and regulations, varying individual decisions and specific policy changes provided the Nazi regime with the opportunity of demonstrating continuous ideas on racial hygiene and, at the same time, to react flexibly and assure the individual German man in "the East" that he would be supported. The ambiguity of the system served precisely to secure the power of the Nazi regime in the often rather fragile situation of the War of Annihilation.

Notes

I would like to thank Uta Balbier, Cornelia Berens, Carsten Gericke, Amy Holmes, Birthe Kundrus, Alana and Ronit Lentin, Emily Levine, Elissa Mailänder-Koslov, and Gaby Zipfel for their inspiring and challenging comments!

[i] This can also be said for other German occupied territories, albeit that the Nazis evaluated the terms and conditions differently (Warring 2003; Meinen 2003; Virgili 2002; Olsen 2002; Drolshagen 2000).

[ii] Different sources indicate that German women, too, had sexual encounters with local men in "the East". Apparently, the Nazi officials treated these in a distinctly different way. However, corresponding policies, the number of these women, their biographies, the places of their deployment etc. have not yet been subject to research. On the deployment of women in general, see Harvey 2003; Kundrus 1999; Schwarz 1997. On sexual encounters of German women with "ethnically alien" men within the borders of the German Reich see Kundrus 2002; Czarnowski 2000; Stephenson 1992.

[iii] This Nazi term refers to the German occupied territories of the former Soviet Union, including the Reichskommissariat Ostland (roughly Estonia, Latvia, Lithuania, and the bigger part of West Byelorussia), the Reichskommissariat Ukraine (roughly central Ukraine), and the occupied parts of Russia. The General Government (Warsaw, Radom,

Lublin, Krakau, Galizien) is not included in the term "occupied Eastern territories". For an introduction on the German administration in the "occupied Eastern territories" see Hilberg 1994, vol. 2: 362. On the Nazi terminology concerning "the East" see Harvey 2003: 20.

[iv] Rede Himmlers auf SS- und Polizeiführer-Tagung, Feldkommandostelle Hegewald bei Shitomir, 16.09.1942, BA [Bundesarchiv Berlin] NS 19/4009: 78—127, 125.

[v] Adolf Hitler. *Mein Kampf*. 2 volumes in one edition: 573—577. München 1940: 311.

[vi] Rede Himmlers auf SS- und Polizeiführer-Tagung, Feldkommandostelle Hegewald bei Shitomir, 16.09.1942, BA NS 19/4009: 78—127, 90. See also Lilienthal 2003: 220.

[vii] Rede Himmlers auf SS- und Polizeiführer-Tagung, Feldkommandostelle Hegewald bei Shitomir, 16.09.1942, BA NS 19/4009: 78—127, 89.

[viii] Germany in its borders of 1937.

[ix] Gespräch vom 23.04.1942, Wolfsschanze, documented in Picker 1997: 332.

[x] Oberkommando des Heeres, von Brauchitsch, 31.07.1940, BA MA [Bundesarchiv-Militärarchiv Freiburg] RH 53-7/v. 233a/167, quoted in Beck 2004: 107.

[xi] Oberkommando der Wehrmacht, Keitel, Betrifft: Verkehr des deutschen Soldaten mit der Zivilbevölkerung in den besetzten Ostgebieten, 12.09.1942, Abschrift, BA MA, RH 26-6/67.

[xii] Aktennotiz, 6.12.1943, UAD, 8/4, 19, quoted in Plassmann 2003: 162.

[xiii] Partei und Wehrmacht im Generalgouvernement und ihre Führungsaufgaben, 24.08.1944, BA NS 55/26, 1499—1506. About the "sexual freedom" of men and women in Nazi Germany see Herzog 2004: 10.

[viv] RKF Himmler an SS-Obergruppenführer Friedrich Wilhelm Krüger, Betrifft: Geschlechtsverkehr von Angehörigen der SS und Polizei mit Frauen einer andersrassigen Bevölkerung, 30.06.1942, BA NS 19/1913, 3—4: 4, printed in Heiber 1970: 156, Doc. 120. See also Beck 1999: 229. Himmler referred to brothels in the General Gouvernement. The establishment of brothels in the Reichskommissariate Ostland and Ukraine, however, suggest a similar attitude.

[xv] The female body figured centrally to symbolize the body of the Volk and the nation (Yuval-Davis 2001; Lentin 1997).

[1] Various incidents are documented in Beck 2004; Gertjejanssen 2004; and Müller 2003. See also Gerlach 2000: 104, 472, 560, 777, 938, 1073, 1080; Krausnick 1981: 53, 76, 82.

[xvi] Schreiben der 18ten Panzerdivision, 17.11.1941, BA MA RH 27 18/177, quoted in Bartov 1985: 126.

[xvii] The designation "*reichsdeutsch*" referred to people, who carried the German citizenship. The designation "*volksdeutsch*" referred to people, who were considered to be "of German origin" and thus of German nationality — regardless of their citizenship.

[xviii] It should be noted that these ideas were gender specific. "Reich German" women who were known to have sexual relations with "ethnic German" men were treated differently (Harvey 2003).

[xiv] Reichskommissar für das Ostland an Reichminister für die besetzten Ostgebiete, 27.07.1941, BA R 90/460, quoted in Müller 2003: 249.

[xvv] Reichsführer-SS an SS-Obergruppenführer Gottlob Berger, Betr: Zu Ihren Aktennotizen, Reval, 28.07.1942, BA NS 19/1772: 5. In the process of "racial inspection" the women, as opposed to the men, were subject to an assessment of their sexual history (Bergen 2001).

[xxvi] Richtertagung in München am 07.05.1943, Bericht und Vermerk zu diversen Besprechungspunkten, BA NS 7/13, Bl. 1—21: 7.
[xxvii] Rede Himmlers auf SS- und Polizeiführer-Tagung, Feldkommandostelle Hegewald bei Shitomir, 16.09.1942, BA NS 19/4009, 78—127: 124.

References

Bartov, Omer. 1985. *The Eastern Front, 1941-1945: German Troops and the Barbarisation of Warfare*. Houndmills, Basingstoke, Hampshire and London: Macmillan.
Beck, Birgit. 2004. *Wehrmacht und sexuelle Gewalt: Sexualverbrechen vor deutschen Militärgerichten 1939-1945*. Paderborn, Munich, Vienna and Zürich: Ferdinand Schöningh.
Beck, Birgit. 1999. Sexuelle Gewalt und Krieg: Geschlecht, Rasse und der nationalsozialistische Vernichtungsfeldzug gegen die Sowjetunion, 1941-1945, in Veronika Aegerter et al. (eds.) *Geschlecht hat Methode: Ansätze und Perspektiven in der Frauen- und Geschlechtergeschichte*. Zürich: Chronos: 223-234.
Bergen, Doris L. 2001. Sex, Blood, and Vulnerability: Women Outsiders in German Occupied Europe, in Robert Gellately and Nathan Stoltzfus (eds.) *Social Outsiders in Nazi Germany*. Princeton: Princeton University Press: 273-293.
Bourke, Joanna. 1999. *An Intimate History of Killing: Face-to-Face Killing in Twentieth-Century Warfare*. New York: Basic Books.
Czarnowski, Gabriele. 2000. Zwischen Germanisierung und Vernichtung: Verbotene polnisch-deutsche Liebesbeziehungen und die Re-Konstruktion des Volkskörpers im Zweiten Weltkrieg, in Helgard Kramer (ed.) *Die Gegenwart der NS-Vergangenheit*. Berlin and Vienna: Philo: 295-303.
Diehl, Paula. 2005. *Macht—Mythos—Utopie:Die Körperbilder der SS-Männer*. Berlin: Akademie-Verlag.
Drolshagen, Ebba. 2000. *Nicht ungeschoren davonkommen: Die Geliebten der Wehrmachtssoldaten im besetzten Europa*. Munich: Propyläen Taschenbuch.
Essner, Cornelia. 2002. *Die "Nürnberger Gesetze" oder Die Verwaltung des Rassenwahns 1933-1945*. Paderborn, Munich, Vienna and Zürich: Ferdinand Schöningh.
Foucault, Michel. 2004. *Geschichte der Gouvernementalität II: Die Geburt der Biopolitik*. Frankfurt am Main: Suhrkamp.
Gertjejanssen, Wendy Jo. 2004. *Victims, Heroes, Survivors: Sexual Violence on the Eastern Front during World War II*. Ph.D. dissertation, University of Minnesota.
Hamburger Institut für Sozialforschung (ed.). 2002. *Verbrechen der Wehrmacht: Dimensionen des Vernichtungskrieges 1941-1944, Ausstellungskatalog*. Hamburg: Hamburger Edition.
Harvey, Elizabeth. 2003. *Women and the Nazi East: Agents and Witnesses of Germanization*. New Haven and London: Yale University Press.
Heiber, Helmut (ed.) 1970. *Reichsführer! Briefe an und von Himmler*. München: Deutscher Taschenbuchverlag.
Heineman, Elizabeth D. 2002. Sexuality and Nazism: The Doubly Unspeakable? *Journal of the History of Sexuality* 11: 22-66.

Heinemann, Isabel. 2003. *"Rasse, Siedlung, deutsches Blut": Das Rasse- und Siedlungshauptamt der SS und die rassenpolitische Neuordnung Europas*. Göttingen: Wallstein.
Hilberg, Raul. 1994. *Die Vernichtung der europäischen Juden*. Frankfurt am Main: Fischer Taschenbuch (Originally published in English in 1961).
Kaminski, Hartmut. 2002. *Liebe im Vernichtungskrieg. Die Frauen im Osten und die deutsche Besatzungsmacht*. TV Documentary, broadcasted on May 20, 2002 on Arte.
Krausnick, Helmut. 1981. Die Einsatzgruppen vom Anschluß Österreichs bis zum Feldzug gegen die Sowjetunion: Entwicklung und Verhältnis zur Wehrmacht, in Helmut Krausnick and Hans-Heinrich Wilhelm (eds.) *Die Truppe des Weltanschauungskrieges. Die Einsatzgruppen der Sicherheitspolizei und des SD 1938—1942*. Stuttgart: Deutsche Verlags-Anstalt: 213-278.
Kühne, Thomas. 1996. Kameradschaft—"das Beste im Leben des Mannes". Die deutschen Soldaten des Zweiten Weltkriegs in erfahrungs- und geschlechtergeschichtlicher Perspektive, *Geschichte und Gesellschaft* 22: 504-529.
Kundrus, Birthe. 2002. Forbidden Company: Romantic Relationships between Germans and Foreigners, 1939-1945, *Journal of the History of Sexuality* 11: 201-222.
Kundrus, Birthe. 1999. Nur die halbe Geschichte: Frauen im Umfeld der Wehrmacht zwischen 1939 und 1945—Ein Forschungsbericht, in Rolf-Dieter Müller and Hans-Erich Volkmann (eds.) *Die Wehrmacht: Mythos und Realität*. München: R. Oldenbourg Verlag.
Lemke, Thomas. 1997. *Eine Kritik der politischen Vernunft: Foucaults Analyse der modernen Gouvernementalität*. Berlin and Hamburg: Argument.
Lentin, Ronit. 1997. Introduction: (En)gendering Genocides, in Ronit Lentin (ed.) *Gender and Catastrophe*. London and New York: Zed Books: 2-17.
Lilienthal, Georg. 2003. *Der "Lebensborn e.V. ": Ein Instrument nationalsozialistischer Rassenpolitik*. 2nd Edition. Frankfurt am Main: Fischer Taschenbuch.
Mallmann, Klaus-Michael, Volker Rieß and Wolfram Pyta (eds.). 2003. *Deutscher Osten 1939—1945: Der Weltanschauungskrieg in Photos und Texten*. Darmstadt: Wissenschaftliche Buchgesellschaft.
Meinen, Insa. 2002. *Wehrmacht und Prostitution im besetzten Frankreich*. Bremen: Edition Temmen.
Mühlhäuser, Regina. 2005. Between Extermination and Germanization: Children of German Men in the "Occupied Eastern Territories", 1942-1945, in Kjersti Ericsson and Eva Simonsen (eds.) *Children of World War II: A Hidden Enemy Legacy*. Oxford and New York: Berg: 167-189.
Müller, Rolf-Dieter. 2003. Liebe im Vernichtungskrieg: Geschlechtergeschichtliche Aspekte des Einsatzes deutscher Soldaten im Rußlandkrieg 1941-1944, in Frank Becker et. al. (eds.) *Politische Gewalt in der Moderne: Festschrift für Hans-Ulrich Thamer*. Münster: Aschendorff: 239-267.
Olsen, Kåre. 2002. *Vater: Deutscher. Das Schicksal der norwegischen Lebensbornkinder und ihrer Mütter von 1940 bis heute*. Frankfurt am Main and New York: Campus.
Picker, Henry. 1997 [1951]. *Hitlers Tischgespräche im Führerhauptquartier: Entstehung, Struktur, Folgen des Nationalsozialismus*. 2nd Edition. Berlin: Propyläen Taschenbuch.

Plassmann, Max, 2003. Wehrmachtsbordelle: Anmerkungen zu einem Quellenfund im Universitätsarchiv Düsseldorf, *Militärgeschichtliche Zeitschrift* 62: 157-173.
Pohl, Rolf. 2004. *Feindbild Frau: Männliche Sexualität, Gewalt und die Abwehr des Weiblichen.* Hannover: Offizin.
Reemtsma, Jan Philipp. 2002. Über den Begriff "Handlungsspielräume", *Mittelweg 36* 6: 5-23.
Roos, Julia. 2002. Backlash against Prostitutes' Rights: Origins and Dynamics of Nazi Prostitution Policies, *Journal of the History of Sexuality* 11: 67-94.
Schwarz, Gudrun. 1997. Frauen in der SS: Sippenverband und Frauenkorps, in Kirsten Heinsohn, Barbara Vogel and Ulrike Weckel (eds.) *Zwischen Karriere und Verfolgung: Handlungsräume von Frauen im nationalsozialistischen Deutschland.* Frankfurt and New York: Campus: 223-244.
Seidler, Franz W. 1977. *Prostitution, Homosexualität, Selbstverstümmelung: Probleme der deutschen Sanitätsführung 1939-1945.* Neckargemünd: Kurt Vowinckel-Verlag.
Stephenson, Jill. 1992. Triangle: Foreign Workers, German Civilians, and the Nazi Regime: War and Society in Württemberg, 1939-1945, *German Studies Review* 15: 339—358.
Timm, Annette F. 2002. Sex with a Purpose: Prostitution, Venereal Disease, and Militarized Masculinity in the Third Reich, *Journal of the History of Sexuality* 11: 223-255.
Ueberschär, Gerd R. and Wolfgang Wette (eds.) 1984. *"Unternehmen Barbarossa": Der deutsche Überfall auf die Sowjetunion 1941.* Paderborn: Ferdinand Schöningh.
Virgili, Fabrice. 2002. *Shorn Women:Gender and Punishment in Liberations France.* Oxford and New York: Berg.
Warring, Anette. 2003. National Bodies: Fraternisation, Gender and Sexuality in Occupied Europe 1940-45, Paper presented at the University of Hamburg, October 29, 2003.
Wilhelm, Hans Heinrich. 1981. Die Einsatzgruppe A der Sicherheitspolizei des SD 1941/42: Eine exemplarische Studie, in Helmut Krausnick and Hans-Heinrich Wilhelm (eds.) *Die Truppe des Weltanschauungskrieges. Die Einsatzgruppen der Sicherheitspolizei und des SD 1938-1942.* Stuttgart: Deutsche Verlags-Anstalt: 281-636.
Yoshimi, Yoshiaki. 2002. *Comfort Women: Sexual Slavery in the Japanese Military During World War II.* New York: Columbia University Press.
Yuval-Davis, Nira. 2001. *Geschlecht und Nation.* Emmendingen: die brotsuppe (Originally published in English 1997).
Zipfel, Gaby. 2001. "Blood, Sperm, and Tears": Sexual Violence in War, *Eurozine*, November 29, http://www.eurozine.com/articles/2001-11-29-zipfel-en.html (accessed December 10, 2005).

PART II

RACIAL STATES AFTER THE 11TH OF SEPTMBER, 2001

CHAPTER SIX

WARS ON OUR DOORSTEP: ISLAMICISING "RACE" AND MILITARISING EVERYDAY LIFE

GARGI BHATTACHARYYA

This chapter started its life as a contribution to a conference on issues of "race" and state, many months into the bloody occupations of Iraq and Afghanistan, but before the London bombings of July 2005. Now I fear that many of the points I make here are all too obvious, the banal knowledge of the everyday, hardly meriting the effort of academic analysis. Who doesn't understand that we are living through a militarisation of everyday life? Such a realisation has become part of the world as we know it.

Unfortunately, part of this realisation has taken the form of acceptance; the world brings new dangers and, whatever our misgivings, this demands new responses. Here I want to argue that the banality of this acceptance is an outcome of a particular confidence and intensity in state racism.

Much of what I have to say builds on a longer debate about the nature of the state, and the very old lesson that the conduct of imperial expansion seeps into governance at home. What seems to be new in this unhappy scenario is the particular contemporary racism of today's imperialism, a racism shaped by the particular history of recent globalisation, and the interplay between this international project and the internal racisms of Western nations.

Thinking about what we mean by racist state—again.

When I was invited to take part in this project I thought for a while about my own understanding of state racism and the racist state. Familiar territory, I thought, part of the technique of national government, a well-established method of disciplining the space of nation and re-asserting its boundaries. My understanding was of a national project, perhaps projected beyond the boundaries of nation for particular reasons of national interest, but largely confined within the national space and, more than that, constitutive of that space.

Now I am not so sure that contemporary state racisms are so tidily contained within national boundaries. What I think is changing in our time is that the particular racisms of particular states are being subsumed into a globally integrated machinery of state racisms. Of course, this too is now a banal claim. The experience of living in a unipolar world and the everyday evidence of absolute US supremacy make it all too easy to comprehend the formation of a global racism shaped by US culture, economy, and most importantly, foreign policy. However, although it is hardly original to suggest that we are facing forms of racism that transcend any one national context, this widespread understanding does not seem to have created new and appropriate forms of anti-racism.

In part the difficulty seems to rest around the challenge of articulating a constant and coherent alternative to the absolute terms of "with us or against us", when the conduct of the war on terror increasingly rallies a transnational resistance to this new imperialism which, whatever we may wish, is not itself always progressive or palatable to the liberal values shaped in the West (as opposed to liberal values as developed elsewhere). In this context, even committed anti-racists can be drawn into the terms of a global racism which purports to be defending "our" way of life.

On a more mundane level, in Britain at least, and in the aftermath of the Lawrence Inquiry (Macpherson 1999), much anti-racist activity has become focused on the conduct of public institutions; a generation of potential activists have been sucked into the bureaucratisation of race equality work. Although this activity, laudably, is focused on the outcomes of service delivery, in the process we seem to have lost our ability to articulate our vision of a different and just society.

When faced with the multiple challenges and lofty rhetoric of the war on terror, an anti racism so focused on the minutiae of public service provision risks appearing parochial and based on nothing more than self-interest. While state racism is being remade as a defence of our way of life, such institutionally based challenges to racism can appear to be little more than bean counting, a diversion from the urgent business of saving civilisation. There is a danger that the war on terror is impacting on the ability of anti-racists to articulate a progressive critique of the racist state or to formulate an alternative to its terms of belonging. After all, we are afraid as well.

Occupation policing: Is this business as usual?

This chapter argues not only that the war on terror has infected the politics of "race" within Britain and other "coalition" nations—as I have said, that is a banal claim that we all know only too well—but also that there is a more specific flavour of occupation to British state activity in our time.

In September 2003 a young African-Caribbean man called Michael Powell was killed on my street, apparently in the course of being arrested. His death joined the long history of other police killings and also the rapidly increasing sub-group of mental health related killings. Reports said that the police were called because Michael was behaving in a manner that indicated that he was in distress and required assistance; the processes of restraint and arrest that were used in this attempt to provide assistance led to Michael's death. Since the much-publicised gang-related shootings in Aston, around the corner from us, and the stabbing of local shop-keepers by another local man with mental health problems, our neighbourhood has been characterised by an anxious police presence, including the semi-permanent presence of an enclosed police booth on the main shopping street. There is an expectation that something is going to kick off, and extreme fear in the faces of local coppers as they patrol our family streets, all expecting Falluja any minute. On the morning after Michael Powell's death this all changed for a moment. That morning the cordoned-off street was filled with cheery young police officers exchanging banter with locals (who mainly did not yet know what had happened). In the days that followed, there was a return to even more extreme versions of occupation policing—including a van of officers armed with sub-machine guns leaping out to make an arrest on a busy shopping street as families and children returned from school and nursery. This was a police presence that echoed the style and body language of the occupation of Iraq. Of course, much of this is a continuation of the racist policing of many years, but now this was also infected by the nightly news images on our screens.

Since I presented an earlier version of this chapter in March 2005, all of this has become far more open. The shooting of Jean Charles De Menezes, an innocent Brazilian man mistaken for one of those suspected of the attempted London bombings of July 21 2005 reveals the extent to which the British police has adopted the methods of occupation. This adoption is not a secret, but instead is proclaimed as a populist strategy, made legitimate by the need to make ordinary people feel safe. In the aftermath of this killing regret was expressed, but, at the same time, the public was told that such events may happen again, desperate times calling for such desperate measures. Occupation policing is being presented as a necessary response to our changing world.

Policing and the racist state

UK discussions of state racism—that extensive literature and politics that explain racism as a technique of governance, rather than a psychological disorder or weakness of character—have focused largely on the workings and impact of the criminal justice system (for influential examples see Keith 1993; Solomos 1993). This is the arena where the outcomes of state racism are most apparent.

This is not the explicit distinction in law that has characterised states that adopt an open and explicit racism—these are not the race laws of Nazi Germany or apartheid South Africa—but instead an identification of the significant and systematic differences in treatment and outcome for different groups. This has been one of the key lessons of the Lawrence Inquiry (Macpherson 1999). The conception of institutional racism that has been propagated from that report has taken the systematic failure of the police and criminal justice system to tackle racist crime or to provide adequate and equal treatment for minority ethnic communities as the central and formative aspect of institutional racism, with similar failures pervading public institutions so that the racism of the state permeates all of its public functions without being stated explicitly anywhere.

Despite the fanfare announcements of repentance that accompanied the publication of the Lawrence Inquiry, these aspects of state racism remain, and in fact continue to be all too prevalent. The key themes of earlier discussion are all areas that have continued into the era of the war on terror. What shifts is the rhetoric by which such events are legitimated and the use of co-operation between different states to augment the practices within each. A cursory review reveals how closely the business of the war on terror at home echoes longer-running practices of state racism.

a) Force and over-reaction

This refers to the levels of force used and the differential manner of policing adopted in relation to racialised minorities. There is a long-standing debate about levels of policing in minority areas; in fact this is the issue that continues to shape discussion about policing and racism. For many years, concern has been expressed over issues such as the levels of force employed in detentions and arrests, injuries sustained during arrest and in custody, the manner in which restraint is used and armed units deployed. All of these issues have led to serious complaints from minority ethnic communities, not least because each has been the cause of serious violence and, on occasion, death. War on terror policing utilises all of these discredited techniques, but now with the added justification that we are dealing with potential terrorists.

b) Tampering with evidence and fit-ups

The history of miscarriages of justice in the British justice system has not always been included in discussions of the racist state. Some of the most high-profile cases have involved Irish defendants, and therefore have been filed under the alternative heading of "the (Northern Ireland) Troubles". The centuries-old racism against the Irish is analysed as a separate chapter in state racism, a set of practices developed as an adjunct to an ongoing imperialist crisis. However, in recent years, there has been a more concerted attempt to chart the continuities between communities, and to uncover so-called miscarriages as all too predictable tactics of containment that are used against a range of communities (see Miscarriages of Justice Organisation 2005). The constant theme in implied defences of police fit-ups, whether the defendant is Irish, black or something else, is the suggestion that the community is being protected, that the requirement for proper evidence lets the guilty go free and that the police are acting in the greater good.

Before the war on terror, such justifications appealed to popular feeling but were not offered as an official account. When long-running miscarriages were finally returned to court, evidence of coerced confessions and tampering with evidence did eventually secure releases and followed the dismantling of the West Midlands Serious Crime Squad due to allegations of corruption. In the official narrative, due process was to be respected and these injustices represented an unfortunate anomaly.

We now live in a time where the intolerant mutter of popular feeling—the dull buzz of murmurs that there is no smoke without fire, that liberal bleeding hearts leave the whole community vulnerable, that fair trials are a trick to protect the criminal—has taken over. Now governments, and most notably the Blair government, no longer trumpet the importance of due process. Instead the niceties of natural justice are described as clunky anachronisms, practices that cannot meet the challenges of the present.

The ruling that "evidence" obtained from torture can be used in British courts, as long as this torture was carried out by someone else, represents an official acceptance of fit-ups. In fact, the acknowledged use of supposed information from the most dubious of international sources is an extension of previous practices of fitting up (Bindman 2005). Now intimidation, coercion and torture have become acceptable strategies to extract information from a range of vulnerable people across the world. Although these unfortunates may not know each other, their desperation can be used to implicate others. In this way, each false allegation in the chain sustains the others. Once again, confessions extracted through torture are being used as the basis for imprisonment, but this time each forced confession cements a global alliance supervised by the United States.

c) Stop and search

Some other aspects of the debate about the racist state also reappear, but in adapted form. The use of stop and search has been a recurrent problem in relation to the policing of black communities. This issue has come to symbolise the larger and more diffuse grievances of communities suffering state violence and systematic discrimination. With the war on terror, stop and search has been rehabilitated again as a tactic. Now ethnic profiling is proclaimed as a legitimate and unavoidable aspect of maintaining national security.

There has been a recent concern about the sharp rise in the stops and searches of Asian men, and this is clearly a reflection of contemporary racial fears (*Statewatch* 2005). However, this is also a continuation of a longer history of enabling police discretionary powers to enhance existing racism and to actively criminalise certain communities. When Kenan Malik argues that there is no increase in Islamophobia, he is basing his argument on this continuity (Malik 2005). African and African-Caribbean men are stopped and searched at more disproportionate rates than Asians and there has been a concurrent increase in the stop and search of white men. Overall, the war on terror has served to legitimate a variety of methods of attributing guilt without a hearing for everyone; civil liberties are eroded for all communities with a parallel outcome of enabling an increasingly open targeting of minority communities. This was admitted by Hazel Blears, a junior Home Office minister, when her evidence to the Home Affairs Select Committee in 2005 included the suggestion that Muslim communities must expect to be targeted disproportionately by anti-terrorist policing.

d) Immigration

Immigration has been and continues to be a central narrative in the mythologies of UK racism. The business of state racism, in particular, returns again and again to the figure of the migrant as the threat that must be contained. UK immigration law and the propaganda that surrounds this issue continue to place entire communities under suspicion and render them vulnerable to policing strategies that can use immigration charges as a default outcome of raids undertaken for other reasons; this has been the outcome of a number of "anti-terrorism" raids.

Taken together, all of the above examples suggest that what I am calling occupation policing has arguably been the practice for a long time. My suggestion is that a new imperial consciousness created via occupation TV and rhetoric has a knock-on impact on the policing of black and minority ethnic communities, in the process resurrecting and revamping all kinds of racist policing strategies.

Does state racism always have a shadow of militarisation?

My overall argument is that the conduct of the war on terror brings the process of militarisation right back home, and most of all into the conduct of state racism. I want to suggest that there are some particular and troubling aspects to this process in our time, something very historically specific that demands an equally pertinent response. However, I am not sure that my argument can be made in such absolute terms. Perhaps state racism has always had a covert affinity with militarisation.

The militarisation of our times is taking place outside the norms of international law. If anything, it is this disregard for such previous contracts of conduct between nations that characterises contemporary militarisation and warfare. This is a scary story that is very much of our time. The struggle to create a new but unacknowledged power bloc in the world is leading to the erosion of such norms plus a concerted propaganda campaign on many fronts to de-legitimise the very idea that international agreement on such issues could be possible.

This retreat from the norms of international law is justified by the often repeated assertion that the world has changed, and, therefore, a new conception of legality and international relations is required. As with so many frightening assertions, there is an element of truth in this claim. Serious attempts to analyse and understand that changing nature of states and of war have identified significant shifts in our world. The fragile equilibrium of the Cold War, despite its own bloody hot spots, maintained the fiction of international law in the conduct of war. Although this period had no lack of highly militarised atrocities, relations between states were regulated by the counterbalancing of two superpowers. The range and conduct of armed conflicts across the globe since the demise of the Soviet Union has revealed new demons—inter-ethnic violence, armies that are not regulated by any recognised state, regions where government does not wield authority over military forces, the emergence of non-state actors who did wield this authority but without the responsibilities of government. These are the characteristics identified in the literature on so-called "new wars", a debate that has proved to be highly influential in shaping foreign policy debates among global powers, and British discussions in particular (Kaldor 1999). Nations that wish to show their influence in the world—primarily the US and its allies—have been rushing to adapt their strategies of statecraft to respond to these warnings of the increasing role of non-state actors and frequency of wars played out on terms not agreed through the fora of legitimate states. The public rhetoric of the war on terror is shaped directly in response to this kind of account; this is how Blair et al seek to legitimise pre-emptive strikes and to argue for new terms of war for "democratic states". Although Robert Cooper's interesting but frightening book, *The Breaking of Nations*, in fact offers a careful defence of diplomacy as the least unsatisfactory method of conflict resolution, despite its slowness, his account of the new security challenges of the contemporary world has served to justify actions that break the previous contract of international law (Cooper 2004). Cooper's suggestion that the world is divided into nations that are pre-modern, modern and post-modern and that the chaos of the pre-modern threatens the security of post-modern nations who no longer conceptualise their interests in purely national terms has been used to justify a defensive imperialism against the perceived threat of attacks by non-state actors and/or rogue states.

This leads to a gloves-off approach and an open embracing of illegal methods of warfare, building on the covert history of war crimes against ethnic others. It is worth remembering that the niceties of international law and terms of warfare always stumbled when it came to the racial other; aerial bombing can be contemplated because the targets are viewed as less than human, Hiroshima is made possible through the distance created by racial othering. Developments in military technology and tactics designed to maximise destruction rely on a dehumanisation of the enemy, because how could we unleash such horror on people like us? In Iraq and Afghanistan we are witnessing another continuation of occupation as race war with apparently widespread use of dehumanising techniques against the local population, even though they are not supposed to be identified as the "enemy" in this instance. From the pictures of prisoner abuse at Abu Ghraib to the brutalisation and murder of Iraqi civilians by coalition forces to the public burning of the bodies of dead Taliban fighters as a warning and provocation to their colleagues, these nation-building occupations are meting out treatment that implies that these places are inhabited by lesser peoples.

In a parallel move, state racism at home in the coalition nations mobilises a rhetoric of emergency and relies on a popular acceptance that membership of the nation does not extend to the demonised and targeted others, thereby rendering militarised tactics legitimate. These violences, committed both abroad and at home, are presented as unfortunate exceptions to an otherwise functioning contract of honour. The implication is that in the normal course of events regulated and respectful relations apply to conflict both within states and between states, but that these honourable arrangements have been spoilt by the sneaky excesses of new enemies. The concept of honour between enemies, even in situations of mortal combat, has relied on an assumption of similarity between combatants. As long as fighting goes on between people like "us", or the coercive power of the state disciplines only those within the ethnic family of nation, so the story goes, the rules work and nobody gets hurt. Mutual respect regulates and limits the violence. Unfortunately, the barriers of racialisation render the other both alien and incomprehensible. This distance debars us/them from the niceties of international law and the protections of citizenship. The racialised other is frightening because there is no way of knowing how s/he thinks or what s/he will do. In these circumstances, and given the ongoing emergency signalled by the war on terror, states seek to persuade the population that it is best to mobilise all the defensive forces at our disposal.

The state racism that I am describing rests on systems of differential citizenship and entitlement, even if these are informal rather than explicit. This category of less than citizen marks the limit to the fiction of benign state activity, because instead of the paternalistic care given to full members of the national family, these others force the state to reveal its coercive teeth. Some people are not amenable to reason; they don't understand the rules. For such people only the more forceful aspects of governance can work. All of which makes me wonder if perhaps those rendered non-citizens or less-than-citizens have always been subject to occupation tactics? Certainly, that was the feeling of earlier campaigns against racist policing.

Now the explicit erosion of the terms of international law feeds back into the idea of emergency at home: internal legislation and practice mirrors the erosions in the international arena.

Racial supremacy and global alliances

Much has been said already about Islamophobia, and how it echoes earlier racisms (Commission on British Muslims and Islamophobia 2004; Sayyid 1997), so it is not necessary to revisit those debates here. I want to argue that what is distinctive about the recent wave of Islamophobia is the global reach of this project. Earlier modes of racism continue, shaped by particular national histories, mobilised for particular local interests. However, now there is a linking of local state racisms to an international network of imperial co-operation. This is the pact that unites the coalition of the willing, the difference between being with us or against us. I am not suggesting here that US military aggression and expansionism is motivated by racism. However, I do want to argue that this highly instrumental project to build invincible structures to protect those most old-fashioned of assets, money and power, harnesses the motivating energies of racial supremacism. I take this to be what Samir Amin is describing when he writes that the liberal virus of US expansionism has created anew the distinction between a "master race" and other peoples.

This "Master Race" has the right to conquer "the living space" deemed necessary, while the very existence of other peoples is tolerated only if it does not constitute a threat to the ambitions of those called upon to be "masters of the world". Hence, in the eyes of the Washington establishment, we have all become "redskins", that is, peoples that have a right to exist only in so far as we do not obstruct the expansion of the transnational capital of the United States (Amin 2004: 77).

In this context, the continuing and enthusiastic deployment of domestic racism by individual states within the coalition consolidates the position of the racialised elites at home while at the same time serving as a sign of allegiance to the imperial project of the remaining global superpower. It is convenient to pretend that Islam—Islam presented as the demon enemy of the West—is the name of the racialised other here, the "challenge" that must be met. Yet the practices that link those in the coalition are more diffuse, scooping up a variety of vilified and/or subjugated groups into the category of enemy combatants at home. The international battle against Muslims, if not against Islam as such, serves to legitimate state racism of all sorts. After all, these unpalatable strategies of statecraft are presented as a last resort, unpleasant but necessary in order to protect the national family against the incursions of the less than human, whoever they may be.

At the same time, the targeting of Muslim communities also serves to re-legitimate longstanding racist policing strategies against a variety of minority communities. For all the talk about new racisms and faith based racism, there is little sign that everyday policing techniques have changed or developed; there may have been a slight expansion of the range of targets, but the techniques of state racism as deployed through racist policing remain all too familiar. As discussed above, the state of emergency rhetoric of the war on terror is used to rehabilitate such tactics. The long years of campaigning against the abuse of stop and search, the exposés of police malpractice, the release of those imprisoned on the basis of fabricated evidence—all of this is dismissed through reference to the new threats that we are facing. Attempts to appeal to natural justice, civil liberties or anti-racism, or to suggest that as a society we should take note of the consequences of abandoning such principles, consequences that can be learnt from our own recent past, are decried as unrealistic and living in the past. Our present, it is argued, is filled with terror, and therefore, the erosion of rights for some is a small price to pay to safeguard the security of the many. The implication is that those who have criticised police racism in the past have now been proved wrong. It turns out that it is not only acceptable to persecute minorities, it may even be necessary for the greater good. It has never been easy to challenge police racism; this has never been a populist campaign. Rather, the challenge has been to counter the populism of appeals to law and order. The rhetoric of the war on terror seeks to shift the debate to such an extent that critics of state racism render themselves suspect. They become enemies of the state and their resistance itself becomes a justification for such extreme responses by the state.

The Islamicisation of "race": how anti-muslim state racism infects racisms against other communities

In part, this is no more than another statement of the obvious. UK racism continues to be shaped by an unseemly attention to physical difference. While mythologies of culture and faith are gaining currency, racist practice can often revert to an old-fashioned attempt to read the body. The term "Muslim" is understood as a physical category and there is a well-documented confusion about who is Muslim. For example, the increases in stop and search use physical markers, Asians, not Muslims as such; after September 11 2001 and now July 7 2005, revenge racism targets dark-skinned people, perhaps in the hope that at least some of them are bound to be Muslim.

Despite our well practised insistence that racism is contextual and historically specific, British narratives of racialised threat have tended to follow established themes. We have been used to ideas of criminality, lack of civilisation, animality, hyper-sexuality and coded references to race science. Of course, such myths are given particular articulations in relation to different communities and contexts. However, and as can be seen in relation to new communities in the UK, versions of these narratives re-emerge in each new incarnation of racism. For each new demonised other, there are familiar triggers to public outrage, the repertoire of narratives that can be adapted to encompass new characters but for similar effect.

UK Islamophobia builds on a long-running debate about cultural racism which is far from new. We might ask ourselves when was there not a confusion of biology and culture in the process of racialisation. Even the most essentialist of racisms imply that physical degeneracy and cultural degeneracy are mutually reinforcing and that the markers of physical difference warn of moral failings or cultural limitations. In recent times, cultural racism has been increasingly articulated as a response to a perceived affront or threat to Western values, in a continuation of the suggestion that some minorities are resistant to civilisation and, perhaps, evolution. The persistence with which some communities hold onto their own cultural practices and beliefs, particularly where such practices are deemed to be backward, oppressive or anti-Western, is presented as a biologically-based culture. These things may be no more than what people do, but they are as hard to change as blood and bones.

The other side of this is that this cultural racism relies on old-style physical ascription: certain bodies are seen to be hiding the dangers of irrationality, now especially articulated through faith. Islam is the archetype for this conceptualisation, but a failure to temper faith with reason can come to be seen as a weakness of other minorities as well. In part, this is a return to Western celebrations of secularism, the body of thought still presented as one of the West's gifts to the world. However, at the same time, there has been a resurgence of religiosity in some mainstream Western politics, most famously embodied in the image, perhaps apocryphal, of Bush and Blair praying together. The implication that some faiths can encompass reason while others remain mired in superstition reintroduces a dangerous suggestion of religious war. In the process, bodies and beliefs become interchangeable, each one a cipher for the other.

It is obvious that the high profile scrutiny of Muslim communities has not stopped the ongoing racism faced by others, despite the continued assertions of particular interest groups that religion has replaced "race" in the practices of institutional discrimination. To cite only a few of the most obvious examples: what has changed in terms of African-Caribbean boys and school achievement; stop and search; levels of imprisonment; disparities in employment and income; deaths in custody?

Islamophobia does not replace other racisms, although it overlaps with them. However, it does add new elements to the repertoire of state racism and raises a seemingly unanswerable legitimation of repression in the spectre of international terrorism—a state racism that is explicitly part of the contract to belong with the free world and which mobilises fear of international terrorism in order to gain support for racism at home.

This call to international realignment is echoed in shifts in British concepts of the "other". Asylum has become a coded scare-word for all migration. In the process, there is some knowledge of but little sympathy with the circumstances of these new waves of migration. Asylum-seekers can be coded, with some accuracy, as victims of conflict and deprivation, another unhappy by-product of the same instability that creates international terrorism, in the popular imagination at least. There is a cultural racism against refugees and asylum-seekers that parallels the rise of Islamophobia, with both regarded as dangerous envoys from the pre-modern world that threatens to corrode our way of life.

How to respond?

When I first presented this chapter I suggested that we were standing at the edge of an abyss, and suffering from a collective sense of vertigo as we realise what we are witnessing. Whereas in a previous era the excesses of empire took place far away, hidden from the view of most of the imperial nation's population, now the ugly machinery of empire is visible everywhere. There is no revelation from the heart of darkness for us. We do not need to be told from afar of the horror, the horror. For us the horror has come right up to our own doorsteps. And there is a danger that we will remain frozen with the shock of our response.

There is an understandable rush to defend Muslim communities against such concerted attacks and this is evident in both the academic commentary on and the community response to recent events. How can we not do this? We all know that this is how it starts—an acceptance of racist violence by both individuals and state, endlessly rehearsed fictions about the sub-human characteristics and practices of one group, a carefully nurtured confusion between peddling racism and protecting the national interest. Let this go and the violence and horror can only escalate.

At the same time, the reinvigorated tactics being used to target Muslims are also impacting on other minority ethnic groups; again, in an echo of previous eras of British racism, the high-profile persecution of one group enables a legitimation of other flavours of racism. An anti-racist response with too exclusive a focus on the Muslim, or any other one community, risks accepting the terms of this new racism and certainly replicates the divide-and-rule tactics of the racist state. As others have commented, a collective failure to organise across communities leaves us all vulnerable to a resurgence of confident state racism. Equally, failure to articulate and understand the changing-same of this new racism leaves racism within minority communities unchallenged and us all unprepared to face what is happening.

I want to argue that our job is to analyse the emergence of new articulations of state racism and to propose a resistance built on the universalism of anti-racist politics. None of which seems to have much space at the moment. But if the militarisation of state racism through the war on terror cannot remind us that racism is about power not identity, then we are all in extreme danger.

As I finish writing this in October 2005, the streets outside my window in Lozells, Birmingham are alight again with blazing cars. A rumour that a young African-Caribbean girl has been gang-raped by Asian men has seeped around the community, leading to public protests and meetings and then to street violence. Despite repeated calls, no-one comes to put out the fires in my street. Instead we get vans full of riot police and later, and all too ironically for me, an unmarked armoured vehicle and armed police who kick down my back gate and rush across the backyards of our row of houses with machine-guns. Whether we like it or not, the war has come to our doorsteps; anti-racists need to be clear which side we are on.

References

Amin, Samir. 2004. *The Liberal Virus, Permanent War and the Americanization of the World*. London: Pluto

Bindman, Geoffrey. 2005. Should Britain be relying on evidence obtained by torture? *The Times,* October 18, 2005.

Commission on British Muslims and Islamophpbia. 2004. *Islamophobia: Issues, Challenges and Action.* Stoke-on-Trent: Trenthan Books.

Cooper, Robert. 2004. *The Breaking of Nations: Order and Chaos in the Twenty-First Century*. London: Atlantic Books

Kaldor, Mary. 1999. *New and Old Wars: Organized Violence in a Global Era*. Cambridge: Polity Press.

Keith, Michael. 1993. *Race, Riots and Policing: Lore and Disorder in a Multi-Racist Society*. London: UCL Press

Malik, Kenan. 2005. The Islamophobia Myth, *Prospect Magazine,* February 2005

Macpherson of Cluny, Sir William. 1999. *The Stephen Lawrence Inquiry: report of an inquiry by Sir William Macpherson of Cluny.* London: Stationary Office

Miscarriages of Justice Organisation. 2005. www.mojoscotland.com.

Sayyid, Bobby. 1997. *A Fundamental Fear: Eurocentrism and the Emergence of Islamism.* London: Zed Books.

Solomos, John. 1993. *Race and Racism in Britain.* London: Macmillan

Statewatch. 2005. *Statewatch Bulletin: UK: Stop and Search: Ethnic Injustice continues unabated*, Vol 15, no.1.

CHAPTER SEVEN

THE PRODUCTION OF THE IMAGINARY TERRORIST AS AN OBJECT OF FEAR: ORIENTALISM IN THE TWENTY FIRST CENTURY

CHRIS SPARKS

In the current theatre of the politics of fear, the mediated image of the hooded, weapon-wielding terrorist has become commonplace on news bulletins across the globe. This chapter examines the manner in which state and counter-state organisations produce mediated images of "the terrorist" as a malleable polymorph of racial and cultural "otherness"—a threatening "global other" and argues that: firstly, the production of the "super terrorist" as "global other" is a dualistically contrived construction produced by two apparently opposed political groupings, terror-inducing anti-western militias and those western governments who are committed to the eradication of unmanageable uncertainties in political and cultural life, both of whom share a commitment to producing and maintaining a global politics of fear; secondly, media transmission and presentation of terror events and the portrayal of polymorphic terroristic images serve the production of a global politics of fear by overwhelming people's capacity for judgement with irrational fearfulness; thirdly, a key factor in the media's production of societal fearfulness is the reproduction of a vulgarised Orientalist pornography of visceral carnage.

In making its argument, this chapter explores the reductive conflict-oriented sensibility produced by the perennial but historically variant condition of fear-ridden politics, and examines the political manipulation of Orientalist imaginings to produce a particularly racialised common sense of threatening enemies lurking within and gathering around "besieged" western society. It examines the strategies deployed in the effective use of terror to create scenarios of societal fearfulness. It also brings into focus the little-discussed strategic production of the cultural/racial "other as terrorist" through a process of "haunting", a process which imprints the terrorist image into the conscious state of continual fearfulness which is core to the current politics of fear.

Fear

I shall begin this discussion by overturning the Hobbesian/Schmittian notion allowed to drift into public consciousness by those who advocate the "war on terror", that the condition of fear is a constant and immovable foundation of human life. Fear is incidental in as much as it is contingent: it comes and goes along with the objective conditions that produce it. Furthermore, contrary to Hobbesian thinking, fear is not necessarily destructive and de-humanising. It has many qualities (being a response to many different situations). Judith Shklar noted that fear can be "much to our advantage in many cases, since alarm often preserves us from dangers" (Rosenblum 1989: 23), and Gugliemo Ferrero used Machiavelli's insight that fear is mother of the vital human quality "courage", to present politics itself as "the school of courage"—the brave encounter with fear-full situations (Ferraro 1941: 34-35). Nevertheless, Hobbes's one-dimensional and historical account of fear in the human condition does perform the valuable task of showing decisively that civility, with all its attending civilising features, is dependent on trust and trust cannot exist in a "desert of lawlessness" (Arendt 1986: 466), neither in the absence of governance nor, as Montesquieu made clear, in the suffocating rule-bound lawlessness of despotism. It is here that we hit on the kind of fear that I wish to discuss in this chapter. It is the fear that functions in the absence of polity which is also fear of a kind that perniciously eats away at the constitution of civil society—of the conditions for trust, for toleration, for co-existence, for the "summum malum" of Hobbes at the bare minimum, or, for the optimists, the pursuit of happiness.

Montesquieu described quietude in despotism as "the silence of those towns that the enemy is ready to invade" (Montesquieu 1949: 59). In this phrase, he points to a kind of fear-driven madness... the constant subjection of the populaces to the cruel caprices of their governors leaves them reduced into a fear-ridden silent expectation of attack from external enemies that may well not exist. The maddening effect of fear in a political void is, of course, both a psychological and a political point. Fear has moving power in our lives that derives from the way it colours our perceptions of what is going on. Fear drags our interest away from the clear definitions produced by rational considerations of our situation and from the likely outcomes of our involvement in it, causing us to dwell instead upon the most unlikely possibilities (this plane may crash, the stranger in the car park may be a killer on the run) creating a sense of the dangerous strangeness, the uncanny or *unheimliche*—as Freud described it—which appears to make itself present as the light and shade of phenomena. This haunting presence can lead us to act inappropriately, if left unchecked, to the point of self-destructive madness. The political point—as stressed, perhaps most notably, by Hannah Arendt (1986) and George Orwell (1954), is that the fall into madness can only be checked by the presence of trusted others who communicate through tried and trusted means in conditions that enable clarity; in short, all the features of a pluralistic public sphere and civil society.

Arendt, as we know, wrote at length about how fearfulness, framed and directed by terror, overpowers polities by reducing plurality to moving masses, fragmenting the public sphere (and its worldly common sense) and with it the conditions of informed judgement, replacing political sensibility with corrupted and corrupting propaganda (Arendt 1986: 341-64). This is the situation we face today and at the centre of the process is the production of terror and the mediated reproduction of the "über-terrorist", both constituent parts of the so called "war on terror".

Orientalism as a feature of the war on terror

Many of the features attributed to the imagined "über terrorist" are familiar to anyone with any knowledge of Orientalist fiction and art. Ironically, they can be found in Montesquieu's presentations of despotism, which are themselves an early form of Orientalism. The irony is not surprising as Orientalism is a highly nuanced and fluid genre of human representation. Thus, while Edward Said's presentation of Orientalism, as a pernicious model of racial inferiority developed in service of imperialism is charged with historical insight, it doesn't encompass all the dimensions of Orientalism. Orientalism is not always necessarily an expression of perceived superiority, of clearly defined difference and of constant potential enmity. That this reduced Schmittian conception of Orientalism has come to dominate the western mindset—a fact that plays heavily in the construction of the imagined super terrorist—is the result of contingent factors.

To make this point clear, let me compare briefly two distinct and significant moments in the development of European Orientalism: the call to arms against the Islamic world made by the Catholic Church at the Council of Narbonne in 1054, and the visits of Peter the Great and Mehemet Riza Bey to France in 1717.

In 1054, the Catholic church, seeking to halt the internecine warfare of a dominant and rampant warrior class which was destroying the barely constructed Carolingan Empire, and faced with the increasing incursions into "Christian" territory by Islamic forces, held the council of Narbonne, which recognised the validity of the warrior class, redefined them as Christian brotherhood, and legitimated their violent plundering by transforming it into holy war in pursuit of a holy duty to drive the "mohamedons" from Christian Europe, cleverly redirecting warfare away from western Europe towards the external but pressing Islamic world. The development of internal peace within

Christendom, dependent on warfare with Islam, centred on occupation of the holy land, which was validated in turn by the construction of a wholly negative nomenclature of Oriental devilry (Strayer 1971: 333-4) .

This exemplifies the crude ways in which Orientalism has been and can be used to attack everything in the Islamic world. Contrast this with the rich and complex dimensions of Orientalism that ran throughout the discussions and writing of the philosophes of the French Enlightenment, and a different aspect of Orientalism emerges.

Although France in the early 1700s was the epi-centre of European "enlightened" civilisation, it was racked by religious and class tensions, by damaging colonial conflict with Britain, and by economic failure. It was a self-regarding but insecure culture; a breeding ground for exploration of "self" and "otherness" displayed in the philosophical interest in the relativity of norms, in the growing interest in cultural "otherness", stimulated by colonial France's growing contact with non-European cultures and newly formed diplomatic relationships with many "eastern" countries (Baum 1979: 36). Public interest in things oriental was whetted by the arrivals in France of Peter the Great of Russia (perceived as oriental), and the dramatic and exotic Mehemet Riza Bey, a trickster who fooled the French court into believing that he was an ambassador of the Shah of Persia (Sparks 1999: 53) and "used the opportunity to act in ways that scandalised" the French public" (Baum 1979: 36). Interest was further stimulated by a flood of fantasy-flavoured Orientalist travel literature. Widely-read travelogues of "oriental" travellers of the time were richly loaded with fantasy elements. The mix of fantasy and supposed fact filtered into the work of possibly the most influential writer and social theorist in Europe at that time—Montesquieu, in his Orientalist fiction *The Persian Letters* (a book which was so popular due to its Orientalist erotic content that it continually sold out across France for years) and later appeared in instances of supposed empirical evidence in The Spirit of the Laws, one of the most influential texts in the whole eighteenth century political cannon and, as some commentators today have noted, one of the first works of sociological analysis. In short, the Orient became fashionable and on this occasion Orientalism, far from promoting mutually exclusive cultures and polities, was manifestly a heavy flirtation of Europeans with the fantastic and fantasy "othernesses" of human possibility.

The contrast between these examples shows that Orientalism isn't simply pure negativity. In the more developed "classical" Orientalism of eighteenth century Europe, there is a dialectic at play: the desire for the exotic, the extraordinary, and the dangerous is matched by fear of the sublime, of terrible beauty, and of terrifying passion. The push and pull of embracing opposed tendencies strongly suggests that it alone cannot be responsible for the production of hostility to otherness. Furthermore it is clear that oriental sensibilities have to be vulgarised, stripped of nuance and complexity if it is to be the simple servant of racism. Thus, external factors must take and use Orientalism to explain its role in developing the west's culture of aggressive fearfulness regarding "oriental" peoples.

The external factor is the (historically perennial) political use of oriental imagination to reduce the common sense of strangeness to a common enmity. The genre of Orientalism, hanging the draperies of its fantasies on a conception of "the east" and hanging the presentations of erotic sensuality, of lawlessness, of passion and the joyful experience of power on the glorified frame of exotic "eastern" men and women provided the Schmittian political mindset with an easy task—the forcing of the complex sophistication of Orientalist imaginings into the crude simplicities of racial stereotypes: "Orientals" are madly passionate, dangerously sexual, lustful for power, prone to extreme violence, corrupt and corrupting and for all these reasons, destructive to civil society wherever they find it. Because this vulgarised Orientalism serves up all "Orientals" this way—be they brown or black, Arabs, Negros or Semites—it serves to reduce the complexity of the multi-cultural and multi-ethnic world to a purely Schmittian binary friend-enemy relationship. At this point, it works as a servant of those who wish to produce a politics of fear.

The war of terror: A dialectic of instigation and eradication

Current discussions of terrorism and fear are based on the long established dualism of governance, producing safety and order, and chaos, fuelled by and reproducing fear and madness. In this context, the dualism between government and terrorism is as follows: if governance is the ordered management of the social conditions of people's existence, terrorism is its opposite. Terrorism is the strategic production of terror to undermine a society's capacity to endure the uncertainties of existence—to make society insecure through the production of a social condition of fear. While this truism is a means to coherently understand the relationship of opposition between governance and terrorism, history is rich with examples of incoherent and ultimately self-destructive marriages between the two. I suggest here that the current relationship between western governments and propagators of anti-western terror is such a situation.

As the War on Terror developed, from New York's "9/11" to London's "7/7", it has become increasingly evident that the protagonists of terror and the self-declared "warriors against terror" have become locked in a strange dance of mutual definition and justification for their warfare, which produces an ongoing, open-ended, un-bordered and debilitating condition of fear.

On one side, we have those labelled in the west as terrorists; this definition which closes off the context of the terror-maker's actions and so shuts off consideration of the social, economic and military factors which might provide these actors some political credibility is a fairly useless identifier when trying to understand intensely political situations. However, from 9/11 onwards, it is clear that the self-defined jihadist bombers are instigators of terror in the western world. These instigators consist of groups who for various reasons oppose the western socio-political order and seek to produce an incapacitating fear in their "western enemies" by undermining the solidity of their world, violently rupturing normality and surreally re-ordering the relationship of objects and activities. Their organisation cannot stand the exposure produced by any kind of transparency, is anti-democratic and destroys the secure order required to establish civil society, but it can be used as a dangerous tool for democratic ends by those unable by other means to establish any power over the order of their lives (Sparks 2004: 200-206).

Currently in the USA and UK these instigators are being "faced off" by governments who are driven domestically and internationally by "a gut level fear" of uncertainty. Uncertainty threatens planned futures and bubbles through the surface of current common sensibilities, always threatening to reduce the smoothing task of public management to crisis management. For this reason, eradicators seek to eradicate the causes of uncertainty "entirely with little regard to cost" (Stern 1999: 34-5). Fear drives the desire to hunt out and destroy agents of danger without and within. Where there is cultural heterogeneity, this fear-driven quest for safety can become twisted into a drive for the security of sameness. The potential cost of such activity is the loss of civil society itself. Overly fearful governments can lurch into panoptic governance, undermining the world they seek to preserve. In such situations, citizens come to be seen as actual or potential enemies within, vigilantes prosper, civility withers and, ironically, the uncertainties and dangers that lurk within the society become its defining features. This is the danger that we see facing us currently, particularly in the domestic anti-terror policies of the USA and the UK.

Media, democracy and rumour mill

As much of the politics of the modern world functions directly through media, the pivotal role of mediating terrorism is the core mechanism by which the rhythmic songs of war and the dance of definition has been drummed out. How and why this is so, or to put it another way, how and why the media has not performed its supposed roles of truth finder, power checker, mediator between citizens and government, becomes clear on reconsideration of the supposed functions of modern media in liberal democracies.

Jean Delemeau defined rumour as "equal acknowledgement and elucidation of a general fear", as "the identification of a threat and the clarification of a situation that has become unbearable" (Delemeau 1978: 247), but rumours seldom provide accurate portrayals of situations and their scary power to drive populations to a kind of maddened and often self-damaging reaction against what they fear (usually something that does not exist as they imagine it) derive from the lack of authorship and the lack of definite details that make it impossible to verify or falsify them. It derives also from the multiple authorship that encourages them to mutate, grow and fragment into a plurality of overlapping, sometimes contradictory tales. This churning of fear-inducing uncertainties (communicated with all the lurid pseudo-certainties that fearful imaginations can conjure) is what has come to be called "the rumour mill", a social milieu of communicated doubt and uncertainty, energising and disseminating fearfulness.

All human societies have the capacity to create rumour mills, only some have the capacity to endure them. Hobbes, for all his is reductionism, hit the nail on the head when pointing out that there can be no kind of society - certainly no civil society - in a world where every person's life is directed by fear. He began the analysis of how civil society could be developed from procedures which acknowledge dangerous uncertainties and the common condition of fear that they nurture and he initiated the discussion about reducing the scope and range of these uncertainties through rational discourse producing tested and verifiable fact rooted in, and giving securing knowledge to, a rule-bound civil society. This idea which is key to the tradition of liberalism, branches into the arguments of Milton, Paine and J.S. Mill for the necessary public nature of truth-rendering rational discourse in the form of a free press—the historical forerunner of our own modern media.

Today, it is generally agreed that the great jewel of modern democracies is the life-enhancing liberty endowed to each and all their citizens by the institutions and processes of civil society, which democratic politics both expresses and protects. John Keane has pointed out in Media and Democracy (1991) that the agencies of the media have become so central to this relationship that modern democracies necessarily function through the sophisticated use of communications media. This is significant, as the role of the media in mediating between governors and governed has historically depended on its special truth-rendering function, which is designed in part to ensure that democratic society progresses in the light of genuine knowledge and well-judged argument. Keane notes that the great virtue of organised mediation of public discourse through a "free press" and broadcasting media is that the location of news-bearing agencies in the public sphere enables identification of the source of every new story and the subjection to public scrutiny of both the factual claims involved and of the analysis involved in the story's narrative (Keane 2001: 9-10). This public transparency reduces the debilitating and corrupting spread of falsity and fear associated with the rumour mills of marketplace and coffee shop and promotes in its stead the relatively certain, rationally analysed, truthful and manageable news. Keane has also noted that media activities have the vital effect "of transforming the nature of fear experienced by civil societies by publicising it" (Keane 2001: 9), exposing its dimensions to clarifying and often demystifying analysis and so enabling effective and affective action to be taken as civil society protects itself. However, he notes the ironic fact that publicising fear dramatises it and such dramatisation can itself function to enlarge and intensify fearful imaginings and start rumours. The outcome of such dramatisations depends on the manner and the conditions in which the dramatisation takes place and these we have to consider in weighing the media's capacity to quell rumour against its tendency to dramatise events. Three factors particularly need to be considered: (1) the psychological function of story telling; (2) the political function of the news in democracies and; (3) the commercially-driven competition between media agencies to out-sell each other, which I now examine.

A core function of story telling is to explore the constituent elements of the familiar and the strange in the living of lives. It is an activity which inherently flirts with fearful imaginings. Interestingly, Freud showed in his essay *Das Heimliche* (Strachey 1985) how this function of exploring the unsettling otherness—the uncanny—in the familiar objects of everyday life is distilled in the thrilling and populist form of gothic narrative, which not only retains enormous cultural power today through its mass usage in popular movies and TV shows, but over-spills into journalistic descriptions of conflicts and natural carnage as forms of "Hell".

Democracies tend to deal with the fear-inducing implications of power relations between social members by pounding the powerful with the raucous rock and roll of common opinion, loudly, and sometimes crudely given. This democratic course is rife with problems. The tendencies for populist politicians and commercial media to promote and exploit fear and the tendencies of mass plebiscites to reduce decision-making to its lowest common denominator can conjoin into the production of mass fear and its use as the lowest common denominator in democratically enabled decision-making.

When the agencies that comprise the mass media contrive to compete for "hot news", the news degenerates into high-speed delivery of catch-all populist sound bites, reducing the complexities of situations into lowest common denominator images: it functions as a rumour mill, energising and disseminating fearfulness.

The combination of these three factors is pertinent to the present times, in which there is much more presentation and discussion of events than in any time in history. There is 24 hour coverage of dramatic events, with rumour-fuelled instant commentary and constant reams of "high brow" journalism presented as academic analysis for the people. The strange result of this is that there is less space and time to consider the things being displayed. Added to this, there is the difficulty faced by people in our society trying to understand the mountains of constantly unfurling images and stories about other worlds. All of this produces a heady brew of strangeness and catastrophes, resulting in widespread misapprehension, bouts of overwhelming fear, and loss of judgement; in short, a kind of fear-ridden intoxication.

This brief overview of the three ways in which modern media tend to promote fear-inducing rumour indicates that not only have modern media failed to eradicate the power of imagination and all its thrilling, fear-inducing constituents, but they actually stimulate it, and our failure to recognise this is a crucial factor in the current production of a kind of general condition of fearfulness that undermines civil society.

To support this argument, I will now consider some examples of how the media has become a digging and spreading tool for exposing terror and spreading fear, a tool which is expertly used by two mutually reinforcing opponents in the current politics of fear.

The political context: the current politics of fear

The current acute state of fearfulness of the western world results from the apparent emergence of a global network of anti-western terrorist groups who seek to inflict massive damage to western peoples using weapons of mass destruction (WMDs). Following the attack on the World Trade Centre, governmental worries about "illicit traffic in nuclear materials" (Galinskiy 2002: 1-24; Hoffman and Claridge 1999: 10-12), the "easy access to intruders and to insiders interested in smuggling nuclear materials" (Gurr 2000: 57) following the opening up of international barriers in pursuit of free trade were rapidly fed by TV and newspapers to the public in compressed and dramatised form. This, combined with the shared psychological trauma of witnessing attacks on western capitals (in a narrated and mediated form) has stimulated a common sense in western society of acute danger.

Since 9/11, the common sensibility, fuelled with imagery of disasters, combined with threadbare knowledge about the availability of WMDs, the presence of anti-western terrorist groups and Orientalist imaginings of Islamic culture as violently unstable, constantly reveals its ready capacity to imagine the most dangerous scenarios for the near future.

The centrality of media activity in this—its function of fabricating apparent threats—became obvious to all in the farce of Colin Powell's media-saturated presentation to the UN, and simultaneously by TV to the western world, of "images of WMDs". Powell's use of blurry satellite images and fragments of bugged telephone conversation created from a series of mundane objects gives an appearance of a dark otherness, a haunting presence of chemical killers which we now know to be an illusion. However, the psychological power of such conjuring tricks is that, even when the truth is known, the impact of the illusion lingers in fear-inducing imaginings. As a result, people continue to scare themselves into non-rational panic-driven activity. In the USA this is exemplified by the reduction of numbers travelling abroad and the frailty of stock markets. In Western Europe fearfulness has been expressed in a right-wing backlash against the ethnic and cultural diversity commonplace in European nations, as the issue of terrorism has become confused with issues of immigration. In May 2002, the anti-immigration/anti-Islam *Front National* (France) and the List Pim Fortuyn (Holland) made significant electoral gains. More recently an overt anti-Islamic flavour has become evident. In Germany and Holland, mainstream parties respond to the eradication politics of the far right by espousing eradication themselves. The German general election of 2002 saw a pledge by the Christian Democrat leader to expel "4000 Islamic fundamentalists" from the country (*The Guardian* 2002).

Two significant points can be drawn from this consideration of the current scenario of fearfulness. We see the political creation of assumed enmity in situations of strangeness. We also see a powerful undercurrent of fear-driven Orientalist imaginings.

Politics and enmity

Political reactions as just described do not occur without some political manipulation. As we shall see, terrorism is a strategy to manipulate mass fear, but eradicationist governments have been equally manipulative in their own way. Political exploitation of mass fearfulness initiated by the attack of 9/11 began with President Bush's "State of the Nation" address in 2002, which introduced a permanent "war on terror". Governmental manipulation of facts such as Bush's description of Iraqi nuclear scientists as "nuclear holy warriors" (Bush 2002) prepared the grounds of popular acceptance for the reductions of civil liberties in areas of communication, movement, and judicial process contained in the Patriot Act later that year. In Europe also, eradication politics exploited commonsense connections of Islam and terrorism. Restrictions on civil liberties in the UK initiated by the Anti-terrorism Security and Crime Act 2001, are to be extended under a 2005 Terrorism Bill "proscribing extremist groups" and banning texts that "are likely to be understood by members of the public as indirectly encouraging the committing or preparation of acts of terrorism"(Travis 2005). Underpinning this fear-promoting Orientalist strategy, is the deceptive reinforcement of the mythology of al-Qa'eda as a unified force, when it has long been clear to observers that this "organisation" is more of a rag-bag alliance of disaffected groups. In this deceit, western governments conflate Islam with Islamism and Islamism with terrorism. In doing so, they effectively act as PR men for Bin Laden and for various terrorists exploiting grievances of violated and oppressed peoples in the non-western world. On immediate consideration, this promotional activity appears baffling, but its purpose becomes clearer when considering the tendency of political actors to reduce the unknown and frightening to a clearly defined enemy.

To a large degree, political activity consists of strategic action aimed at creating or maintaining enough power to order society into a desired form. Such action is by definition taken with reference to potential threats and countervailing forces, usually to some "other" who may seek alternative future arrangements. Such action and the conflictual world of us and them to which it refers, constitute what Carl Schmitt called the "friend/enemy" dimension of political life (Schmitt 1976). Schmitt's insight into the inherently conflictual scenarios, constantly produced by people's attempts to produce collectivity, inadvertently reveals a tendency amongst political actors to conflate uncertainty—expressing the frailty of existence—with the risks inherent in organising forces against threatening "strangers", who may seek to impose another order of life; that is, to reduce the strangeness of "otherness" to a dangerous threat. In his classic essay *The Stranger* (Simmel 1971), George Simmel pointed out that strangeness includes both the uncanny otherness of something (or someone) otherwise completely familiar, and the uncanny familiarity of something (or someone) otherwise completely "other". From the perspective which seeks certainty and security in the familiarity of common identity, strangeness is sensed as threatening; "the other" may wish to destroy them, to impose another, foreign identity upon them. Thus the stranger—in this case the non-western Muslim—is reduced to enemy, even though the actual otherness of "the stranger" may be other to political conceptions entirely.

Post 9/11 Orientalism

Following the explosive rupture of homely normality by the attack on New York, the media's self-imposed pressure to provide instant analysis and constant delivery of "facts" has continued to funnel the complexities of interconnected global conflicts through pressurised restricted time and space, with the result that, as events erupt, observers/discussants reach for some ready forged easy access, common sense imagery with which to read and understand new situations. Here, longstanding cultural prejudices and fearful folk-mythologies have been pulled together at rapid pace in sound bites and visual montage to produce a ghastly post-modern montage—the Islamic monster-terrorist beings known as "al Qa'eda": "a terrorist organisation... comprising thousands of trained and motivated men watching and waiting in every city in every country... to carry out the orders of their leader Osama bin Laden and kill and maim for their cause" (Burke 2004: 1). Clearly, this fusion of "extreme Islamism" and terror in the imagined "al Qa'eda" is a twenty-first century Orientalist image, but it's one that has absolutely stripped its imagery and message of any of the complexity and nuanced sophistication of classical Orientalism. It is odd that the pure negativity of this oriental image is rarely questioned; rather its features are portrayed both by the western media and by the instigators of terror as simple facts.

Comparison of two Orientalist images of beheadings, the first a classical nineteenth century Orientalist fantasy, Henri Renault's painting *"Execution Sans Jugement"*, the second the image of a recent "al Qa'eda" beheading, transmitted on the internet, highlights the way that instigators of the politics of fear and the eradicators of terrorism exploit the rumour-mongering sensationalism of current media to deploy the darkly negative images involved in Orientalism at their disposal to reduce all the elements of complexity and uncertainty, of the part-seen, and the creative interpretation involved in the meeting of strangers into the knowing stand-off between certain enemies.

Henri Renault's painting *"Execution Sans Jugement"* consists of a carefully contrived collection of sensual images, clearly intended to stimulate some kind of mildly erotic fantasy about power, sexuality and death. The internet image produced by people claiming the identity of al-Qa'eda took this commonly understood Orientalist fantasy image and played on its fearful elements, in the live production of a brutal carnal fact—the beheading of a westerner (the fact that it is just some westerner that strayed into the path of these hooded killers further intensifies the scariness of the brutal killing). It is the use of TV channels and newspapers to stimulate and feed off traditional and culturally established Orientalist imagery in order to vulgarise Orientalist erotics into pornographic voyeuristic snuff movie, reducing the imagined content to nil, while massively multiplying the negative symbolic resonances through the production of factual death and the transmission of the possibility that the killers could really come for the viewer. Here we see how readily mass media becomes the servant of terrorists, who use it to disseminate scary, vulgarised Orientalist imagery to produce an intoxicating brew of repulsion and fear in those viewing. It is no surprise that surveys in France (1991) and the USA (1994) found that 51 per cent of the French population felt endangered by the presence in the world of Iraq, Libya, Iran and Algeria, and 61 per cent of the American population considered the resurgence of militant Islamism a direct threat to their person (Cesari 2004: 2-3).

How terrorism works

The first point to note in assessing the workings of modern terrorism is its exploitation of the structural processes that facilitate the mass communication which drives and enables modern civil society's existence. Such mechanisms are in fact juicy targets for terrorists, because they are vital to the inter-subjective construction of a commonly-sensed familiarity and homeliness of our "world" and are therefore the very means by which this sense can be disrupted and subverted to produce incapacitating conditions of general fearfulness.

The trick is to have disorienting and frightening images of terror situations and apparently present terror agents spread wide and fast. In an age when experiences are communicated well beyond the immediate sphere of the event, through radio and visual media, it is the sight and sounds of horrors which spill out and across channels of communication into the consciousness of entire societies. Reflecting on people's reactions to the exposure of conditions in Nazi death camps in radio broadcast and—most dramatically—on film, Hannah Arendt discussed the ways in which "the fearful imagination" of those who saw images of the holocaust in the media "keep thinking about horrors" (Arendt 1986: 441). This comment reminds us of the central role of the ruminating imagination in the ongoing reproduction of fear. Today, those who endured such terrors often can't help but think about them, just as those who witnessed recent terrors often find it hard not to think about them - most notably, perhaps, the destruction of the World Trade Centre. This last point echoes in the recent research findings of the American "Zogby Organisation", as reported in a piece entitled "Four Years on, New York is still bickering about Ground Zero, and burying its dead" (Usborne 2005). The report "showed 69 per cent of Americans still say that that they think about the 9/11 terror attacks at least once a week." The report states that "it is clear that the American public has been deeply emotionally affected by the events of September 11" (Usborne 2005) and, as the title of the piece suggests, this chronic, fear-ridden unhappiness is crippling the dynamism of the West's most dynamic society: New York itself.

Taking up this iconic example of dangers "we have to live with", in a "new age of terror", we can now examine how strategic use of terror exploits mass mediation of fearful imagery, to produce widespread fear. Having done this, we will consider how this mediation is exploited by both the instigators and eradicators to produce an ongoing condition of general fearfulness, which is the core condition necessary to create the Orwellian permanent state of war, which characterises "the war on terror".

The function of mediated images in the inter-subjective construction of a common sense of fearful situations

People (like us) who were not at a terrifying event, but who "witnessed" the destruction of the World Trade Centre via electronic media, can still recall the experience of standing stock-still next to some mediating technology, hearing and /or viewing the agent of destruction at its terrible work. In scenarios such as this, the media functions as a nexus, linking those who view the event of destruction to the experience of terror, even if they are not immediately terrorised.

The effect of such media events is that of the rumour mill, which still works with effect in modern times. In the mediated reproduction of the event, often attended by some rumour-laden commentary, some reduced echoes of awe and dread are communicated to the non-involved voyeur/listener and while they are not enough to produce terror, they can and often do instil a sense of radical uncertainty and, consequently, fearfulness within them. This fear is approximate to the fear attending terror. It has a positive political potential as far as it is not directly connected to terror and reduced by it to a numbed shock. Fear-inducing recollections of distantly observed terrorising events "are useful for the perception of political contexts and the mobilisation of political passions" (Arendt 1986: 441). However, such fear will fade without fairly regular booster shots of terror, and the more closely entwined the fear is with "bestial, desperate terror" (Arendt 1986: 441), the greater the suppression of its politicising potential. It is for this reason that the mass communication of the terrorising event to observers is so significant in the creation of a common sense of fear. The communication of the implications of the event ensures that the intense energy involved in the event of terror, the incapacitating power which floods into and fills the recipients' senses to the point of bursting, spills out and over the limits of the time and place of its occurrence. Thanks to the transmission of the event, all who witness it—those who were there and were terrorised and those who witnessed from a safe distance and were merely scared—share a common tendency to recall and react.

Having witnessed terror, they find that their minds flash back to it at the trigger of an image, sound or smell. Although to radically different degrees, the terrorised have been traumatised and the witnesses merely frightened, the few victims of terror and the hugely sympathetic witnesses share a sense of the moment of terror, and this sharing produces a common sense of fear. Thus, in modern society, the media provide the link between those who were there and all other social members who witnessed the event of terror via the media, which facilitates the latent capacity of terror to generate widespread, enduring, incapacitating fearfulness.

Using mass media to produce incapacitating fear

The instigators of the condition of fear know that it will endure if it is fed and they know too, that the root of fear is not the knowledge that London, or Madrid, or New York has been bombed, but the uncertainty produced by the knowledge that these or in fact any city might be bombed at any time. Such fear has also been cleverly intensified by the creation of common sense of the lurking presence, a harbinger of doom—an active alien violator of the peace— a post—event commentator on the significance of each dramatic terrorising event; in short, a nemesis in this case known as al-Qa'eda. Thus events such as 9/11 or London's 7/7 are usually followed by waves of images and messages effectively exploiting the initial impact of the terror events. After 9/11, the media carried Bin Laden's image, along with messages signalling the possibility of further attacks, possibly radioactive, and possibly biological somewhere and sometime soon in the western world, and this instilled fear into far more people than did the planes crashing into the towers. A wave of secondary events after London's 7/7 attempted to produce a similar effect. Such fear leads to systemic breakdown in social and economic processes. In the USA people were saying that they were scared to fly. In London people were afraid to get on the tube and were advised not to travel to work. So shops closed, roads closed, planes went empty, the bustle of public intercourse was replaced with the mutterings of private discussions held behind closed and locked doors. Now perhaps, with New York and London bustling again, we might think the effect temporary but the report of the Zogby Organisation reveals how the wounds of the initial event, the trauma of the very being of those terrorised, and the fear-inducing experience of witnessing such terror, has, with the aid of continuous terrorist alerts, endured over many years. In this, we see how the use of the mass media by the instigators of terror instils traumatising images into people's future and hangs around as chronic fearfulness in a long-lasting afterlife of panics and anxieties.

The joint production of the cultural/racial "other as terrorist" functions through a process of "haunting" which is made possible by the de-personalising effect of the terrorist image. The militias' production of significant violent destruction, coupled with the anonymity of the disguised perpetrators, stimulate a general obsession among members of the terrorised society that among them lurk people who look and act like citizens, but who are secretly and profoundly other. This effect is being produced exactly by the activities of al-Qa'eda, and it is aided by a US government which puts up wanted posters of the haunting image of Bin Laden, and a Western media which regularly presents video messages from the "mystery man" and consistently runs "al Qa'eda are among us" stories. The subsequent obsession with the "enemy within" is fed by the eradicationist state's very public establishment of panoptic surveillance in public spaces such as airports and by constant negative imagery "encouraging the stereotypical connections between Islam Violence and fanaticism" (Cesari 2004) typified recently by two news-stories. On the anniversary of 9/11 this year, *The Independent* claimed to reveal "How militant Islamists are infiltrating Britain's top companies" (Malik 2005). An *Irish Independent* story stated "Muslim School in Probe" because "Too much time spent on Koran" so "fears that the school could have become a focus for religious extremism" (Walshe 2005). The implicit anti-Islamic link with terrorism in such stories is left unchallenged by state representatives; negative Orientalist imaginings are facilitated, softening up the citizenry so that it will accept the steady reduction in civil liberties and fast increases in panoptic governance extending throughout the western world. All of this is paraded before our bemused and fearful eyes on TV and radio programmes, newspapers and internet outlets. We can see, hear and even commentate, but in the face of such rumour-full fear mongering, we struggle to effectively challenge the entrapment of our society by the contesting co-producers of the war of terror.

References

Arendt, Hannah. 1986. *The Origins of Totalitarianism*. London: André Deutch.
Baum, John Alan. 1979. *Montesquieu and Social Theory*. Oxford: Pergamon Press.
Burke, Justin. 2004. *Al-Qaeda: The True Story of Radical Islam*. London: Penguin.
Bush, George W. 2002. Transcript of President Bush's speech in Cincinnati, *The Guardian*, 7 October, 2002.
Cesari, Jocelyne. 2004. *When Islam and Democracy Meet*. Basingstoke: Palgrave Macmillan.
Delemeau, Jean. 1978. *La peur en Occident XIVe —XVIIIe Siecles*. Paris: Fayard.
Ferraro, Gugliemo. 1941. *The Reconstruction of Europe. Tallerand and the Congress of Vienna 1814-1815*. New York: G.Putnam and Sons
Freud, Sigmund. 1985. *The Uncanny. Art and Literature: Jensons' Gradiva, Leonardo da Vinci and other Works*. Edited and translated by J. Strachey. Harmondsworth: Penguin.
Gilinsky, Yakov. 2002. Political Transition and Crime, paper presented at the annual international meeting of The European Society of Criminology, September 7, 2002.
Gurr, Nadine and Benajamin Cole. 2000. *The New Face of Terrorism*. London: I. B. Tauris & Co.
Hoffman and Claridge. 1999. Illicit Trafficking in Nuclear Materials, *Conflict Studies*, Jan /Feb: 314-315.
Keane, John. 2001. Fear and Democracy, unpublished paper, 19 February, 2001.
Keane, John. 1991. *Media and Democracy*. Cambridge: Polity
Malik, Shiv. 2005. How Militant Islamists are infiltrating Britain's Top Companies, *The Independent on Sunday*, 11 September, 2005.

Montesquieu, Charles de Secondat. 1949. *The Spirit of the Laws* (translated by Thomas Nugent). New York: Hafner Publishing Company.
Oliver, Mark. 2002. German elections: Race, security, unemployment and religion are key issues in Germany's upcoming general election, *The Guardian*, 19 September, 2002.
Orwell, George. 1954. *1984*. Harmondsworth: Penguin.
Rosenblum, N.L. (ed.) 1989. *Liberalism and Moral Life*. Chicago and London: University of Chicago Press.
Shklar, Judith. 1989. Liberalism of Fear, in N.L. Rosenblum (ed.) *Liberalism and Moral Life*. Chicago and London: University of Chicago Press.
Simmel, Georg. 1971. The Stranger, in Donald N. Levin (ed.) *On Individuality and Social Forms*. Chicago and London: The University of Chicago Press. (Originally published as Der Fremde in *Soziologie*, Munich and Liepzig: Humbolt, 1908)
Said, Edward. 1997. *Covering Islam*. London: Vintage.
Schmitt, Carl. 1976. *The Concept of the Political*, trans. George Schwab. New Brunswick: Rutgers University Press
Shackleton, Robert. 1963. *Montesquieu: A Critical Biography*. Oxford: Oxford University Press.
Sparks, Chris. 1999. *Montesquieu's Vision: Uncertainty and Modernity in Political Philosophy*. Lampeter: Edwin Mellen Press.
Sparks, Chris. 2003. Liberalism, terrorism and Politics of Fear, *Politics* 23 (3): 200-206.
Stern, Jessica. 1999. *Ultimate Terrorists*. Massachusetts: Harvard University Press.
Strayer, Joseph. 1971. *Medieval Statecraft and the Perspective of History*. Princeton, N.J.: Princeton University Press.
Travis, Alan. 2002. British police powers toughest in Europe, *The Guardian*, 13 October, 2002.
Usborne, David. 2005. Four Years on, New York is still bickering about Ground Zero, and burying its dead, *The Independent on Sunday*. 11 September, 2005.
Walshe, John. 2005. Muslim School in Probe, *The Irish Independent*, 10 October, 2005.

CHAPTER EIGHT

ELUSIVE GENEALOGIES: CONCEPTUALIZING RACE IN THE WAKE OF 11 SEPTEMBER, 2001

MALREDDY PAVAN KUMAR

The settler makes his history; his life is an epoch, an Odyssey. He is the absolute beginning... over against him torpid creatures, wasted by fevers, obsessed by ancestral customs, form an almost inorganic background for the innovating dynamism of colonial mercantilism (Fanon 1963: 40).

Just none of us is outside or beyond geography, none of us is free completely from the struggles of geography. The struggle is complex and interesting because it is not only about soldiers and cannons, but also about ideas, about forms, about images and imaginings (Said 1994: 7).

Introduction

Recent studies on the politics of September 11, 2001 (9/11) "terrorist attacks" have tended to focus on the egregious conditions that aroused the event. The socio-economic transformations that preceded the event, the political tensions that resulted from the event, the leaders who came forward to orchestrate the event and the issues which were raised by them have been crucial to the emerging perspectives on 9/11. Among a remarkably broad range of issues, the conventional antinomies of South/North, East/West, Orient/Occident were deployed at the forefront of politics, culture, and difference (Barnett 2003). Within this conventional political rift however, as Friedman observes, new forms of global connections were charted "since the terrorists originated from the least globalised, least open, least integrated corners of the world: namely, Saudi Arabia, Yemen, Afghanistan and northwest Pakistan" (Friedman 2002: 11).

Following the "terrorist attacks", not only religion became the *modus oprerandi* of redemptive political violence on a global scale, but the cultural context of religion was indoctrinated into a more sophisticated racial discourse.

The racism Arab Americans encounter in the United States, as Salaita argues (2005), is also directed at other minorities. Therefore it seems only logical for Arab Americans to demystify stereotypes in conjunction with the minorities at whom racism has traditionally been directed and "approach the question of race in relation to other ethnic minorities" (Salaita 2005: 165). Such trans-ethnic identities after 9/11 are manifest in the epochal and multiform interconnections among racially identified communities around the globe.

The looming ethno-political tensions after 9/11 however, in Spivak's view, cannot be discoursed in terms of religion or race alone: "there is neither mourning nor execution without imagining the transcendental, and the transcendental, when imagined, has cultural names" (Spivak 2004: 88). Cultural names as edifices of *difference*, Spivak asserts, transcend all religious identifies as they refashion the "impersonal narratives" of colonised/coloniser, East/West within which *difference* is fetishised. Situating such "impersonal narratives" of *difference* in a historical context, Sivanandan (2006) argues that the post-9/11 differential politics are categorically different from the racism that is directed at those with darker skins from the former colonial territories. Instead, the "new racism" is redefined by the newer categories of the displaced, the dispossessed and the uprooted others, who are beating at Western Europe's doors—the Europe that helped to displace them in the first place. It is, therefore, Sivanandan contends, a racism that is inlaid with xenophobia, a "natural" but historically crystallised fear of the other(s). But in the way it denigrates and reifies people before segregating and/or expelling them, it is a xenophobia that bears all the marks of old racism. In this sense, the post-9/11 racial politics are viewed not necessarily as a particular reaction to the event. It is an entire culture of imperative ideology of the self (patriotism and European/white identity), including all its "*attendant manifestations*, that existed years before 9/11, which was merely strengthened by the anxiety manufactured in the aftermath of the attacks" (Salaita 2005: 166; emphasis added).

After the terrorist attacks on 9/11 the United States government compiled a long list of suspect Muslim countries. Within these mapped territories resided "terrorists", Muslims and native others. Even though the racial mapping of national boundaries is a recent phenomenon, the cultural mapping of native subjects inside of each mapped territory, as Ludden (2003) remarks, is an historical one. Reinforced by competitive political interests, inscribing civilization and culture within mapped social spaces—where natives essentially belonged and others did not—has been a routine course of bureaucratic enterprise throughout colonialism.

Ballantyne's *The Coral Island* (1990) offers a glaring example of the infirmities of the colonial cultural mapping. After recovering from their ill-fated voyage, Peterkin and his two white friends immediately claim ownership of the island on which they *accidentally* land. Upon their arrival Peterkin exclaims to his friends: "We've got an island all to ourselves. We'll take possession in the name of the king; we'll go and enter the service of its black inhabitants. Of course we'll rise, naturally, to the top of affairs" (Ballantyne 1990: 16). For Peterkin and his friends, the coral island awaits not only to be discovered— inhabited by natives who are *de facto* black—but to be conquered and ruled at the emperor's will. Like Peterkin's adventures through the inexorable passages of an unknown world, the cultural mapping of the native subject was a blind ("accidental") exercise; it was the result of a series of European encounters with the natives. Such encounters, first imbued by wonderment and then embraced by imagination, became the most enchanting testimonials to the narration of native typologies, phenotypes, rituals, witchcraft, and other occult performances of many kinds. In Said's view (1994), the deployment of anthropological discourse as a shared cultural passion by colonial ethnologists falls within this typological narrative tradition. However, after the formal end of colonialism,[i] the culturally inscribed "alien native" was no longer discoursed in terms of cultural space. Even though anthropology continued to explore who belongs and who does not belong to cultural spaces, geography emerged as the new imperialist paradigm to determine "who owns territory and who lives there under sufferance and who is naturally native and who needs naturalizing" (Ludden 2003: 1065).

As Spivak and Sivandandan evoke the "historical crystallisation" of "impersonal narratives", post-9/11 racial otherness is inscribed in a largely unseen historical order of convoluted discursive contexts. These discursive contexts, I suggest, are fatally endemic to the indoctrination of anthropology and geography, within whose textual and intertextual fields belies the mapping of racial otherness.[ii] Re-reading of historical contexts, as Dirks (2002) observes, can serve as a reminder of the *materiality* of all texts as well as the institutions that make it possible, comprehensive and serviceable. If we consider contexts as pretexts, history (colonialism/imperialism) cannot be located outsides of texts (anthropology/geography) but remains within an intertextual field, constructed out of genealogical relations between histories of prior texts and the reflective conditions (cultural/territorial mapping) that are constructed by successive readings of these texts.

Colonialism and cultural mapping

The concept of race in particular was first used in the English language in 1508, but "it was only in the late eighteenth century that the term came to mean a distinct category of human beings with physical characteristics transmitted by descent" (Ashcroft et al 1998), and only in the context of colonial empires that the racial categories were deployed in the form of structured inequality (Jackson 1990).

Throughout the history of European empires the notion of a fundamental otherness between Europe and other civilizations to the South and East was prevalent. For Hellenic Greece, it was the Persian Empire that was seen as inherently alien other (a threat); for the Romans, it was confrontation between the ordered Roman-Hellenic world and a jumble of oriental potentates beyond the empire; for medieval and early modern Europe, an apocalyptic religious struggle between Christianity and Islam; and for Hitler, a new crusade of European civilization against the degenerate forces of Judeo-Bolshevism (Winant 2004). For the colonial empires, the alien other was the absolute unknown or, as describes, the "lack of identity": "Until Europeans took the idea [of Africa] to Africa, no African knew that he lived in a continent which could hopefully be thought of as a whole. No African knew he was an African until his European schoolmaster told him so" (Dathorne 1996: 3).

Wherever the Europeans encountered them, the non-European natives were actively drawn into an enormously wide range of relationships with the ascendant or would-be imperialists and were variously cast as temporarily or permanently different, in relation to the Europeans, according to a wide range of conceptions of difference. Even though the previously uninscribed and unexplored world was inhabited by different civilizations, peoples and their custom, the European view of such differential world was inlaid by an epistemic thrust of pan-otherness. It was the "organic unity" of the East, Europeans acclaimed, which was conducive to irremediable otherness, in spite of the marked geographical, cultural and cosmic disjunctures within the Orient (Palat 2004). [iii] Among other categorical devices, the concept of "organic unity" was crucial to the renderings of anthropological, methodic, and other pseudo-scientific approaches to the preview of an all-embracing, all-encompassing, and uncharacteristically homological Orient.

Pioneered by Colonel Wilks (1810), the notion of "organic unity" in particular became a theoretical lynchpin in Henry Maine's (1876; 1916) doctrines on ancient law, economics, and "village communities" in the East. The village community was defined as an organic body of corporate groups *sharing common land* ordered by law and custom. Although both Wilks's and Maine's observations were limited to India, the pan-oriental image of the village community was exemplified in Marx's later writings on the "Asiatic modes of production." Caught in the perils of "despotism", and "communalism", Indian society featured a distinct colonial context to the enthusiastic observer compared to its counterparts in the East. The quintessential character of India, Maine argued, was "the patriarchal family" (Maine 1876: 16). As in the patriarchal family how each member of the household is assigned different social roles, the

Indian village community too, is organised around the assignment of roles to different individuals. In this sense, the Indian village community is more than a brotherhood of relatives and more than an association of parts:

> It is an organized society, and besides, providing for management, of the common fund, it seldom fails to provide, by a complete staff of functionaries, for internal government, for police, for administration of justice, and for the appointment of the taxes and public duties (Maine 1916: 274).

However fascinating, to Maine, these were nonetheless largely theoretical summations. But to British administrators in India they were questions of immense practical importance. The self-contingent model of the village community was appealing to land surveyors and tax collectors as they found that the idea of property as understood in the western sense was completely absent in India. Moreover, as the traditional land tenure settlements of *malguzari, and ryotwari* "resembled" the features of village community, Maine's writings were in defence of many pet-administrative projects. As such, Thomas Munro's induction of private property in the *ryotwari* areas of Madras (in 1812) and Bombay (in 1818) owed a great deal of gratitude to the writings of Wilks and Maine. Murno was in full agreement with Wilks's view that "it was important to keep the communal spirit of the Indian panchayat" in order to implement British law (Wilks 1810: 119). Since the question of landownership in India was hard to specify, Murno's *ryotwari* system enabled the British to endow individual land titles and collect taxes from the individual owners without actually "disrupting" the "communal spirit" of the Indian village (Dumont 1966).[iv]

Once the parameters of the village community were drawn, the idea of "communal production" became an epistemic expression of Indian social organization. The customary modes of communal production, which was variably known as "joint proprietorship" and "collective production" in the colonial literature, was portrayed as an archaic form of social organization; a living museum of history for the curious Westerner. By the time Maine's (1876) *Village Communities in East and West* became influential, a myriad of ethnological surveys on communal production in various parts of India were already underway. Extensively documented in Firminger's *Fifth Report* (1812), the south Indian systems of communal production known as *Padayal, Mirasi* and *kaniachi* rendered an immense anthropological potential to the British ethnologists. As such, these "southern systems" were embodied by a new ethnological category called "village servants." Unlike the north Indian land tenure systems, the village servants in the south were believed to have held property rights in the form of service (not land) as the servants of "entire villages" (Mayer 1993). However, in some cases, the village servants received property rights in "service tenure" such as land grants known as *inams*. In due course, such property rights were also located in north India. The north Indian *batuldari* system for example, consisted of two types of rights to the village servants—one permanent and hereditary or *watandari* right, and two, temporary or *upari* rights. In either case, the servants were granted *inams*, housing-land, and emoluments for the services they rendered to the "entire village." The constitution of "village servants" as the servants of "entire" villages, receiving collective payments by the "entire" village posed an impossible anthropological challenge to later anthropologists (Dumont 1966; Fuller 1977). While they resided in the coterie of archival reports and ethnological texts, the "servants of entire villages" as an empirical phenomenon was hard to specify.

By any arbitrary definition, a village must constitute people, and more importantly, such people must constitute households. Therefore the so-called "village servants" were either the servants of the individual households or non-household individuals. Furthermore, it is impossible to envisage "village" as an active entity providing land grants and payments to the village servants in its entirety, unless the individual subjects of the "village" assumed certain "entirety" in the guise of communal production. However unrealistic the servants of an entire village may be, for the British ethnologists they persisted in the imaginary hinterlands for the sole purpose of reifying communal production. Indeed, repetition and duplication of ideas is a common theme in intellectual history: the village servants were first mentioned by Murno in a report written in 1808 and then reiterated verbatim by Wilks in 1810, followed by Elephantine in 1819, and finally by Maine in 1916. Far from a picture of facts, as Dumont remarks, the servants of the village community in India were a piece of myth, a belief widely shared by administrators of the period (Dumont 1966: 85).

The wheel has turned full circle. While the idyllic notion of village community invoked the new *ryotwari* act, *ryotwari* justified the tenets of communal production. Whereas communal production heralded the arrival of "village servants", village servants rallied around the village community in a *tour de force*. Dubbed variedly by Maine's contemporaries as the "village republic", "little republic" and "Indian republic", village community was celebrated as the stepping stone of Indian civilization. Subsequently Maine's theories and observations, canonised in the writings of British ethnologists, have become accepted truths of anthropological theory. Among the anthropologists of the day writing on the caste system in India, the concept of village community had a profound influence. As in Fuller's (1977) remark, if the customary modes of land tenure structure were the heart of Indian economy, caste system was the "heart" of Indian anthropology. Indeed, the embodiment of caste-based division of labour was seen as organic to the "self-sufficiency" of Indian villages:

The Indian village community consisted of at least twelve occupational-specialists such as the judge, the registrar, the tailor, the watchman, the water distributor, the astrologer, the carpenter, the potter, the washerman, the barber and the smith. These twelve officers or requisite members of the community, receive the compensation of their labour, either in allotments of land from the corporate stock, or in fees, consisting of fixed proportions of the crop of every farmer in the village (Wilks 1810: 119).

Wilks's definition of occupational specialists lent enough anthropological imagination to William Wiser (1936) to develop a more comprehensive paradigm of Indian subcastes known as the *jajmani* system. Introduced in 1855 by H.H. Wilson in the *Glossary of Judicial and Revenue Terms*, the *jajmani* system emphasised the role of occupational specialists in sustaining the self-sufficiency of Indian villages. Soon after Wilks's (1810) *Historical Sketches of South India* appeared, district commissioners in the Southern and Central Provinces began observing Indian castes for strategic use. Some material castes such as the *rajputs* in North India and the *kshatriya* warriors in the South were already recruited into the provincial military regiments. Where absent, private property was introduced (*ryoitwari*) to elevate the status of selected caste elites for the purpose of revenue control. Where needed, castes and tribes were labelled "criminal" with restricted territorial mobility—all in an effort to "reinstitute" the self sufficiency of the Indian village community. [v] The use of caste at an all-India level to categorize the population according to occupation and social structure formed a more sophisticated basis for British attempts at social engineering. As a result, in 1861 the Asiatic Society of Bengal appeared with a Census consisting of "aboriginal" data of Indian "specimens" with the details of their habitat, name, age, parentage, sex, measurements of height, length of upper arm, lower arm, thigh, leg, breadth of chest and body, colour of skin, eyes, pupils, beard and moustache, length or peculiarity of heel, diet and other asinine details of many kind (Bates 1995).

In a seemingly teleological colonial passage, from the meta-cultural foundations of the Indian village community to the micro-narratives of caste, the body of the Indian subject became the new site of anthropological quest. The 1861 report by the Asiatic Society of Bengal captured the attention of Edgar Thurston, who viewed the study of racial types among the Indians as an extension of his daily routine of labeling and pinning butterflies and of collecting and categorizing the varieties of plants. A trained medical practitioner and the president of the Ethnological Museum of Madras, Thurston claimed that anthropometry was the most important branch of anthropology, which he defined "as measurement and estimation of physical data relating to people of different races, castes and tribes" (cited in Dirks 2002: 163). Many of Thurston's anthropometric discoveries revealed that "intelligence is in inverse proportion to the breadth of nose." Thurston obsession with the racial types of Indian subjects took many sinister forms:

> The Paniyan women of the wynaad, when I appeared in their midst, ran away, believing that I was going to have the finest specimens among them stuffed for the museum. Oh, that this were possible. The difficult problem of obtaining models from the living subject would then be disposed of (cited in Dirks 2002: 165).

While Thurston's anthropometric theories were used to label and restrict "criminal castes" in South India, the 1861 Census produced a four volume dictionary of *the Tribes and Castes of Bengal*, a considerable proportion of which is collected by Thurston's anthropological counterpart, H.H. Risely. Both Risely and Thurston's anthropometric data was centred around the assumption that even the minute socio-cultural distinction of castes could, in time, be traced to some difference in physiognomy, skin colour or bone structure.

This almost alien perspective of the Indian native may sound facetious, but Thurston was in full agreement with Risley that the task of the ethnographer is to digest the massive accumulation of material in governmental reports. In India, anthropology worked on society at the level of the native body. Caste was defined as the genetic territory of Indian society, which was measured and explained in relation to a displaced Victorian enthusiasm for the colonised body (Dirks 2002).

Anthropometric Geography and racial mapping

Once the mapping of Indian cultural territory was complete, the spatial ordering of Indian castes became a crucial measure to the function and progression of colonial science. As such, the idea of a racial difference between *Northern* Indians and *Southern* Indians was first mooted by the observations of Sir William Jones (Bates 1995). At the beck of the north and south racial divide in India stood the Aryan Invasion Theory, weakly supported by linguistic and archaeological evidence.

The sole purpose of the Aryan Invasion Theory was to privilege one race over other, and justify the geographical containment of races across the subcontinent. As such, Risley's anthropometric view of India projected seven basic racial types among the Indians: the Mongoloid, the Dravidian, the Indo-Aryan, the Turko-Iranian, the Mongolo-Dravidian, the Aryo-Dravidian, and the Scytho-Dravidian. Risley maintained that each group was the result of incursions by different racial types into the subcontinent, the Scythians arriving from Central Asia sweeping down the west coast in the second millennium, and the Aryans arriving shortly after (Bates 1995). Risley's findings also revealed that the Mongoloid and the Dravidian races hailed from North-eastern India. Based on skin complexion, Dravidians became the original inhabitants of the South, having mixed with the Mongoloid races. Most of these races, thought to be tribal, were described as being of Dravidian or Mongolian stock, whilst the agricultural or peasant classes of North India were either of mixed stock, or were Aryan in origin. All this evidence, Risley believed, could be testified to the simple act of measurement, though he admitted that his own evidence, at best, suggested only a three-fold racial division between Aryan, Mongoloid and Dravidian. He thus asserted:

> If we take a series of castes in Bengal, Bihar and the United Provinces of Agra and Oudh, or Madras, and arrange them in the order of the average nasal index, so that the caste with finest nose shall be at the top, and that with the coarsest at the bottom of the list, it will be found that this order substantially corresponds with the accepted order of social precedence (Risley 1901: 9).

In this panoply of anthropometric geography however, the "laboratory" was not simply India, but the whole of humankind. Geographers in Europe became intrigued with the task of producing anthropometric geography. The prominent British cartographer H.J. Fleure measured Scottish racial types using a variety of characteristics, including cephalic index, head shape, and pigmentation, and he mapped those individuals whose four grandparents had also lived in the immediate surrounding area of Wales. His method was based on interplay between environment and heredity and was intended to reveal the "concentrated essences of locality" (cited in Winlow 2001: 511). Rentao Biasutti, an Italian geographer, gave cartographic expression to the anthropometric measuring of brains and bones in his construction of the geography of racial provinces. Indeed Biasutti's somatometric cartography was embellished with eight world maps showing the distribution of human trait-occurrences (Driver and Rose 1992). Biasutti's maps became crucial sources of analysis to Terry Jordan's European maps of hair colour, average stature, cephalic index, and the distribution of Caucasian sub races (Jordan, 1973). In a similar context, Griffith Taylor's (1919) climatic theory of evolution incidentally gave rhetorical expression to periphery and centrality, Self and the Other. Taylor's entire career was characterised by his fondest desire to establish a scientific connection between environment and the "superior" Nordic race. In Taylor's cartographic vision of the racial world, the most primitive people were dolichocephalic. The races of brachycephalic head form were the product of later evolution. "Negroes", of course, were long headed and as such represented the earliest phases of human evolution. The Aryans were seen as more highly evolved due to their oval-to-round skull. The Mongoloids represented the most recent evolutionary origins, thus not highly evolved. In the course of evolution, Aryans had driven out the black races from the cradle-lands of civilization, while the migrations of the Mongoloids driven out by the Aryans from Asia. Based on these observations Taylor produced an anthropometric world chart in 1919. A few years later, based on Taylor's chart, Huntington (1924: 131) concluded that the evolution had stagnated in the tropics and therefore that tropical peoples were "in reality the children of the human race." Geography had directed that it was wrong to expect that "such people would ever rise very high in the scale of civilization" (Huntington 1924: 131). Thus, whether through the representations of anthropometric cartography or regionalising of evolutionary history, race and geography were umbilically bound together. In the words of Livingstone (1992: 43), "what genetics had failed to accomplish for white northwest Europeans (Nordic) and trans-Atlantic transplants, geography had."

As early as the eighteenth century, the principles and practices of racial maps became familiar to Europeans. Geography was widely understood as being the crucial element of the period's canons of knowledge (Edney 1997). It was placed as the third arena of polite learning to be mastered by children. Subsequently, it became a prominent part of the British Self vis-à-vis the Indian Other. The rhetoric of colonial historiography then was to describe the coloniser/colonised relationship in terms of geographically intertwined histories of cultural twinship between Indians *and* British, Algerians *and* French, Natives *and* Americans, despite the horrors, bloodshed, vengeful bitterness and racial malice (Said 1994). In India, the cartographic mapping was an exercise in discipline: the British surveyed the Indian landscapes primarily with the aim of assessing and *improving* them. The revenue surveyors in Western India entered into considerable logical convolutions in order to bring communal agricultural practices into line with the ideological conception of the *peasant*—the individual cultivator who embodied the essence of a modern India (Chakrabarty 2001). In the aim of breaking up such "communal practices", surveyors had to mark, and transform the agrarian social structure (*jajmani* system) into revenue structures. The most recalcitrant misfits became "criminal castes and tribes" (Ludden 2003). State officials in India counted people who crossed the lines of state territory, and census officials counted the names of the castes born in one territory who lived in another. Uprooting, detachment, separation and ascription of social identities to authentic spaces provided the basis for the imperialist world vision of alien otherness of the now-colonised native a century later.

Imperialism and territorial mapping:

After the end of colonialism "the whole world had fallen into disorder", declared the American geographer Isaiah Bowman (1921). The rise of new nation-states challenged the conventional geographic order of the world. The states created by the disintegration of European empires remained callipers of colonial constructions, often deliberately divided within themselves by arbitrary ethnic and tribal fractures. The new cartographic passions elicited prominently in territorial security, conflict, as the rise and fall of World Wars instilled fear and instability in Europe. The external and internal margins of national territory became more infested with alien menace and threat amid the territorial anxieties of looming national identity. During the global expansion of modern mapping, national territory incorporated all geography (Ludden 2003). Once the histories of all peoples have come to appear within national maps, the racial and ethnic division of national identities posed new challenge for geography.

With the end of World War One, as the Russian, German, Austro-Hungarian and Ottoman empires ceased to exist, the 1919 Paris Peace Conference was a platform for the resolution of ethnic and territorial sensibilities in Europe. In Smith's observation, Bowman measured the conference's limited success in ethnic terms: "at no time in the history of Europe have political boundaries more closely expressed the lines of ethnic division" (Smith 2003: 176). Ethnicity became the focus of territorial conflicts and of the settlements at Paris. The language of ethnicity in the United States was used to rationalise immigrant nationalities which were deemed inferior to Anglo-Saxon racial norms but superior to African-Americans In relation to European immigrants, ethnicity supplanted "race" and flattened intra-European differences into safe pan-Americanism. Yet the transportation of politics and economic conflicts into "ethnic" squabbles had far reaching ramifications. Ethnicity, as opposed to race, claimed to be a more progressive, historically expressive language.

Although ethnicity is conceptually different from race, it is, in some ways, bound up with race. The social construction of ethnicity, like race, begins with acts of power: the process by which groups are marginalised as different and unequal in their access to social resources from the mainstream society (Barlow 2003). The act of defining people as different also defines other people as non-ethnic, or "normal" and privileged. Racism, of course, can make people ethnic as people can also be marginalised from society on the basis of their real or alleged ties to another nation (national minority) or, in societies with established religions, on the basis of religion. For Bowman, the Post-war ethnic sensibilities and nascent nation building featured a tremendous potential to imperialist intervention. As Smith (2003: 176) writes, in order to bring order into disorder, Bowman claimed that "empire builders must think in terms of geography."

As the Chair of the American Geographical Society between 1915 and 1935, one of the greatest achievements of Bowman's career was the production of the Millionth Map. Spawning over three decades between the two world wars, the Millionth Map was largest geographical project of America. This map, as Bowman boasted, imposed cartographic order on the "almost dark countries" of

South and Central America. The blueprints of the map became base signs for the air navigation charts of the region, and the Panama sheet was the official chart for the US Army Air Corps Pilots in the Central Zone. The Map ran a cover page story in Life and was regarded as playing a "crucial role in the political and economic life of the Western hemisphere, adjusting national boundaries, and guiding technological progress into the wilderness" (Smith 2003: 93). After the completion of the Map, at a celebratory dinner hosted by the Rockefeller Centre, Bowman lauded the fact that its makers had gone: "…out into the unknown and vanquished and charted it … it represents the indomitable determination of men to know the world and master it, but also the forces of civilizations advancing in spite of the high-barriers" (cited in Smith 2003: 97).

The Millionth Map represented the completion of nineteenth century geographic business, as much in tune with the exploratory and imperial vision of Bowman's America as with the realities of modern commerce and politics a half century later.

Renowned as Wilson and Roosevelt's geographer during their presidencies, Bowman's proactive politics in the American intelligence was highly influential. After World War Two, Bowman produced intelligence information in collaboration with French and British geographers and advised the American government on the configuration of the New World. Bowman (1921) used that very title for his study of post-war global geopolitics. As the New World became the centre of global geopolitics, the socialist societies were designated the second world. Geographers then reserved the rubric of third world to map the territorial margins of traditional societies in their pristine cultural states.

Bowman's legacy in American geography is rich. By the late 1980s, the emergence of Area Studies as a sub-discipline of geography, largely influenced by Bowmanian ideology, began remapping continental boundaries in the interest of strategic imperialism. America drew maps of Asia by lumping countries into regions that officially define East, Southeast, Central, and South Asia. The boundaries of Asian and Central Asian republics were drawn "not along geographic or ethnic lines but in ways that seemed likeliest to suppress dissent, dividing clans, villages, and ethnic groups" (Rashid 2002: 36). For instance, in Central Asia the Tajiks acclaimed their own republic, while their cultural and economic capitals of Bukhara and Samarkhand were given to Uzbekistan. Although many maps depicted Asia as including most of Russia and touching the Mediterranean, the American government mapped Asia so as to separate the Middle East from Central and South Asia prior to their political interventions in the Middle East.

For the geographers of Bowman's generation, national states or sub-national units were as important as the larger geo-cultural continental areas (Palat 2004). However, the prior national mapping of the world made it often institutionally difficult for the geographers on Asia and of the Middle East to jointly challenge the attribution of contemporary political outcomes to *culturalist* explanations. Since Islam became virtually synonymous with the Middle East in culturalist conceptions—even though more Muslims live in South and Southeast Asia and in Africa—the American invasion of Afghanistan has led to a partial reterritorialisation of the geographical units within Asia and the Middle East. As a result, the then Asian Afghanistan is now relocated as part of Middle East by virtue of the alleged culturalist association of a "Muslim psyche", although it is more closely linked with Central and South Asia than with Arabia or Egypt. Perhaps it is symbolic of this reterritorialisation of the world based on a regionalisation of cultural identities and the association of Islam with the Middle East that, in a Yale University Press catalogue, books on Pakistan are listed under Middle Eastern Studies rather than Asian Studies (Roberts et al 2003). Mired in such a culturalist vision of American imperialism, perhaps Thomas Barnett's *The Pentagon's New Map* (2003) achieves more than Bowman and his contemporary geographers combined.

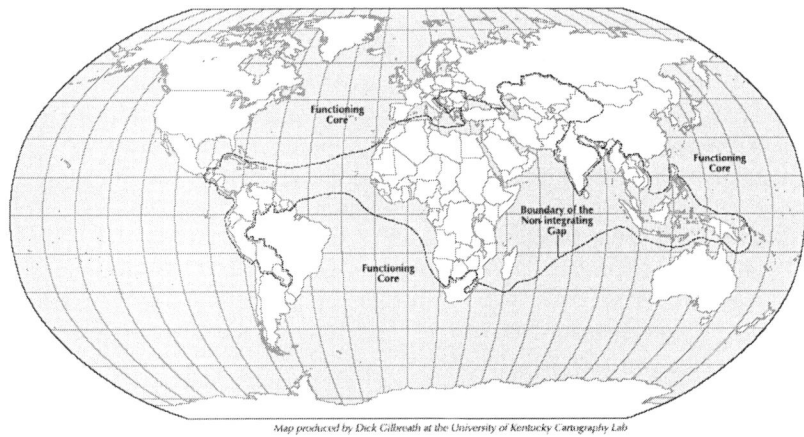

Fig. 8-1: Roberts at. al (2003: 891). *Neoliberal Geopolitics*.

While the arguments in Barnett's work were of recent origin, the ideas underpinning the new cartography were not fresh, as Roberts, Secor and Spark (2003) argue, but have complex genealogies and, as such, reflect much more widespread ideologies of imperialist geopolitics. With its explicit title and descriptive cartography, Barnett's mapping arises from the conspicuous split between "the West" and "the East." A dotted line distinguishes the "Non-Integrating Gap" from the "Functioning Core," while coloured spots mark recent US military engagements of various kinds (Barnett 2003: 174-82):

> The maps on these pages show all United States military responses to global crises from 1990 to 2002. Notice that a pattern emerges ... Draw a line around these military engagements and you've got what I call the Non-Integrating Gap. Everything else is the Functioning Core (Barnett 2003: 181).

In the binary territorial model that the map enframes, "the Gap" consists of regions such as: the Caribbean, Central America (south of Mexico), South America (except for Brazil, Uruguay, Argentina and Chile), Africa (except South Africa), the Middle East (including Turkey), the Balkans, Bulgaria, Romania, Moldova, Armenia, the Central Asian republics, Afghanistan, Pakistan, Kashmir, Nepal, Bangladesh, the Muslim provinces of Western China, and all of Southeast Asia. Barnett seems determined to maintain the Gap as a contiguous area, represented on his West/East globes as a dark blot seeping across the planet from the Caribbean to South East Asia. For Barnett "there is no Gap in the Core, no Core in the Gap", and more importantly, no details that might disrupt his bands of homogenized planetary difference cited in Roberts et al 2003: 889). Instead, the Gap becomes simply an "unfunctional" disposable space, existing only for the purpose of returning to the "functioning core." The Gap is also represented as "a lack", "a hole", "a stain", and "a site of rejection." In Barnett's words, the countries most likely to provoke US military action are those that are either "losing out to globalisation or rejecting much of the content flows associated with its advance" (Barnett 2003: 175). Barnett claims that the two crucial reasons for the Gap's rejection of this advancement are "abject poverty" and "political/cultural rigidity" (Barnett 2003: 175).

In keeping with the expansionist agenda of the Bush administration, Barnett argues that the goal of American foreign policy can no longer be considered in terms of "containment," but rather should follow a more aggressive "shrinking" of the Gap:

> We've got to shrink these parts of the world that are not integrating with the global economy, and the way you integrate a Middle East in a broadband fashion... is to remove the security impediments that create such a security deficit in that part of the world (Barnett 2003: 176).

Containment is inadequate because of the porosity of the "seam" between the Functioning and Non-functioning Cores. It is along this seam, Barnett hopes, that the Core will seek to suppress bad things coming out of the Gap. These "bad things" include terrorism, drugs, disease, instability and (most abstractly) "pain" and so forth. Bin Laden and al-Qaeda are, Barnett writes, "feedback" from the unfunctional Gap to the Functioning Core: "They tell us how we are doing in exporting security to these *lawless* areas (not very well) and which states they would like to take 'off line' from globalisation" (Barnett 2003: 176).

Homogeneity presupposes difference. While Barnett's "shrinking" vision may be coloured by the insurmountable odds of a homogenising world, it is premised on the fundamental difference between the functioning Self and the unfunctional Other.

Conclusion

The day after 9/11, Middle Easterners and South Asians lumped together became the subjects of vengeful retribution. While this exemplifies the arbitrariness of territorialising cultural identities, the necessity of solidarity in the face of nativist discrimination also challenges contemporary ethnic categorisations, since physical differences insulated East Asians, by and large, from those who had the physical appearance of a Muslim, or those who resembled them (South Asians). The ominous Muslim Other is no longer imagined in terms of specific national or territorial identity. The association of "brown skin" with Muslims (and "terrorists") gave rise to collective cultural names and identities. In other words, cultural maps took a territorial form, as the American mapping of the "terrorist" is being inscribed with symbols that contained cultural attachments to spatiality. The Asia that is drawn in Barnett's *The Pentagon's New Map* extends far beyond the old American Astronomical Society map of Asia. It connects the far West and Northwest of Eurasia to South, Central, East, and Southeast Asia to conjure a nameless Asia that also touches Chechnya, Palestine, Armenia, Turkey, Egypt, Sudan, Kenya, Iraq, Saudi Arabia, Turkmenistan, Kazakhstan, Afghanistan, Pakistan, Bangladesh, Indonesia, and the Philippines. Deeply entrenched in popular imaginations, it is this nameless collective other, be it territorial or cultural that appears as a fearsome terrain, filled with volatile, dangerous, irrationally religious people who threaten civilization with deadly chaos.

In contrast, the Western territory persists as the sublime domain, as the enclosure of civility, outside of which lurk the fearsome others in a collective cultural space. Although they are alien people who wander in the traditional ethnographies of the mobile anthropologists, they are incarcerated in native spaces and bounded localities in the cartographies of modern geographers. Anthropologically distinguished, they are alien people who have been carried around in dim memory and its accumulation of detail and authority over time in the cultural cartographies of the Western mind. Geographically distinguished, they are still alien people who are located within or outside the borders of previously colonised territories that vary in scale and coherence from Wales to India and, more generically, to the Orient. If colonialism provided context to anthropology, anthropology as a record of cultural experience is inadequate because, as Bowman asserts, geography "conditions" that experience. In the contemporary discourse of race, however, cultural mapping no more provides context to anthropology, than geography provides context to territorial mapping. It is rather a question of reciprocal constitution.

Notes

[i] Colonialism, a form of imperialism, involves the establishment and maintenance of rule and/or the tangible settlement of people and the displacement or subordination of others (Said 1994). Imperialism is a broader concept, referring to unequal economic, cultural, and territorial relationships based on domination and subordination. However, in this essay, I use the term 'imperialism' with reference to the strategic deployment of metropolitan cultural and capital expansion over the ex-colonial territories, in the post-war context.

[ii] Although both anthropology and geography as imperialist sciences underwent severe criticism, the intricate genealogical lineage between the two disciplines remains largely ignored.

[iii] Unlike the Hellenic concept of the "barbarian" which helped Greeks identify themselves, the Sanskritic concept of *mleccha* did not possess an "otherness" against which one's own identity could be asserted. In the Japanese tripartite view of the world—Tenjiku (India), Kara (China), and Honch (Japan)—Japan was placed not at the centre "but at the end of a geographical succession which moved from the exotic and the sacred (represented by 'Tenjiku') to the mundane and secular (represented by 'Honcho')" (Halbfass 1988: 187; see also Palat 2002: 671).

[iv] One of the District Commissioners from the Central Provinces exclaimed that "surely a more striking example of village communism and of village rights going beyond the ryotwari system of Madras or Bombay could not be imagined" (Bates 1995: 30).

[v] This restriction applied to the occupational mobility of castes as well. To this effect, the 1891 Census was conducted primarily on occupational criteria (see Bates 1995).

References

Appadurai, Arjun. 1998. Putting Hierarchy in Its Place, *Cultural Anthropology*, vol. 3, no. 23: 36-49.

Ashcroft, Bill, Gareth Griffiths and Helen Tiffin. 1998. *Key Concepts in Post-colonial Studies*. London: Routledge.

Ballantyne, M. Robert. 1990. *The Coral Island: A Tale of the Pacific Ocean.* Oxford: Oxford University Press.

Barlow, Andrew. 2003. *Between Fear and Hope: Globalization and Race in United States*. New York: Rowman and Littlefield.

Barnett, S. Thomas. 2003. The Pentagon's New Map, *Esquire*, vol. 139, no. 3: 174-182.
Bates, Crispin. 1995. *Race, Caste and Tribe in Central India: The Early Origins of Indian Anthropometry.* Edinburgh: Centre for South Asian Studies.
Bowman, Isaiah. 1921. *The New World, Problems of Political Geography.* New York: World Book Company.
Chakrabarty, Dipesh. 2000. *Provincializing Europe: Postcolonial Thought and Historical Difference.* Princeton: Princeton University Press.
Cheng, Chu-Chueh. 2002. Imperial Cartography and Victorian Literature, *Culture, Theory & Critique*, vol. 43, no. 1: 1-16.
Dathorne, Ronald. 1996. *Asian Voyages: Two Thousand Years of Constructing the Other.* Westport CT: Bergin and Gravery.
Dirks, Nicholas. 2002. The Crimes of Colonialism: Anthropology and the Textualization of India, in Peter Pels and Oscar Salemink (eds.) *Colonial Subjects.* Michigan: The University of Michigan Press.
Driver, Felix and Gillian Rose (eds.) 1992. *Nature and Science: Essays in the History of Geographical Knowledge.* Cheltenham: Historical Geography Research Group Series.
Dumont, Louis. 1966. The Village Community from Munro to Maine, *Contributions to Indian Sociology*, vol. 9: 67-89.
Edney, Mathew. 1997. *Mapping An Empire: The Geographical Construction of British India 1765-1843.* Chicago: University of Chicago Press.
Fanon, Frantz. 1963. *The Wretched of the Earth.* New York: Grove Press.
Firminger, W. Kelly, ed. 1812. *The Fifth Report from the Selection Committee of the House of Commons on the Affairs of the East India Company.* Calcutta: East Indian Company.
Friedman, S. Thomas. 2002. Globalization Alive and Well, *The New York Times*, September 22, 2002: 10 -11.
Fuller, J. Christopher. 1977. British Indian or Traditional India? An Anthropological Problem, *Ethnos*, vol, 42, no. 3-4: 95-121.
Halbfass, Wilhelm. 1988. *Indian and Europe: An Essay in Understanding.* Albany: State University of New York Press.
Huntington, Ellsworth. 1924. *The Character of Races As Influenced by Physical Environment, Natural Selection and Historical Development.* New York: Scribner's.
Jackson, Peter. 1990. *Maps of Meaning.* London: Routledge.
Jordan, Terry. 1973. *The European Culture Area: A Systematic Geography.* New York: Haprer and Row.
Livingstone, David. 1992. Never Shall Ye Make the Crab Walk Straight: An Inquiry into the Scientific Sources of Racial Geography, in Felix Driver and Gillian Rose (eds.) *Nature and Science: Essays in the History of Geographical Knowledge.* Cheltenham: Historical Geography Research Group Series.
Ludden, David. 2003. Presidential Address: Maps in the Mind and the Mobility of Asia, *The Journal of Asian Studies*, vol. 62, no. 2: 1057-1078.
Maine, S. Henry. 1876. *Village Communities in the East and West.* London: John Murray.
Maine, S. Henry. 1916. *Ancient Law: Its Connection with Early History of Society and Its Relation to Modern Ideas.* London: John Murray.

Mayer, Peter. 1993. Inventing Village Tradition: The Late 19th Century Origins of the North Indian "Jajmani System", *Modern Asian Studies*, vol. 27, no. 2: 357-395.

Palat, R. Arvind. 2004. *Capitalist Restructuring and the Pacific Rim.* London: Routledge.

Rashid, Ahmed. 2002. They are Only Sleeping: Why Militant Islamicists in Central Asia Aren't Going to Go Away, *New Yorker*, January 14, 2002: 34-41.

Risley, H. Herbert. 1901. *Introduction to Ethnographic Appendices.* Calcutta: Government of India.

Roberts, Susan, Secor Anna and Spark Mathew. 2003. Neoliberal Geopolitics, *Antipode*, vol. 35, no. 5: 886-898.

Said, Edward. 1994. *Culture and Imperialism.* New York: Vintage Books.

Salaita, Steven. 2005. Ethnic Identity and Imperative Patriotism: Arab Americans Before and After 9/11, *College Literature*, vol. 32, no. 2: 147-168.

Sivanandan, Ambalavaner. 2006. Race, Terror, and Civil Society, *Race & Class*, vol. 47, no. 3: 1-8

Smith, Niel. 2003. *American Empire: Roosevelt's Geographer and the Prelude to Globalization.* Berkeley: University of California Press.

Spivak, Gayatri C. 2004. Terror: A Speech After 9/11, *Boundary*, vol. 31, no. 2: 71-103.

Taylor, Griffith. 1919. Climatic Cycles of Evolution, *Geographical Review*, vol. 8: 289-328.

Wilks, C. Mark. 1810. *Historical Sketches of South India Vol. 1.* London: Longman.

Wilson, H. Heyman. 1855. *A Glossary of Revenue and Judicial Terms.* Delhi: Munshiram and Manoharlal.

Winant, Howard. 2004. *The New Politics of Race, Globalism, Difference and Justice.* Minneapolis: University of Minnesota Press,

Winlow, Heather. 2001. Anthropometric Cartography: Constructing Scottish Racial Identity in the Early Twentieth Century, *Journal of Historical Geography*, vol. 27, no. 4: 507-528.

Wiser, W. William. 1936. *The Hindu Jajmani System.* Lucknow: Lucknow Publishing House.

Part III

The Racial State(s) of Ireland

CHAPTER NINE

FROM RACIAL STATE TO RACIST STATE? RACISM
AND IMMIGRATION IN TWENTY FIRST CENTURY
IRELAND [i]

RONIT LENTIN

Introduction: Racism in Ireland, the contradictions

Ireland has been confronted with rapid change in circumstances where it was not used to multiculturalism and immigration and the like… It suddenly found itself sucked into a situation which many did not anticipate until it was upon us… I believe this country has been remarkably free from racism. We have not had race riots, thank god, and I hope we never will… (Minister for Justice, cited by O'Regan 2003).

In June 2002 the Irish political parties Fianna Fáil and the Progressive Democrats agreed on a Programme for Government, which epitomises the key contradictions of the Irish debate on racism and immigration. To date, the debate has discussed racism as a societal rather than a state phenomenon (with the exception of Lentin and McVeigh 2006 and Loyal 2003). On the one hand, under the heading "Supporting diversity and tolerance", the Programme for Government promised to *promote greater respect for… the diversity, equality and cultural difference*, to uphold the *entitlement of all people to equal treatment* before the law, to undertake an annual review of the anti-racism campaign in order to identify new avenues to combat racism, and to review the laws on incitement to hatred and ensure that people who incite racial hatred have no place in Irish society. On the other hand, under "Asylum and immigration", the government partners committed to *increase the rate of repatriation* of failed asylum applicants… in order to *maintain the integrity of the asylum policy*, to ensure that new asylum applications *are dealt with within six months,* to deal quickly with outstanding applications, and to keep under review the number of applications from non-nationals to remain in the State on the basis of parentage of an Irish-born child; finally the programme committed to "initiate all-party discussions on the issue of any constitutional or other measures which might be required" (in relation to residency rights of non-nationals) (Department of the Taoiseach, 2002, emphases added).

The June 2003 statement, cited above, by Michael McDowell, Ireland's Minister of Justice, Equality and Law Reform, within whose responsibility lie both immigration control and government-sponsored antiracism initiatives, that Ireland is *not* a racist society, juxtaposed with the commitment in the Programme for Government to both "diversity, equality and cultural difference" and to an "increase in the rate of repatriation", summarised what might seem like the contradictions inherent in the debate on racism in Ireland. While racism is vehemently denied, in-migration is conceived as "new" and "sudden", and the effect of state policies on the lives of racialised populations in Ireland is minimised, the commitment to restrict immigration and increase deportations had never been more explicit. This is in line with what David Theo Goldberg (2002) terms "the culturalist turn" of the past twenty years, according to which denying racism goes hand in hand with state control over incoming and existing populations.

Echoed by a chorus of media commentators, the Minister's insistence that only in the 1990s was Ireland transformed from a "nursery of emigrants" to a destination of in-migration, has been refuted by some commentators (e.g., O'Toole 2000; McVeigh and Lentin 2002). Indeed, multi-ethnicity, in-migration and racism are not new phenomena: Ireland has always been multi-ethnic; Travellers, black-Irish people, Jewish people and other immigrants have been part of Irish society for centuries, and in-migration had always co-existed with emigration (as argued, *inter alia*, by Ward 1999; Tracy 2000). However, together with other socio-economic and political transformations since the mid-1990s, and in particular in the wake of the Good Friday Agreement, recent population transformations have given rise to new articulations of Irishness and to experiences of racism by existing racialised minorities and by new migrant populations.

This chapter conceptualises racism is "a political system aiming to regulate bodies",[ii] rather than the consequence of individual prejudice, involving state, rather than individual or societal formations. I argue that Ireland has been evolving from being, like other nation-states, a "racial state", in which "race" and "nation" are defined in terms of each other—evident in the ethnically narrow framing of the Constitution of Ireland (Lentin 1998)—to a racist state, where governmental "biopolitics" and technologies of regulating immigration and asylum dictate the discursive and practical construction of Irishness and of Ireland's ("new", but also "old") racialised populations. Government constructions of immigrants as progressively "bogus", "illegal", and "economic" discredit them, and via the media, feed into common sense racisms, which manifest in countless everyday incidents of racial harassment and institutional racial discrimination, leading to increasing numbers of racially motivated attacks and murders.

Racial terminology, intent on categorisation and control, constructs the Irish state's response to cultural diversity and the ensuing racism in the wake of increasing immigration since the 1990s, in the shape of "intercultural" politics, which construct cultural difference and ethnic minority "communities" as static and already there, ignoring intra-ethnic heterogeneities and contestations such as class, gender, age, disability or sexuality. Racial state thinking in Ireland has spawned various state-generated euphemisms such as "non-nationals" to describe non-EU migrants (replacing the no-longer-acceptable "aliens" coined by the British-inspired 1935 Aliens Act, which has not been taken off the statute books), and "Irish born children" to describe the children citizen of non-EU migrants. State asylum, immigration and integration policies demonstrate Foucault's theorisation of the modern nation-state as a "state of population", monitoring and controlling through a series of technologies the nation's biological life which becomes a problem of sovereign power (Agamben 1998: 10).

At the heart of state anti-racism initiatives, such as the KNOW RACISM National Anti-racism Awareness Programme, lies the Canadian model of multiculturalism and the "politics of recognition" formulated by Taylor with Canada in mind, according to which "our identity is partly shaped by recognition or its absence, often by the *mis*recognition of others" (Taylor 1994: 75; see Alana Lentin's chapter in this volume). However, this approach, which highlights racism as arising from "lack of knowledge, fear or insecurity, in its more extreme forms (emerging) as racially motivated abuse, direct discrimination and violence",[iii] erases the link between immigration and racism, and unpoblematically conflates "Irishness" and "whiteness", translating "cultural diversity" into "Forty shades of Green".[iv]

In this chapter I examine the seeming contradiction, in contemporary Ireland, between a declared politics of "a caring society" and an increasing tendency to re-define the nation-state's boundaries by controlling not only in-migration, but also the self-definition of existing ethnic collectives within. I begin by exploring David Theo Goldberg's positing the Western nation-state as a "racial state", focusing on the centrality of the law to upholding the racial state. I then discuss Foucault's concept of "biopolitics" which posits the state as controlling while "caring" for the population. My argument that in the twenty first century, the Irish state can be termed not only "racial" but also "racist" is illustrated by the controversy which surrounded Irish citizen children and its centrality to questions of Irishness and otherness. As I argue elsewhere (Lentin 2003), "non-national" mothers giving birth to future generations of "non-nationals", became central to understanding state constructions of nation in relation to the children citizen controversy and to the 2004 Citizenship Referendum. If the 1937 Constitution theorised (Irish) "woman" as central to society's "common good", in the twenty first century ("non-national") woman was seen by the state as "flooding" maternity hospitals, and thus threatening the purity of nation and the security of state boundaries (see Lentin and McVeigh 2006).

Ireland's newly constructed "race relations" industry which is generating resources and income for a large number of statutory, voluntary and community organisations, is keeping out the racialised whose seriously under-funded organisations are rarely consulted, thus making top down (bio)policy decisions *for* the racialised, seen as "not yet ready" to speak for themselves (Lentin and McVeigh 2006). Following Roediger's (2003) and Goldberg's analyses of "racelessness", I conclude by proposing that a critical study of "Irishness" should not place white, settled, Christian "Irishness" at the centre, but rather take seriously the insights about Irishness by its racialised "others".

Ireland as a racial state

David Theo Goldberg posits modern nation-states as racial states, which exclude in order to construct homogeneity—which he sees as "heterogeneity in denial"—while appropriating difference through celebrations of the multicultural. The racial state is *a state of power*, asserting its control over those within the state and excluding others from outside the state. Through constitutions, border controls, the law, policy making, bureaucracy and governmental technologies such as census categorisations, invented histories and traditions, ceremonies and cultural imaginings, modern states, each in its own way, are defined by their power to exclude (and include) in racially ordered terms, to categorise hierarchically, and to set aside. In the modern state, race and nation are defined in terms of each other to produce a coherent picture of the population in the face of a divisive heterogeneity, which may be defined as standing *outside* the state, or about the containment of the "other" within.

Goldberg posits two traditions of thinking about racial states. The first, naturalism, fixes racially conceived "natives" as premodern, naturally incapable of progress. The second tradition, historicism, elevates Europeans over primitive or underdeveloped others as a victory of progress (Goldberg 2002: 43).

Naturalism Irish-style is exemplified in English colonialism, from the seventeenth-century onwards, racialising the Irish, casting them as bestial and incapable of progress. Sinéad Ní Shuinéar (2002) gives several examples of the naturalistic construction of the Irish. Imagining the Irish as homogeneously "wild" and "classless", English racialisation erased linguistic, religious, class and urban/rural heterogeneities, and Irish history was written in the English language in the service of English policy, by the English Ascendancy. Ní Shuineár further argues that just as the Irish were naturalised by the English, they are naturalising their own indigenous others: "popular images of Irish Travellers are merely the most extreme manifestation of an ancient Anglo-Saxon tradition of othering the Irish" (177).

The modern state is about keeping racialised others out and about legislating against the so-called "degeneracy" of indigenous minorities (which explains the persistence of antisemitism and anti-nomadism in the European nation-state regime; see Mosse 1978). For the racial naturalist, the racially subjugated are surplus labour, exploited at best, detritus at worst. For the racial historicist, the racially immature are inserted into historical development, though progress is only possible through mimicry of the Eurocentre (Goldberg 2002: 94-6).

The argument that in-migration and racism are "new" phenomena in Ireland is disputed by Rolston and Shannon (2002), who argue that far from Ireland being a homogeneous society not used to foreigners, especially black people, the "Irish have been encountering people of colour from at least the time of the Vikings" and had "more than enough time to 'get used' to black migrants". The fact that Irish people seem *not* have got used to the presence of people of colour, according to Rolston and Shannon, is due mainly to uneven power relations and unacknowledged privilege. A historicist interpretation of the positionality of people of colour *vis á vis* Irish "whiteness" is another possible explanation. Interpreting in-migration and the presence of people of colour as "new" buys into the elevation of Europeans and the respective racialisation of non-Europeans as working towards progress and equality with the Eurocentre.

While the two traditions overlap, historicism has become dominant since the twentieth century (Nazi and South African Apartheid racial naturalism notwithstanding). Understood as the space of white men of property (see Lentin 1998), the modern state's historicist progressivism aims, through amalgamation and assimilation, to assist its racial others—conceived as not white—to "undo their uncivilised conditions". But beneath its liberalism, historicism camouflages racism, and is ultimately about the ordering zeal of modernity (Goldberg 2002: 80, 92-3).

Zygmunt Bauman (1991) argues that modernity's classifying schemas are about imposing order in the face of the unknown, of control in the face of the anarchic, and are central to the experience of racism. Modernity's struggle to order the world gave rise to chaos and ambivalence; modernity responds to its ambivalence by, on the one hand, repressive state insistence on the *naturalist* order it imposes through law, policy, classificatory modes and immigration controls; and on the other, by revising the categories through which the racial order claims to be known, through, for example, changing citizenship laws (as demonstrated below), but also through racial management technologies such as education, equal opportunities and access, as I argue in relation to the biopolitics regime regulating in-migrants in the Irish state.

While the Irish were naturalised by the British, the Irish state, constitutionally conceived as the space of white, settled men of property, historicises its own racial inferiors. This is achieved firstly[v] through governmental technologies of asylum and immigration control, aiming to restore modernity's order just as all certainties—economic, civil, cultural, sexual—seem to be collapsing; and secondly through biopolitical governmental technologies including regulations governing the lives of migrants, but also equality mechanisms, which reproduce racialised populations as ultimately unequal, since the promise of equality is always conditional.

Biopolitics: From racial state to racist state

In *The History of Sexuality I* Michel Foucault (1990) argues that when natural life becomes included in mechanisms of state power, politics turn into biopolitics, the territorial state becomes "state of population", and the nation's biological life becomes a problem of sovereign power. Through a series of technologies, bio-power creates "docile bodies", and the population—its welfare, wealth, longevity and health—becomes, according to Foucault's "governmentality" theory (1991: 87-104), a *subject*, but also an *object* in the hands of government.

In *Society Must Be Defended* (2003) Foucault uses the concept of "biopower" to demonstrate how the "ethnicisation" of racism shifts its focus from intra-societal degeneration to the threat posed from the outside. Biopower is addressed to living beings and, more specifically, to their mass, as population. The technology of biopower is directed at all the processes that refer to this mass of humans: birth, death, sickness, health, education, welfare, but also the gathering of information about the lifestyle of the population through demography and statistics. According to Foucault, there is a difference between sovereign power of the old territorial state ("to make die and let live") and modern biopower ("to make live and let die"). If the old order exerted the right to kill, the new biopower aims to make the care of *life* the concern of state power, exercised by governmental technologies such as the hospital, the psychiatric clinic, the prison, and, I would add, the refugee hostel and the detention centre.

The modern state, according to Foucault, can scarcely function without becoming involved with racism, which he sees as "the break between what must live and what must die" (2003: 254). Race no longer serves one group against another, but becomes a "tool" of social conservatism and of state racism: a racism that society practices against itself, an internal racism, that of constant purification and social normalisation. In constructing homogeneities, the state therefore is not only denying its internal heterogeneities, it is also a normalising, regulating biopower state. As opposed to scapegoat theories of racism, which argue that under economic and social duress, sub-populations are cordoned off as intruders, blamed and used to deflect anxieties, Foucault's theory of racism is an expression of an ongoing social war nurtured by biopolitical technologies of purification. Thus racism is internal to the bio-political state.

Foucault concludes on an ominous note. While the deadly play between a power based on the sovereign right to kill and biopolitical management of life was exemplified at its worst in the Nazi state, it is not housed there alone but appears in all modern states, and racism is intrinsic to the nature of all modern, normalising states and their biological technologies, occurring in varying intensities, ranging from social exclusion to mass murder.

The rest of the chapter links racialising technologies with the forms biopower takes in the contemporary Irish state, which, in doing all it can to maintain its homogeneity by "managing" ethnic diversity, is not merely "racial" in its formation and use of discourses and practices such as the law, but also "racist" in terms of using biopower governmental technologies to control, in particular, though not exclusively, migrant and minority ethnic populations.

The law in the service of the racial state

> There is no two-tier system of Irish citizenship. It is not disputed that every person born on the island of Ireland is entitled to be an Irish citizen; however, while an Irish citizen child has *certain* rights to remain in Ireland, these are *not absolute*. In cases where the non-national parents of an Irish born child are found not to have an entitlement to remain in the State, the law recognises their responsibility in certain cases to bring their child out of the State with them (Minister for Justice, Michael McDowell 2003).[vi]

Goldberg posits the law as central to modern state formation and a technology of racial rule, promoting racial categorisation and identification, and shaping national identities through legislating on citizenship rights and immigration controls. While under naturalist regimes the law was a means of legitimising physical violence, with historicism, the law shapes race in legal terms, threading it into the fabric of the social. Since the neutrality of the law is no guarantee of equal treatment, constitutions might be suspended (or not extended) in relation to racially defined populations.

While "the narrowing of social heterogeneities in the name of racial conception is not something simply or merely ordered by state instrumentalities" (Goldberg 2002: 149), I want to suggest that Irish naturalism regards non-Irish others as inadequate candidates for citizenship defined as "full membership of the community", employing patently racist legislation to control indigenous and migrant minorities, as I demonstrate in this chapter.

In 2003 the Irish state was explicitly contesting accepted definitions of populations. One illustration of the use of the law by the racial state is the discriminatory policies towards Irish Travellers. It had taken Travellers a long time to be recognised as an ethnic group, yet on October 15 2003 the Minister for Justice could claim that Travellers "do not constitute a distinct group from the population as a whole in terms of race, colour, descent or national or ethnic origin", which is why, he argued, rather circularly, "discrimination against Travellers" was inserted as a "separate ground" into the Equal Status Act and the Employment Equality Act—combining a biopolitics of "caring" for Travellers with their discrimination.[vii] Further limiting their rights, the 2002 Housing (Miscellaneous Provisions) No. 2 Bill, criminalising Traveller camping on public and private property, gives Gardaí (Irish police) powers to arrest people without warrants, allows property to be confiscated and disposed of and trespassers to be jailed for a month or fined up to €3,000.[viii] This despite the fact that commitments to provide adequate accommodation to Travellers made by the government in its Task Force on the Travelling Community (1995) went largely unfulfilled.

In July 2002 the government decided to terminate the funding for the Citizen Traveller project. The Minister for Justice stated that the campaign "did not achieve significant success in its main objective—"healing the divide in Irish society that stands between the settled and Traveller communities"[ix]—thus again avowing "concern" for Traveller welfare. However, the Irish Traveller Movement expressed its disappointment and anger at the suspension of the campaign, due, the ITM claimed, to its decision to run an outdoor poster campaign highlighting the negative implications for Travellers of the "trespass law" and declaring the law "racist" (ITM 2003).

The decision to end the funding illustrates the contradiction between the racial state's racially naturalist approach to indigenous minorities and its alleged commitment to anti-racism, based on a Foucauldian "biopolitics", according to which the role of the state is to "manage" the population. Conversely, Irish historicism seeks to master increasing heterogeneities, which in relation to indigenous minorities translates into assimilationist policies enacted on Travellers by successive governments, but ultimately aiming to segregate them (O'Connell 2002).

At the same time, the Irish state was employing immigration legislation in order to prevent migrants from gaining equal access to the state. Thus the 1996 Refugee Act, hailed as "progressive" at the time of enactment, because it broadened the Geneva Convention definition of "refugee" to include "membership of a particular social group" extending to membership of a trade union, being either male or female, or having a particular sexual orientation, was superseded by the 1999 Immigration Bill and the 2000 Illegal Immigration (Trafficking) Act, before it was itself amended on 15 September 2003. The amended 2003 Refugee Act focuses on issues of applicants' credibility, mandates finger printing of all applicants, makes provisions for detention, and disallows applications from countries designated as "safe countries". In a press release, the Department of Justice, Equality and Law reform (DJELR) combines restrictive measures with "care" for "genuine refugees", making clear that these amendments "are based on the experience of operating the Refugee Act... in particular in dealing with the high level of *unfounded and abusive applications for asylum* and the high number of 'no shows' at interviews, which are tying up large amounts of resources which could be better used to provide support to *genuine refugees"*.[x] However, the amended Illegal Immigration (Trafficking) Act, according to the Irish Refugee Council, shifts the focus from identifying persons in need of protection, "towards techniques devised to *screen out as many applications as possible"*.[xi]

The amended Refugee Act and the Immigration Act also enabled increasing deportations. Since 1999, a total of 2,268 deportations have been carried out. Another 611 left the state voluntarily, bringing the total that have left the state (and informed the authorities) to 2,520 since 1999. In addition, 230 Dublin II transfer orders were signed and 65 were carried out (Irish Refugee Council 2005). In 2004 alone a total of 599 deportations were carried out from 2,866 deportation orders signed by the Minister of Justice. Top countries of origin: Romania: 647 orders issued and 250 people deported; Nigeria: 946 orders issued and 77 people deported; China: 166 orders issued and 18 people deported; Moldova: 134 orders issued and 57 deported (Lentin and McVeigh 2006).

One poignant illustration of the use of the law in controlling the citizenship rights of migrant populations is the relationship between the Irish state and migrant parents of children born in Ireland, who are therefore Irish citizens, as reconfirmed in the amended Article 2 of the Irish Constitution, as part of the 1998 Good Friday Agreement (GFA):

> It is the entitlement and birthright of every person born in the island of Ireland, which includes its islands and seas, to be part of the Irish nation. That is also the entitlement of all persons otherwise qualified in accordance with law to be citizens of Ireland. Furthermore, the Irish nation cherishes its special affinity with

people of Irish ancestry living abroad who share its cultural identity and heritage (Constitution of Ireland 1998).

The debates on immigrants' citizenship and residency rights obscured the fact that citizenship was constitutionally granted to anyone who was a citizen of the Irish Free State before the 1937 constitution. In addition, the 1956 and 1986 Nationality and Citizenship Act grants citizenship to anyone born in the 32 counties of Ireland, except "children of aliens entitled to diplomatic immunity in the State at the time of birth". Thus amending the Constitution to grant automatic citizenship to people born in Ireland as part of the GFA was nothing new; what *was* new was their explicit entitlement to membership of "the nation".

The GFA amendment meant, as was ruled in a 1990 Fajujonu Supreme Court case, that migrant parents of children born in Ireland had a claim to remain in Ireland to provide "care and company" to their citizen child. This process of application for permission to remain was overturned in January 2003 when the Supreme Court ruled in the Lobe and Osayande appeal, that "non-national" parents no longer had a strong case to be allowed to remain in Ireland to bring up their child (Maddock and Mallon 2003). The Lobe and Osayande case involved two families of Czech Roma and Nigerian origin respectively against whom deportation orders were made. In both cases, the parents claimed that their decision to remain resident was in their children's best interest. The Supreme Court, however, privileged the State's right to deport, and the "integrity of the asylum process" over these citizen children's rights, although it did not rescind the citizenship right of persons born in the island of Ireland, nor did it have any impact on the decision of whether to recognise an individual as a refugee (CADIC 2003).

The media debates following the January 2003 Supreme Court ruling exposed two contradictions. One contradiction is between nationality and citizenship. The *ius sanguinis*-based rights to Irish citizenship allows up to third generation Irish emigrants to claim Irish citizenship, while at the same time, the state is contesting the *ius solis* citizenship rights accorded to children of migrants by the insertion of Article 2 into the Constitution. According to Siobhán Mullally (2003), reporting migrant numbers "spiralling out of control" feeds into an irrational fear of the "other", creating a climate of insecurity within which racism and xenophobia flourish. These fears, Mullally stresses, are most evident in the Irish government's attempt to deny the right of residency to migrant parents of children who have *ius solis* citizenship rights, by placing a question mark on these citizen's "absolute" rights of residency (as evident from the above quote by the Minister for Justice).

The second contradiction exposed by the Supreme Court decision is between two constitutional entities, "the nation" and "the family", termed in

Article 41.1.1 of the Constitution as "the natural primary and fundamental unit group of Society". The ruling juxtaposed the "integrity of the asylum process", interpreted as the right of the Minister for Justice to deport, and the right of the racial state to impose order by controlling the residency rights of migrants living in its jurisdiction, and the constitutional integrity of "the family", which, however, was never intended to have an exclusive "birth connection with Ireland" (Binchy 2003).

The court's ruling in the Lobe and Osayande case (Maddock and Mallon 2003; Coulter 2003) illustrates the centrality of the law as a governmental technology employed by the racial state. Chief Justice Ronan Keane's judgment upheld the rights of the state by insisting on the "inherent power of Ireland as a sovereign state to expel or deport non-nationals". Keane gave a socio-political interpretation to his ruling by stressing that while the ruling in the 1990 Fajujonu case was given at a time of low levels of in-migration, "the state could not be expected to disregard the problems which an increased volume of immigration inevitably created". Arguably upholding "control in the face of the anarchic, of order in the face of disorder" (Goldberg 2002: 94), Keane ruled that the State "was entitled to take the view that the orderly system of dealing with immigration and asylum applications should not be undermined by persons seeking to take advantage" of the system. Justice Susan Denham further argued that "it does not follow from the rights of citizenship and residency of a minor child that the child is entitled to the society, care and company of his parents *in Ireland*..." If the common good requires it, Denham added, "the Minister has the right to terminate the residence in Ireland of non-national parents of Irish citizens, leading to either the break up of the family or the *constructive* deportation of the child citizens" (Maddock and Mallon 2003, emphases added). By creating a new category of "constructive deportation", Denham prioritised the racial state over the individual citizen and her family. According to Mullaly, the ruling proves that "the protection of a child's claim to reside within a State (is) made dependent on the legal status and behaviour of her or his parents... in place of a concern with the child's best interests, the State substitutes its own interest in immigration control".

In the wake of the ruling, on February 19 2003, the Minister of Justice removed the process whereby an immigrant parent could seek permission to remain in Ireland solely on the grounds of having a child citizen. Any applications for leave to remain made exclusively on the basis of being the parent of an Irish citizen that had not been determined by then were not going to be processed any longer; parents would only be entitled to apply for residency after a deportation order had been issued. In the summer of 2003 letters began being issued by the Department of Justice Equality and Law

Reform to some 11,500 parents whose residency applications remained pending on 19 February 2003.

The Citizenship Referendum

On June 11 2004 the government of the Republic of Ireland asked the electorate to vote in a referendum to amend article 9 of the Constitution to remove birth-right citizenship from children born in Ireland who do not have at least one parent who is an Irish citizen or who is entitled to Irish citizenship. The amendment did not include the children of the 1.8 million holders of Irish passports not born in Ireland who have one Irish grandparent and who are therefore entitled to Irish citizenship without having to set foot in Ireland. The government's argument was couched in "common sense" terms, persuading 79.8 per cent of the electorate to vote in favour of the proposal, aiming to safeguard the "integrity of Irish citizenship". However, an exit poll conducted by RTÉ, the national broadcaster, found that a significant proportion of those voting "Yes" said they were motivated by "hostility to immigrants" (Love 2004).

Amongst other things, the Referendum resulted in changes in relation to migrant parents of Irish citizen children. For a period of almost two years, the Minister for Justice declared his unwillingness to reverse his decision or entertain any policy recognising en masse migrant parents of Irish children who had lawfully applied for residency. Not only did the government refuse to grant residency to migrant parents, but among the people deported between 2002 and February 2005 there were at least 20 citizen children. As late as November 2004 the Minister said in reply to a Dáil (parliament) question that any amnesty for parents seeking residency on the basis of having an "Irish-born child" would cause "chaos" (O'Brien 2004).

However, rhetoric aside, on January 15 2005, six months after the state won the Citizenship Referendum, the decision was reversed and the Department of Justice, Equality and Law Reform announced the details of the new administrative arrangements for parents of Irish children, born before January 1 2005, to apply for residency in Ireland. By July 2005 some 18,000 people applied for residency, even though they were made to sign away any rights for family reunification. This *volte face* had most probably more to do with the huge cost of potential court cases by migrant parents than with humanitarian reasons, though the Minister did not adequately explain this reversal of fortunes (Lentin and McVeigh 2006).

Market-driven migration in the service of the racial state

Cultural diversity has always existed in Ireland. Of late, it has been highlighted due to a significant increase in inward migration in recent years...There are now more black Irish and other EU and non EU citizens living in Ireland, who experience racism on the basis of skin colour and ethnic origin... (KNOW RACISM).[xii]

The above quote from the government-funded National Anti-Racism Awareness Programme upholds diversity as a positive value, occluding the Irish state's determination to do all it can to restrict immigration. Loyal (2003: 74) argues that the current hegemonic construction of Ireland as an "open, cosmopolitan, multicultural, tourist friendly society", obscures a "harsh reality of capitalist production, exclusionary nationalism and growing xenophobia in relation to both the state and the general populace". The economic boom, instead of allaying racist fears, has "consistently treated non-national immigration as a political problem". However, the capitalist accumulation argument does not fully explain the relationship between the racial state and immigration in an era when "immigration" has become the new name of "race" (Balibar 1991: 222).

While the absence hitherto of an "ethnicity" question in the Irish census of population, makes it impossible to quantify the numbers of "ethnic minorities" residing in Ireland (see King-O'Riain in this volume), the 2002 census of population returned nationality figures, according to which 5.8 per cent of the population were "non-national". Of the 10.4 per cent born outside the state, a substantial number are returning Irish emigrants: for example in 2002, of 47,500 in-migrants, 18,000 were returning Irish migrants (Mac Éinri 2003: 7).[xiii]

According to 2005 Central Statistics Office figures, by April 2005 the number of people who do not describe themselves as "Irish" living in the Republic of Ireland approached 400,000 (or 10 per cent of the population), up from 240,000 in the 2002 census, an increase of 40 per cent. Assuming immigration continues to grow, the CSO predicts the proportion of foreign-born people could increase to 18 per cent, or one million, by 2030. 100,000 people migrated to Ireland between December 2004 and December 2005 from the new EU accession countries, headed by Poland and Lithuania, helping fuel the five per cent increase in the number of people employed over the year, a figure almost unknown in the global economy (O'Brien 2005). In 2005 only 13 per cent of immigrants, or 9,000, came from the "rest of the world", down from 14,900 the previous year and 17,700 in 2003. This puts paid to the notion that the Republic is "flooded" with illegal immigrants and asylum seekers, whose numbers have gone down from a peak of 11,634 in 2002 to 4,766 in 2004, and 4,323 in 2005, due, primarily, to increasing numbers (over 4,000 per annum in

2004 and 2005) being refused leave to land to present asylum applications (Humphries 2005; Mac Cormaic 2005).

Decisions in relation to migrant labour are clearly dictated by the state's market needs, not by the human factor, another obvious illustration of the control exercised by the racial state over its boundaries. In 2000 the Tánaiste (Deputy Prime Minister) Mary Harney that a failure to address Ireland's labour shortage could undermine its economic growth, since wage rates and the availability of skilled workers were central to the concerns of multinational companies making investment decisions (cited in Loyal 2003: 79-80). She also said that once EU enlargement was put in place, the numbers of non-EU migrant workers would fall, a self fulfilling prediction, confirmed by the large numbers of labour migrants from the EU accession states. The key role of migrant workers in Ireland's "Celtic Tiger" economy was highlighted in 2004 by predictions that Ireland will need 50,000 immigrants per year over the next five to twelve years, in order to sustain its economic growth (Hughes and Quinn, 2004; McGarry, 2005).

Despite this reliance on migrant labour, various studies (e.g., Conroy and Brennan 2003; Cunningham et al, 2003; MRCI 2004) document their exploitation and the exclusionist and arguably racist policies operating within the Irish state in relation to migrant workers. Cunningham et al found policies based on collusion between state and business, the "natural result of a neo-liberal and market driven environment", and argue that "the psycho-babbling concept of multiculturalism being proposed in the Irish context fails to address existing problems and may even be creating problems for the future" as it creates serious moral burdens which would be difficult to justify in the light of the abuse and discrimination migrant workers experience.

In the spirit of the racial state's biopower, in 2005 the government established the Irish Naturalisation and Immigration Service (INIS), a "one-stop shop" for immigration, asylum, visas and citizenship services making "key linkages to the work permit system"; according to the Minister for Justice, INIS will provide "a strong foundation for *better service provision* and the *enhancement of enforcement strategies* in these areas" (Mac Cormaic 2005, emphases added).

Furthermore, the fingerprints of biopolitics and the racial state are evident in the recommendations made by some of the studies cited above. Thus Mac Éinri's study for The Immigrant Council of Ireland epitomises the contradictions inherent in the racial state both "managing" its population and policing those wishing to enter its borders. The ICI's report starts by stating the state's market requirements by recognising that migrants are "needed to meet employment shortages in virtually all sectors", but echoes the state by strongly rejecting unrestricted immigration as "impracticable" (due to EU harmonisation, but also to the need to provide health, transport, housing and education services to a putative "flood" of future labour migrants). The ICI demands humane, rights-based immigration policy, while calling for "clear integration policies" and "a managed policy" (which, admittedly, includes issues such as family reunification, issuing employment permits directly to migrant workers not their employers, anti-racism measures, the regularisation of undocumented migrants, etc.). The ICI uses the racial state's language of control in recommending an "integrated" approach, which includes terms such as "regulating" (recruitment agencies), "mandatory licensing" (of language schools), and "mainstreaming" (Mac Éinrí 2003b). In a briefing paper on the proposals for an Immigration and Residence Bill, the ICI proposes to balance the government's proposals on "managing migration to serve the needs and security of the state" with a focus on human rights and entitlements, active integration policies and a recognition of the economic, social and cultural benefits to immigrants. Rather than relax the work permit system, the ICI recommends "greater regulation" of the work permit system while also expressing concern on the government's reliance on workers from the enlarged EU (ICI 2005).[xiv]

Similar language was used by the NCCRI's advocacy paper on migration in Ireland (NCCRI 2002), even though Piaras Mac Éinrí's contribution to the document cautions against increasing EU harmonisation in this regard. Unless accompanied by a (highly unlikely) guarantee of civil rights, Mac Éinrí warns, "the net effect will be to reinforce the creeping marginalisation of immigrants" (Mac Éinri 2002: 51). Likewise, Martin Ruhs's study for the Trinity College Policy Institute (2005) makes recommendations in the spirit of guarding the state's (not necessarily migrant workers') interests. While recommending stricter employment laws and employer sanctions, including a labour inspectorate, Ruhs also recommends tightening the regulations of employing non-EEA students (Ruhs 2004: xv-xvii).

I want to suggest, after Goldberg (2002: 203-5), that the language of harmonisation, integration, management and mainstreaming is part of the construction of homogeneity as "heterogeneity in denial", but, more crucially, of a multicultural discourse of "racelessness", denoting a historicist shift from biologically-driven to culturalist conceptions of race. Assuming an ability to solve almost any problem put before them, including immigration, modern states, including Ireland, make claims to "racelessness", which disavows the everyday racism experienced by racialised populations in the name of a universalist utilitarianism which asserts control over all dimensions of social life.

Conclusion: Multiculturalism, integration, and the promise of "racelessness"

Racism is the exact opposite of the values of respect and welcome and fair play which Ireland is known for... The (KNOW RACISM) National Anti-racism Programme is setting the tone by saying clearly that Ireland wants to be a country free of racism and discrimination against minorities... By saying 'no' to racism... we are saying 'yes' to an honest discussion about where we are, where we want this country to go... *That does not mean adopting an open-door immigration and asylum policy.* No country operates such a system and we are not going to do so either (Taoiseach Bertie Ahern, at the launch of the National Anti-Racism Awareness Programme, 25 October 2001, emphasis added).[xv]

Ireland is now and will remain a country with a significant minority born outside Ireland, coming from diverse ethnic and cultural backgrounds. Our task is to *integrate these diversities* successfully (Minister for Justice, John O'Donoghue, Towards a National Action Plan conference, March 2002, emphasis added). [xvi]

Since the mid-1990s, Ireland's ethnic landscape has changed dramatically. "Multiculturalism", or its Irish version, "interculturaism", has become a common linguistic currency, yet the experiences of "the multiculturals" translate into various versions of Afro-Celtic fusions, while their everyday, institutional and state racist undertones are disavowed in the name of racelessness, as illustrated by the Taoiseach's denial of racism, side by side with his rejection of an open-door migration policy, quoted above.

Integration is unproblematically posited by state agencies implementing interculturalist policies. In a report by the Interdepartmental Working Group on the Integration of Refugees in Ireland (1999) titled *Integration: A Two Way Process,* "integration" is defined as " the ability to participate to the extent that a person needs and wishes in all of the major components of society, without having to relinquish his or her own cultural identity". This definition is founded on a "politics of recognition" type of multiculturalism, eschewing a power analysis and erroneously assuming, as Phil Cohen reminds us, that

> The multicultural illusion is that dominant and subordinate can somehow swap places and learn how the other half lives, whilst leaving the structures of power intact. As if power relations could be magically suspended through the direct exchange of experience, and ideology dissolve into the thin air of face-to-face communication (Cohen 1988: 13).

By stressing integration as a "two way process", the state puts equal onus on migrants and refugees to play their part, obscuring unequal power relations. This document, like similar documents emanating from state bodies dealing with integrating refugees and migrants, in constructing immigrants and asylum seekers as both "new" and a "problem", re-conceptualises "the nation" not only as homogeneous, but also as "invaded" by "floods" of refugees, and therefore as arguably "porous" (see King 1999). Irish public and media debates regarding asylum seekers have been couched in a set of euphemisms that not only disavow racism and silence its victims, but also obscure the invisibility of "whiteness".

Summarising the shift from naturalism to historicism, Goldberg (2002: 200-238) argues that naturalism's "violence of an imposed physical repression" gave way to historicism's "infuriating subtleties of a legally fashioned racial order" where the law is committed to the "formal equality of treating like alike (and by extension the unlike differently)". Despite the fact that since the 1930s race has been dismissed as a premodern marking, it is central to the modernising state, which seeks, through race, to mediate and manage the tensions between the economy and society, and, significantly, to maintain white privilege and power. If naturalist states are about expulsion and exclusion, historicist states modernise by claiming to educate those regarded as less developed, and seeking to marginalise and manage surplus populations. If naturalist states entail a "state of whiteness" as final solution, aiming for racelessness as racial hygiene, historicist states seek the racelessness of absorption and transmogrification of the racially differentiated into a state of rationality defined by white standards and norms. The contemporary promotion of globalised flows of human, social and financial capital, and the rendering of national borders porous mean that modernising naturalist racial regimes become segregationist and historicist regimes opt for racelessness as the mark of modernising global commitment, burying their racial articulations beneath vocal dismissals of naturalism as modernising prehistory.

In Europe the shift to a language of ethnic pluralism and multiculturalism means the relative disappearance of any reference to European colonialism (and in the Irish context the disavowal of Irish involvement in British imperial armies, but also of generations of missionaries arguably engaged in "cultural imperialism"; see Mac Éinri in this volume). The ethnic (re)turn makes it impossible to directly refer to contemporary racism in Europe. While supposedly committed to integration and multiculturalism, in espousing explicit policies against racial discrimination, the multicultural racial state distances itself from the phenomenon:

> Everyday racisms in private spheres proliferate behind the veil of their public disavowal in the name of ethnic pluralist and multicultural decency, on one hand, and the substitution of racial reference by the coded terms of policy concerns over immigration, criminalisation, and the integrity of national culture on the other (Goldberg 2002: 218).

The modern racial state, while promoting racelessness, is always about its own white superiority. While declaring its commitment to equality, care and interculturalism, the Irish version of racelessness, the state seeks to continually redefine the boundaries of belonging in racial ways. Thus the preface to the NCCRI document *Towards the Development of a National Action Plan Against Racism* by the Minister for Justice declares as a government priority "the tackling of racism for promoting an inclusive society, by defining what integration actually means in practical terms" (NCCRI 2002). Yet the document mentions neither state racism and immigration policies, nor Irish white, Christian, settled privilege.

Elsewhere (2002: 230), I argue that multiculturalism Irish style is built on Westocentric assumptions, which do not deconstruct power relations, disempowering migrant and minority organisations through competition for scarce funding. Deirdre Coghlan (2003) demonstrates the way in which the state racialises and racially excludes refugees by charting the trajectory from the paternalistic approach to programme refugees, conceived as "deserving and rights-bearing" by the Department of Foreign Affairs (DFA), to the restrictive approach to asylum seekers, regarded as "undeserving, fraudulent and criminal" by the DJELR. She further argues that criminalising asylum seekers as un-deserving was enabled by earlier DFA constructions of refugees as deserving and *entitled to help* under the Geneva Convention, but also by the dialectical self glorification of the Irish as generous donors and helpers. While officially condemning racism, the everyday experience of racism was kept out of the debate, thus privileging the DJELR discourse. Prophetically, as it turned out, Coghlan argued that her analysis demonstrated that the Minister for Justice was intent on silencing all alternative discourses until his plans were in place (Coghlan 2003: 52-3).

Goldberg suggests that the racial status quo, with racial exclusions mostly favouring middle class whites, is maintained by governmentalities of formalising equality. But behind the formalisms of legally mandated equalities, inequalities of race are routinised. Racelessness, be it US colourblindness, Brazilian "racial democracy", post-Aparheid "non racialism" or European multiculturalism, becomes the public way of "speaking about racial conditions in the face of their... unspeakability... Race supposedly could not even be discussed as a public policy concern save to render its expression off-limits to public political and policy debate" (Goldberg 2002: 221-2).

After Hesse (1999), I propose substituting Irish interculturalism's "politics of recognition" with a "politics of interrogation", which, in the Irish context, entails an interrogation of "the nation" and its heterogeneities, and of the unspeakable privilege of Irish whiteness. Committed to a politics of heterogeneities, I posit, after Roediger (2003), nonwhiteness in thinking about race in Ireland, not meant here as an offensive term, but rather as a starting point to interrogating how the *nation* can become other than white, Christian and settled, by privileging the voices of the racialised and subverting state immigration but also integration policies.

Furthermore, according to Bhattacharyya et al (2002; and as argued by Lentin and McVeigh 2006), racialisation has to be understood in the context of globalisation, which has transformed our conceptions of race and racism. Global factors impinging on migration are increasingly discussed in relation to the coupling of migration with discourses of "security" and "the war on/of terror". These developments, in Ireland and elsewhere, confirm the argument of this chapter, which repositions the racial state as central to discussions of racism and immigration in twenty first century Ireland, as well as the broader context of current global developments in which racial states combine in what Agamben (2005) calls "the global civil war". The contemporary "politics of fear" and the regime of global security dominate the "global migration regime", governed by neo-liberal states and supported by organisations such as the International Organisation of Migration (IOM). Ultimately, this regime, designed, *inter alia*, to construct consensus, aims to bring to an end the long-term settlement of migrants in Western societies, and casts a long shadow on any discussions of the integration of so-called "new communities" into so-called "host societies" in Ireland as elsewhere.

Notes

[i] Thanks to Deirdre Coghlan for permission to quote from her MPhil dissertation, and to Elaine Moriarty and Piaras Mac Éinri for their comments on the first draft.
[ii] C.f. Barnor Hesse, personal communication.
[iii] www.knowracism.ie.
[iv] The Minister of Justice announced an anti-racism programme of that name at the launch of the Equality Authority of its 2002 Annual Report, but this programme was not put into operation. The KNOW RACISM campaign was terminated after three years.
[v] Though not exclusively: see for example the racialisation of Irish Travellers, conceived as 'Irish national' though not always as 'white', as argued by Robbie McVeigh, 1996.
[vi] Written answer to Dáil question no. 1235 by Minister of Justice, Equality and Law Reform, Michael McDowell to Sinn Féin Dáil deputy Aengus Ó Snodaigh, September 30, 2003 (emphasis added).
[vii] Dáil Debates, Written Answers, Minister for Justice, Equality and Law Reform, to Mr Wall, TD, 15 October 2003. www.iregov.ie/oireachtas/frame.htm.
[viii] On the bill, see Irish Council for Civil Liberties. www.iccl.ie/minorities.travellers/02_tresspass
[ix] Department of Justice, Equality and Law Reform press release: 'McDowell published report on Citizen traveller Campaign', 4 November 2002. www.justice.ie.

[x] Press release, September 12, 2003, DJELR (emphasis added). www.justice.ie/802569B20047F907/vweb/pcCAMC5RBJTE.
[xi] Irish Refugee Council press release, Amendments to the Immigration Bill 2002, June 17, 2003 (emphasis added).
[xii] KNOW RACISM Information pack. Dublin: Department of Justice, Equality and Law Reform.
[xiii] The next largest foreign-born populations come from English speaking countries, particularly England and Wales (182,624), Northern Ireland (49,928), the USA (21,541) and Scotland (15,963). The next largest population groups come from Germany and France. Nigerian-born account for 9,225, with South Africa, Romania, China and Australia each numbering about 6,000.
[xiv] In a further twist, in January 2006 an *Irish Times*/TNS mrbi poll found that 78 per cent of those polled believed that people from central and east European states what joined the EU in 2004 should be required to apply for and receive work permits before coming to Ireland to work (Brennock 2006). While the government declared it was unlikely to impose work permits, given its initial decision to allow free access from the ten new EU countries, this was not ruled out if there was to be an economic down turn, constructing migrant workers as merely servicing the interests of the racial state.
[xv] Nuala Haughey, Taoiseach regards racism as opposite of our values, *The Irish Times* online, 25 October 2001.
[xvi] Department of Justice press release, March 28 2002.

References

Agamben, Giorgio. 1998. *Homo Sacer: Sovereign Power and Bare Life.* Stanford: Stanford University Press.
Agamben, Giorgio. 2005. *State of Exception.* Chicago and London: Chicago University Press.
Balibar, Etienne. 1991. Racism and crisis, in Etienne Balibar and Immanuel Wallerstein, *Race, Nation, Class: Ambiguous Identities.* London: Verso.
Bauman, Zygmunt. 1991. *Modernity and Ambivalence.* Cambridge: Polity Press.
Bhattacharyya, Gargi, John Gabriel and Stephen Small. 2002. *Race and Power: Global Racism in the Twenty-first Century.* London: Routledge.
Binchy, William. 2003. Thousands of families at risk after court decision, *The Irish Times*, February 1, 2003.
Brennock, Mark. 2006. 78% want permit system for EU migrants, *The Irish Times*, January 23, 2006.
Bunreacht na hÉireann (Constitution of Ireland). 1998 [1937]. 9th amendment. Dublin: Government Publications Office.
Coalition Against Deportation of Irish Children (CADIC). 2003. *Information for Migrant Parents of Irish Citizen Children.* September 2003.
Coghlan, Deirdre. 2003. *The (Un)Deserving Refugee/Asylum Seeker? Racism and the Irish State*, unpublished MPhil in Ethnic and Racial Studies dissertation, Department of Sociology, Trinity College Dublin.

Cohen, Phil. 1988. Perversions of heritage: Studies in the making of multi-racist Britain, in Phil Cohen and H. Baines (eds.) *Multi-Racist Britain.* London: MacMillan.

Coulter, Carol. 2002. Right of minister to deport upheld by court, *The Irish Times,* 19 January, 2002.

Coulter, Carol. 2003. Supreme court decision in landmark immigrant residency case, *The Irish Times,* 24 January, 2003.

Cunningham, Tony, Emre Işik and Niall Moran. 2005. "Are you being served?": Migrant workers, multiculturalism and the state, in Gerry Boucher and Grainne Collins (eds.) *The New World of Work: Labour Markets in Contemporary Ireland.* Dublin: The Liffey Press.

Department of the Taoiseach. 2002. An agreed programme for government between Fianna Fail and the Progressive Democrats. http://www.taoiseach.gov.ie/index.asp?docID=794

Foucault, Michel. 1990. *The history of sexuality. Vol. I. The will to knowledge.* London: Penguin.

Foucault, Michel. 1991. Governmentality, in Graham Burchell, Colin Gordon and Peter Miller (eds.) *The Foucault Effect.* London: Harvester Wheatsheaf.

Foucault, Michel. 2003. *Society Must be Defended, Lectures at the Collège de France, 1975-76.* London: Allen Lane.

Goldberg, David Theo. 2002. *The Racial State.* Oxford: Blackwell.

Hesse, Barnor. 1999. It's your world: Discrepant m/ulticulturalism, in Phil Cohen (ed.) *New Ethnicities, Old Racisms.* London: Zed Books.

Hughes, Gerard and Emma Quinn. 2004. *The Impact of Immigration on Europe's Societies: Ireland.* Dublin: Economic and Social Research Institute/European Migration Network.

Humphries, Joe. 2005. Immigrant level moves towards 10%, *The Irish Times,* September 15, 2005.

Immigrant Council of Ireland. 2005. *Summary Analysis and Initial Response to the Government's Proposal for an Immigration and Residence Bill.* Dublin: ICI.

Interdepartmental Working Group on the Integration of Refugees in Ireland. 1999. *Integration: A Two Way Process.* Dublin: Government Publications Office.

Irish Traveller Movement. 2003. www.itmtrav.com/newsFeb2003.

King, Jason. 1999. Porous nation: from Ireland's "haemorrhage" to immigrant inundation: discourses of passivity and the effects of out-migration on perceptions of in-migration, in Ronit Lentin (ed.) *The Expanding Nation: Towards a Multi-ethnic Ireland.* Dublin: MPhil in Ethnic and Racial Studies, Department of Sociology, Trinity College Dublin.

Lentin, Ronit and Robbie McVeigh. 2006. *After Optimism? Ireland, Racism and Globalisation.* Dublin: Metro Eireann Publications.

Lentin, Ronit. 1998. "Irishness", the 1937 Constitution and women: a gender and ethnicity view, *Irish Journal of Sociology,* vol. 8: 5-24.

Lentin, Ronit. 2002. Anti-racist responses to the racialisation of Irishness: Disavowed multiculturalism and its discontents, in Ronit Lentin and Robbie McVeigh (eds.) *Racism and Anti-racism in Ireland.* Belfast: Beyond the Pale Publications.

Lentin, Ronit. 2003. Pregnant silence: (En)gendering Ireland's asylum space, *Patterns of Prejudice,* 37/3: 301-22.

Love, Séan. 2004. Ireland: Government fails to stem rise in hostility toward immigrants, *News Amnesty*, June 19, 2004. http://news.amnesty.org/index/ENGEUR296172004.

Loyal, Steven. 2003. Welcome to the Celtic Tiger: Racism, immigration and the state, in Colin Coulter and Steve Coleman (eds.) *The End Of Irish History? Critical Reflections on the Celtic Tiger*. Manchester: Manchester University Press.

Mac Cormaic, Ruadhán. 2005. Year total of asylum seekers is lowest since 1998, *The Irish Times*, December 31, 2005.

Mac Éinrí, Piaras. 2002. The implications for Ireland and the UK arising from the development of recent European Union policy on migration, in NCCRI, *Migration Policy in Ireland*. Dublin: NCCRI.

Mac Éinrí, Piaras. 2003a. Contemporary migration to and from Ireland, *Asyland*, 6.

Mac Éinrí, Piaras. 2003b. *Labour Migration into Ireland*. Dublin: Immigrant Council of Ireland.

Maddock, John and Charles Mallon. 2003. 10,000 parents of Irish babies to be deported, *The Evening Herald*, January 23, 2003.

McGarry, Patsy. 2005. More foreign workers needed, says Brennan, *The Irish Times*, September. 30, 2005.

McVeigh, Robbie and Ronit Lentin. 2002. Situated racisms: A theoretical introduction, in Ronit Lentin and Robbie McVeigh (eds.) *Racism and Antiracism in Ireland*. Belfast: Beyond the Pale Publications, 2002.

McVeigh, Robbie. 1996. *The Racialisation of Irishness: Racism and Antiracism in Ireland*. Belfast: CRD.

Migrant Rights Centre Ireland. 2004. *The Experiences of twenty Migrant Women Employed in the Private Home in Ireland*. Dublin: MRCI.

Mosse, George L. 1978. *Towards the Final Solution: A History of European Racism*, New York: Howard Fertig.

Mullaly, Siobhán. 2003. Defining the limits of citizenship: children, family life and the *jus soli* principle in Irish law, unpublished paper, distributed by CADIC, October 2003 and cited with the author's permission.

NCCRI. 2002. *Migration Policy in Ireland: Reform and Harmonisation*. Dublin: NCCRI.

NCCRI. 2002. *Towards a National Action Plan Against Racism: A Discussion Document to Inform the Consultative Process*. Dublin: Department of Justice, Equality and Law Reform.

Ní Shuinéar, Sinéad. 2002. Othering the Irish (Traveller), in Ronit Lentin and Robbie McVeigh (eds.) *Racism and Anti-racism in Ireland*. Belfast: Beyond the Pale Publications.

O'Brien, Carl. 2004. McDowell rules out residency amnesty, *The Irish Times*, November 17, 2004.

O'Brien, Carl. 2005. A nation in transition, *The Irish Times*, December 28, 2005.

O'Connell, John. 2002. Travellers in Ireland: An examination of discrimination and racism, in Ronit Lentin and Robbie McVeigh (eds.) *Racism and Anti-racism in Ireland*. Belfast: Beyond the Pale Publications.

O'Doherty, Gemma. 2003. The rights to citizenship, *The Irish Independent*, January 23, 2003.

O'Regan Michael. 2003. McDowell rules out identity cards, *The Irish Times*, June 16, 2003.

O'Toole, Fintan. 2000. Green, white and black: Race and Irish identity, in Ronit Lentin (ed.) *Emerging Irish Identities*. Dublin: MPhil in Ethnic and Racial Studies, Trinity College Dublin.

Roediger, David. 2003. *Colored White: Transcending the Racial Past*. Berkeley: University of California Press.

Rolston, Bill and Michael Shannon. 2002. *Encounters: How Racism Came to Ireland*. Belfast: Beyond the Pale Publications.

Ruhs, Martin. 2005. *Managing the Immigration and Employment of non-EU Nationals in Ireland*. Dublin: The Policy Institute, Trinity College Dublin.

Task Force on the Travelling Community. 1995. Dublin: Government Publications Office.

Taylor, Charles. 1994. The politics of recognition, in David T. Goldberg (ed.) *Multiculturalism: A Critical Reader*. Oxford: Blackwell.

Tracy, Marshall. 2000. *Immigration and Racism in Ireland: A Comparative Analysis*, Ethnic and Racial Studies, Department of Sociology, TCD.

Ward, Eilis. 1999. Ireland and refugees/asylum seekers: 1922-1966, in R. Lentin (ed.) *The Expanding Nation: Towards a Multi-ethnic Ireland*, Ethnic and Racial Studies, Department of Sociology, TCD.

CHAPTER TEN

RETHINKING IMMIGRATION AND THE STATE IN IRELAND

STEVEN LOYAL AND KIERAN ALLEN

Introduction

In this chapter we argue that processes of immigration and ethno-racial domination in Ireland need to be understood within a framework which includes concepts of social relations of capitalist accumulation, cultural nationalism, and state regulation and control. To that end this chapter is an attempt to reassert the importance of concrete historical, material and social relationships both as furnishing a more realistic explanatory framework, and as providing a more viable basis for challenging and explaining immigration and ethno-racial domination than theories which singularly focus on difference, diversity and othering. The argument that is proposed here is that an understanding of state practices tied to capital accumulation within the so called "Celtic Tiger" economy are necessary, though perhaps not sufficient conditions, for explaining processes tied to migration and ethno-racial domination in Irish society (Loyal 2003).

The shape of the chapter is as follows. We begin by outlining the cultural turn in sociology, and indicating some of the problems with existing analyses of racism and immigration in Ireland. We then look at the important role of the state in categorising and classifying individuals in terms of social statuses, before discussing the development of the Irish state and examining the treatment and regulation of asylum seekers and migrant workers in Irish society.

The cultural turn in Sociology

Since the late 1970s, following what Gustav Bergmann calls the "linguistic turn" in philosophy, there has been an increasing emphasis on culture and language as explanatory principles in the social sciences generally, and in studies of migration, community formation and racial and ethnic studies more specifically. With reference to the latter, two developments have been of special significance: first, the development of cultural studies which had its roots in the work of Richard Hoggart, E.P. Thompson and Raymond Williams, but reached maturity in the work of Stuart Hall and the Birmingham School of Cultural Studies, and second, the rise of structuralist and post-structuralist philosophy, and postcolonial theory, especially in the work of Homi Bhabba, Edward Said, and Gayatri Spivak. Both theorists of cultural studies and postcolonial thinkers initially acknowledged material social conditions as an aspect of their analysis, however, over time this shifted to a singular emphasis on textualism, signification, semiotics, encoding and decoding. This was reflected in the emergence of a new conceptual vocabulary which emphasises difference, diversity, hybridity, syncretism, intersectionality, alterity, cultural pluralism, identity and otherness.

There are, of course, social and intellectual reasons for this shift. The rise of new social movements, as well as the collapse of the USSR, led to a new focus on identity politics. There were also intellectual attempts to move away from what were considered essentialist and class reductionist analyses of social life. But these twin processes are overlain by what Bourdieu calls the "scholastic view" or *skole* which results from a failure of sociological reflexivity (1979). For Bourdieu, there is no acknowledgement that the intellectualist bias inherent in the scholarly gaze of the modern academic is imposed onto the object studied, hence the preoccupation with language, symbols and meaning. These are, after all, the essential tools and components of the academic standpoint but they have a distorting effect once substituted for an analysis of the broader world of social practices.

The cumulative effect of these processes has been that questions of culture, subjective identity and representation have come to the fore in sociological analysis whereas historical analyses of social relations and material processes have receded. The new writing on racism and immigration has borrowed heavily from abstract post-structuralist philosophy. The concept of otherness for example, has its intellectual roots in Husserl's discussion on the impossibility of gaining access to another's consciousness in the fifth Cartesian Meditation, before being developed by Levinas in *Totality and Infinity* (1969), and later incorporated within Derrida's discussion of "violent hierarchies" which was itself influenced by the Algerian War (Le Sueur 2001). Rather than adopting a sociological reflexivity towards these concepts—as opposed to the self-reflexivity involved in acknowledging one's social position and location in the social world in terms of gender, ethnicity etc.—many writers in Ireland have frequently uncritically adopted these frameworks in their analyses of racism and immigration. A large number of the articles and chapters in a variety of major edited works on racism and immigration in Ireland have, we feel, focused too restrictively on the discursive construction of a narrow sense of Irishness and identity, and its concomitant engendering of otherness (Cullen 2000; Gillespie 1999; Goldstone 1999; Gray 1999; Lentin 2000; Lentin and McVeigh 2002; McDonagh 2002; O'Toole 2000; Sinha 1999; White 2002). Such analyses have tended to concentrate on interrogating the homogenous and exclusionary construction of national discourses of Irish identity as white, settled and Catholic. Such a restrictive notion of identity, it is argued, militates against the construction of a more inclusive and encompassing notion of a multi-ethnic Ireland by stigmatising or racialising an "out-group" or "other". The solution to such exclusionary definitions and processes is to either reduce power differentials in Irish society, or to celebrate diversity, difference and hybridity. The majority of the various theoretical frameworks contained in these works can be accommodated within two broad positions: first, those postmodern positions which rightly emphasise power and racialisation (Lentin 2000; Lentin and McVeigh 2002; Gray 1999; O'Toole 2000; Sinha 2000; 2002; White 2002); and, second, those liberal positions which focus on the importance of celebrating diversity, multiculturalism, and pluralism (Farrell and Watt 2001; MacLachlan and O'Connell 2000; Monshengwo, 2001; Tannam, Smyth and Flood 1998). Notwithstanding their divergent conceptual frameworks in relation to power, both of these broad positions share an emphasis on difference and diversity and also an analytic framework which approaches racism through a self-other, us-them dynamic. Thus, typically, it is suggested that, "othering— denying equal legitimacy to individuals and cultures that do not conform to one's own arbitrary, ever shifting criteria of normality—is a two sided coin. On the one hand it creates a clearly defined undifferentiated "them"… On the other, it forges a bond of solidarity" (Ní Shuinéar 2002: 177). Or that "we cannot understand Irish racism, or the Irish racialisation of the other, without understanding the racialisation of the Irish self" (Lentin 2000: 3).

We wish to argue, however, that the singular emphasis on the construction of Irish identity, Otherness and diversity is problematic for a number of reasons. First, such an analysis fails to explain why these self-other or us-them processes emerge in the first place, and therefore remains at the level of description rather than explanation. Thus, although questions of racialisation are insightfully discussed, there seems to be little analysis of the rationale underlying these processes of group-making (Bourdieu 1987; Brubaker 2005). There are some exceptions which are found in the most interesting of the available chapters, but these rationalisations for group formation are pitched at a very high level of generality and point to endemic tendencies in modernity to exclude others (Lentin, 1999: 8; Gray 2000: 66), or to restrictive forms of ethnic nationalism (Fanning 2002).

Secondly, the focus on difference and otherness ignores the contradictory attitudes—or what Gramsci (1971; 323-343) calls contradictory common sense—which many in the indigenous population have towards immigrants. Far from a general fear about difference, these include more specific concerns about competition for scarce resources, maintaining status and distinction, jobs and pay levels. But these can often co-exist with feelings of mutual identification and humanitarian concern towards asylum seekers and migrants and their social condition. Resentment built up through people's own experience of employment find an outlet in attacks on "spongers" who are defined precisely by their ability to escape the constraints of work. However the generalised identification of immigrants, rather than, say, tax avoiding entrepreneurs or establishment politicians, as "spongers", is itself a function of specific political conjunctures. The crucial point here is to avoid analytically transmuting the complex and contradictory attitudes of the indigenous population into a flattened metaphysical formula about a fear or dislike of the other, but rather to analyse these responses empirically within their specific social context.

There are also specific problems with each of these positions. In terms of the postmodern standpoint, power is seen as de-centered into a host of social spaces. As a result, there appears to be little common ground from which to develop a strategy to oppose racism that involves the majority of the indigenous population. With reference to the standard liberal positions, state, church and media discourses emphasise the values of diversity and pluralism while packaging it within the framework of "interculturalism". Interculturalism is the National Consultative Committee on Racism and Interculturalism's (NCCRI) preferred term to designate cultures which interact with one another. This body is predominantly funded by state agencies and stresses the idea of a partnership between NGOs, employers, the unions and the state to challenge racism. There is little recognition that some of these groups might actually benefit from racism. Thus a 2002 NCCRI publication on diversity at work simply assumes that the business "community" has an automatic interest in eliminating racism. It is further assumed that a harmonious immigration policy can be created which takes into account "the long term (as opposed to event driven) national security concerns; the broad socio-economic concerns of migrants and broad human rights/equality concerns… and the medium to long term needs of the economy (as opposed to annual fluctuation)" (Watt 2002: 14-45).

Although these works have been useful in highlighting the pervasiveness of racist practices in Irish society, and the exclusionary role that Irish nationalism has contributed towards these, we feel that their restricted focus on national identity and othering underplays the constitutive role that the logic of capitalist accumulation—intrinsic to the "Celtic Tiger"—also contributes in processes of ethnoracial domination. That is not to say that class stratification and poverty have not been mentioned in some of these works (e.g., Mac Éinri 2001; Frazer 2001). However, they have not figured as central explanatory concepts. Though we focus largely on economic and state processes in this chapter, our intention is not to simply reverse the continuing shift away from the economy, to politics, to culture, and identity. One would, additionally, have to problematise these clear-cut analytical distinctions in the first place. Rather, it is to understand these processes within capitalism as a *whole*, and in all their interconnections. Our aim is to shift the paradigm for understanding processes of ethno-racial domination towards a more broadly conceived cultural materialist framework. It is our belief that the postmodern and liberal standpoints have disarticulated the social and economic conditions of the emergence of forms of signification and racialisation. As Hall himself noted in his earlier writings:

> The question is not whether men-in-general make perceptual distinctions between groups with different racial or ethnic characteristics, but rather, what are the specific conditions which make this form of distinction socially pertinent, historically active (1980: 338).

The signification of "otherness", as a basis for racialisation and racism, can have effect and meaning only within determinate economic and political relations of social domination. Such perceptual and cognitive distinctions are made by embedded individuals in the real world, in their practices and in their struggles over symbolic and material resources. Language as a practice, as Wittgenstein (1957) rightly notes, is always embedded in other, broader practices or forms of life. Our argument, then, does not aim to replace a one-sided idealism with a similarly conceived one-sided materialism, but to deny the separation of the two spheres in the first place. Instead we need to examine social practices involving "real individuals, their activity and the material conditions of their life [which] can be verified in a purely empirical way" (Marx and Engels 1846: 37).[i] This involves not only moving beyond identity (Brubaker and Cooper 2005), but also beyond some of the inherent theoretical, empirical, and strategic limitations of the postmodern and liberal positions.

State and citizenship

In his important book, *The Suffering of the Immigrant* (2004), Abdelmalek Sayad notes, "the secret virtue of immigration: it provides an introduction… to the sociology of the state" (Sayad 2004: 279). Not only has the denial of the role of immigration in nation-building been central to the creation of national myths of homogeneity, especially in Europe, but the world is so structured according to nation-state principles that these can become so routinely assumed that they vanish from sight altogether. They form what Bourdieu terms a *doxa*:

unquestioned background assumptions of social analysis. The fundamental problem, then, for any sociology of migration is to analyse immigration without reinforcing the nation-state's own categories, schemes of perception, and its structuring organising principles.

Though the pervasive correlation of social research with the nation-state as society has long been questioned in sociological analysis (Elias 1978; Mann 1986), migration research continues to embody what Andreas Wimmer and Nancy Glick Schiller (2002) have called "methodological nationalism". There is evidence of this in much sociological literature. The prominence of such questions as: "What does immigration mean for the state?", "How can migrants adapt to their host society?" all demonstrate the powerful influence on nation-state thinking.

Weber (1968) famously defined the state as an institution which has a monopoly over the means of violence, and Elias extended this to include forms of taxation. By contrast, Marxists have been more concerned with how the state functions as "the committee of management" for the general interests of the capitalist class, acknowledging sometimes that this gives it relative autonomy. Issues are further clouded by the fact that most definitions contain both an institutional level, referring to what the state looks like, and a functional level of analysis, what the state does (Mann 1984: 186).

Most theorists however, recognise the two major dimensions of the state— the domestic economic ideological aspect of the state, and its military international aspect (Hintze 1975; Skocpol 1979; Mann 1984; Giddens 1985). And almost all agree that modern states carry out a multiplicity of functions, including classification, codification, the monitoring and regulation of circumscribed population, binding rule making, the fostering of a restricted narrative of ethnic and national identity, and crucially, the regulation of labour power.

In *Seeing like a State* (1998), James Scott argues that states attempt to make a society legible, to arrange the population in ways that simplified the classic functions of taxation, conscription and the prevention of rebellion. Legibility, he argues, was a central concern for states. Through the development of an increasing knowledge base, the state aims to make the physical and human resources of the nation more productive. Thus, Scott, for example, argues that permanent surnames were largely a project of official legibility.

A very early pre-modern example of the power of state categories is provided by the Qin dynasty in China. It reputedly began imposing surnames on much of its population for the purposes of taxation, forced labour, and conscription. Moreover, the assigning of patronyms by family was integral to a state policy which promoted the status of male family heads by giving them legal jurisdiction over their wives, children and juniors, and this required registering the entire population. Scott argues that a comparable connection between state-building and the invention of permanent surnames also exists for fourteenth and fifteenth century England. As he notes: "Many of the 14th century surnames were clearly nothing more than administrative fictions designed to make a population fiscally legible" (1998: 68).

Equally, as Corrigan and Sayer note in their discussion of state formation, *The Great Arch: English State Formation as Cultural Revolution* (1985), states attempt to regulate the forms of cultural and social activity within their borders. Hence, out of the vast range of human social capacities and possible ways in which social life could be lived, states more or less forcibly "encourage" some, whilst suppressing and marginalising others. Certain forms of activity are officially sanctioned while others are condemned. States thus engage in forms of moral regulation—"a project of normalising, rendering natural, taken for granted, in a word 'obvious', what are in fact ontological and epistemological premises of a particular and historical form of social order" (Corrigan and Sayer 1985:4)

A major component of legislation is to encourage people to identify themselves and their "place" in the world in a specific way. This ability to regulate social life depends in part, as Bourdieu notes, upon the capacity to sustain and impose categories of thought, through which institutions and individuals make sense of the world. "Structures" in the social world lead a "double life" so that they exist twice. Firstly, they exist in the "objectivity of the first order" constituted as objective social positions as fields, and secondly, in "the objectivity of the second order", in the form of systems of classification, subjective bundles of dispositions deposited in individuals in the guise of the cognitive schemata which inform their thoughts, feelings and conduct. The potential to impose what Bourdieu calls a "vision of divisions" is the "power of making social divisions and hence the political power *par excellence*" (Bourdieu 1984: 468).

For Bourdieu, political struggle is a cognitive struggle for the power to impose the legitimate vision of the social world, that is, the power to (re)make reality by preserving or altering the categories through which agents comprehend and construct that world. Thus, an important aspect of this vision of divisions is the way in which individuals are encouraged to identify themselves predominantly in narrow national terms. This of course has important implications for how states regulate forms of ethnic migration (Joppke 2005). The administrative categories and classifications used by the state play an important role in defining broader discourses of identification and exclusion. Both dominant and marginalised groups can come to define themselves and each other through such categorisations.

Yet states, through systems of classification, also individualise in specific ways. Rather than providing all residents with the same civil and political rights, bureaucratic classification schemes engender systematic patterns of discrimination. The legal and administrative categories of "asylum seeker", "refugee" and "economic migrant" are important social statuses which confer different rights and entitlements. These categorisations have been used by state service providers as a basis for judgements about individual entitlements to social, political and economic support. They in turn enter public consciousness as key categories for seeing the social world.

The key framework for regulating social activity is citizenship. Citizens, however, are not immediately recognisable, nor did the discourse of citizenship take life automatically. In conventional thought it is assumed that the idea of citizenship had its roots in Greek thought and practice and was then reborn in the medieval European city as the burghers acquired unique rights. However, this does not explain how the modern concept of citizenship is linked to membership of a nation—which is distinct from both the polities of the absolute monarchy or the petty feudal states which predominated in medieval Europe. Nor does it explain how citizenship acquired a meaning of equality before the law—as distinct from different legal rights attached to social rank. The emergence of free market capitalism, which uprooted local particularisms, and the explosion of political discourse in the French and American revolutions had far more to do with the category of citizenship than a supposed unbroken thread that stretches back to classical Greece.

The material manifestation of modern citizenship is the passport. Originally, the passport was regarded by many as a mark of servitude, as an obstacle to human liberty. Prior to the French revolution, passports barely existed and, where they did, they were often rudimentary identity papers which were used to prevent the movement of the "masterless rabble" to different districts where they might become a burden on the poor relief. During the French revolution, there was often a clamour to remove passports, as the cahiers from the Neuilly-sur-Marne parish indicated:

> As every man is equal before God and every sojourner is this life must be left undisturbed in his legitimate possessions, especially in his natural and political life, it is the wish of this assembly that individual liberty be guaranteed to all the French, and therefore that each must be free to move about, within and outside the Kingdom, *without permission, passports or other formalities that hamper the liberty of the citizen* (Torpey 2000: 22).

For most of the nineteenth century, the passport was indeed an irrelevancy. Few of the one million Irish who fled the famine of 1847 had a passport before they set off for America. Arthur Cooper, a cleric who wrote traveller guides at the end of the nineteenth century, made no mention of immigration controls as he travelled between states, for the simple reason that there were hardly any. He did advise his readers to take a passport, but only to gain access to private art galleries or when collecting money from a local post office. Even then he remarked that he had been informed by the Spanish consul that "the passport was as much out of date as the blunderbuss" (Haynes, 1999: 28).

The passport only returned with the "revolution in identity papers" that came with World War One as part of states' monopolisation of the means of movement. During this first total war, the civilian population became targets of mass conscription, propaganda and efforts to raise or undermine morale. In this context, each country drew the boundaries of citizenship ever tighter and sought to rigorously control "non-nationals." The nationalism born in an imperialist age and the revolution in identity papers gave the state powerful new tools to homogenise its populations.

This then is the broader background against which we need to examine the categories used by the Irish state to construct migrants as social actors. Far from a focus on the social or psychological fear of the other we need to look at the very specific, historical and economic contexts within which the state deploys its categories to serve its needs.

The Irish State and racism

The Irish state was born from a nationalist revolt against imperialism but, like all nationalist revolts, it soon integrated itself into the world order—initially under the aegis of Britain, then later as part of the Atlanticist nexus. British guns were used to suppress former comrades in a bitter civil war, and later the specific administrative forms of the British state were incorporated into the new state structures. Historically, Irish regiments in the British Army had played their part in defending the British Empire and Irish immigrants have frequently clashed with black people in the US. The struggle for political independence therefore did little to undermine the wider racism that prevailed in the advanced industrial world.

Two specific features of the Irish state structure are, however, relevant to the issue of migration. First, the truncated nature of the Irish revolution led to a hyper-Catholicism which served as a compensation for the ensuing poverty and failure to achieve national unification. The Catholic Church took control of schools, hospitals and the administration of many social services. Catholic morality was imposed through bans on divorce, contraception and censorship. The "special position" of the Catholic Church was recognised in the constitution and the state embarked on a cultural policy which defined the notion "Irish" as simultaneously meaning Catholic and Gaelic. Protestantism was identified with being "West British", while the tiny Jewish population was viewed with suspicion. The combination of hyper-Catholicism and underdevelopment meant few immigrants came to Ireland, and those who did found a less than hospitable welcome. A few years after the Aliens Order was promulgated in 1935, there were only 2,354 aliens in Ireland, including 1,143 American (Ferriter 2004: 387). Although the Hungarian refugees who arrived in Ireland after Soviet repression in 1956 were selected according to their adherence to "Christian ideals", even they found the place inhospitable and soon left (Fanning, 2002: 88).

Catholicism reigned supreme in Ireland until the early 1990s, when economic change and an explosion of social struggle involving divorce and abortion broke much of their ideological, though not their institutional, grip. The defeats inflicted on the Catholic Church ensured that there was a greater openness within political elite to re-define Irishness as not necessarily linked to one homogenous Catholic culture. This was important, as the first major influx of immigrants to Ireland coincided with the political displacement of Catholicism. A further consequence was that, after the "sex wars", the Catholic Church re-positioned itself by developing a discourse about "social exclusion". Church agencies such as the Conference of Religious in Ireland (CORI 2006) assumed that there was a "contented" consumerist majority which needed to be morally disciplined so that care and compassion were shown to the "excluded". Ironically, this new discourse meant that the same church which had been the main agent of homogenisation in previous decades often took up a position of support for the new migrants in the nineties. There were, of course, limits to this, as the new Catholicism did not fundamentally challenge the wider racist views that were common in all Western industrialised countries.

The second main feature of the Irish state is the developmental partnership which was forged by its main political party, Fianna Fáil. It established long term hegemony by forging a broad coalition to challenge an agro-export model which was seen as the main legacy of empire. Its founder, Eamonn de Valera, promised to change Ireland's status from being "an out-garden of Britain", and suggested that this would lead to general social advance. Like many other nationalist parties in former colonies, the traditionalist husk of Fianna Fáil contained a deeply modernist project of development. For long periods, it succeeded in integrating the labour movement into this populist project in a manner that was similar to, though weaker than, political patterns found in some Latin American countries. The left-right divide in European politics thus appeared to have little saliency.

By the 1960s, forms of strong corporatism came to replace the older more informal nationalist understandings, as the trade unions took part in state-led projects to promote Irish development and "competitiveness". After brief periods of intense class conflict, this again changed into the institutionally dense forms of social partnership from 1987 onwards.

These two specific features of the Irish state—a fading hyper-Catholicism and a developmental partnership model—were to have important consequences for the categories the state constructed to organise a sudden influx of migrants after 1994. From being the "human resource warehouse" of Europe, Ireland has moved to becoming a major recipient of immigrants. The scale and pace of the change is astounding. The table below illustrates the stock of foreign born populations in selected OECD countries

Country	Foreign Born	Foreign Population
Australia	23%	7%
Canada	19%	5%
Germany	13%	9%
United States	12%	7%
France	10%	6%
Ireland	10%	6%
Netherlands	10%	4%
United Kingdom	8%	6%
Norway	7%	4%
Denmark	7%	5%
Portugal	6%	2%
Spain	5%	4%
Hungary	3%	1%
Poland	2%	0%

Table 1: Source: OECD 2005: chart 1.6

The table illustrates how Ireland is now one of the top EU recipients of immigrants as a proportion to its population. The nearest comparison is with France and the Netherlands, but these countries experienced a long process of immigration shaped by a colonial past and a longer period of economic development.

The focus of the Irish state in managing this influx of migrants has gone through a number of phases which reflect the complex interplay of its political culture and political economy of modern capitalism. Throughout the various phases, however, its method of categorising migrants has had important material effects on both the migrants themselves and the attitudes of the indigenous population to them. This categorisation should not be reified but, rather, understood in terms of how the state wins acceptance for, and serves the accumulation of, capital.

The migrant as asylum seeker

The main polarity in the state's categorisation of migrants is between asylum seeker/refugee and economic migrant, which mirrors the political-economic division that is common in much of bourgeois society. As a result of the trauma of World War Two and the emerging Cold War, the Western powers agreed to the 1951 Geneva Convention on Refugees. This gave anyone the right to apply for asylum and to stay in the country until a determination of their case had been made. The asylum seeker, however, is presumed to have no economic existence. Asylum seekers are subject to persecution rather than poverty, and, while waiting for the bureaucratic structures of the state to deal with their cases, they are not supposed to work. In terms of its own legal and ideological structure, the state therefore creates the asylum seeker as welfare dependent. From the point of view of capital accumulation, asylum seekers are therefore a "cost", and hence, in general, are made subject to the most negative characteristics in society.

The first migrants who came to Ireland in the recent period were typically labelled "refugees". In 1992, Ireland received only thirty-nine applications for asylum. By 1996, this figure had risen to 1,179; by 2001, it had risen to 10,325: by 2002, it rose again to 11, 364, though by 2003 it had fallen to 7, 900 and back down to 4,265 in 2004 (Irish Refugee Council 2004). These figures were presented as dramatic but, in absolute terms, Ireland received one of the lowest number of asylum seekers within the European Union (EU), with only 2.4 per cent of the total number of applications in 2000, for example.

Initially, asylum seekers arrived in Ireland when the "liberal agenda" was dominant. Not only had the church begun to suffer a number of defeats, but in 1992 the Labour Party scored its highest vote since 1928. In the first legislative change on migration since 1935, the Refugee Act expanded the definition of "refugee" to include a person persecuted because of his or her gender, sexual orientation or membership of a trade union. The state promised to be generous in relation to the provision for re-unification of families and also to allow entry of other relatives where a dependency relationship existed.

However, the liberal regime in relation to refugees did not persist. Growing inequality became evident within the "Celtic Tiger", and this led to considerable social resentment. Neo-liberal policies meant that there was a marked contrast between the boom in the economy and the low provision of public services. "A First World economy with Third World public services" became a common description of Ireland. The institutions of social partnership meant that there were limited opportunities for the left to actively respond to the inequality. Not surprisingly, therefore, during the elections in 1997, this resentment was often focused on "refugees" who were constructed as spongers who caused problems for the social services. The official definition of the refugee as a "burden" to be carried for the Western mission of civilisation led to new antagonisms. However it is important to stress that these sentiments did not arise primarily from a psychic fear of the other but were articulated and echoed by all the main political parties (and print media) who participated in constructing the state's categories in relation to migrants.

Nevertheless, a problem emerged at the level of the political economy. The "Celtic Tiger" needed an abundance of unskilled labour and access to particular skill mixes. Because of the state's inexperience in dealing with asylum seekers, it had a less developed bureaucratic apparatus for processing applications. Many remained within the system for quite some time and therefore there seemed no good reason why they might not work. As "refugees" had previously been implicitly constructed as "spongers" by the state's own legislative framework, the obvious answer was to remove their welfare dependency by granting them a right to work. This issue was articulated by a broad coalition ranging from the left to the Catholic Church, and in 1999 the state responded by allowing more than 3,000 asylum seekers the right to work as a "once off" concession (Fanning 2002: 106).

It was, however, only a momentary joining of the logic of humanitarianism with the logic of capital accumulation. Aging capitalism is characterised by a growing use of racist ideologies to occlude its deeper class polarisation. "Fortress Europe" embodies this through its competitive demand that all countries match growing restrictions on asylum seekers, or else be labelled as a "chink" in the armour. The "right to work" was clearly a pull factor and, if allowed to continue, it might eventually have led Ireland to become a much more racially mixed society. The Irish state therefore undertook an about- turn and, from April 2000 onwards, deprived asylum seekers of the right to work, study or receive social welfare. From there on, Ireland aligned itself with current EU policies whose primary strategy was to reduce the number of "uneconomic" asylum seekers.

The result has been a progressive ratcheting up of the restrictions against asylum seekers. Asylum seekers were first "dispersed" throughout the country and subject to "direct provision", receiving only €19.10 a week. In addition, bi-lateral re-admission agreements with Nigeria were signed in 2002 to facilitate deportations. In common with the rest of the EU, greater use was made of "safe country" and "safe third countries" in assessing applications. By 2004, child benefit had been withdrawn from asylum seekers, thereby cutting family income by about 40 per cent. A total of 599 deportations were carried out in 2004 out of 2,866 deportation orders signed by the Minister of Justice. When one considers that less than 300 Irish people were deported from the US is the same period, one gets some idea of the racist parameters of decision making (Irish Refugee Council 2005).

The above discussion suggests that the treatment of asylum seekers cannot adequately be analysed simply in terms which emphasise a fear of the other. As we have seen, there are shifts and changes in the treatment of asylum seekers which are ultimately linked to the manner in which the bourgeois logic of humanitarianism interacts with the logic of capital accumulation.

The migrant as bonded labourer

The scale of the Irish boom meant that, by the end of the 1990s, the Irish government became more concerned with labour supply. Up to 1999, rising labour participation rates, primarily among women, accounted for nearly half the extra labour supply. After that immigration played a larger role in expanding the labour force.

Despite the constant neo-liberal refrain about reducing government interference in the market, the Irish state actually plays a major role in planning labour market supply. Formally it undertakes this planning process through the interaction of state agencies with social partners. In reality, it gave the employers a free hand to tailor make immigration policy towards their requirements. This occurred in a number of ways. In 1997, an Expert Group for Skills Needs (EGSN) was established which was dominated by employer interests. The chairperson of the current board came from Ireland's largest recruiting firm, CPL Resources. There are also four representatives of Irish and multinational firms, two union representatives and one from the employers organisation IBEC. The EGSN worked closely with the Skills and Labour Migration Research Unit, which is a division of FÁS, the National Training Agency. This in turn is chaired by the former director general of IBEC, and co-incidentally the husband of the Mary Harney, Tánaiste (deputy prime minister) and leader of the coalition partner, the Progressive Democrats party. The Skills and Labour Migration Unit maintains a National Database and issues sectoral reports to match the influx of migrants with the market needs within particular sectors. One result of this is that work permits are issued only for what are defined as "eligible" as opposed to "ineligible" jobs. At various times however, depending on market fluctuations, jobs can shift from one category to another.

This high level of state planning is designed to ensure that overheating in the boom is minimised so that wage rates do not rise greatly. While the unions get to have formal representation on the partnership structures which engage in labour market planning, it is evident that they merely legitimate the process and put up little opposition to its pro-business bias.

The main instrument through which immigrant labour was brought to Ireland between 1999 and 2004 was the work permit system. What is significant about the market-driven nature of this process is that it constructs the migrant as a mere economic unit. A large source of demand for work permits came from unskilled sectors, such as hotels and catering, and other low-grade services. As a result, work permits, renewable on a yearly basis, were issued to meet labour demands. However, such permits were tied to specific jobs and employers had to demonstrate that it had not been possible to fill the vacancy with indigenous labour or with EEA workers. Between 1999-2003, 9.8 per cent of work permits went to Latvia; 9.6 per cent to Lithuania; 8 per cent to the Philippines; 7.8 per cent to Poland; 6.1 per cent to Romania; 5.6 per cent to South Africa; 5.2 per cent to Brazil; 3 per cent to China; 2.1 per cent to India. The Top 5 countries accounted for 41.3 per cent of work permits in 2002 (Ruhs 2005: 15).

The work permit system is modelled on the idea of the guest worker system that was devised by the big industrial powers after WW2. It is highly flexible and designed to suit the needs of employers, while denying workers a number of social and political rights. Workers were tied to a particular employer and have to leave the country before applying for new jobs. As they were dependent on their employers, they could not complain about sexual harassment or join a trade union. The system was made deliberately liberal to suit employer interests. Junior Minister Noel Tracey explained the philosophy in a recent speech, "We have had a very liberal regime in place in relation to work permit applications where circa 95 per cent of these were granted" (Tracey 2001). In addition to the work permit system, employers in the services industry in particular were also able to employ the growing number of international students, who were entitled to work for up to 20 hours a week.

The Irish state has turned a blind eye to the growth of undocumented workers within an unbalanced work permit system. Few people who overstayed their work permits were deported. Although employers were supposed to comply with minimal labour standards, less than 50 labour inspectors existed to police them (there are, by contrast, 100 inspectors to monitor the welfare of dogs). The largest permit holder for work permits, the Turkish Gamma Corporation, which won many large construction contracts for the state, was subsequently found to be paying its employees less than the minimum wage.

The migrant as owner of valuable skills

As a result of continuing skill shortages, business organisations and government bodies such as the National Competitiveness Council and the national training agency FÁS called for the creation of a fast-track work authorisation visa system. These fast-track visas were introduced specifically to facilitate the recruitment of workers in specialist categories: professionals in information technology and construction, as well as nurses. Work visas are more flexible than work permits, in that they allow the recipient to move jobs within a specified sector. Unlike work permits, visas are renewable on a two-year basis and permitted family reunion in Ireland. The working visa/authorisation scheme is restricted to specific skilled occupations that are in short supply, such as technicians in IT and computing, professionals, and registered nurses. The scheme was introduced in June 2000 to fast-track procedures for processing applications. Since February 2004, spouses of workers under this scheme have an automatic right to work.

In addition to this, the Irish state developed two other minor procedures for immigration to suit business interests. There was, first, a Business Permission scheme which granted immigrant status to those who set up a business of more than €300,000 and employed two people. There was also an Intra-Company Transfer scheme for senior professionals of multi-nationals corporations (this has temporarily been suspended due to abuse, except for those from "familiar" firms).

The result, then, of the state's strategy of making migrants "legible" is the construction of an elaborate set of social categories which crudely construct human beings according to their relative use for capital. A multi-tiered migrant work regime has been created with differential rights for highly skilled visa immigrants, on the one hand, and lower-skilled work permit immigrants. After the 2004 accession of new EU states, this regime was once again re-modelled to reduce the number of work permits to non-EU Nationals and to use Eastern Europe as the main reserve fund for cheaper labour. Significantly, Charlie McCreevy, an EU Commissioner (and former Irish Minister of Finance), has become the main proponent of the EU Services Directive, which he hopes will allow employers to evade minimum wage responsibilities by paying people according to the laws in "their country of origin". The consistent thread behind the changes, however, has been a strategy to create a super flexible migrant workforce that serves the immediate needs of capital and which is subject to higher forms of exploitation. Recent revelations about abuses suffered by migrants are therefore not accidental, but are rather an intrinsic part of a system designed to serve employer interests.

These narrow economic concerns have always been mediated by a restricted notion of Irish nationhood, in which the Irish government expects non-EU workers to return (voluntarily or otherwise) to their country of origin once their labour is no longer needed. Such a standpoint echoes the restrictive policy of other European nation states and effectively denies the reality of long-term trends in immigration. Although born as an anti-imperialist state, the modern Irish State fits easily into the ethnic and racial hierarchies that were ultimately created by the imperialist conquest of the world. Hence its desire for a flexible migrant labour force is mediated by a preference that they be white rather than brown or black, and culturally similar (Joppke 2005).

Despite the differences between those given work permits—who can be described as "bonded labour"—and those holding visas, both lack social and political rights, including access to free education, medical care and social welfare entitlements. Neither group benefits from any holistic integration strategy or even from proper access to language classes. As a result, asylum seekers and some economic migrants have a great deal in common. They are generally at the bottom end of the socio-economic ladder, share similar racialised disadvantages in terms of housing and educational opportunities, experience low standards of living, poverty and social exclusion, and are equally targets of informal and institutional racism, discrimination and hostility.

Conclusion

The recent development of contemporary Irish society is inherently paradoxical. At the same time as producing unprecedented wealth, it has created poverty and social exclusion. It is largely, although not exclusively, by reference to this paradox that we can attempt to understand the growth of racism in Ireland. Although racism may take the form of a relatively coherent theory, it can also appear in the form of a less coherent assembly of stereotypes, images and attributions, and as an explanation that is constructed and employed by individuals to negotiate their everyday lives. As Miles notes, racism can be characterised as practically adequate, in the sense that it refracts, in thought, certain observed regularities in the social world and constructs a causal interpretation which is presented as consistent with those regularities (Miles 1989).

Such images and stereotypes rarely emerge spontaneously, but often arise from state and media discourses, given their monopoly over the powers of governance, diffusion and representation. Thus, refugees in Ireland, and Europe generally, are often represented as being responsible for a number of social and economic problems (which usually existed well before their arrival), such as housing shortages, unemployment and the general lack of adequate statutory provisions. For many disempowered sections of the population, racist discourses often constitute a description of, and explanation for, the world they experience on a day-to-day basis. Racist discourse is an ideological account of the social world which recognises and offers an explanation for the housing crisis, for the lack of jobs, for the continuance of poverty—experiences which many marginalised groups face. It helps to make sense of the economic and social changes accompanying poverty, urban decline and social exclusion, as they are experienced by sections of the working class within the context of a booming "Celtic Tiger" economy.

The singular focus on othering is unhelpful because it fails to focus on how the Irish state constructs these racist discourses through the social organisation of migrants around particular categories which serve its needs. Instead it replaces such an analysis with an emphasis on psychic fears of difference or on the definition of identities.

By de-centring locations of power, the causal role of the state is often downplayed.[ii] It fails to recognise how the categories it constructs to organise society have a dramatic effect on the perceptions of all social actors. It fails also to understand how there can be an important point of agreement between indigenous workers and migrants when it comes to resisting exploitation. Yet in 2005 and 2006, in cases such as the solidarity demonstrated for Turkish Gama workers, the campaigns of SIPTU for rights for Polish workers who were constructing Dublin's port tunnel or for Brazilian workers in meat plants in Roscommon or migrant workers in Irish Ferries, it is striking how the call for a common front against employers interacts with, and partially undermines, racist discourses in many ways. Such gestures of solidarity are often not strong enough to overcome the state's system of social categorisation, and people can hold contradictory approaches to class and ethnic identity at one and the same time. But, contrary to a theoretical pessimism that pervades the literature on otherness, they do indicate strategic points of contact for anti-racist activists.

Notes

[i] Materialism here is used in contrast to Feuerbach's reductive theory of materialism
[ii] Within the context of acknowledging power relationships there is of course also reference to the state in some of the more insightful accounts, for example Lentin and McVeigh (2002), but this does not detract from our overall argument since the state is discussed rather abstractly and not in terms of its changing historical modalities; that is whether it is dynastic, bureaucratic, etc. or in terms of its relationship to capitalism.

References

Bourdieu, Pierre. 1979. *Outline of a Theory of Practice*. Cambridge: Cambridge University Press

Bourdieu, Pierre. 1979. *Distinction: A Social Critique of the Judgement of Taste*. London: Routledge.

Bourdieu, Pierre. 1987. What Makes a Social Class? On the Theoretical and Practical Existence of Groups, *Berkeley Journal of Sociology*, 32: 1-18

Bourdieu, Pierre and Loic Wacquant. 1992. *An Invitation to Reflexive Sociology*. Cambridge: Polity.

Brubaker, Rogers. 2005. *Beyond Ethnicity*. Cambridge Mass: Harvard University Press.
Brubaker, Rogers and Frederick Cooper. 2005. Beyond Identity, in Rogers Brubaker, *Beyond Ethnicity*. Cambridge Mass: Harvard University Press.
Conference of Religious in Ireland. 2006. www.cori.ie.
Corrigan, Philip and Derek Sayer. 1985. *The Great Arch: English State Formation as Cultural Revolution*. Oxford: Blackwell
Cullen, Paul. 2000. Identity, emigration and the boomerang generation, in Ronit Lentin (ed.) *Emerging Irish identities*. Dublin: Ethnic and Racial Studies, Department of Sociology, Trinity College Dublin.
Elias, Norbert. 1978. *What is Sociology?* London: Hutchinson.
Fanning, Bryan. 2002. *Racism and Social Change in the Republic of Ireland*. Manchester: Manchester University Press.
Farrell, Fintan and Philip Watt. 2001. Responding to racism in Ireland: an overview, in Fintan Farrell and Philip Watt (eds.) *Responding to Racism in Ireland*. Dublin: Veritas.
Ferriter, Diarmuid. 2004. *The Transformation of Ireland 1900-2000*. London: Profile Books.
Forfas. 2001. *The Third Report of the Expert Group on Future Skills Needs*. Dublin: Forfas.
Frazer, Hugh. 2001. Racism, Poverty and Community Development, in Fintan Farrell and Philip (eds.) *Responding to Racism in Ireland,* Dublin: Veritas.
Giddens, Anthony. 1985. *The Nation-State and Violence*. Cambridge: Polity
Gillespie, Paul. 1999. Multiple identities in Ireland and Europe, in Ronit Lentin (ed.) *The Expanding Nation*. Dublin: Ethnic and Racial Studies, Department of Sociology, Trinity College Dublin.
Goldstone, Katrina. 1999. Identity formation and anti-racism, in Ronit Lentin (ed.) *Emerging Irish Identities*. Dublin: Ethnic and Racial Studies, Department of Sociology, Trinity College Dublin.
Gramsci, Antonio. 1973. *Selections from the Prison Notebooks*. London: Lawrence and Wishart.
Gray, Breda. 1999. Steering a course somewhere between hegemonic discourses of Irishness, in Ronit Lentin (ed.) *The Expanding Nation*. Dublin: Ethnic and Racial Studies, Department of Sociology, Trinity College Dublin.
Hall, Stuart. 1980. Race, articulation and societies structured in dominance, in *Sociological Theories: Race and Colonialism*. Paris: UNESCO.
Haynes, Mike. 1999. Setting the limits to Europe as an Imagined Community, in Gareth Dale and Mike Cole (eds.) *The European Union and Migrant Labour*. Oxford: Berg.
Hintze, Otto. 1975. *The Historical Essays of Otto Hintze*. New York: Oxford University Press.
Irish Refugee Council. 2004. www.irishrefugeecouncil.ie
Joppke, Christian. 2005. *Selecting by Origin: Ethnic Migration in the Liberal State*. Cambridge Massachusettes: Harvard University Press.
Lentin, Ronit (ed.). 1999. *The Expanding Nation: Towards a Multi-Ethnic Ireland*, Dublin: Ethnic and Racial Studies, Department of Sociology, Trinity College Dublin
Lentin, Ronit. 2000. Introduction: Racialising the other, racialising the us: Emerging Irish identities as processes of racialisation, in Ronit Lentin (ed.) *Emerging IrishI*

Identities. Dublin: Ethnic and Racial Studies, Department of Sociology, Trinity College Dublin.
Lentin, Ronit (ed.) 2000. *Emerging Irish Identities*. Dublin: Ethnic and Racial Studies, Department of Sociology, Trinity College Dublin.
Lentin, Ronit and Robbie McVeigh. 2002. *Racism and Anti-Racism in Ireland*, Belfast: Beyond The Pale Publications.
Le Sueur, James. 2001. *Uncivil War: Intellectuals and Identity Politics during the Decolonisation of Algeria*. Pennsylvania: University of Pennsylvania Press.
Levinas, Emmanuel. 1969. *Totality and Infinity: An Essay on Exteriority*. London: Martinus Nijhoff
Loyal, Steven 2003. Welcome to the celtic tiger: Immigration, racism and the state, in Colin Coulter and Steve Coleman (eds.) *The End of Irish History*. Manchester: Manchester University Press.
Mac Éinrí, Piaras. 2001. Immigration Policy in Ireland', in Fintan Farrell and Philip Watt (eds.) *Responding to Racism in Ireland*. Dublin: Veritas.
MacLaclan, Michael and Michael O'Connell (eds.) 2000. *Cultivating Pluralism*. Dublin: Oak Tree Press.
Mann, Michael. 1984. The autonomous power of the state: Its origins, mechanisms and results, *European Archive of Sociology*, XXV 185-213.
Mann, Michael. 1986. *The Social Sources of Power: Volume 1, A History of Power from the Beginning to A.D. 1760*. Cambridge: Cambridge University Press.
Marx, Karl and Frederick Engels. 1998 [1845]. *The German Ideology*. London: Prometheus Books.
McDonagh, Rosaleen. 2002. The web of self-identity: racism, sexism and disablism, in Ronit Lentin and Robbie McVeigh (eds.) *Racism and Anti-racism in Ireland*. Belfast: Beyond the Pale Publications.
Miles, Robert. 1989. *Racism*. London: Routledge.
Monswengo, Kenswiko. 2001. The potential of public awareness programmes, in Fintan Farrell and Philip Watt *Responding to Racism in Ireland*. Dublin: Veritas.
Ní Shuinear, Sinéad. 2002. Othering the Irish (Travellers), in Ronit Lentin and Robbie McVeigh (eds.) *Racism and Anti-Racism in Ireland*. Belfast: Beyond the Pale Publications.
OECD. 2005. *Trends in International Migration*. Tables and Charts, OECD, Chart 1.6
O'Toole, Fintan. 2000. Green, white and black: Race and Irish Identity, in Ronit Lentin (ed.) *Emerging Irish identities*. Dublin: Ethnic and Racial Studies, Department of Sociology, Trinity College Dublin.
Rojek, Chris and Bryan Turner. 2000. Decorative Sociology: Towards a critique of the Cultural Turn, *The Sociological Review* 4 (48): 629-48.
Ruhs, Martin. 2005. *Managing the Immigration and Employment of Non-Nationals in Ireland*. Dublin: The Policy Institute, Trinity College Dublin.
Sayad, Abdelmalek. 2004. *The Suffering of the Immigrant*. Cambridge: Polity
Scott, John. 1998. *Seeing like a State: How Certain Schemes to Improve the Human Condition have Failed*. New Haven Conn: Yale University Press.
Skocpol, Theda. 1979. *States and Revolutions*. Cambridge: Cambridge University Press.

Sinha, Shalini. 1999. The right to Irishness: implications of ethnicity, nation and state towards a truly multi-ethnic Ireland, in Ronit Lentin (ed.) *The Expanding Nation*. Dublin: Ethnic and Racial Studies, Department of Sociology, Trinity College Dublin.

Torpey, John. 2000. *The Invention of the Passport*. Cambridge: Cambridge University Press.

Tracey, Noel. 2001. Address to the Expert of Supply Chain Professionals, www.entemp.ie/press/2001/091101.htm.

Wacquant, Loic. 1997. Towards an Analytic of Racial Domination, Domination, *Political Power and Social Theory*, Vol 11: 221-34.

Watt, Philip. 2002. Introduction and Overview, in *Migration Policy: Reform and Harmonisation*, Dublin: NCCRI.

Weber, Max. 1968. *Economy and Society*. New York: Bedminister Press.

White, Elisa. 2002. The new Irish story-telling: media, representations and racialised identities, in Ronit Lentin and Robbie McVeigh (eds.) *Racism and Anti-racism in Ireland*. Belfast: Beyond the Pale Publications.

Wimmer, Andreas and Nancy Glick Schiller. 2002. Methodological Nationalism and beyond: Nation state building, migration and the social sciences, *Global Networks. A Journal of Transnational Affairs* 2(4): 301-334, 2002.

Wittgenstein, Ludwig. 1957. *Philosophical Investigations*. Oxford: Blackwell.

CHAPTER ELEVEN

"SPECIAL POWERS": NORTHERN IRELAND AND RACISM IN A PERMANENT STATE OF EXCEPTION

ROBBIE MCVEIGH

> I would be willing to exchange all the legislation of this sort for one clause of the Northern Ireland Special Powers Act, John Vorster South African "Minister forJustice" 1963 introducing the Coercion Act.[i]

The Northern Ireland statelet has been in a permanent state of emergency since its formation in 1920. The *Civil Authorities (Special Powers) Act (Northern Ireland) 1922* became its hallmark as well as being the envy of totalitarian regimes the world over (CAIN 2005). The Act featured a range of "special powers"—prevention of access of family and solicitors to persons imprisoned without trial, the prohibition of inquests, and the capacity of the minister of Home Affairs to create new crimes by Decree. There is some debate as to the clause that was coveted by the apartheid regime; contenders include retrospective criminality—the ability to make an act that was legal when committed subsequently illegal—and the catch-all ability to arrest a person who did anything, "calculated to be prejudicial to the preservation of peace or maintenance of order in Northern Ireland and not specifically provided for in the regulations". We might suggest retrospectively that the most significant schedule of all was the one that allowed the state to operate outside the regime it imposed on others—"these regulations shall not, save as therein expressly provided, be construed as applying to members of His Majesty's forces when acting within the scope of their duties".

This special powers formation was therefore an early prototype of a concept that has increasingly exercised philosophers and lawyers of late—the "state of exception". Giorgio Agamben suggests that this concept addresses "two points":

> The first is a historical matter: the state of exception or state of emergency has become a paradigm of government today. Originally understood as something extraordinary, an exception, which should have validity only for a limited period

of time, *but a historical transformation has made it the normal form of governance*. I wanted to show the consequence of this change for the state of the democracies in which we live. The second is of a philosophical nature and deals with the strange relationship of law and lawlessness, law and anomie. The state of exception establishes a hidden but fundamental relationship between law and the absence of law. It is a void, a blank and this empty space is constitutive of the legal system (Agamben 2004).

The "state of exception" has particular currency therefore because it is argued that it has become the "normal form of governance". This idea of the *permanency* of the exception is also developed in the work of Michael Hardt and Antonio Negri:

The state of exception has become permanent and general; the exception has become the rule, pervading both foreign relations and the homeland.... The constitutional concept of a 'state of exception' is clearly contradictory—the constitution must be suspended in order to be saved—but this contradiction is resolved or at least mitigated by understanding that the period of crisis and exception is brief. When crisis is no longer limited and specific but becomes a general omni-crisis, when the state of war and thus the state of exception become indefinite or even permanent, as they do today, then contradiction is fully expressed, and the concept takes on an entirely different character (Hardt and Negri 2005: 7-8).

Without forcing the comparison, we can see the Northern Ireland "Special Powers" Act as one of the pre-echoes of the US Patriot Act and the UK Prevention of Terrorism Act 2005, and all the other new phenomena, from "rendition" to "unlawful combatants" that indicate the arrival of a permanent state of exception. The Special Powers Act was modelled in the Defence of the Realm Act 1914 and the Restoration of Order in Ireland Act 1920.[ii] It was renewed annually and then made permanent in 1933. It remained a statute in force until 1971 when it was replaced by the Emergency Provisions Act which was later supplemented by the Prevention of Terrorism Act 1974. These were both superseded by the Terrorism Act 2000, "An Act to make provision about terrorism; and to make temporary provision for Northern Ireland about the prosecution and punishment of certain offences, the preservation of peace and the maintenance of order". So for its *whole* existence, some 86 years, the Northern Ireland state has been governed under emergency legislation despite the fiction that this legislation has been "temporary" in character. This continued despite the "new beginning" that supposedly followed the Good Friday Agreement (GFA).[iii] The criminal justice review promised by the GFA explicitly excluded any review of emergency legislation. Indeed the recent "Stormontgate" *coup d'etat*, which saw the elected government suspended by an intervention by the police and executive in which British state agents were apparently centrally involved, was proof of the continued pathology of the state (Davenport 2005). If recent theoretical activity on the importance of the *permanent state of exception* needs a test case, they can find it here. Northern Ireland is a state of exception which has been *permanent* for much longer than those that have been absorbing state theorists of late.

It is perhaps not surprising therefore, that this pathological state formation has generated its share of racism. In 2000 the BBC reported that, "racism is now twice as common as sectarianism" (BBC News 2000). By 2004 *The Guardian* suggested that Northern Ireland was becoming, "the race hate capital of Europe":

> Northern Ireland, which is 99% white, is fast becoming the race-hate capital of Europe. It holds the UK's record for the highest rate of racist attacks: spitting and stoning in the street, human excrement on doorsteps, swastikas on walls, pipe bombs, arson, the ransacking of houses with baseball bats and crow bars, and white supremacist leaflets nailed to front doors. (Chrisafis 2004)

Even this level of hyperbole was topped in February 2005 when *Der Spiegel* announced that Belfast was the "most racist city in the world" (Matussek 2005). Suddenly racism was the new sectarianism in Northern Ireland.[iv] Everyone from the Irish President Mary McAleese and Jesse Jackson to the KKK had a view on this surge in racism (BBC News, 2004h; Press Association 2004). Concern was mounting everywhere at this new phenomenon—from *Wikepedia* to the governments of the Philippines and Portugal whose citizens had been attacked (BBC News 2004b, 2005a).[v] In the midst of this combination of increasing disquiet and journalistic hyperbole, however, there has been a telling silence around the role of the state, despite its unenviable reputation. This is not particularly surprising since the statelet was supposed to have been reconstituted in the "new beginning" that followed the peace process and the GFA. Moreover, the escalation in racism jarred with the mood music of twenty first century Belfast. The "most racist city in the world" tag didn't sit comfortably with the notion that Belfast was now a shining example of economic development, reconciliation and post-conflict society.

Two striking problematics emerge from this situation. These help us to understand something profound about state racism and racism in the state of exception. First, this particular "state of exception" exists fairly unproblematically inside a formal democracy. Northern Ireland is not some pariah territory but rather a constituent part of the UK state, a state formation more than satisfied of its own virtues, tolerance and general decency.[vi] Second, when Northern Ireland racism hit the headlines, this new racist violence was not associated with the old Special Powers statelet—with emergency powers envied by apartheid South Africa, but rather the statelet that emerged from the peace process and the GFA. This was a state formation that was supposed to be founded on the commitment to human rights and equality and which claimed to be setting a good example for Palestinians, South Africans and Iraqis. The nexus between the Northern Ireland statelet and racism provides a unique vantage point from which to ask the question of what is the specificity of racism in the permanent state of exception. So how does the recent exponential growth in racism in Northern Ireland connect to the issue of the state in this most complex of state formations?

Northern Ireland and the State of Exception

To make sense of all this we need to begin by addressing in more depth the nature of the state formation in the Six Counties (of Northern Ireland) post-GFA. It is clear of course that there cannot be an analysis of the nexus between the state and racism without an analysis of the nature of the state. But this is more complex in the Six Counties than it is in most other locations. As suggested above, Northern Ireland has always been a permanent state of exception. The Northern Ireland statelet emerged from the ashes of the colonial British state in Ireland and an unfinished anti-colonial revolution. It thus inherited the peculiarly repressive apparatus of the Irish colonial state but reshaped these in new hyper-sectarian forms; political boundaries were gerrymandered, the franchise was restricted and the Royal Irish Constabulary (RIC) (which had been predominantly Catholic) was reconstituted as the Royal Ulster Constabulary (RUC) (which was overwhelmingly Protestant) alongside a new Special Constabulary which was totally Protestant. As we have seen, a new legal infrastructure of emergency was introduced to govern the state on a permanent basis.

So the Northern Ireland state formation is palpably complex. The current state formation draws on a long history—a sedimentation of successive states of exception. First, the statelet retains aspects of the colonial British state in Ireland that are missing in both the "post colonial" 26 counties of the Republic of Ireland as well as in Britain itself. Second, the statelet created by partition in 1920 was an archetypal "racial state"; its sole logic was the construction of a polity with a guaranteed British/Protestant majority and prevented separation from the colonial power. Third, since the imposition of Direct Rule in 1972, the relative autonomy of this statelet has been severely curtailed. Fourth, since the GFA there have been attempts to restore this autonomy with a new level of cross community legitimacy. Finally, this settlement is currently (Spring 2006) suspended—with a return to neo-colonial administration from Westminster— and its looks difficult to resurrect. The key point about this is that each of these phases has structured racism in the north in particular ways; each has, in its own way, been a different "racial statelet". Moreover, the complex nature of the contemporary statelet means that the state/racism nexus makes it particularly challenging to theorise.

This historical complexity is compounded by its equally complex location within the British state and other formations. In this sense Northern Ireland can be described as a "racial statelet" (Lentin and McVeigh 2006). We find an autonomous state-like structure inside the British State which is in turn inside "Fortress Europe". The institutions of EU racism are therefore overlaid on the institutions of British state racism overlaid on the institutions of the Northern Ireland state of exception. The state formation therefore has *some* of the attributes of a state while missing others; it is defined by its subordinate relationship to the British state as well as other state structures like the EU, the US and the Irish State.

The limited autonomy of the statelet is illustrated by the continuing distinction between matters for which the Northern Ireland Assembly is now responsible and matters for which the British Government remains responsible. In terms of British Government responsibilities in Northern Ireland, there is a further distinction between "*reserved*" matters and "*excepted*" matters. The distinction is that reserved matters are issues that may eventually be devolved to the Northern Ireland Assembly (if and when it is reconstituted), and "excepted matters", like foreign policy and immigration, that the British Government insists on maintaining control over. Under the GFA, therefore, there is a series of excluded powers which include asylum, migration and citizenship policy which will *never* devolve to the "racial statelet". It hardly requires emphasis that many of these powers are precisely those which most characterise state racism in other states that we examine through the "racial state" paradigm (Goldberg 2002).

We can illustrate this complex state/statelet dynamic through a couple of recent events. At the beginning of 2005, there was much discussion surrounding the story of a young migrant worker who, after she had been made redundant, lost her legs from frostbite as she slept rough in Coleraine, County Antrim. Strikingly, the media coverage hardly ever used the term "racism": it was a "tragedy" but it had, you would have thought, nothing to with race. Yet her experiences were a direct consequence of British state policies—her status as a migrant worker meant that she was unable to access the support available to citizens. But here we begin to see the complexity of the state/statelet dichotomy in Northern Ireland, the policy of encouraging migrant workers and yet denying them basic employment and social welfare rights is a policy of the British state. Even if the Northern Ireland Assembly were not suspended, it could not introduce a more humane regime for migrant workers. While the case attracted a great deal of publicity and sympathy, it pointed to the weakness and lack of autonomy of local state structures.

Likewise, when it was in operation, the Assembly offered consistent crossparty opposition to the internment of asylum seekers in Maghaberry Prison in contravention of the UK's obligations towards refugees. Again, however, the Assembly could do nothing about this. This was a policy developed and implemented by Westminster, by the British racial state, not by the Northern Ireland "racial statelet". Asylum seekers are still being held in high tech, high security prisons that are a legacy of the political conflict in the north, first Magilligan, then Maghaberry and now Crumlin Road. Here we begin to see the infrastructure of the Northern Ireland racial statelet laid bare: asylum seekers who have demonstrably done nothing wrong are incarcerated in the apparatus of the Northern Ireland conflict, while the people whose racist violence has made Northern Ireland the "race hate capital of Europe" remain at liberty. We begin to see that the reality of racism and state policy in the north is constantly structured by the particular state formation there and, more particularly, by its peculiar state repressive apparatus.

Managing racism in a racial statelet

There is no disputing the activity that has been generated by the state management of racism and anti-racism of late. It bears emphasis, however, that this is a new phenomenon. The British Government resisted the introduction of "race relations" legislation in Northern Ireland for over thirty years, not least because it offered the possibility of redress from the sectarian discrimination which so characterised the "Special Powers" state. (The first British race equality legislation appeared in 1965; parallel legislation for Northern Ireland did not appear until 1997). For years the British State had been not just ignoring but actively denying the existence of racism in Northern Ireland. State intervention on racism *just* predated the Agreement—the dynamic leading up to the *Race Relations (Northern Ireland) Order 1997* was independent of the peace process. Subsequent legislation and policy on racism has, however, been firmly embedded in the human rights and equality structures which emerged from the GFA. At one level this represents a new, integrated state intervention on racism. For example, responding to a question on racism in Northern Ireland on behalf of the Government, The Lord President of the Council, Baroness Amos, said:

> The Government have made it clear that there is no place for racism in society. Their anti-racism policy is given effect through legislation including the Race Relations (Northern Ireland) Order 1997 as amended by the Race Relations Order (Amendment) Regulations (Northern Ireland) 2003 and Section 75 of the Northern Ireland Act 1998. The Office of the First Minister and Deputy First

Minister is developing race equality and good relations strategies for Northern Ireland (Hansard June 17, 2004).

Given that ten years before the British State position had been that there was no need for anti-racism legislation in Northern Ireland, this represented progress of sorts. However, the development of state anti-racism is not without its contradictions. In particular we need to critique the palpably limited effectiveness of the new state institutions in the face of escalating racist violence across the north.

Following the passing of the Race Relations Order in 1997, state anti-racism took off enthusiastically in the context of the equality agenda within the GFA. Minority ethnic groups were mentioned in the Rights, Safeguards and Equality of Opportunity section of the Agreement—although the two references are fairly cursory.[vii] Race equality became one of the four core responsibilities of the Equality Commission which emerged from the Agreement. Protection from discrimination on the grounds of ethnicity was also a key element in Section 75 of the Northern Ireland Act (1998) which gave legislative effect to the Agreement through the British Parliament. Some of these developments were much more than tokenism. For example, in the Race Relations Order Traveller ethnicity has been named and protected by legislation in a way that now seems radical in comparison to the current government position in the Irish Republic. Resourcing of some aspects of the work of the EU, particularly in terms of legal intervention and test cases, is much stronger in the north. Moreover, in principle at least, Section 75 provides a template for strong, proactive equality proofing by the state.

Despite these gains, however, as we observe the state management of racism and anti-racism within the peculiar "suspended devolution" state formation currently in place, we get the distinct impression that all is not well. For all the commitments and genuine advances, Northern Ireland is now "the race hate capital of Europe". So how did promise of the "new beginning" in the GFA translate into a policy and practice that has been so disappointing in its realisation? How is it possible that a settlement that was supposed to ground *everything* done by government in equality and human rights should see Northern Ireland soar to the top of the European league of racist violence?

Ironically we have seen a downplaying of state anti-racism and a retreat from equality in the wake of the Agreement. This is startling enough given the central emphasis that the Agreement places on equality and human rights and the commitments it made, albeit in passing, towards minority ethnic groups. But it is even more shocking when it is viewed in the context of the rise in racist violence and the effective declaration of "open season" on minority ethnic people in Northern Ireland. How did this happen? First, the new Equality Commission amalgamated existing equality quangos, including crucially the

Community Relations Education Northern Ireland (CRENI). This move had been resisted by the agencies involved as well as by NGOs, all of whom insisted that the inevitable consequence would be a lowest common denominator approach to equality rather than promised economies and synergies of scale. With regard to racism at least, these predictions have been realised. The dedicated racism-specific work of the CRENI has been absorbed into more general equality work. There is no longer a race development unit within the Equality Commission. The racism-specific work has in theory been mainstreamed into the Divisional structures, so there are workers in Employment Development Division and Promotion and Education Division and Policy and Development Division who are working on race related issues. These workers then contribute to Corporate Plan commitments. The difficulty with this is that the Corporate Plan says very little about racism. There is one mention of "racial harassment" in the EC Corporate Plan, which appears as a "Public Life and Community Safety" "impact measure" which suggests that it expects to see: "Evidence of action tackling racial harassment in the following areas: employment; housing; education; and community safety" (2003: 22). This evidence should exist after three years. It is unclear, however, what it would look like or how we would know it. More bizarrely still, there is only *one mention of racism* in the whole of the Corporate Plan 2003-6 (2003).[viii] This says nothing particularly profound, still identifying racism solely in terms of prejudice:

> Prejudices of many kinds, such as sectarianism, racism or sexism, continue to influence the way people are treated in Northern Ireland..... (2003: 9)

This obviously contrasts starkly with the focused strategy and work of the CRENI on racism. The EC Corporate Plan does emphasis its role in promoting "good relations":

> Our particular role in terms of promoting good relations, between people of different racial groups and in respect of our responsibilities under section 75 of the Northern Ireland Act, is a vital component of this work. (2003: 9)

This emphasis on "good relations" between racial groups appears on several occasions through the corporate plan. This is as problematic as the lack of emphasis on racism since the obligations of the Equality Commission under section 75 clearly involve an instruction to regard equality as trumping good relations.[ix] Equality for racial groups has apparently disappeared off the radar of the Corporate Plan as "good relations" assumes a central importance, now described as a "key duty" in the document introduction. This bears emphasis—the EC has a responsibility to promote good relations between multiple identities; yet "good relations" between racial groups are the only ones mentioned, and therefore presumably prioritised, in the plan. This takes it away from its statutory duty to promote equality towards its lesser responsibility to promote good relations—a space already occupied by another quango, the Community Relations Council (CRC).

The CRC was a body that long pre-existed the Agreement and one that was given no role by the Agreement. It had singularly failed to transform relations between sectarian blocs. Moreover, it had never taken any position on racism in all the years that the state was actively denying the problem in Northern Ireland. Despite this track record, it has eagerly expanded its work to address "racism" in the wake of the Agreement. This was, of course, "racism" constructed out of a CRC paradigm. For example, the chairperson of the CRC could claim:

> It is a fact that there are more racist attacks in Northern Ireland than in England and Wales and that people in Northern Ireland are more likely to be racist than sectarian (2003).

Neither of these assertions is a "fact". Moreover, the notion that racism and sectarianism can be measured comparatively in this way is silly; any cursory glance at the grim tally of sectarian murders over recent years illustrates just how problematic this notion that "people in Northern Ireland are more likely to be racist than sectarian" is. But this idea has taken hold. Within months the Equality Commission and the Community Relations Council were asserting with absolute certainty: "We know from research that people in Northern Ireland are actually more likely to be racist than sectarian" (BBC News 2003a; CRC 2003). It is particularly troublesome that this line is promulgated by the Equality Commission, the body with most immediate responsibility for addressing both phenomena and from which we might expect a deal more sensitivity and sophistication on such a complex question. We find, however, this post-GFA body aping the analysis of the pre-GFA CRC. The CRC has been characterised by its inability to name the state as part of the problem when it is analysing sectarianism (McVeigh 2002). Not surprisingly therefore when it turned its efforts towards racism, it exhibited the same blind spot where the state was concerned. Once again the problem became constructed as one of "community relations" and one in which the state was absolved of any agency or responsibility. Thus, for example, the CRC can boast, "150 events to tackle sectarianism and racism in community relations week" but offers no opinion on the state's inability to prosecute or convict people for racist violence (CRC 2005a).

Put the trajectories of the Equality Commission and the CRC together and we begin to make sense of just how racism was moved down the agenda of government *despite the fact that racist violence has clearly spiralled out of control*. Thus with state anti-racism we see a rather curious and provocative *retreat* by the state in the wake of the GFA. Of course, the relentless convergence of Blairism and Thatcherism would suggest no particular commitment to state intervention of the left reformist kind that brought race equality legislation to Britain in the 1960s and 1970s. But here the state actually *withdrew* in the context of the GFA. It effectively dismantled its own race equality apparatus in a context in which Northern Ireland was becoming the "race hate capital of Europe". In other words, the pre-GFA state was, however belatedly, more focused and targeted in its anti-racism than the post-GFA state. In the present context, the state parades a new form of multiculturalism based on the notion of "good relations" while even its own Equality Commission presents itself as being more committed to good relations than equality.

"Good relations" and state racism

Within the GFA framework, therefore, state interventions have forced "anti-racism", or the state management of racism, into a community relations paradigm in a way that profoundly distorts the project of addressing and dismantling racism. This distorts the way in which the state approaches racism but it also increasingly structures community responses as well. Thus the Equality Commission is increasingly devoid of any anti-racist equality agenda at all, however timid and reformist. Meanwhile, the Community Relations Council which has no competence whatsoever on racism (and arguably very little in terms of its track record on sectarianism) is pushed towards providing the authoritative state voice on racism. This development, however, begins to expose the tension between the community relations paradigm of conflict which has dominated the way sectarian conflict in the north of Ireland is understood and models based on political struggles for justice and equality. From this perspective, the community relations paradigm is threatening to undermine the whole spectrum of anti-racism in Northern Ireland.

Yet, for various reasons, almost everyone has conspired to support the continuance of the community relations paradigm in the north of Ireland, despite the fact that it was accorded no role in the GFA. The community relations paradigm is the survival of an older, state-led intervention which was supposedly bypassed by the GFA (McVeigh 2002). In the Agreement human rights and equality were supposed to copper fasten the peace process, not "community relations training". The continued dominance of the community relations paradigm has now begun to corrupt anti-racist work for two key reasons. First, this approach cannot address the racism of the state at all. Second, it can only address the racism of unionism in community relations balance with a sensitively "equal" engagement of racism within Irish nationalism. Racism—

like sectarianism—is reduced to a problem of "relations" between communities. In being racist—as with being sectarian—"one side is as bad as the other".

The problem is, however, not one of community relations, the so-called "relations" between minority ethnic communities and unionists and nationalists. *The problem is racism,* not race or racial relations that somehow emerge inevitably if there are two ethnic groups sharing the same space. There should be no negotiation on this basic principle of anti-racism. There should be no fudging on organisations that are involved in organised racist violence, no "tolerance", no understanding of cultural traditions, no mediation through loyalist commissions. So while fascism and racism must be understood, this is only because this is a necessary prerequisite to removing them from society. Here the role of the state is absolutely pivotal; there can be no ignoring the state and what it does or doesn't do about organised racism and organised racist violence.

Once we put the state back in the picture, we begin to make sense of just why there has been the recent upsurge in widespread and organised racist violence in Northern Ireland. While there has been an elective affinity between loyalism and racism against minority ethnic groups, the issue is not simply about political culture. The issue is not loyalism *per se* but the nexus between loyalism and the state. To really understand how Belfast became the "most racist city in the world", we must make sense of state racism in the peculiar context of the Northern Ireland "statelet". A key beginning is made in Bill Rolston's article "Legacy of intolerance: racism and Unionism in South Belfast" (2004). As Rolston notes, the rise in racist violence cannot be disconnected from British nationalism in Ireland. Of course, all of this local specificity happens against a backdrop of British state racism. Northern Ireland is party to the broader package of legislation and policy on citizenship and nationality, it is part of the broader regime of British state racism. It is also far from immune from broader British nationalist discourse about "fears" and "threats" in relation to immigration and asylum. And where states lead, others follow. It is hardly surprising then that Northern Ireland unionists, arguably the most pro-state, pro-British community in the United Kingdom, begin to mimic "their" state and "defend their communities" from these racialised "threats". The British state has often pandered to this constituency without any critique of what it represents. Even when loyalism turns its attentions away from Catholics towards minority ethnic people—or at least adds them to the list of people from which the loyalist community and state must be defended—the state says silent. There was no sadder emblem of this than the state funeral accorded the footballer George Best. Amid all the state-led construction of a positive sense of self for unionism, people remained conspicuously silent on the notorious incident when Best said Pelé "wasn't bad for a nigger" (McVeigh 1998: 11).

It is useful to develop this argument with a couple of examples of the contemporary nexus of loyalism and the Northern Ireland state: first, the state's treatment of the Loyalist Commission; and, second, the intervention of the Independent Monitoring Commission (IMC). This analysis is less about the importance of either body, than the way it illustrates graphically how antiracism has been marginalised by political processes and, more particularly, by the apparatus of the Northern Ireland statelet.

Especially in the current international climate, it seems strange for the institutions of state to be keen to sit down and legitimate organisations that the state itself has labelled "terrorist". This is, however, precisely what has happened with the Loyalist Commission.[x] Witness the pillars of state and government lining up to meet with the Commission over recent years (McVeigh 2005; Lentin and McVeigh 2006). These included former Northern Ireland Secretary of State John Reid, the NI Chief Constable Hugh Orde and the Irish Republic Taoiseach Bertie Ahern (BBC News 2002, 2003b, 2003c).

The key point about this in terms of the nexus between racism and the state is that all through this period, organisations represented on the Commission were involved in racist violence across Northern Ireland. This violence was justified by the commitment of loyalist paramilitaries to "defend their communities" (*The Irish Times* 2002). In this context, it is important to remind ourselves of what the Loyalist Commission was doing over this period of "very positive" meetings and "frank exchanges" of views with leading representatives of the British and Irish states. The Commission was the key source of political interventions by the loyalist paramilitaries doing all this community "defending":

> The Loyalist Commission has for a period of time been analysing republican tactics post the Provisional IRA ceasefire and monitoring the recent manifestation of this in interface areas. It is evident the PIRA ceasefire is no longer intact, and that a dangerous policy of systematic republican agitation and aggression, aimed at Protestant communities living in interface areas throughout Northern Ireland, is being organised... Such attacks have caused loyalist paramilitaries to defend their communities and then only after considerable restraint in the face of republican provocation. There are no indications that republican aggression will diminish, rather experience shows they will simply broaden the violence to other areas (*The Irish Times* 2002).

The key methodology for "defending" areas appeared to be the expulsion and exclusion of Catholics and minority ethnic people from those communities. Lest the silence on racism be seen as an aberration, it was clear that Commission members were also involved in other criminal activity:

Reporters from the Irish tabloid *The Sunday World* are enduring their second weekend under loyalist death threats and a boycott from the Ulster Defence Association.... The paper's 'crime' was to expose the activities of the UDA's so-called brigadier in east Belfast, who has amassed a personal fortune through drug-dealing. The 'brigadier' sits on the Loyalist Commission, an umbrella body comprising the main loyalist terror groups, unionist politicians and the Protestant churches. 'The boycott was supported by everyone on the Loyalist Commission, including the Protestant Ministers and the unionists. This is an assault on some of the cornerstones of democracy—free speech and a free press,' said [editor Jim] McDowell (McDonald 2003).

The point of this detail is that through this whole process of British and Irish state engagement with the Loyalist Commission, racist violence—alongside many other nefarious activities—was being perpetrated by people associated with and represented on the Commission. Racist violence had become a key manifestation of the loyalist commitment to "defend their communities". Yet there is no evidence of any of the representatives or institutions of the establishment—the Chief Constable, the Secretary of State, the Taoiseach—taking them to task for this violence, let alone refusing to engage with them until racist violence from Loyalists had ended. This obviously begs the question of how much confidence in the state this would give to a minority ethnic person under siege in a loyalist area. The implication was that *racist violence is not a matter of great concern to the state.*

A second example of this state disavowal of racist violence is provided by the IMC. This body has a specific brief to monitor paramilitary activity:

The Independent Monitoring Commission was set up by the British and Irish Governments on 7th January 2004. Its purpose is to help promote the establishment of stable and inclusive devolved government in a peaceful Northern Ireland. It does this by reporting to the Governments on activity by paramilitary groups, on the normalisation of security measures in the province, and on claims by Assembly parties that other parties, or Ministers in a devolved Executive, are not living up to the standards required of them. The four Commissioners are entirely independent of both Governments (IMC 2006).

Despite this specific responsibility to report on "activity by paramilitary groups", the only mention of racist attacks in IMC reports is a perfunctory reference in the Third Report: "Members of the organisation [the UVF] were responsible for a series of violent racial attacks in Belfast, though we believe these were not sanctioned by the leadership" (IMC 2004: para. 3.17, 15). Thus the IMC's intervention serves to trivialise rather than problematise the relationship between loyalist paramilitarism and racism. It bears emphasis that, as we have seen, this ongoing silence traversed a period in which loyalist paramilitaries were engaged routinely in racist violence. This silence on racism seems especially troubling in the context of the record of the IMC which had often commented publicly on matters where there was very little evidence in the public domain. The IMC has often proved keen to comment on all sorts of activities by paramilitary organisations with only the barest reference to evidence in the public domain (BBC News 2004c, 2005b). Again, and particularly against the background of the IMC stridency on other issues, the implication was that *racist violence is of little concern to the state*. We begin to see therefore the stark reality that racist violence has nothing to do with the "peace process", despite the inherently contradictory implications of this reality. For this state, there is nothing problematic about a "peace process" that is intimately associated with an upsurge in racist violence.

Not surprisingly in the context of the refusal of the state to address the situation, racist violence escalated through 2004 and 2005. In March 2004 a racist leaflet was circulated in Belfast's Donegall Pass by loyalists, claiming that the number of Chinese people living and working in the area "undermines the community's Britishness" (BBC News 2004d). The Chinese Welfare Association has been unable to build its community centre there because of "objections of local residents":

> DUP councillor Ruth Patterson, who has been liaising between ethnic minorities and local residents, said the association should consider a different site. 'The Protestant community living in Donegall Pass have grave concerns about their culture, their identity and way of life being slowly taken away from them,' she said (BBC News 2004e).

The following month racism and sectarianism combined in a successful effort to "ethnically cleanse" Belfast's Sandy Row:

> Leaflets calling for Catholics to be put out of their homes were delivered to homes in the Sandy Row and Donegal Road areas of south Belfast at the weekend. A loyalist protest was held on Wednesday night outside Whitehall Square flats in Sandy Row, where the young Catholic student lives. About 200 men, women and children chanted and carried banners saying: 'Nationalists out, republicans out.' Anti-republican graffiti was also daubed at the flats after allegations were made about the residents in the area... She said it was a shame loyalists in the area could not accept that people from a mix of religions as well as Chinese people lived in the apartment block. (BBC News 2004f)

It is not incidental that the upsurge of racist violence has occurred in marginalised inner city loyalist working class areas. These areas are characterised by poor community structures and an aging population. There is a pool of poor housing stock which provides potential accommodation for a whole range of other marginalised groups: asylum seekers and refugees, migrant workers, students and Catholics unable to find accommodation in the contrastingly congested ghettos of republican west and north Belfast. At one level the arrival of Catholics and minority ethnic people *is* symbolic of the decline of these areas. These communities are in freefall as they lose their industrial base in the shipyard and heavy engineering and their political base in dominant cross-class alliances with the unionist parties and the Orange Order.

When it comes to racism and anti-racism, however, the state compromises with loyalist violence, exposed as inherently problematic. Ignoring racist violence or "constructively engaging" with organisations that are unquestionably involved in this violence is the very antithesis of what the state should be doing. Here we begin to see the elective affinity between community relations responses to sectarianism and racism. Having pretended that organisations are not sectarian, we are now asked to pretend that they are not racist. Witness the Chief Commissioner of the Equality Commission before the Northern Ireland Affairs Committee of the British House of Commons refusing to link racist hate crimes to loyalist paramilitary activity:

> I do not think it is the role of the Commission to actually attribute the attacks. I think that is a matter for the police and for other agencies who work directly in this area (House of Commons Northern Ireland Affairs Committee 2005: Ev 9).

The notion that it is possible to condemn inequality without addressing those directly responsible for that inequality is both bizarre and dangerous. At this point the community relations tradition threatens every aspect of the struggle for equality. We find paramilitary organisations working with a degree of protection from the state, well experienced in terror, well equipped with weapons, systematically engaging in racist violence (BBC News 2004d, 2005c; McVeigh 2005; Rolston 2004). This is a frightening prospect for minority ethnic groups in Northern Ireland. Even more frightening, however, is the notion that the state, especially its equality apparatus, should ignore its responsibility for addressing this violence.

"Good relations" and racism in a permanent state of exception

We can begin to draw broader lessons from the examination of "good relations" and the GFA for other states of exception. For example, the "good relations" modelled in Northern Ireland under the aegis of the Agreement and Section 75 has now appeared in British State anti-racism discourse (CRE 2006).[xi] Thus the multiculturalism which had been repudiated in British state discourse a generation ago has re-emerged in this new form tempered in the fire of British management of the Northern Ireland statelet. This trend continues with the British Government committed to replacing the Commission for Racial Equality with a Northern Ireland-style *Commission for Equality and Human Rights*. The "single commission" model has been adopted despite the palpable failure of the Northern Ireland Equality Commission to address escalating racism (DTI 2004). We need to remember here that the northern paradigm is a particularly bad example of "community relations". It was almost completely state-led with little organic relationship to any progressive non-governmental actors (McVeigh 2002). In other situations multiculturalism has been more genuinely if misguidedly adopted as an appropriate response to a geometric rise in racism. However this is also what makes the "good relations" interventions in Northern Ireland such an interesting case study. Here we see a reactionary state formation take the notion of multiculturalism and forge it into a new tool of oppression (McVeigh 2002).

For all that, however, the same essential truth applies with the model of multiculturalism even in its most benign manifestations; if the model cannot critique the state, *it offers nothing towards the analysis of racism*. Once the state has become a sponsor of the good relations industry, its new role effectively precludes any critical analysis of the state itself. If the state is not understood to be part of the problem, it cannot begin to be part of the solution. Even the most benign readings of the capacity of the state to intervene against racism have to allow that the state itself might need a little reform.

Here we begin to see "good relations" as the motif of racism in the state of exception. Because there is neither rights nor equality agenda here, only the project of re-establishing "good relations" which have, for unspecified reasons, gone awry. These are the good relations of the prison or the concentration camp; the managerial approach to dealing with the profound inequalities that are embedded in the state of exception. The state of exception exists largely because of profound structural inequalities between groups of people, and "good relations" are the key mechanism for managing ideologically the consequences of those inequalities without ever reducing them.

We can also remind ourselves that there is no necessary affinity between autonomy and democracy.[xii] Autonomous anti-democratic formations like the Northern Ireland statelet spring up in the heart of formal democracies with growing frequency. Increasingly imperial powers find and construct these spaces to do things that they cannot do elsewhere. The compromises in justice and equality that these spaces of exception entail also, however, pollute the whole body politic. Another lesson that the British state management of Northern Ireland teaches us is that, sooner of later, the special powers that are supposed to be connected to "terrorism occurring in the United Kingdom and connected with the affairs of Northern Ireland" evolve into special powers that can be used against everyone. For example, the British Government is committed by the GFA and the Joint Declaration to "the removal of the provisions particular to Northern Ireland when the security situation allows". [xiii] This has evolved through different negotiations as a package of "security normalisation measures". Indeed the IMC has a specific responsibility under Article Five to "monitor" *inter alia* "the repeal of counter-terrorist legislation particular to Northern Ireland" (IMC 2003). But this is a Pyrrhic victory for human rights. This "normalisation" is only possible because the "special powers" formerly restricted to Northern Ireland have been *mainstreamed*. Powers that used to specify connectedness to the affairs of Northern Ireland are now available to, and widely and routinely used by, the whole apparatus of the British state.

Within these ever-expanding spaces of exception, racism is rampant. Indeed, racism is institutionalised in the state of exception itself. One of the principal reasons that there is a state of exception is that "normal" rules preventing or mediating racism do not apply. Think here of how odd the ordinary conventions of race equality look when applied to these situations. Could Guantánamo Bay present an "intercultural" view of America if it were more sensitive to cultural difference? Could Abu Ghraib offer a model of "good relations" between Christian guards and Muslim internees if it improved its community relations training? Should the execution of Jean Charles de Menezes be recorded as a "racist incident"? Moreover, the need to construct spaces where racism is acceptable is precisely why immigration, nationality and citizenship processes are exempt from the laws of race equality. After all, these are endemically discriminatory in the first place; they are designed to discriminate against people on the basis of race, ethnicity, nationality and so on. For example, the British State's Race Relations (Amendment) Act 2000—which was, we should remember, passed in the wake of the Lawrence Inquiry with the express purpose of *extending* the operation of the Race Relations Act 1976—*exempts* from "unlawful race discrimination": "(a) either House of Parliament; (b) a person exercising functions in connection with proceedings in Parliament; (c) the Security Service; (d) the Secret Intelligence Service; (e) the Government Communications Headquarters; and (f) any unit or part of a unit of any of the naval, military or air forces of the Crown which is for the time being required by the Secretary of State to assist the Government Communications Headquarters in carrying out its functions". It also does not "make it unlawful for a relevant person to discriminate against another person on grounds of nationality or ethnic or national origins in carrying out immigration and nationality functions". Once we strip it bare, therefore, we begin to see that actions that would "normally" clearly constitute unlawful racial discrimination remain perfectly legal for sections of the state apparatus. Racism remains the preserve of the security apparatus, the apparatus of the state of exception.

So, in these spaces which demand exemption from equality legislation, the incipient state of exception has existed for years. Note, however, than none of them are exempt from "good relations" or multiculturalism or "community relations". In any unequal relationship—between master and slave, bondsman and indentured labourer, factory owner and migrant worker—there is always a place for "good relations". In the absence of equality, inequality must be constantly managed. The ideology of *pacification* is functional in any space, no matter how saturated with racism. Here we begin to unpack the ideological superstructure which accompanies this repressive base: it is *good relations*. At bottom this is the notion that ideological relations can be improved without any change in the power relations that generates them. Racism is endemic in the permanent state of exception and "good relations" has emerged as the key methodology for managing the fallout from this racism.

From this perspective we find that, yes, Northern Ireland does look more like the rest of the "democratic world" than it used to. Not because it has any fewer "special powers", but because the rest of the world has many more. As we approach the "normalisation" that was for years an aspiration of a government at war, the frightening reality is that the rest of the democratic world has progressed to become more like Northern Ireland rather than NI reformed to be like the rest of the world. As the US and Britain entered a permanent state of exception—the Patriot Act, Terrorism Act, detention without trial and justification for the use of torture—we are forced towards the unpalatable conclusion that we cannot tell the difference anymore, not because we in Northern Ireland have caught up with them but rather because they have caught up with us.

The examination of racism in Northern Ireland therefore offers a wider sense of racism in a permanent state of exception. It also suggests that this is very often associated with the trademark presence of "good relations". Moreover, the "good relations" model is exported around the world not because the state is a success but because it has been such a failure. In the absence of genuine delivery of human rights and equality, "good relations" remains a key tool of the emergency state.

Thus we find a curious consistency in the model of the Northern Ireland statelet. Just as its "special powers" heralded the permanent state of exception, so its "good relations" foreshadowed the future management of racism in this new age of empire and global civil war. The characteristic of subordinancy precisely conditions the nature of state racism in the racial statelet. As imperial states come to aggressively manage the consequences of the injustice they visit around the world, they throw up new forms of ideological domination and control. The reality is that "good relations" interventions do nothing to address or reorganise the structural injustices that create "bad relations" in the first place. They mark the point at which the state discards a reformist, equality agenda for the permanent state of exception. They indicate the acceptance that a polity will not be stabilised through reform but rather through normalising emergency.

Conclusion

This chapter has analysed the specific relationship between the growth in racism and the latest phase of the Northern Ireland state of exception. It has located the rise in racism in terms of a specific crisis of the loyalist working class in the post-GFA "racial state", a crisis which has seen "defence" of loyalist communities increasingly manifested in racist violence. At the same time the emergency structures of the state remain profoundly incapable of addressing this racism. This situation is given a further vicious twist by the continuing relationship been the state apparatus and unionism/loyalism. While being careful to avoid journalistic overstatement, the characterisation of the north as the "race hate capital of Europe" and Belfast as "the most racist city in the world" signals a genuinely new and dangerous juncture of the Northern Ireland "racial statelet".

As we have seen, this reality cannot be disconnected from the reality of Northern Ireland as a "state of exception". While most people—including most minority ethnic people—might wish that racism could be disarticulated from the "national question"—the traditional question of the legitimacy of the state in Northern Ireland—this is not possible. Once racism is "live", the state plays a decisive role in managing that racism. The state formation plays a decisive role in determining whether racism will be addressed or exacerbated or ignored. Racism in Northern Ireland has emerged within a "state of exception". The nature of the statelet, its pathological, emergency character, is absolutely determining in the shape that racism takes. This example of racism in a state of exception has two determining characteristics: first, a state apparatus neither interested nor capable of controlling rampant racism; second, a state apparatus with a profligate excess of "multiculturalism": "community relations", "cherishing diversity", "celebrating cultural traditions" and "promoting good relations". In other words, the state trumpets the necessity for an end to racism whilst at the same time asserting its own blamelessness for that racism and its incapacity to do anything about it. Racism in the state of exception is defined by the hegemony of "good relations". Moreover, this ideology is genuinely hegemonic: the state itself begins to believe this is the "solution".

All through the "Troubles" in Northern Ireland, the state encouraged the aspiration for a "return to normality". The GFA saw just such a "normalisation" process. The touchstone to normalisation was an end to Republican political violence, nothing else mattered. As we have seen, this is most graphically illustrated in the silence of the IMC on racist violence, but it characterises the whole approach of the state towards racism. In consequence, endemic racist violence could exist alongside—and sometimes even be taken as an indication of—*normality*. This is not, of course, an unproblematic normality. The statelet lurches from crisis to crisis, from the siege of the Garvaghy Road to the collapsing of government through "Stormontgate". Moreover, the infrastructure of emergency continues to develop in Northern Ireland, from the construction of new peace walls to extending emergency legislation. Yet in many ways the *sense* of emergency has been removed. We might suggest that this is a symbolic point at which the state of exception has become permanent. The "bad relations" of a state in crisis are replaced by the "good relations" of state policy which are not and never will be realised and yet reassure people that something is being done. Furthermore, it may be suggested that his reality has come to characterise not just states of exception like Northern Ireland but the British State and the US State. Here we see the Northern Ireland statelet not as a remnant of the colonial past but a portent of the colonial future. This racial statelet appears less a relic of Britain's first colonial project than a warning of the Anglo-American Empire to come. Northern Ireland catching up with the "mainland" in terms of levels of racist violence is, of course, little to boast about. But this *sameness*, this *integration* indicates an even more profoundly disturbing reality. We see the de-ghettoisation of Northern Ireland through the arrival of the permanent state of exception in the British State. The crowning of Northern Ireland as the "race hate capital of Europe" is thus a symbol of *normalisation*. Northern Ireland has finally achieved "normality" in the context of a British State that has ditched reformism for "good relations" and has come to play a frontline role in the global war on terror and a new age of Empire. Ironically, this new post-GFA Northern Ireland has become, as British Premier Margaret Thatcher once famously asserted, "as British as Finchley". This is, however, hardly cause for celebration for even the most ardent unionist. Northern Ireland is only "as British as Finchley" in the way that Guantánamo Bay and Abu Ghraib are now as American as Disneyland. From this perspective, it is sobering to speculate whether the emergent states of exception in Britain and the USA would now "swap all legislation of that kind" for one clause of the Northern Ireland Special Powers Act.

Notes

[i] Vorster—later Prime Minister of apartheid South Africa—was then Minister for Justice. He made these remarks in the context of introducing a new Coercion Bill in response to radicalization of resistance to apartheid in the wake of the Sharpeville Massacre and the beginning of the ANC's armed struggle (CSJ 1964).

[ii] The Defence of the Realm Act 1914 (DORA) was British emergency legislation passed for the duration of World War One and the Restoration of Order in Ireland Act 1920 which adopted the counter-insurgency measures in DORA for the specific war against independence in Ireland—this legislation governed criminal justice until the Special Powers Act was passed in 1922. While this rich history of Irish-specific emergency legislation is ignored by most work on the state of exception, DORA does attract the attention of Agamben (2005).

[iii] This continuity was neatly symbolised by the recent trial and conviction of Abbas Boutrab—described as an "Islamic terrorist"—in Belfast in a non-jury, emergency "Diplock Court". These courts were introduced in Northern Ireland in response to the "emergency which ... resulted from the escalation of terrorist activities since 1969" and were used to try those charged with "terrorist crimes, defined as scheduled offences" (Diplock 1972). The justification for these courts was always that Northern Ireland juries were specifically vulnerable to intimidation, a factor which seems unconvincing in this case (BBC News, 2004i, 2005d). This new usage in the context of the "war on terror" appears to undermine the British Government's stated commitment to phase out Diplock courts as part of "normalisation".

[iv] This notion was a very specific post-GFA construction. Without much evidence other than the rise in levels of racist violence, it became increasingly commonplace to see racism as a "replacement" for sectarianism. *One* piece of research appeared which made tentative and questionable assertions about "racial and sectarian prejudice": Overall, racial prejudice appears to be around twice as significant than sectarian prejudice in the initial attitudes of the population in Northern Ireland. Around twice as many respondents in the survey stated that they would be unwilling to accept and/or mix with members of minority ethnic communities than they would members of the other main religious tradition (i.e. Catholic or Protestant) to themselves" (Connolly and Keenan 2000). But this fairly tentative finding led many commentators to begin to suggest that racism was "worse" or more prevalent than sectarianism.

[v] In fact the *Der Spiegel* article became an interesting example of the media construction of a situation. The phrase appeared in an article that was highly critical of the Republican movement but also contained the sentence, "It doesn't matter that the Protestant Ulster militias are criminals and drug dealers, that they assault Chinese immigrants, paint swastikas on walls and have manage to turn Belfast into the world's most racist city" (Matussek 2005). There was no source for this assertion, let alone any more structured or objective meter that would allow such an assertion to be made. Still the phrase was reproduced in several Northern Irish media and it connected with a rising moral panic about levels of racist violence (Douglas 2005; Young 2005).

[vi] This is not, of course, to suggest that rest of the UK was unaffected by the permanent state of exception in Northern Ireland. It was because the British government wished to retain the power to detain and question people for up to seven days without charge that it entered a derogation from the European Convention on Human Rights on grounds that the "life of the nation" was under threat. The notion that the situation in Northern Ireland constituted such a threat was last tested in the European Court of Human Rights in 1993 when the derogation was upheld. The Human Rights Act continued the derogation. We might reasonably locate the beginnings of the *entire* British state in a permanent state of exception in this moment. (Statewatch 2001)

[vii] The Human Rights section of the Agreement affirms "the right to equal opportunity in all social and economic activity, regardless of class, creed, disability, gender or *ethnicity*"; The Economic, Social and Cultural Issues section recognises, "the importance of respect, understanding and tolerance in relation to linguistic diversity, including in Northern Ireland, the Irish language, Ulster-Scots and *the languages of the various ethnic communities*, all of which are part of the cultural wealth of the island of Ireland".

[viii] This contrasts starkly with the British Government"s "community relations" strategy *A Shared Future: Policy and Strategic Framework for Good Relations in Northern Ireland* (2005) which uses the term "racism" much more frequently. The implication, however, is that racism is now to be understood as part of the "good relations" rather than equality agenda or, indeed, the agenda of the "peace process".

[ix] In Section 75 "good relations" are explicitly subordinate to equality: "Without prejudice to its obligations under subsection (1) [the need to promote equality of opportunity], a public authority shall in carrying out its functions relating to Northern Ireland have regard to the desirability of promoting good relations between persons of different religious belief, political opinion or racial group".

[x] The Loyalist Commission is comprised of representatives of three Loyalist paramilitary groups: the Ulster Defence Association (UDA), the Ulster Volunteer Force (UVF), and the Red Hand Commando (RHC), and Protestant church and community representatives from north Belfast. Members of the Ulster Unionist Party (UUP) helped to set up the group in October 2001" (CAIN 2005).

[xi] The British Race Relations (Amendment) Act 2000 gave public authorities a new statutory duty to promote race equality, commonly referred to as the "race equality duty". Under the third strand of the duty, public authorities in England, Scotland and Wales are required to "promote good race relations". What exactly good race relations is, and what practical steps a public authority might take to work towards it, remains unclear. The term race relations—let alone "*good*" race relations—is not defined in either statute or case law. However the CRE has "identified five principles that should govern public authorities" efforts in this area. Each is equally necessary to achieve good race relations". These are: Equality, Respect, Security, Unity and Cooperation (CRE 2006). These contrast interestingly with the CRC "three main principles" of "equity, respect for diversity and interdependence" (CRC 2005b).

[xii] For example, devolution, often seen as an inherently positive measure, created the constitutional context for the Northern Ireland permanent state of exception.

[xiii] The GFA includes this detail in the section on "Security": "participants note that the development of a peaceful environment on the basis of this agreement can and should mean a *normalisation* of security arrangements and practices". It also commits the British Government to "make progress towards the objective of as early a return as possible to *normal* security arrangements in Northern Ireland, consistent with the level of threat and with a published overall strategy, dealing with: (i) the reduction of the numbers and role of the Armed Forces deployed in Northern Ireland to levels compatible with a *normal* peaceful society; (ii) the removal of security installations; (iii) the removal of emergency powers in Northern Ireland; and (iv) other measures appropriate to and compatible with a *normal* peaceful society" (The Agreement, emphasis added). It would be diverting to indulge in a deeper reading of all this fetishisation of the "normal".

Suffice to remind ourselves that Northern Ireland has been a permanent state of exception since 1922; special powers are the "normal" in this statelet.

References

Agamben, Giorgio. 2004. Interview with Giorgio Agamben—Life, A Work of Art Without an Author: The State of Exception, the Administration of Disorder and Private Life, *German Law Journal,* No. 5 (May 1, 2004) Special Edition.
Agamben, Giorgio. 2005. *State of Exception.* Chicago and London: Chicago University Press.
Amos, Baroness. 2004. Written Answers. Hansard. June 17 2004: Column WA79
BBC News 2000. Racism growing in NI. April 14, 2000.
BBC News 2002. Reid meets loyalist representatives. March 5, 2002.
BBC News 2003a. NI "needs to tackle racism". March 21, 2003.
BBC News 2003b. Chief Constable Meets Loyalist Commission. March 27, 2003
BBC News 2003c. Ahern in talks with Loyalist Commission. June 11, 2003.
BBC News 2004a. Race Hate on Rise in NI. January 13, 2004.
BBC News 2004b. Filipino leader condemns NI attack. April 2, 2004.
BBC News 2004c. Key role for ceasefire watchdog. September 30, 2004.
BBC News 2004d. Loyalist link to racist leaflets. March 12, 2004.
BBC News. 2004e. Residents object to Chinese centre. October 5, 2004.
BBC News. 2004f. Student fears over loyalist threats. April 29, 2004.
BBC News. 2004g. Rise in racist attacks "slowing". December 3, 2004.
BBC News. 2004h. Racist attacks condemned. June 18, 2004.
BBC News. 2004i . Man faces terror charge. February 4, 2004.
BBC News. 2005a. Minister visiting attack victims. 10 June, 2005.
BBC News. 2005b. Sinn Fein leaders "backed raids". February 10, 2005.
BBC News. 2005c. Loyalists aim to "tackle racism". March 10, 2005.
BBC News. 2005d. Al-Qaeda terror suspect is jailed. December 20, 2005.
CAIN. 2005. Abstracts of Organisations. http://cain.ulst.ac.uk/othelem/organ/lorgan.htm.
Campaign for Social Justice in Northern Ireland (CSJ). 1964. *Northern Ireland: The Plain Truth.* Dungannon: CSJ.
Chrisafis, Angelique. 2004. Racist war of the loyalist street gangs: Orchestrated attacks on minorities raise fears of ethnic cleansing, *The Guardian,* January 10, 2004.
Civil Authorities (Special Powers) Act (Northern Ireland). 1922.
Community Relations Council. 2003. Press Release: Anti-Racism in the Workplace Week, November 4, 2003.
Connolly, P. and M. Keenan. 2000. *Racial Attitudes and Prejudice in Northern Ireland. Executive Summary.* Belfast: Northern Ireland Statistics and Research Agency.
CRC. 2003. Anti-Racism in the Workplace Week. Press Release. November 4, 2003. http://www.community-relations.org.uk/about_the_council/press_releases/31/.
CRC. 2005a. 150 events to tackle sectarianism and racism in community relations week. Press Release March 7, 2005. http://www.community-relations.org.uk/about_the_council/press_releases/37/.
CRC. 2005b. *Community Relations: A Brief Guide* Belfast: Community Relations Resource Centre.

CRE. 2006. Promoting good race relations: a guide for public authorities. London: CRE. http://www.cre.gov.uk/duty/grr/index.html.
Davenport, Mark. 2005. Questions arise from "Stormontgate". *BBC New*, December 18, 2005 http://news.bbc.co.uk/1/hi/northern_ireland/4539550.stm.
Diplock, Lord. 1972. *Report of the Commission to consider legal procedures to deal with terrorist activities in Northern Ireland Chairman: Lord Diplock Presented to Parliament by the Secretary of State for Northern Ireland by Command of Her Majesty December 1972* Cmnd. 5185. London: HMSO.
Douglas, Debra. 2005. Mag brands Belfast most racist city: *Der Spiegel* lays blame on loyalists, *Belfast Telegraph,* March 2, 2005.
DTI (Department of Trade and Industry). 2004. *Fairness for All: A New Commission for Equality and Human Rights White Paper.* London: TSO.
Equality Commission. 2003. Press Release.21 March 2003. International Day Against Racism.
Equality Commission for Northern Ireland. *Corporate Plan 2003-2006.* Belfast: ECNI.
Goldberg, David Theo. 2002. *The Racial State.* Oxford: Blackwell.
Hardt, Michael and Antonio Negri. 2000. *Empire.* Cambridge: Harvard University Press.
House of Commons Northern Ireland Affairs Committee. 2005. *The Challenge of Diversity: Hate Crime in Northern Ireland. Ninth Report of Session 2004-5 Volume Two Oral and Written Evidence.* HC 548-II. London: The Stationary Office Limited.
IMC. 2003. *Agreement Between the Government of the United Kingdom of Great Britain and Northern Ireland and the Government of Ireland Establishing the Independent Monitoring Commission.* Dublin: 25, November 2003.
Matussek, Matthias. 2005. The Madness of Belfast, *Der Spiegel*, February 28, 2005.
McDonald, Henry. 2003. Reporters face death threats, *The Observer,* March 30, 2003.
McVeigh, Robbie. 1998. "There's No Racism Because There's No Black People Here": Racism and Anti-racism in Northern Ireland, in Paul Hainsworth (ed.) *Divided Society: Ethnic Minorities and Racism in Northern Ireland.* London: Pluto.
McVeigh, Robbie. 2002. Between reconciliation and pacification: the British state and community relations in the north of Ireland, *Community Development Journal,* 37: 47-59.
McVeigh, Robbie. 2005. State Racism in the "Race Hate Capital of Europe', *Looking back to see forward: the evolution of community development in a changing climate.* Belfast: Community Work Education and Training Network.
Press Association. 2004. Jackson Slams NI Race Hate. November 1, 2004.
Race Relations (Amendment) Act 2000.
Race Relations Act 1976.
Rolston, Bill. 2004. Legacy of intolerance: racism and Unionism in South Belfast. http://www.irr.org.uk/2004/february/ak000008.html.
Statewatch. 2001. UK Terrorism Act 2000: New definition of "terrorism" can criminalise dissent and extra-parliamentary action.
http://www.statewatch.org/news/2001/sep/15ukterr.htm.
The Agreement. 1998. *The Agreement: Agreement reached in the multi-party negotiations (10 April 1998)*
http://cain.ulst.ac.uk/events/peace/docs/agreement.htm.

The Irish Times. 2002. Full text of the Loyalist Commission statement, June 14, 2002.
Wikipedia. 2006. *Racism: Northern Ireland.* http://en.wikipedia.org/wiki/Racism#Northern_Ireland
Young, Connla. 2005. Belfast: "Most racist city in the world", *Daily Ireland,* March 2, 2005.

CHAPTER TWELVE

"A SLICE OF AFRICA". WHOSE SIDE WERE WE ON?
IRELAND AND THE ANTI-COLONIAL STRUGGLE

PIARAS MAC ÉINRÍ

Ireland: a special relationship with the Majority World?

It has become commonplace for many Irish people to express a sense of shared identity with people of the Majority World and to assert a special link of empathy and understanding of a kind which is felt to distinguish Irish attitudes from those of other countries in the developed world.

This belief is not without foundation. Today's development aid workers may be seen as the successors to the religious missionaries of previous generations. Indeed, this is something which is explicitly recognised in official statements.

> The historical roots of Ireland's Aid programme lie in the remarkable work which has been carried out over many years by Irish missionaries (Department of Foreign Affairs 2002).

This is not the place to fully evaluate the precise nature of the complex relationship between Irish missionary activity (which was not confined to Roman Catholic agencies alone) and the late nineteenth century colonisation of Africa and other parts of the world by an expansionary Europe for which military conquest, trade, aid, religious proselytisation and cultural and economic domination were part of a spectrum of inter-connected projects. It would be beyond the scope of this chapter to offer a critical evaluation of the overall impact of the missionary element of such activity, especially as this remains a contested and under-researched field (Hogan 1990). While there was undoubted paternalism ("helping the Black Babies")[i] there were also beneficial elements, such as the material contributions made in the fields of education and health care. In terms of numbers, the Irish missionary role in the world peaked surprisingly recently. In 1970, there were 7,120 missionaries working in the countries of Africa, Asia and Latin America (Coogan 2000). At that time and more recently there was initial resistance by some Irish missionaries to postcolonial indigenisation of the clergy, but a radicalisation of elements of the Irish missionary church was also evident, as they embraced the socially progressive thinking which emerged within various parts of the Catholic Church, notably in the Americas. Ireland itself has since moved decisively towards a more secular society (Inglis 1998). It seems unlikely that religious vocations in the future will be sufficient to even sustain historical numbers of clergy within Ireland, while vocations to missionary orders have also fallen dramatically (McGarry 1999; Walsh 2001).

In recent decades, official and private development aid has taken over where missionary activity left off. Per capita Irish contributions to such causes are relatively high, although by no means exceptional. The Government reneged on a solemn commitment, given in the context of its successful campaign for a seat on the UN Security Council for 2001/2002, to reach the UN development target for development aid of 0.7 per cent of GNP by 2007 (Department of Foreign Affairs 2001; the website erroneously still carries the older target figure). Nonetheless, official Irish contributions to development aid place the country, if not in the top rank (occupied by the Nordic countries and the Netherlands), relatively close to the top.

International development aid comparisons are notoriously difficult to make for a variety of reasons (including tied trade/aid policies and the practice of counting home-based aid programme expenditure in the overall financial package). However, one such set of comparative data, the *commitment to development index* compiled by *Foreign Policy* and the *Center for Global Development*, enables a comparative estimate of official and private development aid donations to be made for 21 of the richest developed countries in the world.

Country	Official aid in US cents per person per day	Private Aid in US cents per person per day	Aggregate contribution	Ranking
Norway	102	24	126	1
Denmark	84	1	85	2
Sweden	61	1	62	3
Netherlands	57	4	61	4
Ireland	**28**	**6**	**34**	**5**
Switzerland	25	7	32	6
Belgium	28	2	30	7
France	25	1	26	8
Finland	24	1	25	9

UK	23	2	25	10
Germany	18	3	21	11
Japan	20	0.4	20.4	12
Austria	18	2	20	13
Canada	17	2	19	14
Australia	14	3	17	15
USA	13	5	17	16
Spain	11	1	12	17
Italy	11	0.2	11.2	18
Portugal	9	0.1	9.1	19
New Zealand	8	1	9	20
Greece	7	0.1	7.1	21

Table 12-1: Source: *Foreign Policy* 2004

It will be seen that while four countries stand out as being substantially greater contributors than the rest of the list, Ireland is at the head of the "middle group" and well ahead of the very poor performance of a number of southern European countries, New Zealand and the USA. Moreover, Irish private donations are the third highest on a per capita basis. It is interesting to compare this with the often bombastic rhetoric emanating from the US, where a deep hostility towards international aid, the UN and Majority World governments tends to be accompanied by claims that individual donations are the most generous in the world—claims which are without basis in fact (Somberg 2005).

Nowadays, of course, a broader range of criteria, including such factors as policies on trade, investment, migration and sustainable environmental development, would also be included in making a more rounded assessment of a country's posture. In the *commitment to development index* already referred to, Ireland only ranked 18th out of 21 in this broader evaluation, although one could certainly dispute elements of the methodology employed (*Foreign Policy* 2004).

My interest is in exploring discourses of "race" in Ireland in the immediate pre- and post-independence period and with particular reference to nationalist and official state ideologies concerning this issue, ideologies which I think have received inadequate attention, with a few exceptions, such as the work of McVeigh (1992), Garner (2003), Rolston and Shannon (2002), and Fanning (2002) in accounts of the historical specificities of Irish racism. After a brief consideration of official and popular discourses of "anti-colonialism", I propose to explore how well current Irish claims regarding its anti-colonial past stand up historically by focusing on Irish attitudes to the Boer War, the question of "whiteness" at the time of independence and the often ambiguous Irish attitudes to India. I shall also touch on the more genuinely subversive revolutionary underground connections between Irish and other anti-colonialists, connections which over time were all but extinguished as such sentiments became associated with Communism and as official Ireland largely failed to reciprocate the interest and admiration shown in it by other colonised peoples.

Ireland as coloniser and colonised

Looking back, one may discern a number of strands in the construction of the Irish assertion of their solidarity with others. Two stand out: the vexed question of Ireland's status as a colonised nation (or not, according to one's point of view) and the putative role of the Great Famine of the late 1840s in forming Irish responses to deprivation. In particular, Ireland's ambiguous status as part-colonised and part-colonising, white but arguably subaltern, perpetrator and victim, has positioned the country and its people in a very specific way vis-à-vis contemporary debates about the location of core and periphery in a rapidly-changing, increasingly globalised world, even if the collective amnesia of post Celtic Tiger Ireland, as well as a degree of terminal boredom with the whole revisionist/post-revisionist debate, have attenuated this awareness in recent years.

Brown (2001) writes that

> Ireland's experience of imperial oppression and economic underdevelopment undoubtedly gave it a unique empathy with the colonised countries of Africa, Asia and Latin America—unique certainly in comparison with the post-imperial powers of Western Europe. Such solidarity was reinforced by a lingering folk memory of the Famine in the mid-nineteenth century when a million-and-a-half Irish people died of starvation and fever and a further million fled the country. The Great Hunger left deep emotional scars in the Irish national psyche, a syndrome not overlooked by Irish international aid agencies when they drew historical parallels between 1840s Ireland and the developing world in their fundraising efforts.

The Famine still casts a long shadow in Irish folk memory. At the very least, it may be argued that a sense of solidarity with other peoples who have experienced famines in the more recent past, is part of Irish public discourse, while the specific solidarity expressed, for instance, in the campaigning organisation Afri's annual Famine Walk and other projects concerned with justice, peace and human rights, is a more ideologically charged version of this sentiment.

The Afri walk commemorates the Irish famine, as well as expressing solidarity and friendship with the people of today's world who continue to suffer famine, poverty, violence as a result of war, military suppression and injustice (Afri website 2005).

Official discourses

A characteristic feature of official discourses in contemporary Irish foreign policy has been a tendency to connect with these received public and historical discourses in order to assert a specific ethical position for Irish official attitudes and policies in this field. Such perspectives are not entirely spurious. There is a degree of real interaction and interpenetration between popular and official discourses on this issue which cannot simply be written off as an exploitative form of "bandwagoning". Moreover, it represents a highly effective tool in building public consensus for policies which, in the development aid area in particular, involve the commitment of substantial funds. It may also be argued that such discourses have been central in areas other than development aid as well. This has been especially true of Ireland's carefully modulated position of moderate support (albeit a good deal less noticeable in the years after EEC/EU membership) for anti-colonial causes around the world. This tendency to adopt policy positions at the edge of the orthodox did not entirely disappear with EU membership either. A classic example was Minister for Foreign Affairs Brian Lineman's famous Bahrain Declaration of 1980 calling for the establishment of a Palestinian State (Dáil Debates 1980).

> 1980 saw the Bahrain Declaration in which foreign minister Brian Lenihan recognised "the role of the PLO in representing the Palestinian people" and called again for 'the withdrawal of Israel from all territory occupied since the 1967 conflict'. This became the basis of the EC's Venice Declaration later that year, thus confirming Lineman's role as a major architect of ostensible Community policy on the Palestine question (Deane 2005).

Nowadays, even US President George Bush accepts the principle of Palestinian statehood, even if the pro-Israeli bias of the US means that country's commitment is theoretical rather than real (Bush 2002).

From a longer historical perspective, it is perfectly possible to see such initiatives as part of a careful and largely successful policy by an Irish Government emerging from the isolationism of post-World War Two neutrality and positioning itself within an emerging and rapidly decolonising world in a manner which gave the State, so to speak, something useful to do on the world stage. And while, in spite of its oft-proclaimed neutrality, Ireland never went so far, for instance, as to consider joining the Neutral and Non-Aligned (NNA) movement led by states such as India and Yugoslavia, it did seek to advance a number of views, notably on issues of UN peacekeeping, nuclear non-proliferation and support for newly emergent postcolonial states, which enabled a number of distinctive policy profiles to be articulated.

The architects of such policy initiatives were both tough-minded and subtle. As the famous 1957 controversy over a possible UN debate on the admissibility of "Red China" showed, there was a willingness to show real steel when necessary, even if the eminent and powerful Irish-American Cardinal Spellman had to be seen off by officials following the views of then Foreign Minister Frank Aiken (Cruise O'Brien 2002).

There was undoubtedly a long tradition of solidarity between some Irish revolutionary elements and their counterparts elsewhere. There were also instances of individuals who managed to cross over from the revolutionary to the official side, without quite abandoning elements of their earlier "subversive" beliefs. Few examples illustrate this better than the extraordinary career of Seán McBride, son of Maud Gonne and Major John McBride (who had fought for the Boers in the Boer War). A former chief of staff of the IRA, he was Minister for External Affairs for Ireland from 1949 to 1951, recipient of both the Nobel and the Lenin prizes for peace in the 1970s, a celebrated international diplomat and negotiator, and a Paris-born intellectual who spoke English with a strong French accent until the day he died.

However, it is another matter for the Government to claim, as it sometimes has done, that official Irish attitudes in these matters have *always* been progressive. My contention is that this was not the case and that, in particular, the dominant view in the pre- and post-independence period of the early twentieth century was informed by a desire to position the would-be fledgling state as respectable and fit to govern itself—in a word, as white.

Locating the historical perspectives

As I have already suggested, revisionist and anti-revisionist (or post-revisionist) arguments about colonialism and postcolonisalism and whether Ireland was a colony, or complicit in colonialism, or both, have gone on for many years in parallel with what has by now become a rather tedious larger argument about relations between Britain and Ireland. Protagonists such as Akenson (1993), Deane (1990), Foster (1988), Gibbons (1996), Howe (2000), Lloyd (1993) and Peatling (2005), speaking from varying disciplinary and ideological perspectives, have had their say. I do not intend to re-hash their arguments. I am not primarily concerned either with the racialisation of Irishness in other places (see e.g. Ignatiev 1995; Hickman and Walter 1997; Walter 2000), nor with the various and sometimes extensive influences exerted by events and ideas in Ireland on subaltern peoples in other parts of the British Empire and/or Commonwealth (e.g. Silvestri 2000). Both questions—the place of Ireland in the project of colonisation and the reception of Irish nationalist discourses in other British-ruled jurisdictions—nonetheless form a backdrop to this chapter.

First, I shall argue that it would be anachronistic to impute a policy of anti-colonialism or anti-imperialism to pre-Independence nationalists or to the young Free State in the 1920s. On the contrary, it seems to me that the new State was probably more anxious to prove its credentials as a trustworthy member of the Commonwealth by asserting its whiteness (notably in solidarity with South Africa and other white-ruled dominions including Canada, Australia and New Zealand) and its distinctly different status from those parts of the British Empire where the indigenous population was not white and/or a non-indigenous colonial class was in control. In doing so, it drew upon many existing discourses, including the strong pre- and even post-Independence connections with the British Empire, the role of missionaries in an "Irish Empire" of the spiritual realm, received ideas from the Diaspora such as the way in the which Irish-Americans, in Ignatiev's terms, "became white", and existing and largely unquestioned racist ideologies current in both Ireland and Britain at the time. I would also point out that the passage to independence was characterised by continuing close cooperation between the justice and immigration authorities in the UK and Ireland, as is evident from Ireland's draconian Aliens Act 1935 (based on earlier wartime British legislation 1914) and later on in the adoption in the 1950s of the Common Travel Area Agreement which saw the near-total alignment of Irish immigration policy to that of the UK, an approach which continues to this day (Mac Éinrí 2002).

Insofar as an anti-colonialist and anti-imperialist discourse existed—and it did—it was a somewhat attenuated one after the Civil War defeat of advanced (especially left-wing) nationalists and the counter-revolution which saw a political class representing conservative, religious and large farming interests take power (Regan 1999). Those who adopted a position of solidarity with subject peoples elsewhere in the British Empire became identified as marginal elements of Irish society, usually close to a far left position, often Communist-influenced, which gradually fell under ever-greater Church and establishment opprobrium in the 1930s. By the time the Spanish Civil War convulsed the Irish public arena, mostly in support of Franco's Fascist state, it was fairly clear where majority Irish opinion lay (Stradling 1999; McGarry 2000).

The evidence for my assertions will necessarily be rather general but I believe that (although Howe, Garner, and Rolston among others have already posed valuable questions) this subject would repay further detailed study.

Pre-independence

In the first place, as has been said elsewhere (Akenson 1993), the spread of Irish missionary activity so characteristic of the final decades of the nineteenth century was in no way incompatible with the spread of Empire, quite the contrary. This had been eloquently put earlier in the century by Fr John Hand, the founder of All Hallows College (1842) for educating Irish missionaries: "God has coupled with the proud mistress of the seas an humble handmaiden... wherever England is found Ireland is by her side" (Clancy 2005).

Apart from religious expansionism, which was not long in shifting its attention from the protection of the Irish flock overseas to the garnering of new souls for the Lord (Society of African Missions, Irish Province website 2005), there were many accompanying reasons why Irish attitudes to Empire were frequently unquestioning or actively supportive. Unionists and moderate nationalists i.e. the majority of the population at least up to 1918, saw valuable career opportunities in the project of Empire, and over time persons of Irish descent came to be proportionally over-represented in the ranks of the military and administrative classes of Empire (Akenson 1993). Thus, for instance, from the 1850s on, the Irish universities actively prepared their students for the Indian Civil Service and other colonial careers. As Holmes (2000) points out, Queen's College Cork offered courses in Indian history, Indian geography, Hindu law and Muslim law (sadly, this is no longer the case). Other Irish universities did likewise; Trinity College Dublin and the Queens University of Belfast offered Sanskrit and Arabic.

This does not mean that support for the ideology of Empire was wholehearted or universal; there were occasional voices raised in support of the rights of indigenous peoples. But it seems reasonable to argue that the majority did not see much connection between the growing Irish desire for self-government and the treatment of indigenous peoples in other places. Indeed, as Holmes suggests, Irish behaviour in India, for instance, was only to be distinguished from that of their British counterparts insofar as many of the Irish were regarded as unusually harsh. Later, Irish Home Rule MPs in the House of Commons were happy to accept sponsorship at one point from the imperialist adventurer Cecil Rhodes, who provided funds in return for political support. We do not know if either side saw anything particularly problematic about this arrangement (Lowry 1998).

The Second Boer War 1899-1902

The single most dramatic example of the lack of Irish concern with issues of race and nation, where the nations in question were subaltern and not white, lies in the strong popular support in Ireland for the Boers, especially during the period of the Second Boer War in 1899-1902. Irish "advanced nationalists" identified strongly with the Boers as another culturally and linguistically oppressed white people within the British Empire. The question of the treatment of indigenous Black Africans did not enter into the matter at all. Two regiments were raised in support of the Boers in Ireland, Major John McBride became a prominent leader and spokesman for them, and pro-Boer riots and unrest broke out in Dublin and elsewhere in 1899. *The Midland Tribune* reported on February 17, 1900:

> Almost every Saturday at the weekly petty sessions we see men very properly punished for disorderly conduct on the streets. Of course, in the eye of the law this crime is much aggravated by the frequent cheers for the Boers and Kruger with which we are growing so familiar of late. ... it seems as if the contagion of admiration for sturdy old Kruger is extending itself to the softer sex. On Saturday, we suppose the climax was reached when a woman who boasts of the significant name of Power, was fined 5s and costs for indulging in such a treasonable practice. Surely the days of chivalry are gone (*Midland Tribune* 1900).

Although 28,000 Irish troops fought on the British side during the war, compared to fewer than 500 for the Boers (McCracken 2000); the episode left an important legacy of solidarity and folk memory in Ireland. The Irish also saw parallels in the decision of the Liberals in 1907 to grant the Boers a form of self-government and there were frequent contacts between reformist unionists and nationalists like Plunkett and Griffith with Rhodes, Smuts and others (Lowry 1998).

Ultimately the Boer revolt profoundly influenced advanced nationalists including the physical force tradition. As Lowry points out

> 'Whenever England goes on her mission of empire, we meet and we strike at her,' warned Patrick Pearse in 1914, 'yesterday it was on the South African veldt, tomorrow it may be on the streets of Dublin'... The Easter 1916 insurgents wore Boer-style hats known as 'de Wet caps', and a number of ex-Boer rifles were captured by the British (Lowry 1998).

Not only were the links between Ireland and South Africa's Boers strong, but Lowry reminds us that the very title of the new Irish Free State was based on its South African precedent and also recounts that

> ... the Irish delegates suggested using the South African title of high commissioner instead of governor-general, in an effort to reduce dominion titles, until it was pointed out to them that the governor-general applied to the white

population and high commissioner to the native population. They were horrified at the prospect of being 'put on the same level as the blacks' and they therefore agreed to the title of governor-general (Lowry 1998).

There is ample evidence that Irish-South African relations continued to be unusually warm after the Irish Free State was established, most particularly with Boer elements on the South African side. Indeed, some degree of diplomatic acrobatics was required in a later period as Ireland re-positioned itself as a champion of the anti-Apartheid movement. As Lowry notes, speaking of the Afrikaner leadership:

> ...as in Ireland, there was a fair sprinkling of former guerrilla generals-turned-parliamentarians, including Smuts and Hertzog, who had in their time made war on the empire. To Irish leaders, Afrikaner nationalists appeared to be plain-speaking, austere farming folk who had returned from the brink of annihilation, while Afrikaner nationalists in turn often warmed to Irish emphases on language, culture, family, fatherland and faith—even if the doctrines of that faith radically differed from their own. 'I had but to talk the Irish and feel at once that they and I understand one another,' Hertzog later recalled during an official visit to Dublin, 'Our history has been very much a parallel' (Lowry 1998).

Admiration for the Boers was, however, but the explicit sign of a broader belief, summed up by the parliamentarian John Dillon when he said that Ireland deserved Home Rule "because we are white men" (McCracken 2003). Critic Joseph Valente observes that Dillon was a cousin of Dubliner Bram Stoker, whose *Dracula* (1897) can be interpreted as an extended meditation on the troubling nature of Irishness (and Jewishness)—"white" but different (Valente 2002).

This theme of whiteness recurs frequently in both moderate and "advanced" nationalist circles of the time. Thus, English naval officer turned Irish nationalist Erskine Childers, in his 1911 *Framework of Home Rule* wrote:

> No one disputes that the Dutch colonists had grievances, without the means of redress. As usual, we find a land question in the shape of enhanced rents charged by Government after the British occupation; the Dutch language was excluded from official use, and English local institutions were introduced with unnecessary abruptness; but the principal grievance concerned the native tribes. Slavery existed in the Colony, and its borders were continually threatened by these tribes. The Dutch colonists were often terribly brutal to the natives; nevertheless there is little doubt that a tactful and sympathetic policy could easily have secured for them a more humane treatment, and the abolition of slavery without economic dislocation. But a strong humanitarian sentiment was sweeping over England at the time, including in its range the negro slaves of Jamaica and the unconquered Kaffirs of South Africa, but absolutely ignoring, let us note in passing, the

economic serfdom of the half-starved Irish peasantry at our very doors. Members of this school took too little account of the tremendous difficulties faced in South Africa by small handfuls of white colonists in contact with hordes of savages. The Colonial Government, with a knowledge of the conditions gained only from well-meaning but somewhat prejudiced missionaries, endeavoured from 1815 onwards to enforce an impracticable equality between white and coloured men, and abolished slavery at one sudden stroke in 1833 without reasonable compensation. A large number of the Dutch, unable to tolerate this treatment, deserted the British flag (Childers 1911).

Space does not allow any more detailed discussion of the reaction in Ireland to the Boer War of 1899-1902. Suffice to say that while many Irish people probably supported the official British line, nationalists, especially "advanced nationalists", had varying degrees of sympathy for the Boers and, as has been noted, a few took up arms on their side. By contrast, what is almost entirely absent from Irish debates at the time is any sense of solidarity with black Africans. Moreover, it is clear that the leader of "moderate" nationalism, John Redmond, saw an opportunity for an Ireland under Home Rule to become a significant partner in the project of Empire.

Irishness as whiteness?

Those who saw a comparison with South Africa had an interest in presenting Ireland not as a downtrodden and oppressed colony, but rather as a land where free men, that is white men, should be allowed to govern themselves. When the Treaty Debates were at their height on 4 January 1922, Deputy A. McCabe, a Sinn Féin member, put it thus:

> Give us Dominion Home Rule, give us Repeal of the Union. Give us anything that will stamp us as white men and women, but for Heaven's sake don't give us a Central American Republic (Dáil Debates 4 January 1922).

The Mexican theme (presumably a legacy of the Zapata years), as well as an equally explicitly racist reference to African subjects of the Empire, recurs in a speech a year later by Kevin O'Higgins, on January 17, 1923:

> There were negotiations, there was a Treaty. It was endorsed by the Dáil, and I have not heard it disputed that it was endorsed by the people. What I want to emphasise is this, that because the race was being wiped out as a distinct national entity we turned with our puny strength against the British, and because the veins and arteries of the country are being cut, and because we bid fair to be classed with the nigger and the Mexican, as a people unable to govern themselves, we who have a democratic mandate, for the moment, to control the destinies of this

country, will go very, very far indeed against the people who are menacing the life of this country (Dáil Debates, January 17, 1923).

It would, of course, be an exaggeration to claim that the whiteness of Ireland was the key to the ideology of the young Irish Free State. "Irish Ireland" nationalism, religion, class and indigenous ethnic differences were of greater significance in the construction of a new Irish identity, narrower and ultimately more backward-looking than that which characterised an earlier, more exuberant phase of cultural nationalism in the 1890s. It is nonetheless worth noting that in its efforts to position itself as an acceptable new polity, the Irish Free State should have chosen to stress its position within a broader imperial world of subaltern natives and white peoples.

O'Higgins's comments are not untypical and his views were not unique. In the debate on the External Affairs Estimate in May, 1925, Mr. Conor Hogan of the Farmers' Party had the following to say:

> ... what makes up the greatness of England more than that very thing, her success in colonisation? Will they deny that? Within reasonable limits what has been made such a great success by the British can also be made a success by us. I believe if it were possible to get a slice of Africa, such a thing is perfectly feasible. In fact, it could be due to us under the terms of the Imperial connection. Did not the South African Commonwealth take over German West Africa? If we could get some part, say some part of the States taken from Germany during the great war, such, for instance, as East Africa, I believe it would be one of the most advantageous things possible for the Irish Free State. I am perfectly serious in this matter. You have there a virgin soil. Unfortunately, when people have to emigrate from this country, they usually go abroad to other countries that are not under our flag. Suppose we had a colony such as I suggest, and if we could induce the people who are determined to emigrate to go to that colony, can you realise what it would mean? They would still remain subjects and they would still retain the home ties. They would live under our flag and they would do a considerable lot towards increasing our export trade. That colony would be a natural means of securing a good export trade for this country, because the colonists would naturally turn to the home land for Irish products to meet their requirements (Dáil Debates, May 13, 1925).

In sum, there can be little doubt that the "whiteness" of the Irish was accepted as a given, not only in Ireland, but also in Britain, by the early twentieth century. This is in no way to imply that all British people saw the Irish as their "racial" equals or that the Irish were not themselves the victims of a sustained racialisation in one form or another down to the present day, however attenuated it may now be. But I would suggest that many Irish and British people saw few links between Irish identity and nationalism ("advanced" or not) and the various anti-colonial and anti-imperial movements within the broader

British Empire, although there are a few notable British exceptions to this general observation, such as Salisbury's famous comparison of the Irish and the Hottentots in 1886 (Pearce 1997). In that sense, later claims to a continuity or solidarity with what we nowadays call the Majority World need to be strongly qualified by the recognition that any such solidarity reflected a distinctly minority view at the time.

The prevalence of the views on whiteness outlined above can be shown in many differing ways. Thus, for instance, in considering the sensitive question of what to do with those Royal Irish Constabulary men who did not wish to remain on in the new Free State, we find the following from a former county inspector:

> I shall do what I can to get men for that Ontario scheme but…it is no great thing. The men are expected to pay their passage out and work for Canadian farmers at wages which no white man in Canada would look at. A country servant boy in Ireland of a much lower type than our fine ex RIC gets more. If these colonial governments want decent settlers they must come out with a straight-forward scheme. So far none of them has done so. Our men are not fools. What I fear most of them want is cheap labour. In short, they are treating our men as niggers and it won't do (quoted in Fedorowich 1999).

Irish-Indian contacts

Irish attitudes towards Indian nationalists, as opposed to their African counterparts, before and after independence, involved more frequent contacts and a greater degree of solidarity, but were also curiously ambivalent. Already in the 1870s one Irish Home Ruler, F.H. O'Donnell, supported the transformation of the Empire into a Commonwealth of equal partners and argued for the "oppressed natives of India" (Silvestri 2000). Such initiatives were however limited and intermittent. The leader of the Irish Home Rule Party, Charles Stewart Parnell, refused to support the notion that an Indian should be nominated to run for an Irish parliamentary seat. That said, it would appear that contacts between Irish and Indian nationalists were relatively frequent, ironically in the seat of Empire, London, and considerable fellow-feeling seems to have developed on both sides. Nonetheless it would appear to have been a courtship where the Indian side's declarations were ultimately not reciprocated by the Irish, whose example was hugely important in the greater Empire and beyond but who did not themselves greatly reciprocate this interest in them.

An important radical exception to the lack of contact and solidarity in the immediate post-independence period was the *League against Imperialism*, which flourished for about ten years before its eventual demise in 1937 (O'Malley 2003). It brought together some quite remarkable Irish and Indian political figures, including leftist Irish republicans Frank Ryan, Peadar

O'Donnell, Seán McBride, Dónal O'Donoghue; feminist Hannah Sheehy Skeffington, labour activists Helena Moloney and Jim Larkin; Indian nationalists Krishna Deonarini (Rienzi), Philip Rupasangha Gunawardena; and Bombay-born British MP and labour activisit Shapurji Saklatvala. The League also attracted such international notables as Calcutta-born British anti-war activist and longstanding Labour politician Fenner Brockway, Jawaharlal Nehru, nationalist and first Prime Minister of independent India, scientist Albert Einstein, French writer and anti-militarist Henri Barbusse and the American novelist Upton Sinclair. Unfortunately, although meetings took places in various parts of Europe, including Dublin, it eventually came to nothing, largely because of the heavy-handed control increasingly exercised over it by the Soviet Comintern. From the outset it was regarded with suspicion by all of the various police and intelligence forces in those countries where it organised, including Ireland (O'Malley 2003).

One other point worthy of note in connection with Free State Government policy in the 1920s is that, in spite of the closeness of the connection with the Union of South Africa,

> (Ireland was) unwilling (at the 1923 imperial conference) to support the Union's exclusionist policy on Indian immigration, and together with the Newfoundland delegation they wholeheartedly supported the Indians' desire for full equality of citizenship and residential rights throughout the empire. On the other hand, in common with the other dominions, the Free State refrained from commenting on South Africa's discriminatory 'native policy' which was regarded as a purely internal matter for the Union (Lowry 1998).

It seemed, then, that in the hierarchy of racial stereotypes, the Indians were positioned by the Irish authorities above Africans.

Throughout this period there is a curious but ultimately empty, (even downright cynical), subtlety in some of De Valera's views and actions as revolutionary leader and later Taoiseach (Prime Minister). At a 1919 meeting of the Friends of Freedom for India in New York, while on his American visit to raise support for the Irish cause, he "stressed both Irish-Egyptian-Indian solidarity and the need for armed rebellion to throw off the yoke of the British Empire".

> We of Ireland and you of India must each of us endeavour, both as separate peoples and in combination, to rid ourselves of the vampire that is fattening on our blood and we must never allow ourselves to forget what weapon it was by which Washington rid his country of the same vampire. Our cause is a common cause (Silvestri 2000).

As late as 1943, he was capable of sending a congratulatory message to Chandra Bose, the Indian nationalist who took arms on the side of the Japanese and against the British in pursuit of his dream of Indian independence, on the formation of the Japanese-backed "Provisional Government of Free India" or *Arzi Hukumate Azad Hind* (*Hindustan Times* 2006). Yet De Valera had also forbidden the entry into Ireland in the 1930s of Ada Wright, international campaigner and mother of two of the Scottsboro defendants, black men falsely accused of rape in a notorious racist trial of the period (Miller et al 2001).

One surprising example of a mainstream Irish politician who had the grace to admit that Indians might have had just cause to resent the Irish was Seán T Ó Ceallaigh, later President. Speaking to the Friends of Freedom for India in 1924 he acknowledged the hurt caused by the Irish role in the oppression of the Indians:

It was 'largely by the work of Irish brains and Irish brawn,' Ó Ceallaigh asserted, 'that the people of India have been beaten into subjection and have been so long oppressed' (Silvestri 2000).

Conclusion

The establishment of the Irish Free State should of course be understood in the light of the circumstances of the time. It would be fair, then, to say that at that time whiteness was an implicit condition of entry into the club of semi-free nations and that most representatives of Irish nationalism in its various forms constructed their nation accordingly. An honourable and more radical dissident anticolonial tradition also existed but it is hard to see how Ireland as a state can lay claim to this legacy, which at the time it did much to deny or suppress.

The ideologies, policies and attitudes of the early Free State made it a relatively simple step in the later period to develop an ever-closer cooperation, primarily with Britain, on a racialised immigration policy. According to this perspective, a principal task of the Irish State, apart from securing its own borders, became one of preventing the possible dangers posed to the British by any possible "back-door route" as UK policies became narrower and more restrictive, notably after the 1962 Commonwealth Immigration Act. By then, the earlier sense of affinity with India and other parts of the Empire, later Commonwealth, such as it might have been, was history. And yet, at the more personal level, it would be difficult to deny that the modern-day experiences of Irish UN troops, or missionaries, or aid workers, in various Majority World countries are not sometimes influenced in some subtle way by a degree of residual goodwill and understanding which at least sometimes indicates a mutual awareness of a legacy of opposition to hegemony.

Perhaps the least which can be said is that contemporary Irish anti-racism needs to take more accurate stock of the attitudes, policies and experiences explored above. There is a danger of an overly facile claim to empathy or solidarity with oppressed peoples in other places, or with those people who have now come to settle in Ireland. We could start with a more thoroughgoing exploration of the policy positions of official Ireland, but also of the nature of the Irish encounter with the Majority World, past and present, whether through officialdom, missionaries or development aid organisations. It may be easy to speak of partnership and solidarity from a comfortable vantage point of charitable giver, but this is a long way from a more radical partnership based on power-sharing and equity within a more just global society. It is time to move beyond the comfort zone.

Notes

[i] A reference to the once-ubiquitous collection boxes placed in the classrooms of Irish Catholic schools, usually by missionary orders, in order to collect money for the "black babies" frequently pictured on the cover.

References

Afri. 2005. http://www.afri.buz.org/management.htm, accessed January 8, 2006.
Akenson, Donald Harmon. 1993. *The Irish Diaspora: a primer*. Belfast: Institute for Irish Studies.
Brown, Rob. 2001. Green Faced Tiger. *New Internationalist*. No. 339, October. http://www.findarticles.com/p/articles/mi_m0JQP/is_2001_Oct/ai_79628817, accessed February 10, 2006.
Bush. George. 2002. President Bush calls for new Palestinian leadership. http://www.whitehouse.gov/news/releases/2002/06/20020624-3.html, accessed January 7, 2006.
Childers, Erskine. 1911. *The Framework of Home Rule*. Project Gutenberg: http://www.gutenberg.org/etext/15086, accessed January 7, 2006.
Clancy, Dermot. 2005, Murdoch University: Centre for Irish Studies. http://wwwsoc.murdoch.edu.au/cfis/abs/clancy.html. accessed January 7, 2005.
Coogan, Tim Pat. 2000. *Wherever Green is Worn*. London: Hutchinson.
Cruise O'Brien, Conor. 2002. She saw me as McBride's stooge and despised me. *The Sunday Independent,* April 7, 2002.
Dáil Debates. 4 January 1922. http://www.ucc.ie/celt/published/E900003-001/text007.html, accessed January 19, 2006.
Dáil Debates. January 17, 1923. http://historical-debates.oireachtas.ie/D/0002/D.0002.192301170007.html, accessed January 19, 2006.

Dáil Debates. May 13, 1925. http://historical-debates.oireachtas.ie/D/0011/D.0011.192505130008.html, accessed January 18, 2006.
Dáil Debates. February 26, 1980. http://www.oireachtas-debates.gov.ie/D/0318/D.0318.198002260011.html, accessed January 18, 2006.
Deane, Seamus. 1991. General Introduction, in *The Field Day Anthology of Irish Writing*. Derry: Field Day Publications: xv-xxv.
Department of Foreign Affairs. 2001. Ireland and Development Aid. http://www.un.int/ireland/dev_aid.htm, accessed January 18, 2006.
Department of Foreign Affairs. 2002. *Ireland Aid Review 2002*, Department of Affairs/Development Cooperation Ireland.
http://www.dci.gov.ie/about_missionary.asp, accessed January 18, 2006.
Fanning, Bryan. 2002. *Racism and Social Change in the Republic of Ireland*, Manchester: Manchester University Press.
Fedorowich, Kent. 1999. Reconstruction and Resettlement: The Politicization of Irish Migration to Australia and Canada, 1919-29. *English Historical Review*, vol. 114, no. 459: 1143-78.
Flynn, Seán and Oliver, Emmet. 2000. "Mercy nuns to cut schools role due to fall in vocations". *Irish Times* March 10, 2000.
Foreign Policy. 2004. Ranking the Rich. http://www.foreignpolicy.com/story/cms.php?story_id=2540&page=7, accessed January 18, 2006.
Foster, Roy E. 1988. *Modern Ireland 1600-1972*. London: Allen Lane.
Garner, Steve. 2003. *Racism in the Irish experience*. London: Pluto.
Gibbons, Luke. 1996. *Transformations in Irish Culture*. Cork: Cork University Press.
Hickman, Mary J. and Bronwen Walter. 1997. *Discrimination and the Irish Community in Britain*. London: Commission for Racial Equality.
Hindustan Times. 2006. Indian National Army in East Asia, http://www.hindustantimes.com/news/specials/Netaji/enlisting3.htm, accessed February 8, 2006.
Hogan, Edmund M. 1990. *The Irish Missionary Movement*. Dublin: Gill and Macmillan.
Holmes, Michael. 2000. The Irish and India: Imperialism, Nationalism and Internationalism, in Andrew Bielenberg (ed.) *The Irish Diaspora*. London: Longman.
Howe, Stephen. 2000. *Ireland and Empire*. Oxford: Oxford University Press.
Ignatiev, Noel. 1995. *How the Irish Became White*. London: Routledge.
Lloyd, David. 1993. *Anomalous States*. Dublin: Lilliput Press.
Lowry, Donal. 1998. "A fellowship of disaffection": Irish-South African relations, circa 1921-1961. *Political Studies Association*. http://www.psa.ac.uk/publications/psd/1998/lowry.htm, accessed January 18, 2006.
McCracken, Donal P. 2000. Odd man out: the South African experience, in Andrew Bielenberg (ed.) *The Irish Diaspora*. London: Longman.
McCracken, Donal P. 2003. Collaborators or Liberators? Irish Race attitudes in the South African Historical Context, in Guðmundur Halfdanarson (ed.) *Racial discrimination and ethnicity in European History*. Pisa: Universita di Pisa.

Mac Éinrí, Piaras. 2002. The Implications for Ireland And The UK Arising From The Development Of Recent European Union Policy On Migration, *Migration Policy in Ireland: Reform and Harmonisation.* Dublin: National Consultative Committee on Racism and Interculturalism.

McGarry, Fearghal. 2000. *Irish politics and the Spanish Civil War.* Cork: Cork University Press.

McGarry, Patsy. 1999. Seminary closes as vocations decline, *The Irish Times,* May, 29, 1999.

McVeigh, Robbie. 1992. The specificity of Irish racism, *Race and Class,* 33, 4.

Midland Tribune. 1900. Tullamore notes. http://www.offalyhistory.com/content/reading_resources/old_newspapers/tribune_fe b1900.htm, accessed January 16, 2006..

Miller, James A., Susan D. Pennybacker and Eve Rosenhaft. 2001. Mother Ada Wright and the International Campaign to Free the Scottsboro Boys, 1931—1934, *The American Historical Review* April. http://www.historycooperative.org/journals/ahr/106.2/ah000387.html, accessed January 10, 2006.

O'Malley, Kate. 2003. The League against Imperialism: British, Irish and Indian Connections' *Communist History Network Newsletter* Issue 14, Spring. http://les1.man.ac.uk/chnn/CHNN14LAI.html, accessed January 18, 2006.

Pearce, Edward. 1997. Anglo-Irish affairs between the bid for Irish Home Rule in 1886 and the outbreak of civil war, *History Today.* Vol 47, Issue 10: 6-8.

Peatling, Gary. 2005. The Whiteness of Ireland under and after the Union, *Journal of British Studies* 44: 115-133.

Regan, John M. 1999. *The Irish Counter-Revolution 1921-1936.* Dublin: Gill and Macmillan.

Rolston, Bill and Michael Shannon. 2002. *Encounters: How Racism Arrived in Ireland,* Belfast: Beyond the Pale Publications.

Silvestri, Michael. 2000. The Sinn Fein of India: Irish nationalism and the Policing of Revolutionary Terrorism in Bengal, *The Journal of British Studies.* Vol. 39, No. 4: 454-486.

Society of African Missions. 2005. http://www.sma.ie/default.asp?article=Foundation_and_Early_History_of_SMA, accessed January 7, 2006.

Somberg, Ben 2005. The world's most generous misers, *Fairness and Accuracy in Reporting* http://www.fair.org/index.php?page=2676, accessed January 10, 2006.

Stradling, Rob. 1999. *The Irish and the Spanish Civil War.* Manchester: Manchester University Press.

Valente, Joseph 2002. *Dracula's Crypt: Bram Stoker, Irishness and the Question of Blood.* Illinois: University of Chicago Press.

Walsh, Declan. 2001. Irish Missionary movement coming to an end, bishop admits, *The Irish Times,* October 29, 2001.

Walter, Bronwen. 2000. *Outsiders Inside: Whiteness, Place and Irish Women.* London: Routledge.

CHAPTER THIRTEEN

RE-RACIALISING THE IRISH STATE THROUGH THE
CENSUS, CITIZENSHIP, AND LANGUAGE

REBECCA CHIYOKO KING-O'RIAIN

This chapter analyses contemporary processes of racialisation within the state in the Republic of Ireland through an examination of three empirical examples: the introduction of a racial/ethnic census question on the Irish census, changes in Irish citizenship laws and changes in Irish language requirements for application to the An Garda Síochána, the national police force.

Recent state theories have demonstrated that modern states are racial in their constitution and operation (Goldberg 2002) and the Irish racial state is no exception (Garner 2004). However, the examples analysed here illustrate that by no means is there a consistent "logic" to state racialisation in Ireland and that the outcomes of each of these programmatic state policies highlights contradictory racial projects in the process of Irish state racialisation. In the case of the census, the "ethnic" question appears to reinscribe racial meanings in Ireland by using technologies of the state to categorise and quantify people along "racial" (visible minority status) lines. The recent changes in Irish citizenship laws to remove *jus solis* (becoming a citizen by being born in Ireland) as a basis for bestowing Irish citizenship distils Irishness as based primarily on *jus sanguinis* or ancestry, which is often assumed to be linked to biological bloodlines and hence "race." The change in the Irish language requirement to apply to be a member of the Irish police force signals a loosening of the link between Irishness and cultural practices such as language. By examining the Irish racial state through its racial/ethnic categories, citizenship laws and language requirements, this chapter illustrates how the Irish racial state is re-racialising itself in different and sometimes contradictory ways.

Race, Racialisation and the Racial State

There has been on-going debate in the social sciences about the fact that race is not a sound scientific concept (e.g. Ali 2004; Gilroy 2000; Murji and Solomos 2005), and some have suggested that to use the concept "race" in social science research is racist in its reification of the concept of race. For many authors, the solution is to bracket "race" as a concept, but then to proceed to use it in studies of racialisation (Murji and Solomos 2005). John Martin and King-To Yeung discuss this catch-22 ontological position with reference to race. They write,

> There is an old Zen koan in which the master Shuzan Osho held up his staff before his disciples and said, 'You monks! If you call this a staff, you oppose its reality. If you do not call it a staff, you ignore the fact. Tell me monks, what will you call it?' The discomfort felt by the monks, who had to choose between denying their insight into the fundamental oneness of the universe and making the absurd counterfactual denial of self-evident fact, is also felt by many sociologists when it comes to race (Martin and Yeung 2003: 521).

We don't want to use the concept for fear of reifying it, but to ignore its role in social life would be denying the obvious. For example, just because the French state does not collect racial and ethnic data does not mean that they do not racially profile racial minority groups in France or that their state is not racialised.

> Just because the French government does not formally articulate such a taxonomy does not mean that the French do not use such a taxonomic system. Few in France are confused by what is meant when Le Pen and his followers cry out 'France for the French' (Duster 2002: 551).

As Duster claims,

> The major task before us is to be vigilant about how and when the concept of race is used and for what purposes, not to advocate a categorical renunciation that, under certain circumstances, redounds benefits of entrenched racial stratification (Duster 2002: 551).

One way to do this has been to focus not on the concept of race, but instead upon the social construction of race, the process through which the concept is given power and meaning in social life, or, in other words, racialisation. Racialisation has become the dominant framework for understanding the process of creating racial meanings, helping social scientists to understand how racial meanings become embedded in ideology and discourse (Murji and Solomos 2005). But the process of racialisation, based on race, is also problematic. Racial ideas are often used and embedded in social institutions in ways that perpetuate privilege for certain groups over others.

These institutions included not only the executive, legislative and judicial branches of government, business interests, trade unions and the mass media, etc., but also political movements within the minorities. Just as they can all be seen as contributing to race making, so in some measure they have contributed to race unmaking. It is a complicated story (Banton 2005: 59).

Perhaps the place to see most clearly the process of racial meanings becoming embedded is in the formation of the modern state. In his seminal book *The Racial State* (2002), David Theo Goldberg offers an impressively detailed analysis of how modern states are by definition racial:

The sociocultural embeddedness of race—its forms and contents, modes and effects of routinisation and penetration into state formation and order—has been basic to fashioning the personality of the modern state (Goldberg 2002: 246).

While race and racialisation are strongly determined by the state, they are not solely the terrain of the state and can bleed into other realms of social life not controlled or shaped directly by the state.

...Race is ultimately uncontainable by state formation. There is always the possibility for race to be mobilized as a counter-history, as counter-performativities and counter-practices to prevailing state design, though the social space for racial counter-performance is invariably contained and restrained (Goldberg 2002: 247).

Therefore, the state, for Goldberg, can be more strongly or more weakly racial. In lagging behind other modern states in terms of racial technologies like racial census categories, the Irish state may still be forming its racial position and indeed may be more flexible or even provide a possibility for the counter-practices that Goldberg speaks of in its racial formation.

Omi and Winant (1994) understand the racialisation of the state as a more processual element in their theory of racial formation by illustrating exactly how racial meanings are embedded and perpetuated through the institutionalisation of race in state institutions and how state composition, policies and discourses perpetuate certain sets of racial meanings. They point out that "the state is composed of its institutions, the policies they carry out, the conditions and rules, which support and justify them, and the social relations in which they are embedded" (Omi and Winant 1994: 83).

However, the state is not a monolithic organism. Various parts of the state may not work together to support some overall racial ideology or claim and in some cases may even contradict each other. There may be hegemonic notions of race, which get perpetuated clearly over time, but it would be unrealistic to see the state as having just one racial ideology, agenda or policy. Rattansi reminds us that,

> ...it is a mistake to treat the state as monolithic. Different ministries and departments of state are charged with carrying out specific governmental tasks and in the process develop relatively autonomous interests, are subject to relatively separate sets of pressures, and have to compete with other branches of state for financial resources (Rattansi 2005: 284).

So while the state may have various racial projects in operation at any one time, and may or may not have a consistent racial ideology, which it articulates at every turn,

> The state is a central player in racial matters. The modern state carries out racial classification, surveillance, and punishment of the population; it distributes resources along racial lines; it simultaneously facilitates and obstructs racial discrimination; and it is both structured and challenged by political mobilization along racial lines (Winant 2004: 3).

In their analyses of the gendering of the state, feminist theorists have critiqued the ways in which the state subordinates women in its composition, policies, legal/bureaucratic norms, modes of institution building and notions of citizenship to find that, "The state is not simply an abstract, macro-level structure; it is also a complex of concrete institutions with which women interact in direct and immediate ways" (Haney 1996: 759). The state then strongly structures the experiences of not only women, but people of colour as well as containing the contradictions and "institutional frictions" mentioned above (Orren and Skowronek 1994: 321). Feminist analyses of the state have reiterated this multiplicity in the state to better understand the state, not only as a monolithic macro-level structure, but also as a "network of differentiated institutions, layered with conflicting and competing messages about gender" (Haney 1996: 759). In doing so, Haney and others (e.g. Orloff 1993) have refocused analyses of the state on the role of resistance within the state by women themselves as well as constraining discourses and policies created by gendered states. Closer analyses of different "arms" of the state, such as the legal, judicial and welfare branches of the state, entailed different approaches to the gender regimes, which took different gendered forms and formats perpetuated throughout the state (Haney 2000: 641).

Much can be learned from feminist state theory, which could be applied to racial state theories. The ethnic differentiation of the category "women" can be glossed over or homogenised in some of these feminist critiques of state theory. Nira Yuval-Davis (1997) argues that this can elide the category of "woman," which does not consider the significant differences among and between women who actually are defined by and interact with the state. This can lead to a reification of the concept of gender in the state, which doesn't also recognise the racialisation of women in diverse ways. This is an age-old tension. The state then prioritises not only gendered, but racialised projects promoted by powerful social actors with certain outcomes in mind.

The different levels at which racial projects operate within different branches of the state may contain different social actors, processes, ideologies and forms which result in very different social effects based on the understanding of race which is embedded in them. Clearly, the state may also play a strong role in structuring the experiences of people of colour (through immigration, citizenship and work policies), guiding the discourse on race, and providing a backdrop to racially bureaucratic policies in, for example, the legal and judicial spheres. By bringing the state back in to theories of race and racialisation much can be learned about how states "work" empirically on race. Theoretically, this chapter tries to stretch state theories to account for how states are not monolithic, but made up of sets of concrete institutions, which can and are often contradictory in terms of racial ideology.

Irish Racial State

The state in the Republic of Ireland is no stranger to racialisation. Even though "racialised others" (Garner 2004; Fanning 2002) such as Jews and Travellers have been present over a long period of time, racial state theorising is relatively new in Ireland. The formation of the nation state in 1922 was subtly infused with racial meanings, which prioritised white, Catholic Irish definitions over others (Garner 2004). Promoting the Irish language was a major way of trying to ethnicise the Free State as stamped clearly "Irish": "...it was possible to choose one's language in a way in which it was not possible to choose one's religion: to choose Irish was to make a conscious commitment to the Irish nation" (Tovey et al 1989: 19). The nationalist movement and the push for independence clearly "coloured" the racialisation of the Irish state as white and Catholic since its inception (Fanning 2002). In its contemporary guise, this politically constructed imaginary homogeneity of the Irish state is challenged by socio-economic change, the weakening of the church, emigration/in migration and globalisation.

The Irish state today is clearly struggling to redefine itself and how it will increasingly deal with the arrival of more diverse ethnic, religious and linguistic groups. Analyses of the Irish State and its racial antecedents argue that the Irish racial state is moving from being racialised to being racist (Lentin 2003; 2004a). The presence of migrant mothers and their "Irish Born Children" now ineligible for citizenship, "subverts traditional understandings of citizenship and 'the nation' dragging Irish modernity kicking and screaming into the chaos of the post-modern" (Lentin 2003: 301). Lentin examines one of the clearest discourses produced by the state, that of integration and harmonisation:

> The state-spawned language of harmonisation, integration, management, and mainstreaming in policy recommendations regarding migrant labour is part of the construction of homogeneity as 'heterogeneity in denial' on the one hand and of a multicultural discourse of 'racelessness' denoting a shift from biologically driven racism to culturalist conceptions of race on the other....The Irish racial state, while promoting racelessness, is always about its own white (Christian, settled) superiority. While declaring its commitment to equality, care and interculturalism—the Irish version of racelessness—the Irish racial state has already begun deporting migrant parents whose applications for residency on the ground of having an Irish citizen child have failed, together with their Irish citizen children (Lentin 2004a: 4).

The case of the change in citizenship laws may actually illustrate a backward slide from cultural understandings of who can be Irish (i.e. if you are born here and live here all your life you are Irish) to biological (ancestral) understandings of who is Irish. The contradictions in the Irish state are clear; we can "KNOW Racism" (the National Anti-Racism Awareness Programme)[i] and try to eliminate racial prejudice through sport and the like at the same time that we are deporting the most vulnerable of the vulnerable in asylum seeking children. Lentin's theorising of the Irish racial state gives us scope to examine the inherent contradictions of empirical racial projects in Irish state racialisation.

In order to better understand how the Irish racial state negotiates these contradictions in the contemporary era, and the process of state racialisation in the Irish context, I now analyse three cases of racial projects within the state. I argue that the Irish state has become more rigid in terms of citizenship and enumeration during the current period of rapid economic growth and prosperity. At the same time, the state has also expanded or showed signs of expanding its notions of Irishness in its approach to ethnic diversity in the police force. However, this expansion of the Irish racial state has happened only to some and along certain lines.

Census

There has been a census in Ireland since the establishment of the Free State in 1922, but the form of the census has changed over time. The collection of racial data is controversial — the state's right to classify and categorise is a form of social control to dictate the terms and terrain on which race and racial meaning will be constructed, embedded and used. Many sociologists such as David Theo Goldberg, (2002) and Alana Lentin (2004) have used Michel Foucault's (1991) analysis of governmentality to understand the micro technologies of the state, such as the census, used to normalise governmentality as part of a conceptualisation of racial or racialised meaning (Rattansi 2005). Most clearly in other countries and eras, the census has been used to rank and order people to accord or deny them certain rights (King-O'Riain, 2005). The Irish state has the capacity for "monitoring and controlling through a series of technologies the nation's biological life" (Lentin 2004b: 1). Clearly, the establishment of racial categories in Ireland could mean that they are conceived for and set out to control and punish ethnic minorities, even though racial/ethnic categories have been used in the US and UK also to promote civil rights and legal claims to prove institutional "racial" discrimination.

In order to reflect the changing demographics in Ireland, the Irish Census has added new questions about income, live births, and racial/ethnic backgrounds. The census has long had a question about nationality, but in the late 1990s it was decided that perhaps enumeration along racial/ethnic lines was needed. The move to add a racial/ethnic question on the census was less controversial than one would have thought; in fact the question on live births provoked by far the strongest response and was dropped. After proposing a format of the question and pilot testing it in 1999, the government rejected the chance to add it onto the census in 2000 (King-O'Riain, 2005). The census question was so "sensitive" in part because there is a distinct absence of legally binding racial and ethnic categories despite the articulations of such categories in Ireland's equality legislation.[ii]

Ethno-racial categories could become crucial to proving instances, if recorded, of discrimination, but that will only be possible based on the categories themselves. It is a field fraught with potential power struggles because it sets the terms of racialisation. In the lead up to the 2006 census, the Central Statistics Office (CSO) responsible for the census, pilot tested a new "ethnic" question (Report of the 2004 Census Pilot Survey 2004) and the government agreed to add the following question to the 2006 census[iii] as illustrated below:

What is your ethnic or cultural background?
Choose ONE section from A to D, then tick the appropriate box to indicate your cultural background.

A.   White
___ Irish

___ Irish Traveller
___ Any other White background

B. Black or Black Irish
___ African
___ Any other Black background

C. Asian or Asian Irish
___ Chinese
___ Any other Asian background

D. Other including mixed background
___ Other including mixed background, write in description.

Even though the question is not billed as a "race" question, and the ticks themselves are on "ethnic" identifiers, they do, in fact, use colour and meta racial designations. No one has to tick black, but can tick under black. The evolution of the categories moved away from national ethnicities i.e. the elimination of "British", which was on a very early draft of the question, towards racial designations as white, black and the like. It creates an ironic situation where the "ethnicity" question on the census actually has meta racial categories of white, black and the like, with Irish (nationality/ethnicity) added and with ethnic identifiers underneath these racial categories.

The evolution of a race/ethnicity question on the Irish census tells us much about the racial meanings embedded in the Irish state through enumeration. I want to make three points here: first, the question is not just an ethnicity question enumerating cultural or ethnic background. It is about capturing data on "visible minority" status and identity, which, it is assumed, could serve as a basis for anti-discrimination legal regulation (Aspinall 2000). Second, the question was formed through an interaction of racial/ethnic meanings in a process of negotiation within the state; this included debate between the CSO, the Equality Authority and the National Consultative Committee on Racism and Interculturalism (NCCRI) who helped to format the wording of the question with little or no consultation with the racialised and with immigrants. The question was also shaped by interaction within racial states and sub-state entities in the UK/Northern Ireland, whose models of race/ethnicity dominate the discourse of ethnicity in the southern Irish state. The discourse and racial meanings thus far embedded in the census test questions have been predominantly state produced and focused on possible bases of discrimination. Third, according to the NCCRI, racial/ethnic meanings are being more formally embedded in the state through the census in the hope that they may be able to provide information to guide the allocation of resources to those underrepresented and underserved groups. They focus primarily on tracking discrimination both individually, but also institutionally. "Employing racial categories may lead to a presupposition of their non-problematic reality.... But ignoring them may lead to a denial of crucial aspects of lived experience" (Martin and Yeung 2003: 539).

Whether we agree or not with the right of the Irish state to ask people to classify and categorise themselves through the census, we should proceed with caution and be vigilant about who is collecting the statistics, along which lines and to what purpose they are being used. The census is not neutral nor does it have the power to dictate the entire conversation about racial equality in Ireland. "Formal taxonomic equality will only be meaningful if it is sustained by more equitable social and political practices..." (Hattam 2005: 69).

The state sponsored racial/ethnic agenda seems to be focused on the tracking of possible racial discrimination in the current racial/ethnic question on the census. The "rights" discourse employed by the Equality Authority and the NCCRI which dominates the form, is a reactive discourse, arguing that to claim rights because of discrimination you need categories to monitor the denial of those rights. These categories are defined in part by those who perpetrate racist acts. Therefore, "other black" is a category because state authorities anticipate having black people face racial, not ethnic, discrimination. Black Irish people are perhaps ethnically Irish, but that is not the basis of their anticipated discrimination. It is the colour of their skin which state authorities think may make them "visible minorities" and vulnerable to discrimination. The ontological catch-22 of speaking of race here is difficult to predict. Can we undo racism by having no categories? If we have the categories, aren't we just anticipating racist acts and reifying them in advance along racial lines by having racial categories? I would argue that we need the categories, if and only if they do indeed capture the basis of race discrimination. Without them, we will have no way to know the scope of racial discrimination in institutional settings, but this has to happen with a vigilant eye on how the data is collected and used.

Citizenship

A second way that states racialise is through their citizenship policies which define who will "be of the nation" with the rights concomitant with that status. For many states, citizenship is dependent upon ancestry and "prior" connection with the nation state. Prior to 2004 (and since the establishment of the state in 1922), Irish citizenship was accorded either through ancestry or through birth i.e. being born in Ireland or having an Irish grandparent made one an Irish citizen. The Irish state was clearly racialising when it changed the constitution in the Citizenship Referendum in June 2004, which formed the basis of the Irish Nationality and Citizenship Bill 2004:

> Notwithstanding any other provision of this constitution, a person born in the island of Ireland, which includes its islands and seas, who does not have, at the time of his or her birth at least one parent who is an Irish citizen or entitled to be an Irish citizen is not entitled to Irish citizenship or nationality, unless otherwise provided by law (Irish Nationality and Citizenship Bill 2004).

The fact that the referendum passed with the support of nearly 80 per cent of those who voted demonstrates the attitudes towards people assumed to be "non-Irish nationals" in Ireland. The campaign was influenced in the media by the portrayal of "Irish born children" with migrant parents versus "Irish children", with the former racialised as undeserving of citizenship rights over the latter. In June 2004, the Citizenship Referendum led to increased restrictions on "non-nationals" and created a racialised two-tier system where *jus sanguinis*, or ancestry, hence *race*, becomes the basis and prime criterion for being an Irish citizen. This gives citizenship priority to third generation Irish Americans who are possibly far removed with no connections at all with Ireland over "Irish Born Children" (often of colour) born and raised in Ireland. The racial distillation of Irishness (read here as whiteness) will be purified through these policies and perpetuate the state's obsession with rules of descent, i.e. race. The ethnic (racial) census categories in the Republic of Ireland are developing within a context of increasing legal and political efforts to control immigration (citizenship) and at the same time to extend racial/ethnic rights and equality (through the census). The census allows for an ethnic concept of Irishness to be combined with different races and promotes a "rights" agenda. The citizenship law however, narrows ethnic and racial Irishness and excludes large numbers of people on "racial" grounds.

The questioning of Irish homogeneity as the "old Catholic nationalist Irish identity" was "disappearing anyway, as part of a process that had already gathered an unstoppable momentum long before significant numbers of immigrants started to arrive" (O'Toole 2005). The fear over what this would mean for Irish society was clearly articulated in the passage of the citizenship bill. Summarising this fear, Kevin Myers, a provocative *Irish Times* columnist, wrote,

> The economist Jim Power of Friends First says Ireland must attract 300,000 migrant workers in the next ten years if we are to achieve our 'growth potential', whatever that means. With dependents, that could be around a million people. So how are we going to cope with the consequences of such a large influx? Should we not, in the longer term, be more modest in our expectations of 'growth potential' and more ambitious in the creation of social harmony? (Myers 2005).

The economic argument gets conflated with a cultural one and is part of the framing of the issue as a zero-sum game for Irish people. The assumption that the bodies of non-nationals threaten social harmony was arguably one reason why people voted to limit citizenship to those who culturally had a "right" to be here. It was clear that the Citizenship Referendum for some distilled Irishness along racial lines and in doing so, "encouraged those with racist tendencies" (Siggins 2004). The referendum was "just another twist in the incapable anxiety of a state seeking to regulate the bodies of its citizens, and most often those, including women, asylum seekers and refugees, whose bodies are at once vulnerable and threatening"(Graham 2004).

Irishness has also become narrowed racially with the less publicised change in the rules for post-nuptial citizenship. Until November 2005, spouses of Irish citizens were given Irish citizenship after a period of three years of marriage, regardless of residency. They could become Irish citizens and reside anywhere in the world as long as they were married to an Irish citizen. The change in the rules means that Irish citizenship will only be available to spouses of Irish citizens married three years or more *and* residing in Ireland (Department of Justice 2004). Under the Irish Nationality and Citizenship Act of 2001, the Irish citizen and his/her children (passing Irishness through ancestry) are Irish citizens, but the non-Irish spouses are not if they do not reside within the state. Irishness through marriage is now limited by residence.

It is clear that the referendum result creates a two-tiered system of citizenship, those with full rights as Irish people, and those who happen to be born here or are here for other reasons (assumed to be nefarious), who, though not considered Irish, can vote in local elections, access social welfare (after proving themselves by living here for two years), and pay taxes to the Irish state.

Language

After independence, language has played a strong role in defining the Irish state as clearly "Irish" and not "English". The rationale was to have the first official language of the state be Irish and to try to re-establish Irish as the primary language. The idea was that if one chose to interact with the state (fill out state forms, work as a civil servant, or testify in the court of law), one could and should be able to do so through the "national language" of Irish. The EU recognition of Irish as an official and working language from January 1, 2007 has strengthened the use of Irish in Brussels as well as in Ireland (Directorate-General for Translation EU 2005). Language then has been a field of battle for Irish identity within the state. This was a racially contradictory position as O'Toole writes,

In one context, they (*the Irish*) were pushed towards a desire to be seen as part of 'the white race', which also included the English. In another, they were pulling against that very notion, attempting to establish through the revival of the Irish language, the creation of national literature and the codification of national sports, a distinct identity in which the possession of a white skin was not in itself a unifying factor sufficiently strong to over-ride difference of culture, religion, and race (O'Toole, 2000: 22, emphasis added).

This appears to be a strongly ethnic conception of the nation and was able to accommodate some difference within it. The role of the Irish language embedded in all state institutions gave Irish a status as the state's first official language of the state. However, according to Tovey et. al.,

the new state did not seriously try to live its own life through the language, or to undertake the heroic efforts, which would have been necessary had it genuinely attempted to fulfil the Gaelic League Programme.[iv] The linguistic and cultural revolution through popular participation which, had been begun by the League, became rationalised and bureaucratised by the state through formal and technical means (Tovey et al. 1989).

Writing in 1989, Tovey et al argued that the state had plays a huge role in developing, maintaining and determining what it means to be Irish through many means including the Irish language, but that this was waning. "The role of the state in maintaining Irish ethnic identity—like the role of the Irish language—has become more symbolic and ritualistic than dynamic" (Tovey et al. 1989: 26).

In the past in order to apply to the Garda Síochána, applicants had to be proficient in the Irish language, which was linked to the requirement that all defendants had rights to be heard in court in either Irish or English. In practice, it was difficult for those who had not been educated in Ireland where Irish is a required subject throughout primary and secondary education, to pass the Irish language proficiency test.

In 2005, in response to falling numbers of recruits and, arguably, to Ireland's new, multiethnicity, it was proposed to change the language requirement for entry into the Irish police force (An Garda Síochána) and do away with the requirement that all applicants have proficient Irish upon entry. This change needs to be seen within analyses of the Irish state as a major shift in the link between the Irish language (if only symbolic) embedded in the state and what it means for "Irishness" racially. The change in October 2005, to allow applicants to have English and one other language and take up the study of Irish within training at the Garda College signalled a significant change in the understanding the Irish state as unitary in requiring Irish language capacity of all its workers and law enforcers. Linguistically homogenous states are not unusual, but the link of nationality to notions of the nation and citizenship figured largely in the rationale given by the Minister for Justice, Michael McDowell, for the change in language requirements, when he said he was recommending the change in part because "...the demand for proficiency in the Irish language could be seen as 'practical discrimination'" (Breaking News 2004).

The Sinn Fein political party responded that the proposal was an "insult to Irish speakers". Sinn Fein Donegal Councillor Pearse Doherty said that "the Department of Justice has consistently acted in deliberate breach of this provision and if they go ahead with their hair-brained proposal the result is that members of the gardai will be unable to work effectively in many communities across the state" (Breaking News 2004). The rationale given by the Department of Justice was that the relaxation of the rules would achieve a force "more representative of multi-cultural society" (Breaking News 2004). The discourse of anti-racism and multiculturalism was clearly being enfolded into the state by actors in the Department of Justice to rationalise the opening up of the criteria for membership in the gardai.

From within the force, the Association of Garda Sergeants and Inspectors (AGSI) had mixed reactions, but in the end voted in favour of keeping the language requirement. Sergeant Padraig Dolan from the Galway West Division said he had no objection to recruits from new ethnic communities "...but let them learn the ways of *our* Irish society, the ways of *our* Irish culture and community and have at least the minimum respect and support for *our* own native language" (Breaking News 2005a, emphasis added). It is clear that the assumption was that all these new recruits would also be new to the country, which probably won't actually be the case, since the rules also stipulate that one must be legally resident in Ireland for five years or more to apply. The assumption that ethnic minorities applying to the force are *not* Irish culturally or an integrated part of the community serves to make them "perpetual foreigners" regardless of how long they have been here. In reality, many who attended the information session when the rule actually did get changed have been in Ireland for many years. Tovey et al's 1989 argument that the support for the Irish language was waning as a sign of lack of confidence cannot be substantiated anymore as Ireland has found confidence economically, politically and socially alongside an increasing visibility for the Irish language at the international, particularly EU level.

Others at the AGSI meeting felt that An Garda Síochána needed to become more multicultural. Sergeant Liam Tighe of the Garda National Immigration Bureau said he was concerned that the motion (to support the Irish language requirement) would be seen as exclusive. "We should be inclusive because we have to police the entire country not just the Irish speakers" (Breaking News

2005b). In fact, the majority of the nation would not need or possibly want to interact with the state through its police force in Irish. It is fairly clear that the need to "hold on to" the Irish language is not primarily for practical reasons such as being able to use it in court if a defendant wishes or in the course of policing, but instead for culturally nostalgic and principled reasons (one should be "able" to speak Irish in all state interactions if desired). Most who speak Irish are assumed to be Irish and therefore "white." Another reason perhaps is to lower the barrier for cross border exchange of police with Northern Ireland so that An Garda Síochána can recruit from the Police Service of Northern Ireland without a language requirement to stand in the way of Northern recruits.

The assumption (and fear for some) is that opening up the Irish language requirement signals a loss of culture and identity for the force, but also for Irish state and society. This is racialised in the nuanced assumptions of the ethnic minority recruits as "new" and "not of the Irish culture." Key to this assumption is that one who is linguistically able to "not speak" Irish means one who probably will speak another "foreign" language instead. Foreigners who speak other languages are clearly "not Irish" and therefore cannot be expected to speak Irish. Those who speak Irish thus are racialised as Irish and therefore white.

The problem with assumptions that connect language to race is that "non-national" or "foreign" police officers are assumed to be better able to "police their own". One sergeant was quoted as saying,

> With them (new people) comes an awful lot of good, but also there are, among some of these communities, some criminal elements. And we have to incorporate good people from these communities into the Garda Siochána to help us keep track of the bad that comes too (Breaking News 2005b).

The assumption is that the "foreign" language capability that these "new" minority police would bring would only be useful in policing the bad element in their own communities. This is confusing given that there are no strong ethnic enclaves, villages, or even towns within Ireland where minority police could be sent. The NCCRI, the state funded advisory group on racism, made clear that this may not be the case:

> In respect of the provision of service it is to be welcomed that the Garda have already made clear that officers from minority ethnic groups are not being recruited with the purpose of policing their own communities, but will be generally deployed in line with the guidelines already laid down within the force (Watt 2005: 4).

In October 2005, with the support of the NCCRI and as a way to meet the goals of the National Action Plan Against Racism, the Garda recruitment began with a series of workshops to give information and encourage applications from ethnic minorities and legally resident "non-nationals" into the force. This move was presented through the discourse of multiculturalism, but the Minister insisted that:

> ...the Irish will continue to have an important place in An Garda Síochána...This initiative clearly shows the commitment of the Government and An Garda Síochána to effective policing in a more diverse society (Department of Justice 2005: 1).

The rhetoric of a multicultural and anti-racist society is re-appropriated from anti-racist groups outside of the state and turned on its head to increase minority representations in the police force and some might point out, converge towards a homogenous (English language based) culture.

> ...the equation of one language with one culture was endowed with political significance: a linguistically united community ('nation') when tied to a territory, could claim to deserve a state of its own (Gal and Irvine 1995: 968).

The state has a language, which reflects the nation and its people. Only as we have seen, it reflects only certain people (those with the right ancestry) and assumes that they have the language as part of the authenticity that helps them to make claims to be members of the "nation". Ireland is a particularly interesting example, where Irish is not a "living" language for many (the majority do not claim that they speak it or are proficient in it: in 2004, the CSO estimated that approximately 1.5 million people in the Republic of Ireland indicated that they were Irish speaking with over 2 million saying that they were not), even though it is taught, by law, through the primary and secondary school curriculum. The opening up of the "state" through language policies could be read as a move to broaden the racial state to incorporate not only different languages, but also the different (diverse) people that speak those languages who now reside in Ireland. However, as the nation becomes more linguistically diverse, English seems to become ever more dominant as the global language. In fact, it is the presence of Ireland as an English speaking country that has contributed in part to increased migration and hence ethnic and racial diversity, which calls the Irish language requirements into question.

Conclusion

This chapter has argued that the racial projects of racial/ethnic census enumeration, changing citizenship and Irish language requirements in the Irish state illustrate that the Irish racial state is not monolithic or even coordinated.

Different racial projects have different discourses of race attached to them, created through them, and the implications in policy and practice are different. At times these conflicting projects operate through the same body, the Department of Justice, and even with the same actor, the Minister for Justice, but in different ways.

In the case of the census, racial and ethnic meanings are used to categorise members of the nation along racial/ethnic lines avowedly in order to track possible discrimination. The census uses a mode of racialised ethnicity (i.e. racial meta-categories with ethnic enumerators underneath), which is self-enumerated and has mutually exclusive categories in order to make claims for rights. The citizenship law changes narrow the basis of citizenship removing post nuptial and residential bases and making ancestry the hegemonic way to be an Irish citizen. This distillation of Irishness re-emphasises the racial (blood quantum and some might say, biological) element of national belonging. In the example of the change in the requirement for Irish language proficiency in An Garda Síochána, it appears to be a move to incorporate linguistic (seen also as ethnic or racial) difference into the police force. The mode of racialisation here is through language and the assumption that non-nationals don't speak Irish or understand Irish culture. In some sense, this reinforces the equation of language with cultural identity, which is racialised white within Ireland.

These three racial projects within the Irish state vary greatly in their modes, discourses, and outcomes. The three examples illustrate the complexities of these different racial projects within the state and point to the increasing flexibility of the state to create a possibility of multiple racialisations, which may include room for a possibility of counter-practices and counter-hegemonic notions of race held by racialised and ethnic minority groups themselves which are multiple, flexible, and context driven.

Notes

[i] The KNOW National Anti-racism Awareness Programme was a three year programme which "aimed to contribute to creating the conditions for building an inclusive and intercultural society in Ireland, where racism was addressed and cultural diversity valued." It was followed by the 2005 National Action Plan Against Racism, which has not really been implemented, to date. http://www.knowracism.ie/.

[ii] The main equality legislation is in two laws the Employment Equality Act (1998) and the Equal Status Act (2000). The Employment Equality Act, 1998, came into operation on 18 October, 1999. The Act outlaws discrimination in relation to employment on nine grounds, namely age, disability, family status, gender, marital status, membership of the Traveller community, race, sexual orientation and religious belief. The Equal Status Act, 2000 came into operation on 25 October 2000. The Act deals with discrimination outside the employment context, including education, provision of goods, services and accommodation and disposal of property on the same nine grounds as those covered by

the Employment Equality Act, 1998. These were both altered slightly in the Equality Act of 2004. http://www.equalitytribunal.ie/index.asp?locID=74&docID=-1.

[iii] The information on the evolution of the racial/ethnic question on the census in the Republic of Ireland was done as a part of a larger project on the process through which census questions evolve. I conducted interviews with CSO officials, examined documents of census makers (both historical and contemporary) in the UK and on the island of Ireland to better understand this process. Most census documentation can be found at: http://www.cso.ie/census/. For more information see King-O'Riain, Rebecca Chiyoko (2005) Stating Your Race: Adding Ethnic Census Categories in the Republic of Ireland (available on request from the author).

[iv] The Gaelic League or Conradh na Gaeilge was founded in 1893, by Douglas Hyde and his friends to encourage the traditional Irish language. The league's aims were to first, preserve Irish as the national language of the country, and extend its use as the spoken tongue; and second, the study and publication of existing Gaelic literature, and the cultivation of a modern literature in Irish. They also supported the development of Irish traditional music and Gaelic Athletics. http://www.usna.edu/EnglishDept/ilv/gaelic.htm

References

Ali, Suki. 2003. *Mixed-Race, Post-Race: Gender, New Ethnicities and Cultural Practices.* Oxford: Berg.
Aspinall, Peter. 2000. The Challenges of Measuring the Ethno-Cultural Diversity of Britain in the new Millennium, *Policy and Politics* 28, 1: 109-118.
Banton, Michael. 2005. Historical and Contemporary Modes of Racialisation, in Karim Murji and John Solomos (eds.) *Racialisation: Studies in Theory and Practice.* New York: Oxford University Press: 51-68.
Breaking News. 2004. SF Slams Move to Relax Garda Language Requirement, *Breaking News.ie.* October 15, 2004.
http://archives.tcm.ie/breakingnews/2004/10/15/story171263.asp.
Breaking News. 2005a. Garda Sergeants back Irish language requirement, *Breaking News.ie.* March 22, 2005. http://breakingnews.iol.ie/email.
Breaking News. 2005b. Irish Language Role in Garda "will continue", *Breaking News.ie.* October 6, 2005. http://home.eircom.net/content/irelandcom/breaking/.
Department of Justice, Equality and Law Reform. 2005. Minster announces Government Approval for major changes to the criteria for entry to An Garda Sióchana, September 7, 2005.
http://www.justice.ie/80256E01003A02CF/vWeb/pcJUSQ6G2CJS-en.
Department of Justice, Equality and Law Reform. 2004. McDowell announces commencement of remaining provisions of the Irish Nationality and Citizenship Act 2001, http://www.justice.ie/80256E01003A02CF/vWeb/pcJUSQ5ZYJK8-ga.
Directorate-General for Translation. European Union. 2005. Irish Becomes the 21st Official Language of the EU.
http://europa.eu.int/comm/dgs/translation/spotlight/irish_en.htm
Duster, Troy. 2002. Caught Between "race" and a hard place, *Ethnicities* 2, 4: 547-553.
Fanning, Bryan. 2002. *Racism and Social Change in the Republic of Ireland.* Manchester: Manchester University Press.

Foucault, Michel. 1991. Governmentality, in Graham Burchell, Colin Gordon and Peter Miller (eds.) *The Foucault Effect: Studies in Governmentality.* Chicago: University of Chicago Press: 87-104.
Gilroy, Paul. 2000. *Against Race: Imagining Political Culture Beyond the Color Line.* Cambridge, MA: Harvard University Press.
Gal, Susan and Judith T. Irvine. 1995. The Boundaries of Languages and Disciplines: How Ideologies Construct Difference, *Social Research* 62, 4 :967-1001.
Garner, Steve. 2004. *Racism in the Irish Experience.* London: Pluto Press.
Goldberg, David Theo. 2002. *The Racial State.* Malden, MA: Blackwell Publishers.
Graham, Colin. 2004. Racism in the Irish Experience (review), *Variant.* http://www.variant.radomestate.org"20texts/racism.html.
Haney, Lynne A. 2000. Feminist State Theory: Applications to Jurisprudence, Criminology, and the Welfare State, *Annual Review of Sociology* 26: 641-666.
Haney, Lynne. 1996. Homeboys, Babies and Men in Suits: The State and the Reproduction of Male Dominance, *American Sociological Review.* 61 (October): 759-778.
Hattam, Victoria. 2005. Ethnicity and the Boundaries of Race: Rereading Directive 15, *Deadalus.* (Winter): 61-69.
Irish Nationality and Citizenship Bill. 2004.
King-O'Riain, Rebecca Chiyoko. 2005. Stating Your Race: Adding Ethnic Census Categories in the Republic of Ireland, unpublished paper.
Lentin, Alana. 2004. *Racism and Anti-Racism in Europe.* London: Pluto Press.
Lentin, Ronit. 2003. Pregnant Silence: (En)gendering Ireland's Asylum Space, *Patterns of Prejudice,* 37, 3: 301-322.
Lentin, Ronit. 2004a. Strangers and Strollers: Feminist Notes on Researching Migrant M/others, *Women's Studies International Forum.* 27, 4: 301-314.
Lentin, Ronit. 2004b. From Racial State to Racist State, *Variant* 20 (Summer 2004), http://www.variant.randomstate.org/20texts/raciststate.html.
Martin, John Levi and King-To Yeung. 2003. The Use of the Conceptual Category of Race in American Sociology, 1937-99, *Sociological Forum.* 18, 4: 521-543.
Murji, Karim and John Solomos. (eds.) 2005. *Racialisation: Studies in Theory and Practice.* New York: Oxford University Press.
Myers, Kevin. 2005. An Irishman's Diary: What are we? A community or an economy? *The Irish Times,* August 5, 2005.
O'Brien, Carl. 2005a. Garda Entry Rules to Change in Effort to Attract Ethnic Minorities, *The Irish Times,* August 23, 2005.
O'Brien, Carl. 2005b. Udaras Member Criticises Plan to Waive Irish Rule for Garda Entry, *The Irish Times,* August 24, 2005.
O'Brien, Carl. 2005c. Garda Entry Changes Set to Allow Non-Nationals to Join, *The Irish Times,* September 8, 2005.
O'Hara, Daniel. 2003. *Yu Ming Is Ainm Dom.* Dough Productions.
Omi, Michael and Howard Winant. 1994. *Racial Formation in the United States: From the 1960s to the 1990s.* New York: Routledge.
Orloff, Ann Sheila. 1993. Gender and the Social Rights of Citizenship, *American Sociological Review,* 58: 303-328.

Orren, Karen and Stephen Skowronek. 1994. Beyond the Iconography of Order, in Lawrence C. Dodd and Calvin Jillson (eds.) *New Perspectives on American Politics.* Washington D.C.: CQ Press: 310-330.
O'Toole, Fintan. 2005. Myths of Immigration, *The Irish Times,* September 1, 2005.
O'Toole, Fintan. 2000. Green, white and black: race and Irish Identity, in Ronit Lentin (ed.) *Emerging Irish Identities.* Dublin: MPhil in Ethnic and Racial Studies, TCD: 17-23.
Rattansi, Ali. 2005. The Uses of Racialisation: The Time-spaces and Subject-objects of the Raced Body, in Karim Murji and John Solomos (eds.) *Racialisation: Studies in Theory and Practice.* New York: Oxford University Press: 271-301.
Central Statistics Office. 2004. Report of the 2004 Census Pilot Survey. http://www.cso.ie/census/census_pilot_2004.htm.
Siggins, Lorna. 2004. Citizenship Poll has "encouraged" racists, *The Irish Times,* November 22, 2004.
Tovey, Hilary, Damien Hannan and Hal Abramson. 1989. Why Irish? Language and Identity in Ireland Today. *Bord Na Gaeile (Foras Na Gaeilge)*: 14-26.
Yuval-Davis, Nira. 1997. *Gender and Nation.* London: SAGE Publications.
Watt, Philip. 2005. Monitoring Ethnic Garda Progress Will Be Crucial Task, *Metro Eireann,* October, 2005:4.
Winant, Howard. 2004. *The New Politics of Race: Globalism, Difference Justice.* Minneapolis: University of Minnesota Press.

CHAPTER FOURTEEN

ROUTINISED PRACTICES AND TECHNOLOGIES OF THE STATE: DIALECTICAL CONSTITUTION OF IRISHNESS AND OTHERNESS

ELAINE MORIARTY

Introduction

Conceptualising Ireland over the past decade has changed profoundly—the emergence of what has been coined "the Celtic Tiger economy", the Good Friday Agreement on Northern Ireland and net immigration following decades of emigration, have all contributed to this change and opening up the question of identity in Ireland.[i] In 1991, as Hughes and Quinn (2004) demonstrate, the gross outflow and inflow of migrants were almost balanced, thus migration had little impact on the population.

However, by 2004, net outflow had halved and net inflow had significantly increased leading Hughes and Quinn (2004:6) to argue that "a remarkable transformation in Ireland's migration experience [occurred] in the second half of the 1990s".[ii] In 2002, foreign nationals amounted to 181,800 or 4.7 per cent of the total population, 80,400 of these were from non-EU countries, accounting for 45 per cent of all immigrants. Immigration levels increased from 33,000 per annum in 1991 to 67,000 in 2002 before falling to 50,000 in 2004 (Hughes and Quinn 2004: 7). Consequent public discourses have generated debates about what it means to be Irish, mediated primarily through the contest of location and the status of belonging. Whilst some attention has been given to questions around race and the relationship with the state (e.g. Lentin, this volume), much of the focus has been on applied aspects of such phenomena including managing immigration (e.g., Ruhs 2005), asylum seekers and the right to work (e.g., Fanning et al 2000) and the experiences of refugees in dispersal centres (e.g., Comhlámh 2001). However, I want to propose that the relationship in Ireland between official state policies and practices and everyday practices has been under-researched.

In this chapter I argue that a dialectical process is at work in the constitution of who belongs and who doesn't in early twenty first century Ireland. In doing so, I conceptualise a routinised construction of modern living which both acknowledges state mechanisms such as the law, policy formation and mechanisms of biopower in creating racist regimes but crucially recognises how racism is routinely created and reinforced through everyday practices. I explore this claim by examining a newspaper article published in *The Sunday Independent*[iii] on June 20, 2004, which discusses events that occurred in Longford, a midlands town in the Republic of Ireland in June 2004.

Fig. 14-1: Laura Bradley, *The Sunday Independent*, June 20, 2004

This newspaper article documented events which occurred on June 7 in Longford. On June 11, 2004 a referendum on citizenship was held in Ireland. The electorate was asked to vote on an amendment to the constitution which, if passed, would end the automatic citizenship conferred on any child born on the island of Ireland, thus children who do not have at least one citizen parent would no longer be entitled to automatic Irish citizenship. 79.8 per cent of the electorate, who voted, voted Yes. Longford, with 84.37 per cent, had the highest Yes vote in the country with a turn out of 71.29 per cent.[iv]

According to the 2002 census, Longford is a county of 30,919 people. Of these, 28,667 describe themselves as Irish and 66 people or 0.21 per cent are asylum seekers, living in Longford as part of the Irish government's dispersal policy which designates where asylum seekers reside pending asylum decision (Quinn and Hughes 2005: 9). Despite such small numbers, a level of unrest had been documented in Longford more than twelve months prior to the events under review. *The Irish Examiner*, an Irish national daily newspaper, reported on February 28, 2003 that

> The Department of Justice is to meet local authority members in Longford following claims the town is a dumping ground for refugees... Town councillors had expressed concerns about 'a refugee influx of an estimated 700 refugees'... living in the town (I Care 2003).

This report coincided with another media reported incident where,

> ... during a court case involving two non-national women accused of shop-lifting, Judge John Neilan, warned that '... shopping centres... will be putting a ban on access to coloured people if this type of behaviour does not stop'... The judge later apologised for his remarks but Longford's mayor said the judge had highlighted 'a local problem'... (Brennock and Haughey 2003).

These discourses demonstrate the eliding of distinction between refugees and asylum seekers and illuminate the imagined invasion by the euphemistic asylum seeker into Longford, despite the fact that refugees are allowed to live where they choose. As I have already highlighted only 66 asylum seekers are based in Longford and many of those perceived erroneously as asylum seekers are in fact working in local mushroom factories, meat factories and engineering firms (Bradley 2004).

Following Michel Foucault (1980) and Stuart Hall (1997), I describe this process as contributing to a regime of representation. Regimes of representation can be analysed as sites of constitution where identities are constructed through routinised social practices and deliberate interventions; as places of encounter of languages of the past and languages of the present; as inter-relations of reflexive and ideological negotiation.

To develop the argument, this chapter draws from a number of schools of thought: postmodernism's deconstructionism, a shift in the general theorising of knowledge (Jaworski and Coupland 1999), a broadening of perspectives in linguistics as well as recognition that language and discourse have the capacity to construct meaning and identity in society (Said 1978; Hall 1997). Michel Foucault's (1980) rejection of a distinction between ideas and material existence shifted attention from language to discourse as a system of representation. Foucault asserted that it is through discourses that the world is brought into being and the individual's subjectivity is constructed. Foucault argued there is an intrinsic relationship between discourses understood as signifying practices and symbolic systems, and 'reality' which cannot achieve meaning outside of discourse. Here it is suggested that social life cannot be constituted as meaningful outside of the discursive conditions of its representation.

In drawing from these linguistic and discursive intersections, critical discourse analysis (Fairclough 1989; Van Dijk 1993) has gone beyond a one-dimensional discursive structural perspective to a position which sees social subjects capable of reshaping practices, thus highlighting the role of agency (Giddens 1984; Chouliaraki and Fairclough 1999). This approach enables a more varied view of the relationship between language and social context, retaining emphasis on the power of discourse while highlighting the role of agency in relation to its use, which emerges through highlighting social practices. In focusing on practices, tacitly repeated habits are emphasised, which condition (Elias 1968/1994) or dispose (Bourdieu 1990) actors to draw from stocks of knowledge (Habermas 1987), providing people with common background convictions with which to deal with social life on an everyday basis, what Anthony Giddens (1984) calls "ontological security". Highlighting actors' routine practices in the performance of meaning making, through the usage of systems of representation, suggests that meaning is created through routinised, yet enacted social use.

While this approach allows me to put forward an analysis of the formation of discourse and examine how discourses are embedded in institutional practices and power relations, it also emphasises how actors' practices are essential in the construction and reproduction of discourses and systems. Drawing from these schools of thought, I examine the newspaper article as a site of engagement with contemporary changes in Ireland, illuminating the interrelationships of representations, power and identities. In this chapter I propose a dialectical approach to understanding the current debate in Ireland around immigration and racism, considering three principal themes to explore this proposal.

Firstly, I set out an analysis of the representations and discourses apparent in the newspaper article while suggesting that these discourses serve to dialectically construct self/other and us/them dichotomies. In examining the forms of knowledge through which this newspaper article is constituted and elaborated into concepts, theories and constituted realities, I argue that racialised representations not only become routinised but are also always contextualised locally and globally.

Secondly, I examine how such discourses are embedded in institutional practices and power relations, both enabling and constituted by a racialised regime of representation. In examining these systems of power, I suggest that the Citizenship Referendum of June 11, 2004 enabled the official rejection of those constructed as "other".

Finally, I problematise the apparent ethical engagement in the meaning making of this newspaper article. Here I highlight the links between the re-invoking of discourses of identification with the "other" through remembering "our" history of emigration, clarifying the prejudicial minority and thus reimagining a generous and caring Irishness

Racialised regime of representation

> It was a scene reminiscent of the darkest days of the Klu Klux Klan [sic]. But this was not America's deep South—it was Longford on a Monday morning two weeks ago…Two men, wearing balaclavas, … videotaped themselves… hanging a life-size black doll from the railway bridge … of Longford. The doll had a paper bag over its head and a sign around its neck saying 'Niggers go home—you'll never be Irish' … A few days later, a Black couple spray painted an image of the murdered gansta rapper Tupac Shakur on the same railway bridge with the words, 'Tupac still I rise' (Bradley 2004).

The primary representations in the newspaper article construct the relevant characters, in this case, the perpetrators, the two men wearing balaclavas and the black couple who are acting back through their use of Tupac Shakur. Tupac Shakur, despite being killed in 1996, continues to be one of the most successful artists in rap history, becoming notorious, according to his website (2005), for rapping about gunfights, rough sex, gang rivalries and "thug life". It is this eternal presence that is enacted in "Tupac, still I rise" and read by one of those interviewed in *The Sunday Independent* article as "You can't get rid of us". Although the graffiti was painted over, those interviewed said

> …the paint cannot hide the racial tension they feel pervades the town. Some fear Longford may become a ghettoised town with clear divisions between the black and white populations… (Bradley 2004).

Thus the already arresting use of Ku Klux Klan imagery, asserting that racism appears to be rife in Longford and describing the location as an emerging ghetto, all build toward demonstrating the racial differences in Longford.

Racial difference links racialised knowledge with visual discourse through the process of signifying practices. This process includes "reducing the culture of black people to nature" and thus fixing differences, through essentialising and stereotyping (Hall 1997: 245). Within these processes of essentialising and stereotyping, the power of representation becomes visible. Thus, we recognise the white "population" in the newspaper article through its difference from the constructed black couple; there is no further mention of white in the article, yet it is constituted through the dialectical relationship with the black couple. With this understanding, identity is relational—it is through the relation to the other, the relation to what it is not, that identity is constructed. Identity is thus marked out by difference and in this sense, following Stuart Hall (1996), identity is processual, constructed through, not outside difference, and functions through its ability to exclude.

As well as constructing the "other", the article also constructs the "self", albeit through distancing from the central characters discussed above. Here identity can be examined as expressing a more primordial or common sense view (Hall 1996: 2). In the newspaper article, the narrator's self is assumed to a large degree and defined through clarifying the difference with both the black couple *and* the men wearing balaclavas. I suggest that this process of identity construction is achieved through differentiation and the presumed common recognition of the inappropriateness of the Longford events, highlighted through presenting the events in Longford as shocking, unbelievable and perpetrated by a minority. The Gardaí (Irish police) who removed the black effigy, said:

> This is the first time we have ever seen this type of thing in Longford…It is a very worrying development (Bradley 2004).

Thus, we recognise the white and good "us" through the dialectical relationship with the black and evil "other" (both black couple *and* men wearing balaclavas). These processes of symbolic and social differentiation facilitate the creation of classificatory systems which utilise a principle of difference in order to divide a population into opposing elements, thus facilitating the othering process (Woodward 1997).

This, I suggest, contributes to racialised representations and discourses constituting the identitarian process. In addition, I wish to argue that this process is embodied and therefore expressed through routinised practices which can appear fixed and natural through processes of reification and essentialisation. In other words, what is routinely naturalised in Irish public culture becomes the obvious primary reading of such a set of representations and discourses found in this article, namely, what is not black and is not evil is white and good, thus affirming a recognisable collective sense of "us". In this sense, practices are constituted ideologically, generated through previous stocks of knowledge (Habermas 1987) and memory traces (Giddens 1984), thus enabling the fabric of familiarity which provides continuity and pattern and hence security in everyday life. However, I wish to argue that, being unstable and requiring work to articulate their knowledges, discourses are also open and reflexive.

This approach highlights a dialectic of colonisation/appropriation which is focused on the migration of discourse from one social practice to another within what I have suggested is a racialised regime of representation. This becomes apparent when the racial divisions in the newspaper article are constructed through multiple images presented or suggested including the Ku Klux Klan and Tupac Shakur, but also an allusion to Abu Ghraib; furthermore, in the context of the Northern Ireland conflict, the imagery of paramilitaries is evoked:

> Schoolgirl Samantha Riggs, 17, said: '...This town is getting like the North. There is a backlash against political correctness and a lot of disputes between white and foreign people'... (Bradley 2004).

Despite the shock and horror which greeted the publication of a series of images of prisoner abuse in Baghdad's Abu Ghraib jail in early May 2004, particularly the iconic photograph of an Iraqi prisoner perched on top of a box in a makeshift shroud, the Longford incident signifies a level of appropriation with the image of a black doll with a bag over its head. This was also a time of extensive media coverage of the videotaping of beheadings of western captives in Iraq. I want to suggest that there are clear linkages between some of the representations witnessed in these global events and the local Longford events: videotaping was used both by American and British soldiers in their abuse of Iraqi prisoners but also by Iraqi militia in the beheadings of western prisoners.

I argue that this newspaper article can be analysed both representationally and ontologically. By this I mean that the article can be explored as the site of representations of knowledge which are imposed on social life to extract meaning, but can also be examined as an ontological condition of social life whereby identity is constituted through the article. Thus this article cannot be examined outside the broader contexts of its constitution as I now go on to argue.

The routinisation of racialisation in the Irish State

This newspaper article can be examined in the context of the global changes of recent times which Zygmunt Bauman (1998) suggests have heralded a wave of fragmentation, dislocation and uncertainty leading people to blame "the stranger next door", particularly the asylum seeker who is seen as challenging the control of borders, the sovereignty of nations and hence, the security of identity and belonging. While the movement of asylum seekers occurs on a global scale, responses to asylum seekers' arrival occur primarily in national contexts where a perceived threat to the nation-state emerges as do potential opportunities to renationalise the nation (Luibhéid 2004: 2). I want to suggest that these apparent paradoxical understandings of the stranger's presence both challenge *and* enable the reproduction of the nation-state through opening up the categories and boundaries of who belongs and who does not.

Theorists such as Omi and Winant (1994), Goldberg (2002) and Ronit Lentin (this volume) argue that the concept of race and the emergence of the nation-state are intrinsically related. Goldberg (2002) asserts that the racial state defines the population of a nation-state through constitutions, border controls, law, policy, bureaucracy and governmental technologies such as census categorisations, invented histories and traditions, ceremonies and cultural imaginings, which facilitate the linking of race and nation. These apparatuses and technologies represent a constitutive matrix, utilised by modern states to reify and underpin racial terminologies and activities leading to the invisibility of the intrinsic relationship between race and state as well as the consequent reproduction of racist exclusions and subjectivities. This approach enables the highlighting of the key point of this chapter. Technologies of racialisation need constant "work", or enacted conduct, to be engaged meaningfully and dialectically; the routinisation of their usage enables the recursive reproduction of a racialised nation-state system as I now examine in the context of the Longford events.

When asked by the journalist to comment on the events outlined in *The Sunday Independent* article, those interviewed immediately linked it to the national context, primarily the Citizenship Referendum:

> ... There wasn't a single poster up in town calling for a No vote in the referendum...Nobody campaigned for a No vote... There were lots of Yes posters, but not a single No poster because there wouldn't be any No votes around here... (Bradley 2004).

The rationale provided by those interviewed around this strong No vote was clear:

> ... People feel they [immigrants] get away with more, as, if they are arrested or kicked out of a pub, they can accuse everyone of being racist... immigrants seem to get houses, cars and more money. They are out in expensive clothes all the time while the citizens are scraping by. There is a feeling they have been dumped here... The big Yes vote was to cut down on the number of asylum seekers. I

thought it was a racist vote, but we are polluted with refugees. The government has been far too liberal giving them top-notch brand new things, money and houses when local people want council houses... I voted Yes. I don't mind immigrants in the town, but they seem to be overrunning it. We have to fight to get anything from the social, but they seem to get everything a lot quicker... (Bradley 2004). [v]

I want to argue that this story begins long before June 2004 and suggest that it is informed primarily through government and media discourses but reproduced and circulated through hearsay and urban legends (see Moriarty 2005). With increased in-migration to Ireland since the early 1990s, the perceived "influx" of refugees and asylum seekers has become a widely discussed topic in Irish public culture. The media coverage of asylum, immigration and racism has been accused of being complicit in developing an anti-immigrant agenda (Guerin 2002: 92); more importantly, the Irish media have played a formative role in shaping public opinion about refugees and asylum seekers (Curry 2000: 149). Key government representatives, particularly Ministers for Justice, Equality and Law Reform, have served to construct asylum seekers as being associated with crime, welfare abuse, exploitation, cultural dilution, economic pressure and a threat to Irish citizenship.

On March 10, 2004, Minister for Justice, Equality and Law Reform Michael McDowell announced that the government was to put forward a referendum on citizenship. When announcing his intention to seek the referendum, the Minister said "...it was a measure to remove an incentive for foreign mothers to give birth in Irish hospitals" (Beesley 2004a). In outlining what he considered as significant evidence,

> Mr McDowell had said the masters [of the Maternity Hospitals] 'pleaded' with him for government action to do something about the large numbers of foreign nationals presenting late in their pregnancies to give birth in Ireland... The Masters subsequently denied that they had sought any constitutional or legislative change. Ms Harney [Tainaiste/Deputy Prime Minister], said 'I doubt very much if the masters would have come to it looking for change in legislation, but I know from private discussions with people working in the maternity hospitals that there is enormous concern about what is happening'... (Beesley 2004b).

There has been little directly attributed to the masters of the maternity hospitals themselves during the debate apart from denials; nevertheless, hearsay and urban legends (Moriarty 2005)[vi] have played a significant part in constructing the threat to "our" Irish hospitals due to a link being established between pregnant migrant women and overburdened maternity services.

Ms Harney insisted that nobody had been more liberal or open on immigration issues than she was, but the 'fact remains that the law in this country is being abused and it cannot be acceptable that people can fly in here from anywhere in the world for the purposes of giving birth' and she said that non-national births accounted for 22% of all births in the Dublin maternity hospitals (O'Halloran, 2004).

The Minister for Justice continued to return to this central discourse during the referendum campaign. Hennessey reports in *The Irish Times* that on a radio report in mid April, the Minister said that

> ... 'In 2003, 787 Nigerian children were born to Nigerian parents in Ireland in Irish hospitals,' he told Today FM's Sunday Supplement programme... He went on: 'I am not shifting my ground. I am saying our citizenship law is being abused. There is plenty of evidence of it. Anyone who has two eyes in their head can see it'... (Hennessy 2004a).

The racialisation of the debate is clear: at the time of this programme, that is, in advance of the referendum, those 787 Nigerian children that Minister McDowell is referring to are in fact Irish citizens. The normalisation of this claim is reinforced by his common sense appeal to "anyone with eyes in their head", again a clearly racialised regime of representation whereby abuse of "our" citizenship can be seen in the streets in people of colour, regardless of their status—citizen, refugee, asylum seeker or tourist.

On April 9, 2004 Minister McDowell's reasoning around the need for a referendum shifted somewhat. *The Irish Times* reported that

> Michael McDowell has said that ... a growing crisis in our maternity hospitals, ... was a side issue. The real driving force behind the referendum, he said, was the integrity of Irish citizenship law... (Brennock 2004a).

Over recent years, the negative presentation of asylum seekers as abusers of the asylum system has become established as has the implicit link with crime and illegality as evidenced by the Minister's address at a 2002 seminar on immigration.

> There are certain principles that no government can jettison. Principles such as the rights of a sovereign state to control access to its territory and to determine who can and who cannot cross its borders, for example, immigration policy in any state must reflect the needs of the state and the wishes of its people... If a state fails to undertake such controls, the consequences for the state are serious. The fruits of such failure will include resentment towards migrants and all that this can bring (McDowell 2002).

What is of particular interest is the threat migrants pose to "subverting our systems" and the implication that if the government does not control illegal immigration, the general public will not accept the "genuine" asylum seeker. Therefore, there is a presumed onus on government to "do something". This forms the basis of the need to intervene to meet the wishes of the people but for the benefit of the migrant also. It also appears to pre-empt and anticipate, but this, I would argue, constitutes the asylum seeker as criminal and bogus.

This is linked to what became known as the Chen case which played a part in providing so-called evidence of the abuses the government claimed were occurring on a large scale. In this case, Ms Chen, a Chinese woman who had her baby in Belfast, on a deportation appeal "was claiming the right to live in the United Kingdom on the basis of being the parent of a child born on the island of Ireland" (Coulter and Brennock 2004; see Moran and Garner in this volume). Ms Chen had taken her case to the European Court of Justice which found in her favour. This case highlighted a number of the elements of this debate. Ms Chen claimed her child had a right to Irish citizenship based on the Good Friday Agreement through the child being born in Northern Ireland; the British government was seeking to deport Ms Chen and her child, which in effect represented deporting an Irish and European citizen. Here the Irish government argued it was seeking to achieve alignment with the European style of citizenship but was forced to do so in the context of fairness. As the Tanaiste (deputy prime minister) Mary Harney argued:

> We are entitled to bring our constitution and our laws into line with European Union countries on citizenship, so that we do not create unintended incentives that are unfair to us or to other E.U. member states (Brennock 2004b).

As a result of Ms Chen's success in the European Court of Justice, the Irish government urged voters to support the Citizenship Referendum. As Minister McDowell argued:

> ... 'There is an overwhelming case for the passage of this referendum and I appeal to the Irish people to put aside the arguments from people who are trying to manufacture doubt where there isn't doubt'... But he warned: '... We have to face up to this issue. It can only get worse from now. The Chen decision will go out right across Europe: if I want to resist being sent home all I have to do is get to either part of Ireland and have a child there. In my view delay would be irresponsible...' (Hennessey 2004b).

The Minister for Foreign Affairs, Brian Cowen, referred to the Chen case when he "urged voters to support the referendum to enable 'genuine migrants' to come to Ireland free of aspersions as to their motives" (Beesley 2004c).

Reading together the dominant themes of the citizenship debate, namely, pleading masters of the maternity hospitals, bogus asylum seekers and "our" responsibilities to Europe, I suggest that such discourses have contributed to links being made between the presence of asylum seekers and a threat to the "Celtic Tiger" as well as causing the dilution of Irish culture and citizenship. These discourses built on the already established discourses about the "bogus", "sponging" and "criminal" asylum seeker and refugee in Ireland as documented by, for example, Watt (1997). I further suggest that it was through such discourses that a dominant set of ideas about asylum seekers, the threat they pose and what comprises legitimate strategies for governing such a threat, were developed, circulated and legitimated.

However, in the context of the Citizenship Referendum, this has largely revolved around the notion that Ireland has no choice but to implement changes but also that these changes will benefit "genuine refugees". Thus the production and circulation of such discourses enabled a public culture in which the State could act to propose legislation which changes the meaning of Irishness. I suggest it becomes "common sense" and "natural" for those who were entitled to vote in the constitutional referendum to vote to change the constitution in order to protect Irish citizenship *and* "genuine refugees". This focus on the constructed caring nature of Irishness is what I turn to in my final section.

The ethical engagement

I want to now shift the emphasis away from the texts of representation and context of enablement to the question of the constitutive meaning making process. I have already argued that there is a complex set of interrelationships between the text through which a racialised regime of representation is reproduced and circulated and the systems which govern its discursive capacities. I furthermore suggest that meaning is constituted not in the text itself but in the articulation between narrator and audience, between the power of the representations to signify and the audience's capacity to interpret meaning, and this leads me to consider the question of ethical dialogue.

It is of interest that Independent Newspapers who published this article, has been singled out by a number of academics and media commentators in recent years for its sensationalising, criminalising and essentialising reports about asylum seekers and refugees in Ireland (Pollak 1999; Curry 2000; Guerin 2002). On initial reading, the newspaper article under review appears to project the need for a more ethical engagement with what is happening in Ireland around immigration. To this end, I focus on the final paragraphs of the newspaper article where

Hostel manager, and Fine Gael councillor, James Kehoe is quoted as saying that 'We have short memories when you think of the number of people who have gone abroad from Ireland. ... It is *now* time for us to look at the issue and try to get people to integrate more. We are not a racist town but some may be misinformed'... (Bradley 2004, emphasis added).

I want to argue that this newspaper article strives to promote empathy, identification and solidarity with the "other" through firstly appealing to "our" history of emigration, secondly, clarifying the prejudicial minority and thirdly focusing on the need to "look at the issue". To examine this, I want to highlight the temporal issue of this media intervention, which appeared on June 20, 2004, just over a week *after* the Citizenship Referendum had taken place. The reference in the quote above to "It is *now* time for us to look at the issue and try to get people to integrate" is very revealing. *Now* that Irish citizenship is perceived as safe, it is time to appeal to "our" national image of Irishness as caring and generous to overcome the racial implications of the Citizenship Referendum.

The invoking of "our" experience of emigration through discourses of identification with the "other" have been discussed by theorists such as Breda Gray (2004) and Ronit Lentin (1998) particularly highlighting the power of memory to appeal to our common experience of emigration and thus highlight "our" obligations in the present. This is a counter discourse that has been apparent in Irish public culture since the mid 1990s, particularly associated with former President Mary Robinson, *The Irish Times* editorials and columnists such as Fintan O'Toole (Moriarty 2000). Utilising discourses of emigration and diaspora, a new less boundaried sense of Irishness is emphasised which is less concerned with territory and sovereignty and attempts to portray a new cultural confidence, portrays a positive image of immigration, encouraging a view of "our" gains through immigration and implies a moral obligation in the present based on "our" national history of emigration.

While there is a clear attempt to differentiate and distance from the prejudicial minority in the newspaper article, I again propose there are parallels with the Abu Ghraib situation where, as Susan Sontag (2004) suggests, despite politicians' protestations about a few bad apples spoiling the barrel, the Western public had a sense that the abuse photographs represented something deeper about the societies that sent such troops to Iraq. In Britain, the significance of the photographs became mired in a debate about the veracity of the photographs but interestingly, there was a level of debate about whether they continued to be representative of actual events, even if re-enacted. Similarly, in *The Sunday Independent* article there appears to be a recognition of something beyond the individual prejudice of the men wearing balaclavas and hence the need to reimagine or reclaim an empathetic Irishness.

These overlapping themes can be examined in the context of the public debate that took place around the deportation of 35 Nigerians in March 2005 and Ireland's "new-found solidarity" with so-called failed and aged-out (i.e. unaccompanied minor asylum seekers who have reached 18 years of age) asylum seekers. This became particularly focused on the plight of Olukunle Elukanlo, a so-called aged out asylum seeker who was deported three months in advance of sitting his Secondary School Leaving Certificate examination. What was evidenced in the public response was the "concerns", "anger" and "protests" (Healy 2005) of Olukunle's school friends, teachers, local politicians and church officials at the treatment of Olukunle, along with more reflective commentary highlighting the ethical obligations based on the link to "our" honourable past. Thus an editorial from *The Irish Times* asserts that

> Ireland's national saint was an immigrant to these shores, coming here first as a slave from Britain and returning later as a missionary who successfully converted the Irish to Christianity. A notable theme in the reconfiguration of his legacy has been Ireland's diasporic identity as a migratory nation. This makes it all the more reprehensible that 35 Nigerian nationals should have been deported apparently summarily, on the eve of the national holiday. Such an unworthy betrayal of St Patrick's legacy should prompt a fight back against this callous policy (*The Irish Times* 2005).

I want to suggest the deportation provided just such an opportunity to reclaim "our" past memories and experiences and reinvoke a perception of "ourselves" as charitable and generous. Following intensive lobbying on the part of Olukunle's campaigners and having "rejected renewed appeals for the deportation …to be overturned", Minister for Justice, Equality and Law Reform, Michael McDowell capitulated and decided to allow the Nigerian student to return to Ireland. The Minister described this decision as:

> … the right thing to do… I did this because having looked at the situation afresh I came to the conclusion that it was a little bit harsh as a decision… I think if I had had a second chance to think about the matter I would have given him enough time to finish his Leaving Cert... (Hennessy 2005).

With nothing short of euphoria, campaigners welcomed the victory in having Olukunle returned. Newspapers reported "Pupil power brings McDowell to book" (Cullen 2005a) and "Shades of World Cup fever as Kunle is carried aloft" (Cullen 2005b). However, as the Minister discussed his decision further, another more revealing reason became apparent:

I think that in the circumstances to maintain public confidence in the deportation system it was correct to give him time to complete his Leaving Certificate (Hennessy 2005).

From these remarks it becomes apparent that the integrity of the asylum system is articulated as the primary rationale for reversing the deportation order regarding Olukunle. Thus, an interesting situation presents itself whereby Minister McDowell, in order to protect the integrity of the asylum system decides to circumvent it, temporarily as it transpires.[vii] Minister McDowell in acknowledging potential and actual disquiet around the human and material consequences of the state's technologies around immigration and citizenship provides a means to re-imagine an ideal Irishness through enabling the generosity and charity of Irish people to be realised.

Hence, the Palmerstown students who had campaigned for the return of Olukunle received the Rehab Young Irish Person of the Year Award (2005) and as Fintan O'Toole suggested,

> ...there is a nice irony in the way the influx of strangers who were supposed to threaten our traditional values have actually revivified them. What's been marvellous is the way words that were so often used to exclude... have been wielded in the campaigns against the deportations as weapons of genuine solidarity... it has taken the removal of foreigners from our midst to make us, for once justifiably, proud to be Irish (O'Toole 2005).

However, Conor Lally's report on October 20, 2005 that "...a group of 39 people deported from the State in the early hours [included]...five ...minors ...born in Ireland..." makes visible an alternative picture of the implications of the Citizenship Referendum.

Conclusion

I have argued that the Longford events represent a site of engagement in the struggle between the representational means by which race is identified and signified but also the institutional forms in which it is routinised and normalised, ultimately facilitating the naturalisation of who belongs and hence who doesn't. In examining *The Sunday Independent* article, I suggested that it could be examined both representationally and ontologically, arguing that it is necessary to utilise a dialectical approach when examining the processes involved in the debates around immigration and racism in Ireland.

In examining the constitution of identities in contemporary Ireland, I suggested that everyday practices and governmental technologies are dialectically integrated in that the structural exclusion and repression of those constructed as other are consistent with and rationalised by regimes of representation which problematise and inferioritise the other. Thus, particular representations and discourses have been utilised by government and media agents who have succeeded in constructing an other against which the state is mobilising its efforts through reasserting the threat to the self. These discourses have focused on the linking of asylum seekers with exploitation and threat to the Irish nation and the normalisation and expectation that the state will "take care of" and protect the nation through legislative control over citizenship. Thus, I argued that government and media discourses migrate and are embodied in everyday practices such as racialised representations, euphemisms and urban legends but crucially such official discourses are dialectically shaped and enabled by routinised practices.

Finally, I have suggested that, in the safety of a post Citizenship Referendum space, articulating "our" traditional values of generosity and solidarity provides an opportunity to reimagine the good "us" and reclaim "our" Irishness. In the process, a denial of the implications of the Citizenship Referendum, which fundamentally changed how Irishness is constituted, is illuminated.

Acknowledgements

I would like to acknowledge the financial support of the Irish Research Council for the Humanities and Social Sciences. I would like to thank Brian Farrell and *The Sunday Independent* for permission to reproduce the images opening this chapter. I would also like to thank Ronit Lentin for her helpful comments.

Notes

[i] Ireland in this article refers to the space of the Republic of Ireland. Ireland has gone through a process of change in the past century, moving from the colonial experience to the Free State which played a dominant role in shaping class and status structures reinforced by the church's role (Breen et al 1990; Lee 1989). Modernisation in Ireland since the 1980s has entailed an emphasis on external investment, and a heightened awareness of Ireland's position globally leading to the prioritisation of economic globalisation principles through cultivating what has been coined the "Celtic Tiger" project characterised by significant economic growth and associated labour needs (See O'Riain 2000; MacÉinrí and Walley 2003: 3).

[ii] While the reliability of relevant statistics has been questioned (MacÉinrí and Walley 2003: 6), immigration constitutes a significant aspect of social change in Ireland. There are an increasing number of non-EU migrant workers—aggregate annual number of employment permits, work visas and work authorisations rose from approx. 3,000 in 1995 to 47,551 in 2003 (Dept of Enterprise 2003), representing an increase of more than 600 per cent since 1999 (MacÉinrí and Walley 2003: 7, 11). The numbers seeking asylum in Ireland has increased from 39 applications in 1992 to 11,634 in 2002 (CSO

2003), declining in 2003 to 7,900 (ORAC 2003). Nigerians have consistently been the largest number of asylum seekers followed by Romanians.

[iii] *The Sunday Independent* is part of the country's largest newspaper group, Independent Newspapers, accounting for two-thirds of the national daily newspapers sold in the state and 95 per cent of the Irish-owned Sunday newspaper market (Pollak 1999: 36).

[iv] The 2004 constitutional amendment followed a number of other legislative interventions. Following the Fajujonu Supreme Court case (1990), the migrant parents of children born in Ireland had a claim to remain in Ireland to provide "care and company" to their children. This process of application for permission to remain was overturned in January 2003 when the Supreme Court ruled that "non-national" parents no longer had the right to remain in Ireland. The Supreme Court further argued that the "integrity of the asylum process" was privileged over the child's right to the care and company of her parents (see Lentin in this volume). The Good Friday Agreement of 1998 had re-asserted the right to citizenship of all those born on the island of Ireland confirming the *jus soli* approach to Irish citizenship that had in fact been in existence since the 1922 constitution.

[v] The presence of the euphemistic asylum seeker (encompassing anyone of colour) is directly linked in the newspaper article to a high No vote backed up by figures from other counties. For example, County Sligo which has an asylum seeking population of 0.04 per cent had the lowest Yes vote, and County Westmeath with a much larger asylum seeker population of 0.52 per cent had the second highest Yes vote (Bradley 2004).

[vi] Urban legends perpetrate a type of folklore or myth, circulated primarily by word of mouth, repeated in news stories and popular press. In this case, myths about pregnant migrant women "getting free prams, phones, cars etc from social welfare" (Comhlámh 2004) have been evidenced in urban legends circulating in Dublin in early 2004 (Moriarty 2005).

[vii] As this chapter goes to print, Olukunle Elukanlo has been served with a second deportation order. Minister McDowell asserts that it would be "...contrary to the common good" to allow Olukunle to stay as this would have implications for "the integrity, coherence and efficiency" of the asylum system (Cullen, 2006). The contingency of what is in "the common good" is illuminated through Minister McDowell's contradictory actions.

References

Bauman, Zygmunt. 1998. *Globalisation: The Human Consequences*. New York: Columbia University Press.
Beesley, Arthur. 2004a. Referendum to be held to restrict citizenship rights, *The Irish Times*, March 11, 2004.
Beesley, Arthur. 2004b. Rabbitte stands over criticism of immigrant poll, *The Irish Times*, March 24, 2004.
Beesley, Arthur. 2004c. Voters urged to aid "genuine migrants", *The Irish Times*, June 4, 2004.
Bourdieu, Pierre. 1990. *The Logic of Practice*. Cambridge: Polity Press.

Bradley, Lara. 2004. Racial Tensions spark fears of midlands ghetto, *The Sunday Independent*, June 20, 2004.
Breen, Richard, Damian Hannan, David Rottman and Christopher Whelan. 1990. *Understanding Contemporary Ireland: State, Class and Development in the Republic of Ireland*. Dublin: Gill and MacMillan.
Brennock, Mark and Nuala Haughey. 2003. Judges apologise to non-nationals for remarks about immigrants, *The Irish Times*, February 21, 2003.
Brennock, Mark. 2004a. McDowell changes argument on referendum, *The Irish Times*, April 9, 2004.
Brennock, Mark. 2004b. Tanaiste staunchly defends citizenship poll plan, *The Irish Times*, April 20, 2004.
Central Statistics Office. 2002. *Population and Migration Estimates*. Dublin: CSO.
Central Statistics Office. 2003. *Population and Migration Estimates*. Dublin: CSO.
Chouliaraki, Lili and Norman Fairclough. 1999. *Discourse in Late Modernity: Rethinking Critical Discourse Analysis*. Edinburgh: Edinburgh University Press.
Comhlámh. 2001. *Refugee Lives: The Failure of Direct Provision As a Social Response to the Needs of Asylum Seekers in Ireland*. Dublin: Comhlámh.
Comhlámh. 2004. *myths/FACTS: About Immigrants, Asylum Seekers and Refugees*. Dublin: Comhlámh.
Coulter, Carol and Mark Brennock. 2004. UK case may have bearing on citizenship referendum. Women claim Irish born child allows her to live in UK. *The Irish Times*, April 3, 2004.
Cullen, Paul. 2005a. How pupil power brings McDowell to book, *The Irish Times*, March 26, 2005.
Cullen, Paul. 2005b. Shades of World Cup fever as Kunle is carried aloft, *The Irish Times*, April 2, 2005.
Cullen, Paul. 2006. Nigerian who was allowed to sit Leaving to be deported again. *The Irish Times*, January 26, 2006.
Curry, Philip. 2000. "She never let them in": Popular Reaction to Refugees Arriving in Dublin, in Malcolm MacLachlan and Michael O'Connell (Eds.) *Cultivating Pluralism:Psychological, Social and Cultural Perspectives on a Changing Ireland*. Dublin: Oaktree Press.
Department of Enterprise. 2003. *Monthly and Annual Work Permit Statistics*. Dublin: Government Publications.
Elias, Norbert. 1968/1994. *The Civilising Process*. Oxford: Blackwell Publishers.
Fairclough, Norman. 1989. *Discourses and Power in Language and Power*. London and New York: Longman.
Fanning, Bryan, Steven Loyal and Ciaran Staunton. 2000. *Asylum Seekers and the Right to Work in Ireland*. Dublin: Irish Refugee Council.
Foucault, Michel. 1980. *Power / Knowledge*. New York: Pantheon Books.
Giddens, Anthony. 1984. *The Constitution of Society*. Cambridge: Polity Press.
Goldberg, David Theo. 2002. *The Racial State*. Oxford: Blackwell.
Gray, Breda. 2004. Remembering a "multicultural" future through a history of emigration: Towards a feminist politics of solidarity across difference, *Women's Studies International Forum*, 27, 4: 413-429.

Guerin, Patrick. 2002. Racism and the Media in Ireland: Setting the Anti-Immigrant Agenda, in Ronit Lentin and Robbie McVeigh (eds.) *Racism and Anti-Racism in Ireland*. Belfast: Beyond the Pale.

Habermas, Jurgen. 1987. *The Theory of Communicative Action Volume II: A Critique of Functionalist Reason.Lifeworld and System*. Cambridge: Polity Press.

Hall, Stuart. 1996. Who needs identity? in Stuart Hall and Paul du Gay (eds.) *Questions of Cultural Identity*. London: Sage Publications.

Hall, Stuart. 1997. The spectacle of the "other", in Stuart Hall (ed.) *Representation: Cultural Representations and Signifying Practices*. London: Sage/Open University.

Healy, Alison 2005. Concern over deportation of Nigerian student, *The Irish Times*, March 17, 2005.

Hennessy, Mark. 2004a. Taoiseach trying to win over SDLP on referendum, *The Irish Times*, April 19, 2004.

Hennessy, Mark. 2004b. McDowell insists his action heads off 'threat', *The Irish Times*, May 19, 2004.

Hennessy, Mark. 2005. U-turn was right thing to do, says McDowell, *The Irish Times*, March25, 2005

Hughes, Gerard and Eimear Quinn. 2004. *The Impact of Immigration on Europe's Societies: Ireland*. Dublin: ESRI. http://www.esri.ie

I Care Newsarchive. 2003. Town Meeting over Refugee Influx (Ireland), *Irish Examiner*, February 28, 2003. http://www.icare.to/archivefebruary2003.html.

Jaworski, Adam and Nikolas Coupland. 1999. *The Discourse Reader*. London and New York: Routledge.

Lally, Conor. 2005. Irish-born minors deported, *The Irish Times*, October 20, 2005.

Lee, Joseph. 1989. *Ireland 1912-1985: Politics and Society*. Cambridge: Cambridge University Press.

Lentin, Ronit (ed.) 1998. *The Expanding Nation: Towards a Multi Ethnic Ireland Conference Papers*. Dublin: Ethnic and Racial Studies, Department of Sociology, Trinity College Dublin.

Luibhéid, Eithne. 2004. Childbearing against the State? Asylum Seeker Women in the Irish Republic, *Women's Studies International Forum*, 27, 4: 335-349.

MacÉinrí, Piaras and Patrick Walley. 2003. *Labour Migration into Ireland*. Dublin: Immigrant Council of Ireland.

McDowell, Michael. 2002. Address at a Seminar on Migration Policy in Ireland and Europe—Proposals, Issues and Experiences, December 10, 2002. http://www.michaelmcdowell.ie/releases/10_dec_02.html.

Moriarty, Elaine. 2005. Telling Identity Stories: The Routinisation of Racialisation of Irishness, *Sociological Research Online*, 10, 3. http://www.socresonline.org.uk/10/3.

Moriarty, Elaine. 2000. *A Critical Consideration of the role of Intellectuals in Interrupting, Perpetuating or Subverting Hegemonic Discourses of Irishness and Otherness in Ireland*, unpublished MPhil in Ethnic and Racial Studies Thesis. Dublin: TCD.

O'Halloran, Marie. 2004. Citizenship referendum date not set, says Harney, *The Irish Times*, March 24, 2004.

O'Riain, Sean. 2000. The flexible developmental state: Globalisation, information technology and the "Celtic Tiger", *Politics and Society*, 28, 2: 157-193.

O'Toole, Fintan. 2005. Ireland's new-found solidarity, *The Irish Times*, March 29, 2005.
Office of the Refugee Application Commissioner. 2003. *Monthly Asylum Statistics.* Dublin: ORAC.
Omi, Michael and Howard Winant. 1994. *Racial formation in the United States: from the 1960s to the 1990s.* London: Routledge.
Pollak, Andy. 1999. An Invitation to Racism? Irish daily newspaper coverage of the refugee issue, in Declan Kiberd (ed.) *Media in Ireland: The Search for Ethical Journalism.* Dublin: Open Air.
Quinn, Eimear and Gerard Hughes. 2005. *Reception Systems, Their Capacities and the Social Situation of Asylum Applicants within the Reception System in Ireland.* Dublin: ESRI. http://www.esri.ie
Rehab. 2005. People of the Year Award, 2005. http://www.rehab.ie/foundation/winners.aspx
Ruhs, Martin 2005. *Managing the Immigration and Employment of Non-EU Nationals in Ireland.* Dublin: The Policy Institute, TCD.
Said, Edward. 1978. *Orientalism.* London: Routledge and Kegan Paul.
Sontag, Susan. 2004. What have we done? *The Guardian*, May 23, 2004: 3-5.
The Irish Times. 2005. St Patrick still retains his appeal, *The Irish Times*, March 17, 2005.
Tupac. 2005. Tupac Amaru Shakur. http://www.2PACLegacy.com.
Van Dijk, Teun A. 1993. *Elite Discourse and Racism.* London: Sage.
Watt, Philip. 1997. Reporting on Refugees, *Focus*, No 57/58: 29-30.
Woodward, Kathryn (ed.) 1997. *Identity and Difference.* London: Sage Publications.

CONTRIBUTORS

Kieran Allen works in the School of Sociology, University College Dublin. He is the author of the *Celtic Tiger: The Myth of Social Partnership* (2000) and *Max Weber: A Critical Introduction* (2001).

Les Back teaches sociology at Goldsmiths College. His recent books include *The Auditory Cultures Reader* (with Michael Bull, Berg 2003), *Out of Whiteness* (with Vron Ware, University of Chicago Press 2002), *The Changing Face of Football* (with John Solomos and Tim Crabbe, Berg 2001). He is working on new book provisionally titled *The Art of Listening: Sociology in a Divided World*.

Gargi Bhattacharyya lives and works in Birmingham. She has published a number of books and articles on issues of race and racism, sexuality and globalisation, including *Tales of dark-skinned women* (UCL Press, 1998), *Race and Power* with John Gabriel and Stephen Small (Routledge 2001) and *Sexuality and Society* (Routledge 2002). Her latest book is *Traffick: The Illicit Movement of People and Things* (Pluto 2005).

David Theo Goldberg is the Director of the systemwide University of California Humanities Research Institute, and Professor of Comparative Literature and Criminology, Law and Society at the University of California, Irvine. His authored books include *The Racial State* (2002), *Racial Subjects: Writing on Race in America* (1997) and *Racist Culture: Philosophy and the Politics of Meaning* (1993). His edited books include *Anatomy of Racism* (1990), *Multiculturalism: A Critical Reader* (1995), *Race Critical Theories* (2001) and *A Companion to Racial and Ethnic Studies* (2002). His current book, *The Threat of Race*, will appear in 2007.

Rebecca Chiyoko King-O'Riain is a lecturer in the department of Sociology at the National University of Ireland, Maynooth. Her research interests are in race/ethnicity, multiraciality, qualitative methods, children, and gender. She is completing a an ethnographic manuscript entitled *Race Work, Body, Culture and Japanese American Beauty Pageants* which examines the use of blood quantum rules to define who is authentically Japanese American enough to represent the collective community as the beauty queen. She has also written about racial/ethnic formation in the US Census and the multiracial movement.

Steve Garner is Senior Lecturer in the School of Sociology at the University of the West of England, Bristol. He teaches on racism and immigration, and is the author of *Racism in the Irish Experience* (Pluto 2003) and *Guyana 1838-1985: Critical Perspectives on Ethnicity, Class and Gender* (Ian Randle Press 2006). He has published articles in *Sociology*, *Ethical Perspectives* and *Irish Review*, and is currently working on an ESRC-funded research project (with Simon Clarke) on white identities in the UK, and other projects on the politics of immigration.

Festus CRA Ikeotuonye is a Modular Fellow at the Sociology Department, University College Dublin. He is also a Part Time Sociology Lecturer at the College of Arts and Design Dublin. His educational background is in History, Integrated Humanities and Sociology. His research interests are as follows: Historical Systems, Border and Non-Modern Thinking, Global processes of Coloniality and Liberation Philosophy.

Malreddy Pavan Kumar has studied History, Anthropology, Sociology and Political Science in India, Netherlands, Singapore and Canada. He is currently working on his PhD in sociology at the University of Saskatchewan. His research interests include sociology of knowledge, knowledge society, cultural studies, intellectual histories and genealogies of colonialism and the intersections of literary and social theory.

Alana Lentin is a writer, political sociologist and anti-racist activist. She is the author of *Racism and Anti-Racism in Europe* (2004) and *Racism: A beginner's guide* (forthcoming). She has written many articles on racism, anti-racism and the migration regime in journals including the *European Journal of Social Theory, Ethnic and Racial Studies, Social Identities, Patterns of Prejudice and Sociological Research Online*. She also participates in online fora such as OpenDemocracy.net. Her writing can be found on her website www.alanalentin.net.

Ronit Lentin is director of the MPhil in Ethnic and Racial Studies, Department of Sociology, Trinity College Dublin. Her books include *Conversations with Palestinian Women* (1982), *Gender and Catastrophe* (1997), *Israel and the Daughters of the Shoah: Reoccupying the Territories of Silence* (2000), *(Re)searching Women: Feminist Research Methodologies in the Social Sciences in Ireland* (with Anne Byrne, 2000), *Racism and Anti-racism in Ireland* (with Robbie McVeigh, 2002), *Women and the Politics of Military Confrontation: Palestinian and Israeli Gendered Narratives of Dislocation* (with Nahla Abdo 2002), *Re-presenting the Shoah for the 21st Century (*2004), and *Representing*

Migrant Women in Ireland and the EU (with Eithne Luibhéid, 2004, special issue of *Women's Studies International Forum*). Ronit has published extensively on racism in Ireland, gender and genocide, Israel and the Holocaust, Israel and Palestine. Her latest book, with Robbie McVeigh, is *After Optimism? Ireland, Globalisation and Racism* (2006).

Steven Loyal is a College Lecturer in Sociology, in the School of Sociology, University College Dublin. His Previous books include *The Sociology of Anthony Giddens* (2003), and with Stephen Quilley, *The Sociology of Norbert Elias* (2004). He is currently working on a global analysis of Punjabi-Sikh migration and on labour migration in Ireland.

Piaras Mac Éinrí was Director from 1997-2003 of the inter-disciplinary Irish Centre for Migration Studies at University College Cork, focusing on Irish and comparative international migration research. He is an advisor to the Dublin-based NGO the Immigrant Council of Ireland and a member of the National Consultative Committee on Racism and Interculturalism. He has lectured and published extensively in the fields of Irish and comparative migration studies, with a particular interest in immigration and integration issues. He is a Geography lecturer at University College Cork and is currently Visiting Professor at the Institute for the Study of European Transformations, London Metropolitan University. He previously served in the Irish Department of Foreign Affairs, with postings in Brussels, Beirut and Paris.

Robbie McVeigh is a human rights activist and researcher from Derry. He runs a research company, An Dúchán, which specialises in community research and evaluation projects. His publications include Harassment—It's Part of Life Here (1994); There's no racism because there's no Black people: Racism and anti-Racism in Northern Ireland and Between Reconciliation and Pacification: The British State and Community Relations in the north of Ireland. He is co-editor, with Ronit Lentin, of *Racism and Anti-racism in Ireland* (2002). His latest book, with Ronit Lentin, is *After Optimism? Ireland, Globalisation and Racism* (2006).

Anthony Moran is a Research Fellow in the Politics Programme, School of Social Sciences, La Trobe University, Australia. He researches and teaches on political culture, nationalism, settler/indigenous politics, the politics of race, and the sociology of risk. His work has appeared in *Ethnic and Racial Studies*, *Political Psychology*, *Free Associations*, and *The Australian Journal of Politics and History*. His most recent books are *Australia: Nation, Belonging and Globalization* (Routledge 2005), the co-edited collection (with Sean Watson)

Trust, Risk and Uncertainty (Palgrave 2005), and (co-written with Judith Brett) *Ordinary People's Politics* (Pluto, forthcoming).

Elaine Moriarty teaches on the MPhil in Ethnic and Racial Studies in Trinity College Dublin. She has a B.Soc.Sc from UCC, an MPhil in Ethnic and Racial Studies from Trinity College and is currently reading for a PhD in the Department of Sociology, Trinity College. This work critically explores the processes involved in the production of discourses and representations of Irishness and Otherness articulated by intellectuals in relation to Ireland's changing cultural makeup (supported by the Irish Research Council for Humanities and Social Sciences and a Trinity Post-Graduate Award).

Regina Mühlhäuser is working on her PhD dissertation: "Between Extermination and 'Germanization': Children of German Men and 'Ethnically Alien' Women in the occupied territories of the Soviet Union, 1941—1945" (funded by the Hamburg Foundation for the Benefit of Research and Culture). She is a contact person for the working group on "War and Gender" at the Hamburg Institute for Social Research.

Chris Sparks is Lecturer in Politics and Sociology at the Institute of Technology Sligo and Associate Lecturer at the Open University. He is author of *Uncertainty and Identity: The Enlightenment and its Shadows* (University of Westminster Press 1994), *Montesquieu's Vision: Uncertainty and Modernity* (Edwin Mellen Press 1999), joint author of *Political Theorists in Context* (Routledge 2004), *Equality* (IT Sligo, Equality Authority, Comhairle 2004), and has written several articles on political uncertainty and the politics of fear. He is currently working on two books, *The Politics of Fear* and *Twentieth Century Political Theorists*.

Index

Aboriginal Australians, 112
Abu Ghraib, 145, 248, 251, 300, 306
Agamben, Giorgio, 37, 46, 51, 104, 118, 190, 206, 207, 232, 233, 252, 254
al-Qa'eda, 162-163, 166
Amin, Samir, 146-47, 151
An Garda Siochána, 275, 286-93
Anthropology, 70, 99, 184-85
anti-racism, 2, 10-11, 53-55, 57, 61, 63-64, 66-67, 139, 147, 188, 190, 195, 202, 206, 229, 237-38, 241-43, 246, 272, 287
Arendt, Hannah, 3-4, 14, 45, 50-51, 153-54, 164-65, 167
asylum seekers, 10, 12, 35, 45, 47, 65, 68, 103, 104-06, 110-18, 200, 204-05, 209-11, 214, 222-24, 227, 237, 246, 285, 294, 296, 301-03, 305, 307, 309-10
Australia, 38, 40, 103-06, 110-20, 207, 221, 259, 263, 273
Balibar, Etienne, 3, 5-6, 14, 59, 69, 104, 118, 200, 207
Barnett, Steve, 169, 181-83, 185
Bauman, Zygmunt, 3-4, 14, 41, 48, 51, 72-73, 79, 82-83, 99, 105, 118, 192, 207, 300, 310
biopolitics, 189-90, 193, 195, 201
Blears, Hazel, 143
bloodlines, 108, 110, 275

boatpeople, 111, 113
bonded labour, 224, 227
border (s), 22, 32-33, 37, 38, 41, 43, 46, 104-06, 110-11, 113-15, 118, 191, 288, 301
Bowman, Isaiah, 178-79, 180, 184-85
Brauchitsch, Walther von, 125, 132
categories, racial/ethnic, 12, 61, 80, 97, 104-05, 111, 123, 130, 170, 172, 193, 216, 217-19, 221, 223, 226, 228, 275, 277, 281-84, 290, 301
Catholic Church, 154, 219-20, 223, 258
Césaire, Aimé, 3, 56
Chen case, 109-10, 117, 304
children, 1, 9, 11, 34, 47, 65, 105, 107-10, 113-14, 122-24, 129, 140, 178, 190, 196-97, 199, 209, 216, 245, 280, 284-85, 296, 303, 310
citizenship, 11-12, 32, 34, 37, 40, 46, 59, 75, 106-10, 115, 119-20, 132, 146, 193-99, 201, 209, 215, 218-19, 236, 242, 248, 270, 275, 278-80, 283-85, 287, 289-90, 296, 302-06, 308-10
Citizenship Referendum, 12, 105, 107-09, 117, 191, 197, 199, 275, 283-85, 291-93, 298, 301, 304-06, 308-09
class, 5, 20, 23, 25, 27, 39, 97, 154-55, 190, 192, 205, 212,

214, 216, 221, 223, 228, 245, 250, 253, 263, 268, 309
classification, 4, 55, 84, 95, 104, 216-18, 278
Colonialism, 171, 184-85, 229
constitution of identities, 308
Cooper, Robert, 145, 151, 215, 218, 229
CRC
(Community Relations Council), 240-41, 253-54
culturalism, 54
De Menezes, Jean Charles, 140
detention (centres), 1, 9, 34, 45, 65, 106, 112-14, 193, 196, 249
dialectical process, 295
discourse, 5, 7, 12-13, 39, 54-55, 63-64, 66-67, 69, 77, 93, 106, 111, 158, 169, 171, 184, 202, 205, 218, 220, 227, 242, 246, 260, 263, 276, 279, 280, 282-83, 287, 289, 297, 299, 300, 303, 306
ECNI
Equality Commission for Northern Ireland, 255
ethical engagement, 298, 305
everyday practices, 294-95, 308
Fairclough, Norman, 297, 311
Fajujonu ruling, 107
Fanon, Frantz, 3, 14, 53-64, 66, 68-70, 169, 185
Fianna Fáil, 188, 220
Foucault, Michel, 2, 3, 5, 11, 14, 19, 31, 79, 84-86, 94, 99, 100-01, 129, 133, 190, 193-94, 208, 281, 292, 296-97
Fraternisation, 135
Geography, 176, 178, 185-86, 316

Germanization, 133-34, 317
Germany, 37-38, 110, 122-23, 125-26, 128, 130, 132-33, 141, 161, 168, 207, 221, 259, 268
GFA
Good Friday Agreement, 108, 189, 196, 197, 233-38, 240-41, 246, 248, 250, 252-53, 294, 304, 310
Giddens, Anthony, 79, 216, 229, 297, 300
Gilroy, Paul, 41, 46, 49, 51, 64, 70, 276, 292
globalisation, 11, 34, 39, 44, 46, 49-50, 84, 103, 105, 138, 182-83, 206, 279, 309
Goldberg, David Theo, 3, 6, 7, 12, 14, 16-17, 31, 56, 61, 66, 70, 72, 83, 100, 189-92, 194-95, 198, 202, 204-05, 208, 210, 236, 255, 275, 277, 281, 292, 301
good relations, 238-39, 241, 246-51, 253
Hall, Stuart, 23, 32, 51, 212, 215, 229, 296-97, 299
Hanson, Pauline
One Nation Party, 112
Hesse, Barnor, 3, 6, 14, 59, 61, 70, 205, 206, 208
Himmler, Heinrich, 121-24, 126, 129, 130, 132-33
historicism, 11, 191-92, 194-95, 204
Hitler, Adolf, 7, 123-26, 132, 172
Holocaust, 4, 6, 7, 14, 55, 92, 99, 101
homosexuality, 125

320   Index

Howard, John (Australian PM), 3, 83, 92, 102, 111-16, 118-19, 186, 209, 292-93
identity, 8, 10, 27, 37, 53-54, 56-58, 60-62, 67, 69, 73, 77, 84, 88-89, 92, 150, 162-63, 170, 172, 179, 183-84, 190, 197, 203, 209, 210, 212-16, 218-19, 228, 230, 245, 257, 268, 282, 284-86, 288, 290, 294, 297, 299, 300-01, 307
IMC
Independent Monitoring Commission, 243-44, 248, 251, 255
immigration, 1, 7, 9-12, 22, 32, 33, 35, 37, 39, 45- 47, 49, 69, 105-07, 109, 111, 116, 118, 143, 161, 188-90, 192-94, 196, 198, 200-06, 209, 211-12, 214-16, 219, 221, 224, 226, 236, 242, 248, 263, 270-71, 279, 284, 294, 297, 302-06, 308-09
imperialism, 75-76, 138-39, 145, 154, 171, 180-81, 184, 204, 219, 263
interracial sexuality, 122
Irish born children, 190, 284
Irish citizenship law, 275, 303
Irish Constitution 1937, 196
Irish language, 253, 275, 279, 286-91
Irish nation, 10, 107, 109-10, 116, 196, 206, 214, 226, 241, 260, 263, 266, 271, 274, 279, 284, 296, 309
Irishness, 107, 189-91, 208-09, 213, 220, 229, 231, 262, 266, 267, 274, 275, 280, 284-85, 286, 290, 294, 298, 305-06, 308-09
Islamophobia, 8, 143, 146, 148-49, 151
ius sanguinis, 197
ius soli, 107, 109, 197
Keane, John, 158, 167, 198
Keitel, Wilhelm, 125, 132
Ku Klux Klan, 299-300
Loyalist Commission, 243-44, 253-54, 256
Macey, David, 53, 56, 58, 60, 63, 68, 70, 100
MacPherson, 14
Maine, Henry, 172-74, 185
mapping, territorial, 170-71, 176, 178-81, 183-84
mapping, cultural, 170-71, 176, 178-81, 183-84
marriage, 5, 122, 128, 285
masculinity, 20, 122, 125-26
McDowell, Michael, 106-08, 110, 189, 194, 206, 209, 244, 287, 291, 302-04, 307-08, 310
Merleau-Ponty, Maurice, 56, 62-63, 70
migration of discourse, 300
militarisation, 13, 25, 138, 144, 150
mixité sociale, 9
Montesquieu, 153-55, 167, 168, 317
Mosse, George, 3, 14, 192, 209
multiculturalism, 34, 43, 56, 115, 188, 190, 201, 203-05, 208, 213, 241, 246-47, 249-50, 287, 289
Muslim, 22, 42, 92, 114, 143, 147-50, 162, 167-68, 170, 181-83, 248, 264

MV Tampa, 113
nationalism, 5, 37, 57-58, 71, 75, 84, 110-11, 118, 200-11, 213-14, 216, 219, 241-42, 267-68, 271, 274, nation-state, 3-7, 10, 12, 55, 63, 75, 82, 84, 92, 103-04, 115-16, 178, 189-92, 215-16, 301
naturalism, 6, 191-92, 195, 204
Nazi racial ideology, 124
new wars, 144
Ní Shuinéar, Sínéad, 191, 209, 213
non-nationals, 103-07, 109, 188, 190-91, 198, 219, 284-85, 289-90
Northern Ireland, 10, 106, 117, 142, 207, 232-44, 246-47, 249-50, 252-56, 282, 288, 294, 300, 304
occupation politics, 122, 129, 131
Operation Relex, 113-14, 116
organic unity, 172
Orientalism, 76, 152, 154-56, 162-63
othering, 145, 192, 211, 213-14, 228, 299
Palat, Arvind, 172, 180, 184, 186
passport, 33, 46, 218-19
Poland, 121, 125, 129, 130, 200, 221, 225
policing, 1, 17, 19, 20, 104, 139, 140-41, 143, 146-47, 201, 288-89
politics of recognition, 54, 56-59, 68, 190, 203, 205, 210
postmodernism, 297
poverty, 22-24, 27, 35, 65, 182, 214, 219, 222, 227, 261

Powell, Michael, 22, 140, 160
power, 5-6, 11, 22, 27, 34, 37, 45, 55, 65, 73-74, 76-77, 84, 87, 90-92, 97, 104, 123-24, 131, 144, 146, 150, 153, 156-63, 165, 179, 190-94, 198, 203-05, 213-14, 216-17, 228, 230, 235, 249, 252, 263, 272, 276, 281, 283, 297-99, 305-07
PSNI
Police Service of Northern Ireland, 288
public culture, 50, 299, 302, 305-06
public opinion (and manipulation of), 302
race, 2-5, 7-8, 10, 12-13, 16-17, 21-22, 32, 35, 37, 41, 46, 55, 58, 64, 69, 70, 72-74, 76, 83-85, 90, 95-97, 99, 101, 121, 123-24, 126, 131, 138-39, 141, 145-46, 148-49, 169-71, 176-77, 179, 184, 188-89, 191, 194-95, 200, 202, 204-06, 234, 236-39, 241-42, 248, 250-51, 253, 255, 259, 264, 267, 275-84, 286, 288, 290-91, 293-94, 301, 308
racelessness, 7, 12, 191, 202-05, 280
racial formation, 277
racial politics, 170
racial state, 10-11, 13, 20, 34, 188-91, 193-95, 198, 200-01, 204-07, 235-37, 249-51, 275, 278-80, 282, 289, 301
racial statelet, 10, 236-37, 249-51
racialisation, 1, 13, 54, 146, 148, 192, 206, 208, 213, 215, 229,

262, 268, 275-77, 279-81, 290, 300-01, 303
racialised, 5, 9-11, 13, 41, 54, 57, 63-64, 66-67, 107, 110-11, 141, 146-48, 152, 189, 191-93, 202, 206, 227, 231, 242, 271, 276, 279-82, 284, 288-90, 298-301, 303, 305, 309
raciology, 64
racism, 1-14, 16-17, 28-29, 32, 37, 39, 41, 53-55, 57-61, 63-67, 69, 71, 74, 76, 80, 82-83, 89, 91, 97, 100, 106, 138-50, 156, 170, 188-90, 192-95, 197, 200, 202-09, 211-12, 214-15, 219, 227, 229, 230-31, 234-55, 259, 272, 274, 280, 283, 287-88, 290, 292, 295, 297, 299, 302, 308
rape, 121, 122, 126-27, 130, 271
refugees, 35, 40, 45, 52, 65, 68, 111, 113-18, 149, 196, 203, 205, 210, 220, 222-23, 227, 237, 246, 285, 294, 296, 302, 305
regimes of representation, 309
representations, 178, 231, 289, 297, 298-300, 305, 309
Republic of Ireland, 10-11, 96, 99, 103-06, 199-200, 229, 235, 273, 275, 279, 284, 289, 291-92, 295, 309, 311
Roediger, David, 191, 206, 210
Romantic Relationships, 134
routinisation of racialisation, 300
routinised practices, 299, 309
Ruddock, Philip (Australian Minister for Immigration), 112-14, 118, 120

Said, Edward, 47, 52, 154, 212
Sarkozy, Nicolas, 9
Sartre, Jean Paul, 56, 60-62, 70, 87
Schmitt, Carl, 162, 168
Scott, Joan Wallach, 61-62, 70, 216-17, 230
sectarianism, 234, 239, 240-42, 245-46, 252, 254
September 11 2001, 37, 41, 148, 164, 169
September 11, 2001, 8, 22, 156-57, 160-62, 164, 166-67, 169-71, 183, 186
site of engagement, 297, 308
sovereignty, 37, 104, 113-14, 116, 301, 306
Soviet Union, 121-22, 125, 127-28, 130-31, 144, 317
Special Powers Act, 232-33, 251-52
SS, 121, 127, 129, 130, 132-35
state, 2-13, 17- 20, 23, 25- 28, 30, 32, 34, 37, 39, 40-41, 46, 54-55, 63-64, 66, 72, 74-76, 78-80, 82- 86, 89-91, 93-97, 102-13, 115-17, 123, 129, 138-50, 152, 160, 164, 166, 178, 188-09, 211, 214-17, 218-28, 230-38, 240-50, 252-55, 259, 262-63, 271, 275, 276-90, 294-95, 301, 303, 308-10
state of exception, 232-36, 246-54
Taylor, Charles, 54, 56, 68
technologies of the state, 275, 281
terrorist, 22, 37, 43, 74, 78, 91, 143, 152, 154, 160, 163, 166,

169, 170, 183, 243, 248, 252, 255
The Irish Examiner, 296
The Sunday Independent, 272, 295, 298, 301, 306, 308, 309, 310
torture, 142, 151, 249
Travellers, 96, 189, 192, 195, 206, 209, 230, 279
Traverso, Enzo, 3
Tupac Shakur, 298, 300
UNESCO, 8, 69, 70, 229

venereal disease, 127
village community, 172-75
visas, 114-15, 201, 225, 227, 309
Voegelin, Eric, 2-4, 14, 80, 83, 87, 101
War of Annihilation, 122, 131
War on Terror, 2, 8, 156
Wehrmacht, 125-28, 132-34
Winant, Howard, 102, 186, 293
World War One, 179, 219, 252
World War Two, 180, 222, 261